Lecture Notes in Computer Science 13414

More information about this series at https://link.springer.com/bookseries/558

Mario Trapp · Francesca Saglietti ·
Marc Spisländer · Friedemann Bitsch (Eds.)

Computer Safety, Reliability, and Security

41st International Conference, SAFECOMP 2022
Munich, Germany, September 6–9, 2022
Proceedings

Editors
Mario Trapp
Fraunhofer IKS
Munich, Germany

Francesca Saglietti
University of Erlangen-Nuremberg
Erlangen, Germany

Marc Spisländer
University of Erlangen-Nuremberg
Erlangen, Germany

Friedemann Bitsch ⓘ
Thales Deutschland GmbH
Ditzingen, Germany

ISSN 0302-9743   ISSN 1611-3349   (electronic)
Lecture Notes in Computer Science
ISBN 978-3-031-14834-7   ISBN 978-3-031-14835-4   (eBook)
https://doi.org/10.1007/978-3-031-14835-4

This Springer imprint is published by the registered company Springer Nature Switzerland AG
The registered company address is: Gewerbestrasse 11, 6330 Cham, Switzerland

Preface

The SAFECOMP conference series was initiated in 1979 by EWICS TC7, the Technical Committee on Reliability, Safety and Security of the European Workshop on Industrial Computer Systems, with the aim of offering a regular platform for knowledge and technology transfer across academia, industry, research, and licensing institutions.

Since 1985, the International Conference on Safety, Reliability, and Security of Computer-based Systems (SAFECOMP) has taken place on an annual basis, and this year the 41st event took place in Munich under the local organization provided by the Fraunhofer Institute of Cognitive Systems (IKS).

The reaction following our call for papers was gratifying both in terms of the number and technical background of submissions: we received 93 full articles originating from 12 European and 10 extra-European countries, including a considerable amount of cooperative effort across geographical and institutional boundaries.

Each article submitted was evaluated by at least three independent reviewers; the decision on the conference program was jointly taken during the International Program Committee meeting in April 2022. In total, 24 articles were finally accepted for publication within the present proceedings volume as well as for presentation in September 2022 during the conference.

We trust that the readers of this volume will appreciate the wide range of topics and application domains addressed and – if not yet the case – may feel motivated to consider joining the EWICS TC7 and SAFECOMP communities.

Our heartfelt thanks go to all who have contributed and will contribute to the success of the SAFECOMP conferences – past, present, and future authors, reviewers, organizers, and attendees!

September 2022

Mario Trapp
Francesca Saglietti
Marc Spisländer
Friedemann Bitsch

Organization

EWICS TC7 Chair

Francesca Saglietti   University of Erlangen-Nuremberg, Germany

Conference Chairs

Mario Trapp   Fraunhofer Institute for Cognitive Systems, Germany
Francesca Saglietti   University of Erlangen-Nuremberg, Germany

Publication Chairs

Marc Spisländer   University of Erlangen-Nuremberg, Germany
Friedemann Bitsch   Thales Deutschland GmbH, Germany

Industry Chair

Simon Fürst   BMW, Germany

Local Organization Chair

Simon Burton   Fraunhofer Institute for Cognitive Systems, Germany

Local Organization Committee

Martin Simon   Fraunhofer Institute for Cognitive Systems, Germany
Eva von Wardenburg   Fraunhofer Institute for Cognitive Systems, Germany

International Program Committee

Magnus Albert   SICK AG, Germany
Uwe Becker   Draeger Medical GmbH, Germany
Peter G. Bishop   Adelard, UK
Friedemann Bitsch   Thales Deutschland GmbH, Germany
Sandro Bologna   Associazione Italiana Esperti Infrastrutture Critiche, Italy
Andrea Bondavalli   University of Florence, Italy
Jeroen Boydens   Katholieke Universiteit Leuven, Belgium
Jens Braband   Siemens AG, Germany
Simon Burton   Fraunhofer Institute for Cognitive Systems, Germany
António Casimiro   University of Lisbon, Portugal
Peter Daniel   EWICS TC7, UK

Ewen Denney	SGT/NASA Ames Research Center, USA
Felicita Di Giandomenico	ISTI-CNR, Italy
Wolfgang Ehrenberger	Fulda University of Applied Sciences, Germany
John Favaro	Intecs, Italy
Francesco Flammini	Linnaeus University, Sweden
Simon Fuerst	BMW Group, Germany
Barbara Gallina	Mälardalen University, Sweden
Janusz Górski	Gdańsk University of Technology, Poland
Erwin Grosspietsch	Euromicro, Germany
Lars Grunske	Humboldt University of Berlin, Germany
Jérémie Guiochet	LAAS-CNRS, France
Ibrahim Habli	University of York, UK
Wolfgang Halang	Fernuniversität Hagen, Germany
Maritta Heisel	University of Duisburg-Essen, Germany
Andreas Heyl	Robert Bosch GmbH, Germany
Yan Jia	University of York, UK
Bernhard Kaiser	Ansys Germany GmbH, Germany
Joost-Pieter Katoen	RWTH Aachen University, Germany
Phil Koopman	Carnegie Mellon University, USA
Núria Mata	Fraunhofer Institute for Cognitive Systems, Germany
John McDermid	University of York, UK
Frank Ortmeier	Otto-von-Guericke University Magdeburg, Germany
Ganesh Pai	KBR/NASA Ames Research Center, USA
Philippe Palanque	ICS-IRIT, University of Toulouse, France
Yiannis Papadopoulos	University of Hull, UK
Michael Paulitsch	Intel, Austria
Holger Pfeifer	Technical University of Munich, Germany
Peter Popov	City, University of London, UK
Andrew Rae	Griffith University, Australia
Matteo Rossi	Politecnico di Milano, Italy
Martin Rothfelder	Siemens AG, Germany
Francesca Saglietti	University of Erlangen-Nuremberg, Germany
Behrooz Sangchoolie	RISE Research Institutes of Sweden, Sweden
Daniel Schneider	Fraunhofer Institute for Experimental Software Engineering, Germany
Erwin Schoitsch	AIT Austrian Institute of Technology, Austria
Christel Seguin	Office National d'Etudes et Recherches Aérospatiales, France
Oleg Sokolsky	University of Pennsylvania, USA
Wilfried Steiner	TTTech Computertechnik AG, Austria
Mark Sujan	Human Factors Everywhere, UK
Kenji Taguchi	CAV Technologies Co., Ltd., Japan
Stefano Tonetta	Fondazione Bruno Kessler, Italy
Martin Törngren	KTH Royal Institute of Technology, Sweden
Mario Trapp	Fraunhofer Institute for Cognitive Systems, Germany
Elena Troubitsyna	KTH Royal Institute of Technology, Sweden
Hélène Waeselynck	LAAS-CNRS, France

Supporting Institutions

European Workshop on
Industrial Computer Systems

Technical Committee 7 on
Reliability, Safety and Security

Fraunhofer Institute for
Cognitive Systems

Chair of Software Engineering,
University of Erlangen-Nuremberg

Technical University of Munich

Thales Deutschland GmbH

Lecture Notes in Computer Science
(LNCS),
Springer Science + Business Media

Gesellschaft für Informatik (GI)

Informationstechnische Gesellschaft
(ITG) im VDE

Technical Group ENCRESS
in GI and ITG

Austrian Computer Society

Electronics and Software Based
Systems (ESBS) – Austria
(formerly Electronic Components and
Systems for European Leadership – Austria)

European Research Consortium for
Informatics and Mathematics

Verband Österreichischer
Software Industrie

Contents

Security and Safety

Fault Injection

Object Detection and Perception

Testing

Safety Analysis and Certification

Analysing the Safety of Decision-Making in Autonomous Systems

Matt Osborne(✉) ⓘ, Richard Hawkins ⓘ, and John McDermid ⓘ

Assuring Autonomy International Programme, Department of Computer Science,
University of York, Deramore Lane, York YO10 5GH, UK
{matthew.osborne,richard.hawkins,john.mcdermid}@york.ac.uk

Abstract. We characterise an autonomous system as one that has the capability to take decisions independently from human control. This independent and autonomous decision making could give rise to new hazards or hazard causes not present in an equivalent human-controlled system, e.g. through lack of human real-world understanding. Despite the increased adoption of autonomous systems there has been a dearth of research in the area of safety analysis and assurance of decision-making for autonomous systems. This paper is intended to be a first step to fill this gap. We compare and contrast the differing causal models of autonomous and non-autonomous systems, and build on existing safety engineering techniques in order to define a process (Decision Safety Analysis) for the analysis of autonomous decision-making. We show, using a real-world example, how this process supports the development of safety requirements to mitigate hazardous scenarios.

Keywords: Decision-making · Autonomous systems · Safety analysis

1 Introduction

As the use of autonomous systems (AS) for safety-related tasks continues to increase, safety-related decision-making has consequently started to transfer from the human to the AS. There is a clear and pressing need to assure the safety of (the AS making) those decisions. There are well established safety analysis approaches that have been shown to be effective in assuring the safety of traditional systems. In this paper we investigate how autonomous decision-making challenges the use of these existing approaches [1]. We identify a lack of understanding of how these approaches may be applied effectively to autonomous decision-making. For example, there are existing techniques for the analysis of human error and erroneous human decision-making but it is not clear that these could be applied to decision-making *by AS*. We therefore propose a process for analysing autonomous decision-making (Decision Safety Analysis (DSA)) that addresses these limitations.

This work is funded by the Assuring Autonomy International Programme https://www.york.ac.uk/assuring-autonomy.

This paper makes the following contributions:

1. We provide a process for analysing the safety of decisions made by an AS
2. We show how the process can be used to specifically focus further, efficient safety analyses of the AS
3. We demonstrate how the outcomes of the process can help to elicit safety requirements in mitigation of unsafe decisions that could be made by an AS.

We present the background and discuss the problem space in Sect. 2 before presenting our proposed DSA approach in Sect. 3. We present an evaluation of the process in Sect. 4, before describing the results, wider applications, and future work in Sect. 5.

2   Background

AS can be characterised as systems that have the capability to take decisions free from human control. From a safety perspective it is therefore the ability of an AS to make *safe* decisions that is of primary concern. It is crucial where the actions of an AS may lead to hazardous events, that such decisions are analysed for their safety impact and sufficient mitigations, or barriers, put in place.

The decision-making of an AS could give rise to new causal/failure paths that would not be present in an equivalent, human-controlled system (such as an autonomous robot operating in a typical office environment being 'unaware' of the dangers presented by blind corners, or water on a floor). Alternatively, autonomous decision-making could bring new causes to existing hazards (for example an office robot failing to detect a door that is comprised of transparent material). Figure 1 shows a representation of an accident model for a system. The system is represented as an agent that must:

– Sense the environment in which it operates using exteroceptive sensors
– Understand the information provided from the sensors (and other information) in order to create a model of the environment
– Decide how the system should respond based on its environment model
– Act in order to implement the decision made.

This is a continuous process for the system as it responds to changes in the environment by updating its understanding in order to make new decisions. For the case represented by the grey boxes at the top of Fig. 1, both the understanding and deciding aspects are dealt with by a human who forms a mental model of the environment from the information presented by the sensors and then, based on that mental model, decides on the best option to ensure the system meets its operational objectives in a sufficiently safe manner. Figure 1 illustrates that some of the actions the human may choose could result in an accident. The system would be designed with a combination of human and system checks that are intended to prevent failures resulting in accident outcomes. These are represented in Fig. 1 as barriers at multiple points in the model.

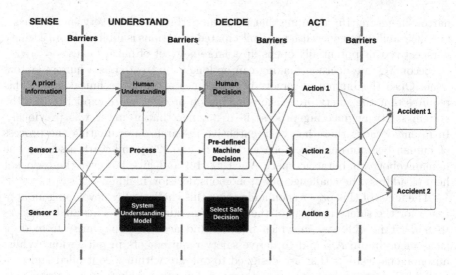

Fig. 1. A causal model of accidents for different types of system

For a traditional software-controlled system, as shown in Fig. 1, information is processed by the system (the unshaded boxes) and decisions either made by the human, or suggested by the system, with human oversight. The decisions made by the software are in fact pre-determined rules which have already been hard-coded into the design by a human. Analysis and assurance of safe decisions is primarily a human factors issue for such traditional systems - through analysis of human behaviour and mitigation through human factors measures such as procedures, training and supervision (although it does depend on the veracity of information provided by the system).

Figure 1 shows a similar causal model for an AS, represented with dark boxes. *In this case, only the bottom line of the understand and decide elements are relevant.* Here the system has primary responsibility for understanding the environment, creating an accurate model, and making safe decisions. A key difference here, as well as the removal of human over-sight, is the fact that the decisions are not hard-coded at design time as they were for traditional software systems [2], rather the system is given autonomy to determine the best action, given its understanding of the environment. Although the level of autonomy given to an AS can vary, we focus here on the case where there is no human oversight. From a safety perspective this represents a significant challenge for two important reasons.

Firstly, for traditional systems, humans have a particularly important role in dealing with unanticipated or unusual situations that the system may encounter. A human operator is able to use their contextual knowledge and general intelligence to react safely to unexpected occurrences. This innate ability to generalise often plays a crucial role in ensuring safe decisions are taken. Although machines may present a high level of artificial intelligence, this intelligence is typically very narrow in nature [15], meaning that they can perform well for very specific tasks, but their ability to generalise to unanticipated situations is limited. From a safety perspective this potentially opens up a large new set of hazard causes.

Secondly, safe decision-making can no longer be treated as a human factors issue. Once the human is removed, it becomes a purely technical issue. This requires that the safety of decision-making be brought more explicitly into the system safety engineering process in a manner that it never was previously. In recent decades there has been extensive research on evaluating the process of human decision-making (such as [10–12], and [20]) and work assessing the human-robot collaborative space (such as [14] and [6]), however these do not help to address the challenge of autonomous decision-making, *per se*.

The focus of this paper is on addressing this challenge by developing an approach for the safety analysis of the decision-making in AS. This analysis seeks to understand the way in which hazards and accidents may arise from decisions made by an AS, and to derive safety requirements in mitigation. Whilst autonomous systems that are designed to operate within a controlled and controllable environment (such as automated passenger railways) can reasonably rely on 'classical' safety engineering techniques, a different approach is required for assuring the safety of decision-making by AS when its operating environment is more complex.

Although a lot of work has considered the implementation and verification of AS decision-making, there is an assumption that what constitutes safe behaviour is known (examples include [19] and [16] but these are by no means exceptions), we have found very little work on safety analysis and identification of mitigations for such systems. This paper begins to address that gap.

3   A Decision Safety Analysis Process

Key to the safe operation of an AS is the establishment of a suitably-defined Operational Domain Model (ODM) (often referred to in the automotive industry as an Operational Design Domain (ODD) [13]). The ODM defines the scope of operation within which the AS is to be shown to be acceptably safe. This will include any assumptions made, the features of the operating environment (e.g. people, road type and layout, weather conditions) which the AS is expected to sense, understand, and potentially interact with prior to making decisions as it carries out its tasks. If the ODM is insufficiently defined then the AS may encounter scenarios during its operation that were not considered during the development of the system, and which could therefore be unsafe and for which no assurance is provided. It is crucial therefore that all relevant aspects, features and interactions within and of the operational domain are defined - including those non-mission interactions [8]. Despite the importance of a sufficiently defined ODM, the assurance of an ODM is out of the scope of this paper.

Use cases can be created for each of the tasks which identify the elements of the ODM which the AS must understand and with which it may interact. Examination of these use cases reveals the occasions when key decisions must be made by an AS. These decisions must be modelled and analysed to determine the nature of any hazardous scenario that may arise as a result of the AS decision.

We consider hazardous scenarios to be special cases of the Operating Scenarios for the AS, which are identified as those which could result in an unsafe outcome. 'Scenarios' describe the combination of the AS Operating Scenario and the relevant environment variables. Potentially hazardous scenarios for an AS arise due to decisions taken which are unsafe in a given environmental state when performing a particular operating scenario (the same decisions might be safe in other circumstances). Hazardous scenarios for the AS can therefore be described using the general form:

<AS operating scenario><relevant environment variables>AND <decision>, where:

- An AS Operating Scenario describes what task(s) the AS is undertaking
- A Relevant Environment Variable is **one or more** features of the environment relevant to the decision point
- The Decision is the selected course of action as a result of the scenario and relevant environment variables.

As an example, for an autonomous passenger shuttle undertaking the task of navigating a (UK) roundabout, we can identify a decision point for whether the shuttle should enter the roundabout. For this case, an example of a 'relevant' environment variable would be a cyclist on the roundabout to the right of the AS. A pedestrian on the footpath 20 m behind the AS would not be considered relevant as they will not influence the decision taken by the AS. Other variables could concern the road state, or weather conditions at the time a decision is required to be made.

Decisions taken by the AS can only be in relation to variables that the system can control, i.e. speed and/or direction - as the environmental variables are outside of the control of the AS. As such, the options for the passenger shuttle at this 'decision point' are:

1. Enter the roundabout (at variations in speed)
2. Stop and wait.

The approach we present in this paper can be used to identify hazardous scenarios by considering the real world state in combination with the belief state of the AS, and each of the options at the decision point, e.g. the 2 options for the shuttle identified above. This analysis would thus identify hazardous scenarios such as:

- <the passenger shuttle is approaching a roundabout><with a cyclist on the roundabout to the vehicle's right> **AND** <the passenger shuttle enters the roundabout> or,
- <the passenger shuttle is approaching a roundabout><with no cyclist present> **AND** <the passenger shuttle stops and waits>.

Whilst the first case presents an obvious risk, the second case may not always be safe, as should the AS decide to brake rapidly and unexpectedly, a hazardous outcome may be realised in the form of a rear-end collision.

3.1   The Decision Safety Analysis Process

Before we discuss the DSA process in detail, we must first consider what we mean by 'decision-making' in AS. The nature of the decisions made by AS can vary enormously depending on the type of system and the application domain. For example:

- An autonomous cancer-screening system decides on the appropriate patient referral based upon information from scans and other medical data
- An autonomous vehicle decides on a safe course of action if it detects an object in its path. The decision must take account of multiple other environmental variables, such as the presence of other road users, and weather conditions.

For the DSA Process it is important to distinguish between what is actually the decisions of interest for the safety analysis and what is part of the understanding task. This distinction can be highlighted in the second example above, which can be split into two parts:

- **Understand** - is there an object in the path of the vehicle?
- **Decide** - what am I going to do about it?

For AS the complexity of the operating environment can have a much greater impact on safe behaviour than for traditional systems, as this increases the chance of unanticipated and unusual events (sometimes referred to as 'edge cases'). This can be a particular challenge since AS typically operate in highly complex environments that often cannot be fully specified at design time [3]. Whilst dealing with complex environments is not limited to AS, traditional systems operating in complex environments place a lot of reliance on the human ability to deal with any unanticipated events. With an AS we cannot rely on a human to ensure a safe state is maintained, and must rely on the AS to respond safely under all situations within the entire operating domain. This requires that the analysis incorporates consideration of the operating environment in a more systematic and explicit manner than is currently the case.

Guiochet advocates the use of Use Cases and Sequence Diagrams (and then State Charts as required) as the models for undertaking HAZOP-UML analysis [7]. However, we have found that these do not make good models for analysing AS decisions as they do not make the decisions explicit, nor do they lend themselves to methodical analysis with defined start/finish points. Instead our approach uses Activity Diagrams for each use case (as shown in Fig. 3 for the example of an autonomous robot) with the following explicit information included:

- *Decision points* (annotated 'DP' within the diamonds) identified from the Use Cases and ODM. These represent the instances where a decision must be made by an AS due to a required interaction with the environment.
- *Options* associated with each decision point (represented as circles). These represent the options that an AS **could** select for each decision point.
- *Understanding points* in the use case represent the points at which the AS requires information about a particular relevant environment variable (non 'DP' diamonds).

In addition, for each Activity Diagram it is important to explicitly model all relevant assumptions and preconditions as these must be considered as part of the analysis.

It is important that the model is a complete representation of the operating scenario, particularly that the decision and understanding points have been adequately elicited. We can gain confidence in this through utilising an explicit domain model, but further work is required, and research such as that presented in [17] has started to address the completeness of ODMs via modelling and simulations, but further work is required.

Having established the Activity Diagram(s) for the system, we then analyse that model to determine hazardous scenarios, i.e. the way in which the decision could lead to selecting an option that is unsafe given the relevant environment variables. As for many similar safety analysis tasks, we propose the use of deviation-based analysis of those decision points in order to identify plausible unsafe behaviours. We considered a number of existing deviation-based techniques that have been applied to software-based systems and could be adapted to decision analysis such as FFA/FHA [5], STPA [9], and HAZOP [4]. In particular we considered HAZOP-UML [7] which was developed as a method for analysing UML models of robot systems. In general, the use of a HAZOP-based approach does seem reasonable, yet it does not support the analysis of the decision models we propose, nor explicitly consider the impact of the operating domain as part of the analysis. In addition the HAZOP-UML approach is exhaustive but unfocused, and will therefore quickly lead to a state explosion requiring substantial analysis effort without necessarily revealing the safety issues of most concern.

We have therefore developed our DSA approach to ensure the analysis is driven by consideration of the identified decision points to establish potentially hazardous deviations. As well as identifying hazardous scenarios associated with decision points, our process also provides the focus for further, more detailed analysis using, for example, HAZOP-UML. Our process is summarised in Fig. 2 and is described below. A more detailed description is provided at [18].

STEP 1. The DSA requires the identification of the relevant environment variables pertinent to the scenario under analysis. These variables are identified through recourse to the ODM, as discussed earlier. One potential approach would be to use [8], but the decision model we present does not presume any particular method.

STEP 2. Decision Points are identified by considering the decisions required to be made as a result of the interactions between the AS and the environment. Once the decision point is identified, the options available to the AS are enumerated through considerations of the system variables, as discussed previously.

In the example at Table 1 in Sect. 3.2, as the AS can only amend system variables it has control over (speed and/or direction), we defined 4 options in this case:

1. Continue on the current path at current speed
2. Continue on the current path at reduced speed

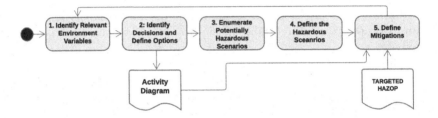

Fig. 2. The decision point analysis process

3. Take and alternative route at current speed
4. Stop and wait.

It is now possible to create an Activity Diagram that includes Understanding Points identified in Step 1 and Decision Points identified in Step 2. An extract of an Activity Diagram for an example system is provided at Fig. 3.

STEP 3. The potentially hazardous scenarios must be determined (represented in the 1st column of Table 1). This is done by firstly considering the possible options defined at Step 2 in combination with both the real world state, and the system belief state at the point at which that decision is made. Real world and system belief states are often represented as Booleans. In the example we give in Sect. 3.2, the state of 'True' for the real world state means a blind corner is present, and a state of 'True' for the system belief means that the AS "knows" this. The potentially hazardous scenarios will also consider false negatives (i.e. a real world state of 'False' and a system belief state of 'True').

For the extract in Table 1 in Sect. 3.2 we can see 14 of the scenarios which are enumerated by considering the 4 options along with the real world, and system belief states regarding the presence of a blind corner and a static object.

STEP 4. The outcome of each potentially hazardous scenarios enumerated in Step 3 must be determined by considering the real world impact should that scenario manifest. For any scenarios with hazardous outcomes, the hazardous scenarios can be specified using the general form described in Sect. 3.

STEP 5. The process then focuses on mitigating hazardous outcomes. Such mitigations could be in the form of design changes (e.g. adding a diverse sensor), or through derived safety requirements. These mitigations can be levied against the sense capability, detection capability, against the decision-making algorithm itself or on supporting infrastructure, where appropriate.

Identifying effective mitigations requires further more detailed analysis. The hazardous scenarios defined at Step 4 are used to identify the logic nodes of interest in the Activity Diagram (such as Understanding points) against which a targeted analysis such as HAZOP-UML can then be applied. The extract at Fig. 3 shows, in red font, the logical nodes of interest to which the Targeted HAZOP will be applied.

The findings of the targeted HAZOP are used to elicit further safety requirements to mitigate potential causes of hazardous scenarios. This targeted approach to undertaking the HAZOP is explained in full and illustrated on a mobile robot at [18].

It is only because we have already assessed the possible outcomes using DSA that the HAZOP can be targeted in this manner. It allows us to focus the analysis on the logic points of interest that could contribute to an erroneous decision being taken. This approach prevents the state explosion that manifests from applying HAZOP guidewords against every logical node in an Activity Diagram by allowing scenarios resulting in safe (if not always efficient) outcomes to be removed from further analysis.

In the next section we present an example of applying our approach to robots that are designed to be used for delivering small packages within one of our University buildings [18].

3.2 Robot Delivery System Example

We are developing a number of small robots that are capable of delivering packages around a university building. Building occupants may request a robot to come to them anywhere in the building and deliver a package to a desired destination. The building comprises 3 floors containing offices, laboratories of varying size, meeting/conference facilities, and various comfort/rest areas. A large goods lift in the centre of the building provides access to all floors, and a large shared atrium houses the reception area for visitors. The building benefits from a building management system (BMS) that provides automation and control of climate, lighting, doors, and the lift.

Through interacting with the BMS the robot is able to open/close doors and use the lift to move around the building. A central server (Robot HQ) is used to coordinate the allocation of tasks amongst the multiple robots that operate in the building at any time, but all movement around the building is controlled locally by each individual robot. In addition to the basic delivery and messenger tasks, the robots must interact with human occupants and other robots within the fabric of the building. The primary overall use case (01) for the robots is 'Package Delivery'. We broke this down to the following, more detailed use cases:

02. Request robot
03. Load package
04. Travel to destination
05. Unload package.

Within use case 04 a number of exception cases were identified, including:

A. Dynamic object in path of robot
B. Static object in path of robot
C. Forbidden zone on planned path
D. Use Lift

E. Pass through doorway

F. Blind corner on route.

Within use case 04 a number of preconditions were also identified, including:

- **Precondition1:** Robot is available
- **Precondition2:** Sender and receiver are in accessible locations
- **Precondition3:** Robot battery charge is sufficient for task.

The identified use cases relates to 4 different actors:

- Sender
- Receiver
- Building Management System
- Robot HQ.

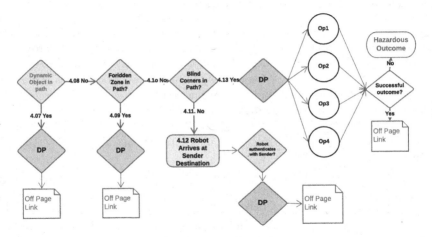

Fig. 3. An extract of the decision activity diagram for use case 04 - "travel to destination"

These, along with the elements of the operating environment defined in the ODM, assumptions, normal flows, alternative flows, and safety requirements/invariants represent the primary interactions that the robots make.

We have used the DSA Process to analyse the system described above. As described in Sect. 3.1 the first thing we require is a model of the decisions taken by the delivery robots. Figure 3 shows an example decision activity diagram for Use Case 04. Through consideration of the interactions of the robot with the elements of the defined ODM, a number of scenarios were identified including the robot approaching a blind corner. By blind corner we mean one the robot cannot "see" around, and these might be permanent, e.g. due to walls, or temporary, e.g. due to a bag being placed against the side of a desk blocking the normal line

Table 1. Extract of a decision safety analysis table

Operational scenario: travel to destination					
Environment variables: \<Robot approaching blind corner\>\<Static object in path\>					
Potentially hazardous scenarios	Real world state	System model belief	Option	Outcome	Safety Reqmt
1	T	T	Continue on current path at current speed	Hazardous - collision	#1 #2 #3
2			Continue on current path at reduced speed	Hazardous - though severity may reduce	#2
3			Take an alternative route at current speed	Correct decision	#2 #3
4			Stop and wait	Safe but inefficient	
5	T	F	Continue on current path at current speed	Hazardous	#4
6			Continue on current path at reduced speed	Hazardous - though severity may reduce	#5
7			Take an alternative route at current speed	Safe - but predicated on erroneous understanding	#3
8			Stop and wait	Safe but inefficient	
9	F	T	Continue on current path at current speed	Safe - but predicated on bug in path planning	#6
10			Continue on current path at reduced speed	Safe - but predicated on bug in path planning	#6
11			Take alternative route at current speed	Safe - but predicated on bug in path planning	#6
12			Stop and wait	Potentially unsafe (sudden stop)	#6
13	F	F	Continue on current path at current speed	Correct decision	
14			Continue on current path at reduced speed	Safe - but predicated on bug in path planning	
Safety requirements					
1	The robot shall take into account blind corners when route planning				
2	The robot shall reduce its speed to 0.25 m per second when approaching a blind corner				
3	The robot shall provide audio and visual alerts when approaching a blind corner				
4	The Building Management System shall enforce robot speed reductions in areas of blind corners				
5	The robot shall be aware of blind corners on its planned path				
6	The robot shall not falsely detect the presence of blind corners				

of sight for the robot's optical sensors. Table 1 shows the results of the analysis of this scenario, showing 14 identified scenarios and their potential outcomes. Note that requirement #4 deals with permanent blind corners but will be unable to deal with temporary problems caused by placing of bags, etc. Requirement #5 requires the robot to sense blockages that create temporary blind corners – for example determining, using a depth camera, that it cannot "see" as far as normal in the relevant direction at this location. This is therefore a requirement on the understanding component of the system, which also requires information about the layout of the building (from maps or the BMS) to detect temporary blind corners and to inform the decision-making algorithm accordingly. Details such as the above would be added as the safety requirements are allocated to the system components and refined.

This analysis elicited a number of hazardous scenarios, for example:

<the robot is travelling to its destination><approaching a blind corner with a static object in its intended path> AND <the robot continues at current speed>.

In conjunction with a targeted HAZOP we were able to identify a number of mitigations levied against both the robots and other actors (e.g. the BMS being required to enforce robot speed reductions in areas including permanent blind corners). The mitigations identified from the DSA can be seen in Table 1, and mitigations from the targeted HAZOP can be found in full at [18].

4   Process Evaluation

We have so far evaluated our DSA process in two ways. Firstly, we assessed the usability of the approach by applying it to a real-life case study. This showed the process was able to successfully generate a set of safety requirements in mitigation of identified hazardous scenarios. Secondly, we have evaluated the efficiency of the process by also carrying out a full HAZOP-UML analysis, and comparing the effort and outputs for both the DSA and HAZOP-UML.

When we applied our DSA process to the robots, we elicited 32 safety requirements, of which 3 were allocated to the BMS and the rest to the robots themselves. The process was simple to apply using the Activity Diagrams that had been created for the robot tasks. In carrying out this evaluation it was noted, however that well-defined use cases and a clearly structured and complete ODM were essential to the efficacy of the process. For example, if the ODM is missing any of the key elements of the operating environment, this would mean that potentially critical interactions could be missed. The challenge of specifying use cases and ODMs is widely reported ([13] for example) and requires further work which is outside the scope of this paper.

It was also noted that for the requirements definition phase, it is often necessary to specify constraints as part of the derived safety requirements. As is always the case for complex systems and environments, defining these safety constraints can be challenging. For example eliciting the required range, bearing, and detectable distance of static and dynamic objects will be influenced by the size, speed, and braking capability of the AS. Defining such constraints as part of the safety requirements is something we intend to explore further, but is out of scope for this paper.

We have described how our process enables further focused analysis of causes of unsafe decisions through the use of a targeted HAZOP that enabled safe scenarios to be excluded from the analysis. This allows a complete analysis without the need for exhaustive state coverage. In order to test this, a full HAZOP-UML was undertaken on the entire use case for our system (considering all logic nodes in the activity diagrams). We found that this full HAZOP analysis was a very time consuming activity due to the expected state explosion (generating 834 lines of analysis). Despite this, it did not identify any safety requirements to be placed on the robots in addition to those elicited much more efficiently from applying our process and subsequent targeted HAZOP. The full use cases, DSA results, HAZOP, and safety requirements elicited in mitigation can all be found at [18].

5   Discussion and Conclusions

This paper has made the following contributions. Firstly, we have demonstrated a process for analysing the safety of AS decision-making. Secondly, we have demonstrated how the process can be used to facilitate a targeted approach to HAZOP, that avoids analysing safe (but perhaps inefficient) outcomes and prevents the state explosion associated with applying guidewords to every logical node of a use case. Thirdly, our approach enables the elicitation of safety requirements in mitigation of hazardous decisions made by an AS.

We have, so far, only applied the DSA approach to a single robot system in a controllable environment, and do not yet make an argument regarding the generalisability of our approach. In order to check the wider applicability of the approach we are applying the process to more complex, less controllable operating domains, including outdoor operation. This will also be further extended to consider a multi-robot system, and concurrent and consecutive decision-making. Our current case study considers robots that operate in an environment that includes humans, but it has not yet been applied to systems involving robot-human collaboration (where humans work together with the robots to fulfil tasks). We therefore also plan to apply the process to a COBOT [6] system.

We anticipate carrying out additional applications of our approach in order to further validate its efficacy and to demonstrate its wider applicability.

References

1. Safety and ethics of autonomous systems project overview. Technical report, Royal Academy of Engineering (2020)
2. Adler, R., Feth, P., Schneider, D.: Safety engineering for autonomous vehicles. In: 2016 46th Annual IEEE/IFIP International Conference on Dependable Systems and Networks Workshop (DSN-W), pp. 200–205. IEEE (2016)
3. Burton, S., Habli, I., Lawton, T., McDermid, J., Morgan, P., Porter, Z.: Mind the gaps: assuring the safety of autonomous systems from an engineering, ethical, and legal perspective. Artif. Intell. **279**, 103201 (2020)
4. International Electrotechnical Commission: IEC 61882 (2016)
5. Ericson, C.A., et al.: Hazard Analysis Techniques for System Safety. Wiley, Hoboken (2015)

6. Gleirscher, M., Johnson, N., Karachristou, P., Calinescu, R., Law, J., Clark, J.: Challenges in the safety-security co-assurance of collaborative industrial robots. arXiv preprint arXiv:2007.11099 (2020)

7. Guiochet, J.: Hazard analysis of human-robot interactions with HAZOP-UML. Saf. Sci. **84**, 225–237 (2016)

8. Harper, C., Caleb-Solly, P.: Towards an ontological framework for environmental survey hazard analysis of autonomous systems. In: SafeAI@ AAAI (2021)

9. Ishimatsu, T., Leveson, N.G., Thomas, J., Katahira, M., Miyamoto, Y., Nakao, H.: Modeling and hazard analysis using STPA (2010)

10. Kahneman, D.: Thinking, Fast and Slow. Macmillan (2011)

11. Klein, G.A., Orasanu, J., Calderwood, R., Zsambok, C.E., et al.: Decision Making in Action: Models and Methods. Ablex Norwood, New Jersey (1993)

12. Koehler, J.J.: The influence of prior beliefs on scientific judgments of evidence quality. Organ. Behav. Hum. Decis. Process. **56**(1), 28–55 (1993)

13. Koopman, P., Fratrik, F.: How many operational design domains, objects, and events? In: SafeAI@AAAI (2019)

14. Lesage, B.M.J.R., Alexander, R.: SASSI: safety analysis using simulation-based situation coverage for cobot systems. In: Proceedings of SafeComp 2021, York (2021)

15. Marcus, G., Davis, E.: Rebooting AI: Building Artificial Intelligence We Can Trust. Vintage (2019)

16. Medrano-Berumen, C., İlhan Akbaş, M.: Validation of decision-making in artificial intelligence-based autonomous vehicles. J. Inf. Telecommun **5**(1), 83–103 (2021)

17. Oberheid, H., Hasselberg, A., Söffker, D.: Know your options-analysing human decision making in dynamic task environments with state space methods. Hum. Centred Autom. 285–300 (2011)

18. Osborne, M.: ISA Robot Safety of Decision Making. https://www-users.cs.york.ac.uk/mo705/isarobot.html

19. Stansbury, R.S., Agah, A.: A robot decision making framework using constraint programming. Artif. Intell. Rev. **38**(1), 67–83 (2012)

20. Walker, G., et al.: Modelling driver decision-making at railway level crossings using the abstraction decomposition space. Cogn. Technol. Work **23**(2), 225–237 (2021)

BayesianSafety - An Open-Source Package for Causality-Guided, Multi-model Safety Analysis

Robert Maier[✉] [iD] and Jürgen Mottok[iD]

Regensburg University of Applied Sciences, 93049 Regensburg, Germany
{robert.maier,juergen.mottok}@oth-regensburg.de

Abstract. Development and verification of modern, dependable automotive systems require appropriate modelling approaches. Classic automotive safety is described by the normative regulations ISO 26262, its relative ISO/PAS 21448, and their respective methodologies. In recent publications, an emerging demand to combine environmental influences, machine learning, or reasoning under uncertainty with standard-compliant analysis techniques can be noticed. Therefore, adapting established methods like FTA and proper tool support is necessary. We argue that Bayesian Networks (BNs) can be used as a central component to address and merge these demands. In this paper, we present our Open-Source Python package *BayesianSafety*. First, we review how BNs relate to data-driven methods, model-to-model transformations, and causal reasoning. Together with FTA and ETA, these models form the core functionality of our software. After describing currently implemented features and possibilities of combining individual modelling approaches, we provide an informal view of the tool's architecture and of the resulting software ecosystem. By comparing selected publicly available safety and reliability analysis libraries, we outline that many relevant methodologies yield specialized implementations. Finally, we show that there is a demand for a flexible, unifying analysis tool that allows researching system safety by using multi-model and multi-domain approaches.

Keywords: Fault Tree Analysis · Event Tree Analysis · Bayesian Networks · Causality · Package BayesianSafety

1 Introduction

Today's view on Functional Safety (FS) and reliability was developed over decades. Throughout this evolution, multiple techniques to manage different aspects of system safety emerged. Modern standards like IEC 61508 or its automotive relatives ISO 26262, ISO/PAS 26448, and UL 4600 encourage and support these modelling approaches. Consequently, methodologies like Fault Tree Analysis (FTA), Event Tree Analysis (ETA), Failure Mode and Effects Analysis (FMEA), or Goal Structuring Notation (GSN) form the basis that allows building complex, highly dependable [2] systems like autonomous driving cars.

M. Trapp et al. (Eds.): SAFECOMP 2022, LNCS 13414, pp. 17–30, 2022.
https://doi.org/10.1007/978-3-031-14835-4_2

Practitioners and researchers working with these modelling approaches demand appropriate tool support. Even though there are proprietary as well as Open-Source solutions available, most of them are optimized to work with one methodology only.

In recent years, researchers noted that system safety is a multi-aspect endeavour. Feth et al. [8] state that various of the above disciplines should be combined to form a joint safety engineering process in the automotive context. Similarly, Mosleh et al. [13] outline that different frameworks (here FTA, a modified ETA, and BNs) can be merged on a conceptual level. This allows addressing many requirements such as model maintainability and justifiability, incorporation of uncertainty, or high fidelity while staying compatible with various standards [18].

In the autonomous driving domain, research questions of interest include how reasoning under uncertainty, handling operational and environmental conditions, or a combination of abstract influences from multiple domains can be combined with ISO 26262 or ISO/PAS 21448. Modelling uncertainty is often addressed by resorting to BNs [12]. Moreover, Bayesian-based graphical models allow researching causality to answer questions like "what if" and "why" [15]. BNs are commonly used in conjunction with established, standard-compliant methods (e.g. Hybrid Causal Logic (HCL) [13]) and for model-to-model transformation [4,5,11].

Usually, the various FS and reliability methodologies have their own semantics, modelling assumptions, or mathematical frameworks to calculate metrics of safety evaluation like Average Probability of Failure on Demand or Probability of Failure per Hour. Due to this, software supporting these various methodologies differs drastically and renders a multi-method often a multi-tool approach. Additional features, like the incorporation of environmental aspects (e.g. adapting FTA as required by HCL) or combining various frameworks (e.g. Bow-Tie models (BTs)) are typically not supported by commercial tools like Ansys® medini analyze[1] or Open-Source packages like $SCRAM$[2]. Nonetheless, these capabilities are of high interest to researchers and practitioners alike. Ideally, software supporting the outlined combination of methodologies should be easy to adapt and modify, extensible, and foremost available for all.

The contribution of this paper and associated research is an Open-Source Python package called $BayesianSafety$[3], which can serve as a basic implementation to address the demands outlined above. Our aim is to provide a novel, extensible software environment with a focus on harmonizing the combination of various modelling approaches by using BNs.

First, we will cover the basics of BNs and how they can be used as a universal model to transform established standard-compliant methodologies. We will do so by addressing how our currently supported modelling approaches FTA and ETA can be mapped to BNs as a mathematical core framework. By doing so, we gain access to methods that can learn environmental models from data, combine them

---

[1] https://www.ansys.com/.

[2] https://github.com/rakhimov/scram.

[3] https://github.com/othr-las3/bayesiansafety.

with transformed models, and allow causal reasoning as outlined by [15]. Next, we give a brief overview of the resulting modelling possibilities by combining simple models and the currently implemented features of *BayesianSafety*. Based on requirements for a novel FS and reliability analysis software package, we review and compare related work. We close this paper with a summary as well as future research and implementation intentions.

2 Preliminaries

The following section highlights the key ideas behind our proposed software package *BayesianSafety*.

2.1 Bayesian Networks

Probabilistic Graphical Models (PGMs) like BNs are often used as suitable mathematical frameworks for reasoning under uncertainty [12]. BNs are directed acyclic graphs that are able to convey assumptions on how variables interact. They specify and represent a joint probability distribution and allow efficient computation of probabilistic information. When connections between variables are given a causal (i.e. cause and effect) interpretation, they can be used as causal models to facilitate causal reasoning [15].

Given the assumption that variables are only directly influenced by their Markovian parents pa_i (i.e. immediate predecessor nodes), the underlying joint probability distribution $P(\mathbf{X})$ can be factorized as a special case of the chain rule of probability:

$$P(\mathbf{X}) = \prod_i P(x_i|pa_i) \tag{1}$$

A conditional probability distribution can be interpreted as a causal mechanism mapping the influence of parent nodes to the distribution of the child node. Causal models allow interventions (i.e. locally changing a causal mechanism) and estimating how probability distributions would change. These mechanisms can be used to model stochastic as well as deterministic relationships. This property is exploited in model-to-model transformations.

2.2 Model-to-Model Transformations

Bobbio et al. [4] show that Fault Trees (FTs) can be mapped into BNs without loss of expressiveness. The deterministic relationship between input nodes (e.g. basic events) and a node of interest (e.g. gate) can be modelled by adjusting the respective conditional probability distributions (i.e. implementing a truth table). In contrast to FTs, a straightforward topological transformation of Event Trees (ETs) [3] is usually not possible. Instead, the model's structure is defined by some properties of the paths between an initiating event and associated consequences. Both model transformations are reversible without any loss of information. A resulting topology, together with the conditional distributions associated with each node, encode all required information of the original model in the resulting BN. To support reasoning under uncertainty, adapting formal methodologies like FMEA [11] or GSN [14] is also researched by using model-to-model transformations.

Casting various modelling approaches into the same mathematical framework allows merging them. In the case of BNs, this requires adjusting the causal mechanisms of nodes that link transformed models. This is possible as long as the modularity assumption (i.e. changing a local mechanism does not affect others, e.g. parents of a node) holds. Consequently, environmental models can be used to serve as input for standard-compliant approaches (e.g. rain and light conditions as basic events in a FT [18]).

Figure 1 gives an informal example of how (mathematically) independent frameworks can be transformed into BNs and combined to a single model. On the left side of the figure, a FT is mapped into a BN according to [4]. In the centre, an ET is transformed based on [3]. Combining FTs and ETs can be done via BTs [10]. On the right side, a HCL model is built from the individual parts. An environmental model with influences (E_i) is added and replaces two basic events of the FT via the nodes $E4$ and $E5$. The top-level event of the transformed FT is considered as initiating event of the ET with outcomes $FE1_{1a}$ and $FE1_{1b}$. FT, ET, and environmental influences together form an instantiation of the HCL framework. Additionally, the conditional probability tables for the transformed ET are given, showing the preservation of determinism after mapping.

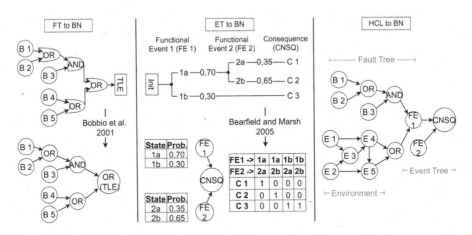

Fig. 1. Informal example of how a FT and an ET can be transformed into a BN. On the right side, both models are combined and extended by an environmental network, forming an instantiation of the HCL framework.

2.3   Bridging the Issue of Multiple Domains

Due to the increasing complexity of technical systems (e.g. autonomous driving cars) FS and reliability analysis is non-trivial. Components of a system can be broadly categorized into three groups: software, hardware, or artificial intelligence-based. Depending on the individual category, different standards like ISO 26262 or ISO/PAS 21448, or UL 4600 might apply. Each of these standards encourages the use of different modelling approaches. As [8,16,18] among others point out, a combination of these methods can be reasonable.

A problem that arises when trying to merge methodologies, is how to adequately link them. Interactions between components as well as between model elements are often treated as causal. As mentioned above, BNs can be utilized to handle such relationships in the form of causal mechanisms and therefore qualify as a framework for a joint multi-domain, multi-model system evaluation.

With respect to the increasing popularity of Machine Learning (ML) based components, the issue of explainability emerges. This is due to black-box learning methods (e.g. Neural Networks) and the data used for their training.

A trend called "causal revolution" started recently in the ML community. Its core idea is to employ causal knowledge in the form of causal graphs to train learning algorithms more efficiently and robustly [17]. This allows working with white-box models (i.e. causal graphs). In the context of FS and reliability, they can serve as input to standard-compliant methodologies like FTs and may be used to verify parts of an ML algorithm.

Causal models can also be used to interpret the underlying data and encoded relationships (i.e. correlation and causation) between variables [15]. Causal discovery describes the approach to algorithmically learn causal models from data, by estimating the topology and conditional probability distributions of the graph [19]. This is especially valuable in light of data-driven safety assurance, as it allows the processing of collected data as a source of causal knowledge (i.e. as an environmental model). As a consequence, the modelling of environmental, operational, or scenario-relevant influences can be decoupled in parts from human experts. Therefore, causal models might serve as an objective way to address parts of scenario-based testing approaches (e.g. evaluation of sensor data or simulation results) as outlined in ISO/PAS 21448.

As mentioned in Sect. 1, each modelling approach typically builds on different assumptions. This ties the calculation of relevant metrics to specialized mathematical constructs. For example, FTs are based on boolean logic and can be used to calculate the likelihood of component failure (e.g. top-level event) given influencing factors. Based on boolean algebra or via a Binary Decision Diagram (BDD), risk worth or importance measures of a component can be derived. ETs on the other hand model logical combinations of events that lead to different consequences. Corresponding likelihoods are calculated as a product of branching probabilities based on paths between an initiating event and a consequence.

These different paradigms yield tailored and highly customized software packages. Researching combinations of these methodologies or of potential environmental influences leads to a multi-tool endeavour. Even though combining different domains is reasonable, to the best of our knowledge, currently, no Open-Source tool supports it. Our contribution is intended to address this demand.

3   Package BayesianSafety

In the following, we will describe our Python package *BayesianSafety*. The descriptions given below refer to FTs as an example.

3.1   Models and Their Combinations

As described by [13] a suitable combination of methodologies can jointly address various demands of system safety. Looking at Probabilistic Safety Assessments (PSAs) the two main frameworks used are FTA and ETA. Both analysis methods can be combined and transformed into BNs and extended in different ways (see Sect. 2). Due to this fact, they were chosen as the core functionality of *BayesianSafety*. Description and exchange of classic PSA models are supported by the Open-PSA initiative model exchange format [7]. Relevant combinations of the above methodologies include:

- stand-alone "classic" FT or ET,
- ET and BN (environmental influences) (see e.g. [3]),
- FT and BN (environmental influences) or common causes (see e.g. [4]),
- FT and ET (BT, see [10]), or
- FT and ET and BN (environmental influences) (HCL, see e.g. [13,18]).

BayesianSafety was developed to allow specifying models by hand if no description file can be provided. Listing 1.1 shows the code to set up the FT model of Fig. 1. Probability nodes (i.e. basic events) have a name parameter, can be given a static probability of failure, and are assumed to have two states: working and failing. A flag can be set to indicate time dependency. The probability of failure is then treated as failure rate λ for a default time behaviour of $1 - e^{(-\lambda t)}$. Logic gates (i.e. boolean gates) are given a name, a list of parent nodes, and a logic type to connect these arbitrary inputs.

Listing 1.1. Example listing for defining a simple FT in *BayesianSafety*.

```
1  from bayesianfaulttree.FaultTreeProbNode import
       FaultTreeProbNode as FTProb
2  from bayesianfaulttree.FaultTreeLogicNode import
       FaultTreeLogicNode as FTLogic
3  from bayesianfaulttree.BayesianFaultTree import
       BayesianFaultTree as BFT
4
5  B_1 = FTProb('B_1', 0.5e-3)
6  B_2 = FTProb('B_2', 1.6e-3)
7  B_3 = FTProb('B_3', 2.7e-3)
8  B_4 = FTProb('B_4', 3.8e-3)
9  B_5 = FTProb('B_5', 4.9e-3, is_time_dependent=True)
10
11 OR_1 = FTLogic('OR_1', ['B_1', 'B_2'] , 'OR')
```

```
12  AND  = FTLogic('AND', ['OR_1', 'B_3'], 'AND')
13  OR_2 = FTLogic('OR_2',  ['B_4', 'B_5'], 'OR')
14  TLE  = FTLogic('TLE', ['AND', 'OR_2'], 'OR')
15
16  probability_nodes = [B_1, B_2, B_3, B_4, B_5]
17  logic_nodes = [OR_1, AND, OR_2, TLE]
18  model = BFT("Example", probability_nodes, logic_nodes)
```

FTs and ETs can be imported either as individual models or as a joint model in case of a BT if a suitable Open-PSA file is available. An importer parses the provided tree structures and preprocesses relevant information. Based on the model type, a mapper is invoked. It instantiates a BN that serves as the default internal model-class of *BayesianSafety*. A *networkX DiGraph*-object [9] is used as a container for the graph representation of the BN topology. Mapping all imported networks to a BN allows combining models and joint inference. Listing 1.2 shows how a simple ET and FT can be imported.

Listing 1.2. Example listing for loading an ET and a FT from an Open-PSA file.

```
1  from bayesianeventtree.EventTreeImporter import
       EventTreeImporter
2  from bayesianfaulttree.FaultTreeImporter import
       FaultTreeImporter
3
4  bay_FT = FaultTreeImporter().load('./Example.xml')
5  bay_ET = EventTreeImporter().load('./Example.xml')
```

Working with Fault Trees. FTs can be used either as a quantitative or qualitative representation of a modelled system. Some basic metrics of interest include minimal cut sets and different importance measures (e.g. Risk Reduction Worth, Risk Achievement Worth, or Birnbaum importance). *BayesianSafety* supports all of the above, including the ability to run a time simulation between a start and end time. For a time-dependent evaluation, the respective time behaviour of time-dependent nodes is evaluated at each time step and the resulting probability of failure is updated for each affected element in the BN. For each node of the tree, the evolution of the probability of failure can be plotted or saved as a figure. A FT can also be evaluated at a given mission time t.

All probability evaluations are done by inferring the BN (i.e. the transformed model). It should be noted, that some method-specific results like nodes contributing to a minimal cut set are currently calculated based on the original FT structure (via the MOCUS algorithm) if equivalent methods using a BN are not available.

A missing feature in most Open-Source packages is the ability to freely specify a custom time behaviour for basic events. The default assumption for an underlying reliability function is usually to be exponential. This holds during the system's lifetime, but neglects for example end-of-life effects. *BayesianSafety* allows modelling time dependency for any probability node of a FT model by specifying a custom function. Listing 1.3 gives a short example of how a full network evaluation including the definition of a custom time behaviour can be implemented.

Listing 1.3. Example listing for evaluating a FT where two nodes have a customized time behaviour (i.e. sigmoid and cosine).

```
1  import numpy as np
2  def time_fn(time, kind="cos"):
3    if time <= 0:
4      return 0
5    sig = 1 - 1 / (np.exp(1.23e-4 * time) + 1)
6    return np.cos(time) if kind == "cos" else sig
7
8  ft_model = ...
9  node_1 = ft_model.get_elem_by_name("target_node_1")
10 node_1.change_time_behaviour(time_fn, {"kind":"sigm"})
11 node_2 = ft_model.get_elem_by_name("target_node_2")
12 node_2.change_time_behaviour(time_fn)
13
14 ft_model.run_time_simulation(start_time=0, stop_time=1e5,
       simulation_steps=50, plot_simulation=True)
```

Extension by Linking Environmental Models. Since FTs are internally represented as BNs, combining them with environmental models can be done straightforward. Boolean gates in a FT are interpreted as potential mounting positions that can be extended by target nodes of one or multiple environmental models. Additional mapping information needs to be provided to define links between gates and external variables. In a resulting *extended* FT, environmental influences are treated as new binary basic events, allowing any calculation of the metrics mentioned above. Since environmental variables can have an arbitrary number of states (e.g. weather with states rain, fog, and snow), one of them needs to be selected and will be treated as "failing". An associated probability is then interpreted as a static probability of failure. Figure 2 shows the idea of linking a FT with multiple environmental models.

Environmental influences may not only serve as basic events. Depending on the modelled effects (e.g. occlusion of a camera lens due to precipitation), an underlying assumption about the failure behaviour of a component (e.g. camera) may change. In *BayesianSafety* this can be implemented by treating an environmental node as a trigger and in response modifying an *existing* basic event based on external influences. Consequently, a time-independent node can be given a custom time behaviour. A modification changes the static probability of failure or the default reliability function $R(t) = e^{(-\lambda t)}$ of a node based on selected state probabilities $P(env_i)$ of environmental nodes and predefined thresholds. Note

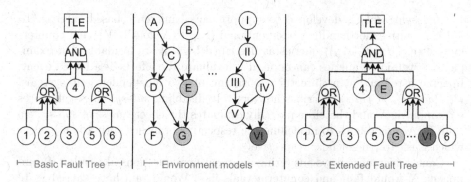

Fig. 2. A FT can be combined with multiple environmental models. Adequate mapping information needs to be provided, specifying which gates will be extended. Selected environmental nodes are treated as new basic events in a resulting *extended* FT.

that nodes independent of external influences can still be modified as described above. The following alterations are currently supported:

Replacement: $R(t) \to P(env)$
Addition: $R(t) \to \omega_0 R(t) + \omega_{env} P(env)$
Weighting: $R(t) \to \omega_0 R(t) \prod_i \omega_i P(env_i)$
Rate: $R(t, \lambda) \to R(t, \lambda^\star)$
Parametric: $R(t, \lambda) \to R^\star(t, P(env))$ as a special case of "Rate"
Functional: $R(t, \lambda) \to R^\star(t, \mathbf{X})$ where $\mathbf{X}$ is a set of parameters.

3.2 Model Inference

Typical metrics calculated in FTA and ETA represent prior probabilities. Posterior distributions (e.g. $P(X|Y, W)$) can be calculated easily due to the use of BNs as a mathematical core framework.

In *BayesianSafety*, inference is tied to a single, independent BN. Queries and their results are only computed on that network instance. In combined models, this leads to a problem for some evaluations due to the current implementation. Suppose we want to extend a FT by linking environmental influences as described above. The resulting composite BN is a newly instantiated model, containing copies of all nodes of the FT and new binary basic events based on the specified environmental nodes. A problematic query of interest would be, how an observed top-level event in the FT part affects the posterior probability for an environmental node $Weather$ (e.g. $P(Weather|TLE = failure)$). Even if $Weather$ is formally linked to the FT, a distributional update will only consider the newly created basic event node $Weather_{new} = state\ x$ in the composite BN and not the original node in the environment network. Consequently, this means that the environmental model will not be considered at all. If an update is required, the joint model needs to be created accordingly.

BayesianSafety is developed to support causal inference based on BNs. To do this, routines for handling interventional (e.g. $P(X|do(Y), W)$) and counterfactual (e.g. $P(y\prime_{x\prime}|x, y)$) queries as described by [15] are available. For example, interventional queries can be used to evaluate the effects of a forced event. Imagine a redundant architecture consisting of two independent sub-systems. $P(X|do(sub_1 = fail))$ describes how actively disabling *sub-system 1* influences a component X and therefore partially evaluates the effectiveness of *sub-system 2*. In FTA, this relates to modelling the respective branches with a house event which is set to true or false respectively.

Causal inference allows answering interventional questions like "What if component X would fail" and counterfactuals like "Would rain have caused X to fail, given we know it was sunny and X worked". This may especially be relevant for generating insights for environmental models by researching causal influence among variables.

3.3 Technical Ecosystem

BayesianSafety is developed in Python 3.9+ and currently spans around 6500 lines of code with an average cyclomatic complexity of 4.76. Source code, including examples treating FTA and ETA, can be found in our GitHub repository under https://github.com/othr-las3/bayesiansafety.

Instead of implementing inference algorithms ourselves, we rely on two different computational back-ends, namely *pgmpy* [1] in version 0.1.17+ and *pyAgrum* [6] in version 0.22.5+. Both provide a wide variety of approximate and exact inference and structure learning algorithms, are actively developed, and are established in the Open-Source PGM software community. They enable causal inference and support other PGM families like Markov Networks.

A key feature of both packages is state-of-the-art causal discovery methods. Consequently, this renders our package ready for an extension to provide an end-to-end (i.e. data to insight) capability. Environmental models could then be learned and combined with standard-compliant approaches to system safety, as outlined throughout this paper. Relying on third-party back-ends allows focusing on the implementation of required methodologies. BNs serve as generic containers to run all probability calculations on. As long as a modelling approach can be cast into the formalisms of BNs, it is expected to be implementable in *BayesianSafety* with minimal effort.

Parsed trees, as well as the underlying graph structure of a model, are internally represented as *networkX DiGraph*-objects [9]. *NetworkX* is one of the richest libraries for managing graphs in Python and provides a vast amount of graph algorithms. It allows plotting graphs, has export and import capabilities to different graph exchange formats, and allows adding custom data to graph elements. Figure 3 gives an informal overview of the ecosystem and the architectural idea of *BayesianSafety* described above.

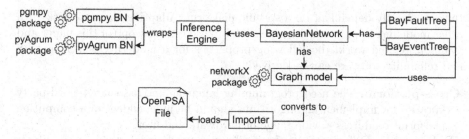

Fig. 3. During inference, *BayesianSafety* acts as a wrapper for back-end packages *pgmpy* [1] and *pyAgrum* [6]. Graph representations are implemented as *networkX DiGraph*-objects [9] and can be loaded from Open-PSA model exchange format files. FS and reliability methodologies like FTA or ETA and their respective algorithms can be implemented as custom modules building on BNs as a core framework.

4 Related Work

Zurheide et al. [20] recently developed a Python package called *pyBNBowtie*[4] to work with BTs mapped to BNs. They support the Open-PSA exchange format[5] to provide models and cast them directly into a *pgmpy BayesianNetwork*-object. Technically, they build on the model-to-model transformations described in [3, 4,10] but support only parts of the arc simplifications described by [3]. Features like Minimal-Cutset calculation in FTs are not implemented.

Open-PSA and therefore treatment and evaluation of individual FTs and ETs are also supported by the C++-based library *SCRAM*. The R package *FaultTree*[6] focuses on FTA, partially builds on *SCRAM*, and adds a basic graphical user interface. Both use BDDs for the calculation of gate probabilities and efficient inference of large models.

JReliability[7] is a Java-based package that also uses BDDs to model trees that are connected via boolean functions. It supports calculating different reliability metrics like Birnbaum importance, Risk Reduction Worth, or Mean-Time-To-Failure, and allows the visualization of metrics and distributions over time.

meta4ics[8] is another Java-based tool for generic AND/OR-connected graphs and can be used to identify critical nodes by calculating a custom weighting metric. *SCRAM*, *JReliability*, and *FaultTree* are highly optimized to work with FTs and support additional boolean gate types other than AND/OR. All of these tools lack the capability to support emerging demands as described in Sect. 1.

Most publicly available software packages for risk assessment and reliability evaluation address FTA and ETA. They are typically monolithic, rendering extension non-trivial. Due to various languages or visualization capabilities used,

---

[4] https://github.com/zurheide/pybnbowtie.
[5] https://open-psa.github.io/joomla1.5/index.php.html.
[6] https://github.com/jto888/FaultTree/.
[7] https://github.com/SDARG/jreliability.
[8] https://github.com/mbarrere/meta4ics.

they are mostly dependent on a specific platform. Adapting them to work with other modelling approaches is not feasible. Based on the scope of this paper and available related work, the following properties for a modern Open-Source FS and reliability software can be derived:

Cross-platform. The used programming language and associated third-party libraries for implementing algorithms should be independent of a computing platform to address a wide range of hardware and users.

Exchangable. Different algorithmic libraries (back-ends) should be available to access required features with minimal changes to the package code.

Exact. Implemented methodologies produce the same results as their classic (e.g. BDD) implementations.

Extensible. Implementing custom functionalities should be possible with low effort if they can be cast to a common mathematical framework (e.g. BNs).

Uncertainty. The central mathematical framework used should allow reasoning under uncertainty and modelling of deterministic relationships.

Modular. Standard-compliant methodologies can be used stand-alone or combined with other methods or environmental models.

Data oriented. ML learning approaches, as well as treatment of environmental data, should be possible in the same tool.

Causal. Support of causal inference to facilitate causal reasoning.

The above Open-Source packages are not intended to incorporate environmental influences. A combination of models as described throughout Sect. 2 is not possible. They lack any support for causal inference, with the only exception being *pyBNBowtie* due to it using *pgmpy*. Neither do they have the option to be extended by data-driven approaches.

As generic, multi-purpose PGM libraries, *pgmpy* and *pyAgrum* support modelling, learning, and inference of BNs and other of the above requirements. Therefore, they qualify as candidates to bridge multiple domains at the cost of implementing standard-compliant methodologies by hand.

In the light of the recent trend of incorporating uncertainty and the demand to consider environmental influences (e.g. scenarios as suggested by ISO/PAS 21448) all of the above packages lack some functionality. As a consequence, multi-methodology approaches as encouraged by [8,18] and others require the use of multiple software tools. Our proposed package *BayesianSafety* is the first to address all of the above requirements.

5   Conclusion

Bayesian Networks are an established framework to deal with uncertainty. In the light of researching system safety, they have desirable properties like versatility, comprehensibility, and support of causal reasoning. In recent years, multiple model-to-model transformations from classic analysis methodologies into BNs have been researched. Many of these publications state that addressing causality is feasible by using PGMs. Since BNs are agnostic to *what* they model, dealing with environmental, socio-technical, or abstract influences, is possible. This enables the combination of models with different scopes and formalisms.

In this paper, we outlined some emerging areas of interest in the FS and reliability community (e.g. researching environmental influences and their effects on reliability functions). Currently, no Open-Source software package is available that satisfies desirable properties like the support of causal reasoning, the ability to reason under uncertainty, or a combination of multi-domain models. To help address this, we propose our Open-Source Python package *BayesianSafety*. To the best of the authors knowledge, *BayesianSafety* is the first attempt to focus on the above-listed requirements and is intended to fill the demand for a causal, multi-domain, multi-model, analysis tool.

Our goal is to create a software environment, where common analysis methods can be treated together, by harmonizing the way each is processed mathematically. Due to the early implementation stage, only essential functionality to work with FTs, ETs, and environmental models is available. We plan on extending the provided capabilities as well as adding support to work with environmental models based on data. We hope *BayesianSafety* can serve as a baseline implementation for researching the combination of methodologies and encourage causality-guided system safety.

Acknowledgment. The present paper is supported by *Bayerisches Staatsministerium für Wirtschaft, Landesentwicklung und Energie* through the granting of the funding project *HolmeS³* (FKZ: DIK0173/03). We thank L. Grabinger and D. Urlhart for valuable discussions.

References

1. Ankan, A., Panda, A.: pgmpy: probabilistic graphical models using Python. In: Proceedings of the 14th Python in Science Conference (SCIPY 2015). Citeseer (2015)
2. Avizienis, A., Laprie, J.C., Randell, B.: Fundamental concepts of dependability. Technical report series. Department of Computing Science (2001)
3. Bearfield, G., Marsh, W.: Generalising event trees using Bayesian networks with a case study of train derailment. In: Winther, R., Gran, B.A., Dahll, G. (eds.) SAFE-COMP 2005. LNCS, vol. 3688, pp. 52–66. Springer, Heidelberg (2005). https://doi.org/10.1007/11563228_5
4. Bobbio, A., Portinale, L., Minichino, M., Ciancamerla, E.: Improving the analysis of dependable systems by mapping fault trees into Bayesian networks. Reliab. Eng. Syst. Saf. **71**(3), 249–260 (2001). https://doi.org/10.1016/S0951-8320(00)00077-6
5. Cai, B., Liu, Y., Liu, Z., Chang, Y., Jiang, L.: Bayesian Networks for Reliability Engineering. Springer, Singapore (2020). https://doi.org/10.1007/978-981-13-6516-4
6. Ducamp, G., Gonzales, C., Wuillemin, P.H.: aGrUM/pyAgrum: a toolbox to build models and algorithms for Probabilistic Graphical Models in Python. In: 10th International Conference on Probabilistic Graphical Models. Proceedings of Machine Learning Research, Skørping, Denmark, vol. 138, pp. 609–612, September 2020. https://hal.archives-ouvertes.fr/hal-03135721

7. Epstein, S., Rauzy, A., Reinhart, F.: The open PSA initiative for next generation probabilistic safety assessment. Kerntechnik **74**, 101–105 (2009). https://doi.org/10.3139/124.110020
8. Feth, P., et al.: Multi-aspect safety engineering for highly automated driving. In: Gallina, B., Skavhaug, A., Bitsch, F. (eds.) SAFECOMP 2018. LNCS, vol. 11093, pp. 59–72. Springer, Cham (2018). https://doi.org/10.1007/978-3-319-99130-6_5
9. Hagberg, A., Swart, P., Chult, D.S.: Exploring network structure, dynamics, and function using NetworkX. Technical report, Los Alamos National Lab. (LANL), Los Alamos, NM, United States (2008)
10. Khakzad, N., Khan, F., Amyotte, P.: Dynamic safety analysis of process systems by mapping bow-tie into Bayesian network. Process Saf. Environ. Prot. **91**(1), 46–53 (2013). https://doi.org/10.1016/j.psep.2012.01.005
11. Kirchhof, M., Haas, K., Kornas, T., Thiede, S., Hirz, M., Herrmann, C.: Root cause analysis in lithium-ion battery production with FMEA-based large-scale Bayesian network. arXiv:2006.03610 [stat], June 2020. https://doi.org/10.20944/preprints202012.0312.v1
12. Koller, D., Friedman, N.: Probabilistic Graphical Models: Principles and Techniques. Adaptive Computation and Machine Learning, MIT Press, Cambridge (2009)
13. Mosleh, A., Dias, A., Eghbali, G., Fazen, K.: An integrated framework for identification, classification, and assessment of aviation systems hazards. In: Spitzer, C., Schmocker, U., Dang, V.N. (eds.) Probabilistic Safety Assessment and Management, pp. 2384–2390. Springer, London (2004). https://doi.org/10.1007/978-0-85729-410-4_383
14. Nešić, D., Nyberg, M., Gallina, B.: A probabilistic model of belief in safety cases. Saf. Sci. **138**, 105187 (2021). https://doi.org/10.1016/j.ssci.2021.105187
15. Pearl, J.: Causality: Models, Reasoning and Inference, 2nd edn. Cambridge University Press, Cambridge (2009)
16. Rudolph, A., Voget, S., Mottok, J.: A consistent safety case argumentation for artificial intelligence in safety related automotive systems. In: ERTS 2018: 9th European Congress on Embedded Real Time Software and Systems (ERTS 2018), Toulouse, France, January 2018
17. Schölkopf, B., et al.: Toward causal representation learning. Proc. IEEE **109**, 612–634 (2021). http://arxiv.org/abs/2102.11107
18. Thomas, S., Groth, K.: Toward a hybrid causal framework for autonomous vehicle safety analysis. Proc. Inst. Mech. Eng. Part O J. Risk Reliab. (2021). https://doi.org/10.1177/1748006X211043310
19. Vowels, M.J., Camgöz, N.C., Bowden, R.: D'ya like DAGs? A survey on structure learning and causal discovery. CoRR abs/2103.02582 (2021). https://arxiv.org/abs/2103.02582
20. Zurheide, F.T., Hermann, E., Lampesberger, H.: pyBNBowTie: Python library for bow-tie analysis based on Bayesian networks. Procedia Comput. Sci. **180**, 344–351 (2021). https://doi.org/10.1016/j.procs.2021.01.172. Proceedings of the 2nd International Conference on Industry 4.0 and Smart Manufacturing (ISM 2020)

Safety Certification with the Open Source Microkernel-Based Operating System L4Re

Kai Lampka[1,2], Joel Thurlby[1], Adam Lackorzynski[3,4(✉)] [iD],
and Marcus Hähnel[3]

[1] Elektrobit Automotive GmbH, 91058 Erlangen, Germany
{kai.lampka,joel.thurlby}@elektrobit.com
[2] TU Kaiserslautern, 67663 Kaiserslautern, Germany
lampka@cs.uni-kl.de
[3] Kernkonzept GmbH, 01097 Dresden, Germany
{adam.lackorzynski,marcus.haehnel}@kernkonzept.com
[4] TU Dresden, 01062 Dresden, Germany
adam.lackorzynski@tu-dresden.de
http://www.elektrobit.com, http://www.uni-kl.de/,
http://www.kernkonzept.com, http://www.tu-dresden.de

Abstract. We report on recent efforts to certify the open-source operating system framework L4Re [2] and its commercial variant EB corbos Hypervisor [1]. Certification is carried out in adherence to ISO 26262 and targets an Automotive Safety Integrity Level B (ASIL-B). Unlike existing work on OS verification [3], the presented work discusses how a complete software system can be taken to certification. The paper identifies challenges arising from the re-use of open-source legacy software in a safety context and provides strategies for its certification without re-implementing major parts of the system. To achieve this, the paper introduces a new safety architecture based on the L4 style of "system-call forwarding", hierarchical memory management and configuration-based setup of inter-process communication relations. Collectively, the proposed innovations isolate safety applications from hidden errors in components not developed in adherence to the ISO 26262, in this case the feature-rich software stack implementing the L4Re userland.

Keywords: Automotive safety certification · L4Re-based hypervisor · Microkernel · ISO 26262 · Open source software

1 Introduction

Motivation. Software development according to the ISO 26262 entails, among other things, the application of relevant best practices for the entire V-model of software development based on the software's assigned safety level. For example, with the second lowest Automotive Safety Integrity Level, ASIL-B, the ISO

M. Trapp et al. (Eds.): SAFECOMP 2022, LNCS 13414, pp. 31–45, 2022.
https://doi.org/10.1007/978-3-031-14835-4_3

26262 highly recommends that not only exhaustive line coverage is provided, but branch coverage and static code analysis as well.

For pre-existing software, the ISO 26262 standard provides software component qualification methods as an alternative to unwarranted re-development according to the safety standard. In this case, the safety standard recognizes that pre-existing software may likely not have been developed with the same methods recommended for safety-related components. To ensure that the safety assurance is sufficient, the standard prescribes a range of measures to verify that the resulting quality of the software components is sufficient for their use in a safety context. Software qualification for pre-existing software can be excluded when it can be shown that the software will not interfere with software contributing to the safety function. As safety-related development and safety qualification can easily become insurmountably expensive, the safety functionality is reduced to a bare minimum. In turn, mechanisms and justification must be provided addressing why (hidden) error propagation from any unqualified component to a safety component has been excluded. One way to do this is to ensure that interference is strictly ruled out by the design and configuration, in hardware and software. This is the method of choice followed in this work.

Contribution. This paper demonstrates how a complete software stack based on an open source microkernel can be certified to the ISO 26262, without qualifying a majority of its pre-existing software according to the ISO 26262 standard or even re-implementing it.

As an example we take the L4Re microkernel system as used in the commercial product EB corbos Hypervisor [1] to certification. The presented approach leverages IPC forwarding, static memory partitioning between safety and quality-managed (QM) applications[1] and restriction of IPC in a way that avoids denial-of-service scenarios directed from QM applications towards safety ones. In this way, we design a safety partition with minimal impact in L4Re and derive arguments why software components executing in the safety partition are not experiencing any (hidden) error propagation from the feature-rich QM software components L4Re is commonly made of, see [9] for an overview. This differs from traditional strategies which commonly rely on exhaustive monitoring of relevant safety features and therefore may suffer from a performance penalty.

Related Work. L4Re is an L4-based open-source microkernel system framework [2], that is composed of the L4Re microkernel and a set of user space components and libraries, which can be used for building systems with real-time, security, safety and virtualization requirements.

The first L4 kernel was developed by Jochen Liedtke in 1994 [10], in assembly language. TU Dresden developed a kernel in C++ that was API compatible. Later on, the L4 API evolved and different kernels were ported to other architectures, such as Arm, Alpha and MIPS. The development of TU Dresden evolved into today's L4Re, which has been spun out to the company Kernkonzept.

---

[1] We call software not meeting ISO 26262 requirements quality-managed (QM).

An important milestone in the domain of secure systems has been the formal verification of the seL4 microkernel [7]. seL4 became the world's first OS kernel with a machine-checked functional correctness proof at the source-code level. It showed that a functionally correct OS kernel is possible, something that until then had been considered infeasible [6]. The verification work around seL4 and its applicability to security properties shows that microkernels provide an important building block in building secure and safe systems.

Unlike the vast body of work related to seL4, the presented work extends beyond the microkernel and drivers. We show how a complete software stack based on the L4-microkernel idea, including a fully fledged userland, can be taken to certification and that the deployment of highly complex software applications of different safety levels executing on a modern multicore processor is possible.

Proprietary systems have been following the microkernel-based principles for similar reasons and have been certified for a wide range of use-cases.

Organization. Section 2 introduces relevant concepts from the domain of operating systems. Section 3 presents the proposed approach, where Sect. 3.1 presents the relevant essentials of L4Re, Sect. 3.2 discusses aspects of qualification with legacy software system and Sect. 3.3 introduces the architectural alignment and gives evidence why freedom from interference goals are met.

2   Background Material

Microkernel-based operating systems (OS) follow a design principle that puts all OS functionality into modules, in such a rigid fashion that even the kernel itself is reduced to a minimal set of required features. The set of kernel features is primarily derived from the requirements of using privilege separation features of the hardware architecture.

With at least two privilege levels, software can be run in de-privileged mode while the software running in the privileged mode exercises control over it. This software component is typically called the kernel, or hypervisor. Software running in a de-privileged mode are typically called programs, applications, tasks, or processes. The kernel provides the functionality required for ensuring isolation between the user-level components and means for basic communication. Isolation must be ensured memory-wise, using virtual memory, and temporally, using preemption, i.e., being able to preempt execution of an application and switching to another one. Communication is provided by a mechanism called Inter-Process-Communication (IPC), allowing applications to exchange messages and call functions implemented in other applications (so-called servers).

Because the kernel only needs to implement this basic functionality, its size is close to minimal and justifies the name microkernel. All other functionality is built on top of the microkernel using small components, including drivers, file systems, memory management and virtualization. Applications depend only on components they use and because each module has specific responsibilities, this results in a small Trusted-Computing-Base (TCB). This design principle supports building secure and safe systems, as functionality only depends on software modules actually required, whilst modules themselves are isolated from each other.

3   Certification Approach

In the following we describe the architecture of a conventional L4Re system, the qualification strategy and the challenges we faced. We then present the newly developed safety architecture, building on the strength of the compositional nature of the existing system while introducing new components that provide essential freedom-from-interference guarantees while still allowing us to use the versatile and flexible environment of the traditional L4Re system for QM applications.

3.1   Architecture of the EB Corbos Hypervisor

The EB corbos Hypervisor is based on the L4Re microkernel system initially researched and developed at TU Dresden and now developed and commercialized by Kernkonzept GmbH. The system consists of the L4Re Microkernel and multiple L4Re userland components, as described in Sect. 2.

L4Re and Its Microkernel. The core module of the system is the microkernel, which is the only component running in the privileged mode of the processor. It provides basic mechanisms for spatial isolation, temporal isolation, execution, and communication. Spatial isolation is realized by means of virtual memory, using the MMU (Memory Management Unit) to protect access to memory and implemented in *Tasks*. Execution is provided through *Threads*. Multiple threads can run within one task. Temporal isolation is implemented through preemptive scheduling. Inter-process communication (IPC) is the principal communication mechanism, both between applications and to invoke the kernel. IPC is synchronous and un-buffered. High-bandwidth asynchronous communication can be built through shared memory between tasks, using software interrupts as a notification facility.

The rights management of the system is based on capabilities. Capabilities are pointers to objects, protected by the microkernel. By modeling all functionality into objects, the objects can be pointed to by capabilities, which then act as access rights to those objects. Calling methods of those objects, referred to as method invocation, is a universal mechanism in the system used for both invoking the kernel as well as invoking user-level implemented functionality.

Capabilities implement a local naming scheme and represent the state-of-the-art in rights management systems for operating systems. The initial set of capabilities for a task must be provided by the loader of the task, as with an empty set of capabilities a task cannot communicate anywhere and thus not use any service nor hardware. The system provides so-called factories, at both the kernel and user-level, to create new objects, such as threads and tasks. Access rights to objects can be passed on to other tasks by sending them to those tasks by IPC.

Memory for tasks is managed in a similar fashion, but is typically made available through a fault-based mechanism. When a thread in a task causes a page fault, the microkernel will generate a page fault IPC message to the pager of this thread. A *pager* is a thread that is able to resolve a page fault by mapping a page of memory to the faulting thread's task such that the thread is able to continue execution. A similar mechanism is used for exception handling.

The microkernel implements a priority-based round-robin scheduling scheme. Each thread has a priority assigned and the thread with the highest priority runs until its quantum runs out (the next thread with the same priority is selected), the thread blocks through IPC, or a higher priority thread becomes ready. Upon blocking, the next ready thread is selected.

The L4 Runtime Environment (L4Re) provides the environment to facilitate easy implementation of user applications on the Hypervisor. It abstracts from the kernel's APIs and allows to build complex use-cases. L4Re is composed of a set of libraries and system services, among them *Sigma0*, *Moe*, *Io*, and *Ned*.

Sigma0 is the root of the pager hierarchy in L4 systems. By allowing tasks to pass on access rights to memory pages, a hierarchy is established with Sigma0 being the root of it. Sigma0 is special for the kernel and gets all the memory from it, allowing to build user-level memory management.

Moe The microkernel starts two initial user-level components and hands control over to them. One is the aforementioned Sigma0, the second is the boot task known as Moe. Moe is responsible for starting the application loader Ned and provides further basic abstractions, such as *namespaces* (directories of named capabilities), *dataspaces* (containers for memory), *boot file-system* (a special namespace of the boot modules as dataspaces), *region management* (managing virtual memory within tasks), *logging* (multiplexing of output from applications), and *interfacing the kernel's scheduler* (core allocation and scheduling parameters).

Io manages the platform's hardware peripherals, comprising I/O memory and interrupts. Further, it provides virtual PCI buses as well as interfaces for clients to iterate and access I/O memory and interrupts. To realize this, it maintains a global view of the system as well as a per-client view. The client view is modeled around a vbus (virtual bus) which a client can query for their peripherals.

Ned is the init process and is used as initialization component. It is started by Moe and executes a Lua script which sets up and starts the remainder of the system. Ned's built-in Lua interpreter provides access to L4Re functionalities such as starting new components and setting up their communication channels, creating resources and setting up the environment for applications.

New services can be added by implementing new components or by exploiting the ability to virtualize the processor and run entire OS and their userlands inside virtual machines.

The boot process is initiated by a component called Bootstrap which is started by the platform bootloader, e.g. u-boot. Bootstrap loads the binaries of the

L4Re Microkernel, Sigma0 and boot task to their linked locations and makes the locations of the latter two known to the microkernel. It provides a description of the systems memory layout and then hands over control to the microkernel.

The kernel proceeds to initialize the essential hardware and internal management structures and loads root pager and boot task as described above.

3.2   General Thoughts on the Qualification Strategy

Since the L4Re system was not developed according to a safety standard, it must be qualified for use in a safety-context. While the ISO 26262, part 8 provides requirements on the qualification of pre-existing software components, which applies to the L4Re system, the qualification process itself is in many ways unclear. A reasonable strategy for the qualification of the L4Re system was needed with the following options at hand: (a) Formal specification and verification of the L4Re system, (b) Qualification of the L4Re system as a single component and (c) Qualification of the L4Re system components separately. A detailed assessment of each of the qualification routes follows below.

Formal Specification and Verification of the L4Re System. Insights to the practical use of formal methods as a basis for OS kernel development are given in [7]. The described development process builds around a set of formal verification tool chains, where the high-level specification is transformed into an executable prototype which is subject to formal verification and tool-based transformation into C code. We identified the following obstacles:

- If tools used in software development can secretly introduce errors in the specifications or secretly fail to identify errors in the specifications, they must be qualified according to the ISO 26262. Depending on the tool impact and likelihood of identifying problems in a tool, the required effort to do so can easily become much higher by orders of magnitude compared to any effort spent for (re-)development of the target software in accordance with the ISO 26262, part 6.
- For use in a safety-context, formal verification must address all software parts that may impact a safety-related component running on the microkernel. Excluding user-space components due to their complexity is not possible.
- Safety analysis of the formal specifications on the software architecture level is still required to identify conditions that can potentially lead to violations of assumed safety requirements.
- Modeling and analysis of non-determinism as inherent to interrupt handling and concurrency is advised. For keeping the model checking problem tractable, the model and in turn the implementation needs to be kept as simple as possible. To address this, the seL4 project focused on essential parts of the system and used techniques relating to the bounded model checking approach [4]. This clearly limits the solution space or may lead to gaps between a model and the actual implementation of a system.

For the above reasons, the qualification route of [7] was not applicable in our context and an alternative path was developed.

Qualification of L4Re as a Single Component. Qualification according to the ISO 26262 is performed on the software component level only. Unfortunately, the term software component is not formally defined by the standard. As a result, the most appropriate abstraction level to qualify the L4Re system is not immediately clear. The most straight-forward strategy would be to qualify the L4Re system as a single software component, irrespective of its modular structure.

Qualifying a software Safety Element out of Context consisting of a single software component impacts the safety lifecycle significantly. In particular, the following tailoring of the ISO 26262 safety lifecycle is sufficient: (a) Part 2, Safety management; (b) Part 6, Specification of software safety requirements; (c) Part 8, Supporting processes.

Notably missing in this tailoring are the recommended methods for the specification and verification of the software architecture as well as the safety analysis on the software architecture level, which reduce the risk of unwanted behavior at run-time. As a result, a decision was taken to minimize the safety footprint of the EB corbos Hypervisor and focus the design and verification efforts on the critical components of the L4Re system.

Qualification of the L4Re Components Separately. The last qualification route considered was to identify critical sub-components of the L4Re system through software safety requirements tracing combined with dependent failure analysis and to qualify these according to the ISO 26262, part 8. This qualification route leads to the following ISO 26262 safety lifecycle tailoring: (a) Part 2, Safety management; (b) Part 6, Specification of software safety requirements; (c) Part 6, Software architecture design; (d) Part 6, Software integration and verification; (e) Part 8, Supporting processes; (f) Part 9, Automotive safety integrity level (ASIL)-oriented and safety-oriented analyses.

This qualification route focuses re-engineering efforts to qualify software components according to the ISO 26262, part 8, clause 12 onto those components which have a clear impact on safety requirements allocated to the system. This posed the challenge to re-compose the system in such a way that freedom from interference (FFI) for individual parts can be enforced either by configuration or by implementing new components where appropriate or limiting, resp. enriching the feature set of the re-used ones. The results in the following chapters show that this strategy is effective for reducing the safety footprint and thus enabling a feasible certification by an external assessor. As a result, it was the selected qualification route.

3.3 New Safety Architecture

As first step towards FFI between components, we introduce the concept of a safety and a quality managed (QM) partition to L4Re. This complements the standard view, where applications are looked at as being in general isolated from each other. Applications of the QM partition do not contribute to any safety function. It must be ensured that they do not interfere with the applications of the safety partition in an unforeseen way.

A partition consists of a set of L4Re tasks, constant sets of physical memory pages and CPU cores. The partitioning concept is based on the idea that all software executing in the safety partition is developed or qualified to the same safety level. It is assumed that safety-related applications are developed in such a way that timeout surveillance for IPC calls is not needed and that data returned from a service does not need to be checked for data corruption. As a result, an application can safely use services by another application inside the safety partition. This strategy limits our efforts w.r.t. ensuring FFI. What remains is the analysis and mitigation strategy for controlling potential interactions between the partitions, resp. their applications. Before we carry out this analysis, we briefly introduce the main parts of our safety partition (see Fig. 1).

Overview of Proposed Architecture. When running the Hypervisor in a safety context, it is loaded and started by a safe bootloader (① in Fig. 1). It boots in a similar fashion to traditional Bootstrap as described in Sect. 3.1 but is reduced to the minimum functionality required to load the system and provide modules to it. In particular, the memory layout is configured statically and the advanced features of Bootstrap such as module compression, device tree parsing, and configuration through command-line arguments have been removed.

After being loaded and started by Bootstrap, the kernel initializes the relevant hardware (e.g., interrupt controller) and creates its internal management structures such as mapping databases and kernel memory pools. The kernel marks memory it reserves for its own use as used in the Kernel Interface Page (KIP) memory descriptors such that Sigma0 will not hand it out to user applications. Subsequently, the kernel creates task and thread objects for the boot task and the root pager, maps their expected capabilities and schedules them.

For the safety partition, we designed a new partition manager called the Safe Application Launcher Task (SALT, ③ in Fig. 1). It serves as the boot task to the safety applications. SALT is launched in place of Moe, which is relegated to be the boot task and abstraction provider for the QM side only (④ in Fig. 1).

Implementing a new boot task, instead of re-using Moe and Ned for the safety partition, comes with the advantage of not being forced to qualifying the latter. Specifically, the qualification effort would be prohibitively high. For example, Ned's Lua interpreter would require significant documentation and testing effort. On the other hand, the feature set available in SALT is significantly reduced. This is practicable, as safety functions are currently assumed to be of low complexity and are mostly static during run-time with respect to resource allocation. They would have limited benefit from the flexible abstractions provided by the L4Re QM applications, which are more tailored to more complex applications running in the QM partition and managing device access for multiple virtual machines.

Sigma0 initializes its memory managers for physical and I/O memory, reacts to memory mapping requests and acts as pager for the boot task (② in Fig. 1). This directly implies that Sigma0 must be qualified as safety component. This is feasible as Sigma0 only consists of a few hundred lines of C++ code and a post-development certification is therefore economically acceptable.

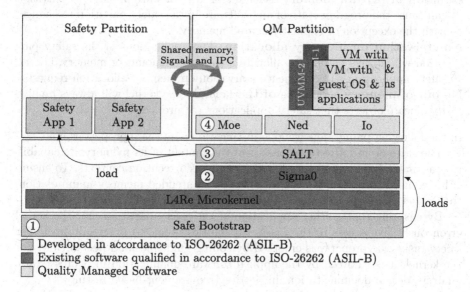

Fig. 1. Safety architecture for L4Re

SALT loads the configured safety applications and maps non-overlapping physical memory to each of them, enforcing their isolation from another. Memory is requested from Sigma0 and guaranteed to be handed out to SALT only.

If there is need for exchanging data among applications, SALT facilitates this by using dedicated memory for that. To do so, the safety applications reference such memory through dedicated named sections in their ELF binary and SALT ensures that sections with the same name receive the same physical memory. If there is need to share data with the QM partition, the hand-over of the related memory pages must be explicitly programmed into SALT's integrator-provided `setup` function, otherwise the memory is not visible to the QM partition.

After setting up their tasks and threads SALT launches the loaded safety applications. Once all of them have successfully passed their initialization phase, SALT starts Moe as the boot task of the QM partition and acts as a scheduler proxy to the QM side of the system.

What follows is the normal boot-up of the L4Re user space, see Sect. 3.1. The main difference concerns the fact that Sigma0 only allows Moe to acquire the remaining parts of the memory with the safety partition being the owner of all of the memory previously mapped to SALT. Moe's scheduler capability invokes SALT which restricts requests to schedule a thread to cores not occupied by safety applications. Device memory requests from the QM partition needs also to be routed through SALT to avoid its unintended sharing.

Spatial freedom from interference (sFFI) requires these three properties:

Isolation of private memory. No fault in any software in the QM partition can cause the program state of any software in the safety partition to change, with the exception of explicitly shared memory.

No starvation on memory allocation. The applications of the safety partition will always be able to allocate a sufficient amount of memory, i.e., no safety application will experience starvation on memory allocation requests.

No out-of-memory scenarios of the kernel. The kernel will always be able to allocate objects that safety applications require.

In the following paragraphs we give justification why these properties hold.

The state of an L4Re task consists of the content of its memory, its capabilities as maintained by the kernel and its threads' execution contexts. To ensure sFFI we need to reason over (a) absence of unintended memory manipulation, (b) protecting access to a task's capabilities and (c) correct context switching.

By ensuring that neither application of the safety partition, nor the kernel erroneously give access to the task's capabilities, item (b) is trivially met. For safety tasks, the property is enforced by coding guidelines and peer-review. For the kernel, it is enforced by the applied software qualification measures (static analysis, design documentation, inspection, requirement-based testing).

Item (c) is ensured by verifying that the microkernel correctly handles thread contexts, which once again can be established by the software qualification measures as applied for the qualification of the microkernel.

This leaves item (a) as the most challenging one, which we discuss now.

Virtual Memory. Each task is given a virtual memory address space which limits the physical memory its threads can access. The threads of a task can only access physical memory which has first been mapped into its address space. This is the core feature upon which memory isolation is built. It is ensured by qualification measures that the physical memory of a task is never mapped unintentionally into the virtual address space of another task. The only exception to this is the intentional sharing of memory to exchange data between applications. This property is ensured by the microkernel as long as a task with access to a physical memory page does not erroneously hand it out to different clients.

Single Ownership for Private Memory. To limit access to non-shared physical memory to a single application Sigma0, which as the root of the memory hierarchy has access to all memory, must not hand out any memory region already mapped to a safety application to another client. By handing out memory regions only to the first client requesting access to them and tracking this ownership Sigma0 ensures that no memory is handed out to two clients at the same time. Clients are identified by the label of the capability they use to access Sigma0.

SALT partitions the memory by requesting all needed memory on behalf of the safety applications during startup. This includes memory explicitly shared between tasks of the safety partition and with tasks of the QM partition. Afterwards SALT requests Sigma0 to create a new client capability that it then passes on to Moe as the boot task of the QM partition. This allows Sigma0 to identify Moe as a different client. As memory mapping requests from the QM partition only occur once SALT has requested all of the memory needed by the safety application, isolation on private memory of the safety partition is ensured.

Due to this construction Sigma0 is a safety application which handles IPC requests from QM applications. This creates the potential for a kind of denial-of-service attack on safety applications the threads of which are running on the same core as Sigma0, necessitating further restrictions as presented below.

Temporal freedom from interference (tFFI) means that any error in any QM application cannot interfere with the timing behavior of applications in the safety partition. E.g., any undetected delay in an IPC response from a QM application shall not result in an unmonitored deadline violation. Achieving tFFI, however, depends in many parts on the used hardware. For example, invalidation of a shared cache by a faulty QM application changes the cache miss rate and easily increases the load on the memory bus prolonging the execution times of safety applications in an unforeseen way [5,8]. Due to the high dependency of SW-based solutions to such problems and the underlying hardware, tFFI is commonly reduced to guarantees relating to the software. For maintaining the generic character of L4Re, we follow this strategy as well and do not consider the vast body of solutions for implementation. For eliminating tFFI at application level, we restrict the L4Re configuration as follows:

1. Exclusive mapping of cores to safety applications
2. Independence of execution by (a) restricted IPC relation and (b) static allocation of resources to safety partition

Below we will justify the restrictions introduced.

Exclusive Mapping of Cores to Safety Applications. Allowing threads of both the QM and safety partition to run on a core can lead to *CPU time stealing*. The responsiveness of a safety application running on the affected CPU may be reduced whenever less CPU time than expected is available. Possible causes are:

IPC-induced CPU time stealing. When an L4Re application acts as a server IPC requests sent to it are directed to the core the receiver thread is running on. In case the receiver is not ready for serving the request immediately, the IPC is queued and the IPC initiator is blocked. Each time a QM thread invokes this server through an IPC request the currently running thread on the core is preempted and the kernel either queues the IPC or schedules the receiver thread for serving it immediately. With a large number of IPC requests directed towards a low priority QM thread, significant CPU time would be spent on IPC queuing, instead of being available for high priority safety functions scheduled on that core.

Memory mapping induced CPU time stealing. When memory mappings are altered, cores running threads of the affected task must be informed to enforce the new mapping. To do so an inter-processor interrupt (IPI) is sent to the relevant cores interrupting their currently running threads. Excessive mapping and unmapping of memory yields CPU time stealing as CPU time is spent for the IPI handler rather than for safety functions.

For suppressing the above scenarios, threads of the QM partition and the safety partition must not share a core. This is enforced by configuration. In addition, SALT must serve as scheduler proxy to the QM partition such that the root task of the QM partition cannot instruct the kernel to migrate a QM thread to a core exclusively mapped to the safety tasks. This together with Sigma0 gives two applications of the safety partition which, besides the kernel itself, serve IPC requests for QM applications at run-time.

Independence of Execution. Each server application can be contacted by applications which have the respective capability. IPCs block until the IPC request has been delivered. However, for each task any thread can execute a new IPC request even if earlier invocations of the capability by other threads are still blocked. Consequently, a faulty QM application may instantiate a large number of threads, each placing an IPC request on an application it holds a capability to. This can induce the aforementioned CPU time stealing.

To avoid such scenarios, we generally forbid that safety applications can act as servers to QM applications. A QM thread may reply to IPC calls by a safety application but cannot hold a capability to directly communicate with it. An exception to this are the kernel, Sigma0 and SALT. These applications potentially act as servers or proxies to QM applications.

With the kernel, this does not pose a problem, as it is only invoked on the core the corresponding IPC request was issued on. For Sigma0 and SALT the IPC request is directed to the core(s) they are running on. As a result, a large number of IPC requests placed by QM applications on them results in unaccounted CPU time stealing. To avoid this scenario, Sigma0 and SALT must not share any core with other safety applications. Since we are statically mapping memory to the safety applications, they will not place any IPC request towards Sigma0 or SALT once SALT has started. This way, we rule out that safety applications experience unexpected delays. The respective IPC requests simply do not occur by construction.

Handling of Devices. Drivers to the physical devices are hosted in L4Re user applications that act as device server. Device services are provided through IPC or shared memory. HW-rooted isolation and protection mechanisms for device usage are offered by hardware vendor specific IP blocks, such as LifeC by Renesasi, XRDC by NXP, or via I/O memory management units (IOMMUs) such as the SMMU by ARM. The availability of HW-rooted isolation mechanism is fundamental to guarantee sFFI with DMA-capable devices, as their memory accesses must be restricted when operated by QM-partition rooted device servers.

It is also assumed that interrupt routing is configured and functions as expected, i.e. device interrupts are delivered to the configured core. This rules out that a device server in the QM partition can generate interrupts delivered to a core running safety applications. The absence of storms of device interrupts caused by device servers running in the safety application is ensured by software design guidelines and quality assurance measures such as static analysis and requirements-based testing.

For the device server, three scenarios must be considered: clients accessing the server are (a) exclusively safety applications, (b) exclusively QM applications and (c) from both partitions. Scenario (a) and (b) are in adherence with the requested restriction we established for the IPC relation, provided the device server is part of the same partition as its clients. With scenario (c), the restrictions postulated for the IPC relation so far appears to be too restrictive as the mixed case would simply be ruled out by configuration. As one may recall, it is requested that a safety application which acts as server for any QM application and is reachable via IPC means from QM side must not execute on the same core as any other safety application. This is irrespective of the application being used by safety applications or not. For easing this constraint, we request the following:

1. A device server located in the safety partition serving clients from the QM partition must operate in polling mode when serving QM clients. No IPC service requests from QM side are allowed other than using a reply capability. The use of a polling period enforces an upper bound on the workload injected by the QM clients and rules out unexpected situations of overload.
2. A device server located in the QM partition may serve both clients from the QM and the safety partition. The clients from the safety partition must implement timeout surveillance when placing an IPC request on the device server. Furthermore, they must not rely on the result of that service.

The above refinement allows us to run device servers on both partitions. Still, the question about sFFI w.r.t. I/O memory has not been touched yet. Unlike with physical memory, Sigma0 does not track ownership for I/O memory.

Currently Sigma0 gives a guarantee that allocations never fail when sufficient memory of the requested type is available. Tracking ownership of memory regions requires a book-keeping facility. Allocation requests for I/O memory may lead to a RAM allocation when a new entry in the management structure is required. Potentially, Sigma0 could run out of internal memory and reject the mapping with an out-of-memory error, breaking the aforementioned guarantee.

For maintaining the interface specification for QM applications while still guaranteeing sFFI we implement a Sigma0 proxy as safety application. The proxy gets a list of all I/O memory regions mapped to safety tasks. As all I/O memory used by safety applications is mapped during startup, the list is effectively static. Consequently, safety applications must not request I/O memory themselves after startup. The Sigma0 proxy relays mapping requests of QM applications to Sigma0 and rejects requests for I/O memory regions overlapping with ones claimed by safety applications. As no ownership is tracked by the Sigma0 proxy, no memory allocations are required and QM requests for I/O memory will never fail due to an out-of-memory error. This maintains the previously mentioned allocation guarantee. Like SALT and Sigma0, the Sigma0 proxy must also not run on a core mapped to the safety applications to guarantee tFFI.

4 Conclusion

In this paper we presented a concept to certify the pre-existing open-source microkernel-based hypervisor L4Re according to ISO 26262 for automotive safety, targeting ASIL-B. The presented concept builds a foundation for mixed-criticality systems, which is enabled by the implementation of components to support partitioning and re-organization of the boot process to prevent possible interference. This approach avoids re-implementation of the complete L4Re system, keeping the re-engineering effort at a minimum, and prevents unnecessary re-certification due to local changes to the QM partition. The compositional design of L4Re supports extension safety concept when the safety partition is further developed.

The presented approach has been found feasible by TÜV Süd as part of a general certification of EB corbos Hypervisor under ISO-26262.

Acknowledgments. The work is funded in part by the German Federal Ministry for education and research, grant numbers: 16ME0450, 16ME0452, 02K18D014.

References

1. EB corbos Hypervisor. https://www.elektrobit.com. Accessed 26 May 2022
2. L4Re Runtime Environment. https://l4re.org. Accessed 26 May 2022
3. The seL4 Microkernel. https://sel4.systems. Accessed 26 May 2022
4. Biere, A., Kröning, D.: Sat-based model checking. In: Handbook of Model Checking, pp. 277–303 (2018)
5. Flodin, J., Lampka, K., Yi, W.: Dynamic budgeting for settling DRAM contention of co-running hard and soft real-time tasks. In: Proceedings of the 9th IEEE International Symposium on Industrial Embedded Systems, SIES 2014, pp. 151–159 (2014)
6. Heiser, G.: The seL4 Microkernel An introduction. https://sel4.systems/About/seL4-whitepaper.pdf. Accessed 26 May 2022
7. Klein, G., et al.: seL4: formal verification of an OS kernel. In: Proceedings of the ACM SIGOPS 22nd Symposium on Operating Systems Principles, SOSP 2009, pp. 207–220. ACM, New York (2009)
8. Lampka, K., Lackorzynski, A.: Resolving contention for networks-on-chips: combining time-triggered application scheduling with dynamic budgeting of memory bus use. In: Remke, A., Haverkort, B.R. (eds.) MMB&DFT 2016. LNCS, vol. 9629, pp. 137–152. Springer, Cham (2016). https://doi.org/10.1007/978-3-319-31559-1_12

9. Lampka, K., Lackorzynski, A.: Using hypervisor technology for safe and secure deployment of high-performance multicore platforms in future vehicles. In: 26th IEEE International Conference on Electronics, Circuits and Systems, ICECS 2019, Genoa, Italy, 27–29 November 2019, pp. 783–786. IEEE (2019)
10. Liedtke, J.: On micro-kernel construction. In: Proceedings of the fifteenth ACM Symposium on Operating Systems Principles, SOSP 1995, pp. 237–250. ACM, New York (1995). http://doi.acm.org/10.1145/224056.224075

Data-Driven Inference of Fault Tree Models Exploiting Symmetry and Modularization

Lisandro Arturo Jimenez-Roa[1]([⊠]) [iD], Matthias Volk[1] [iD],
and Mariëlle Stoelinga[1,2] [iD]

[1] Formal Methods and Tools, University of Twente, Enschede, The Netherlands
{l.jimenezroa,m.volk,m.i.a.stoelinga}@utwente.nl
[2] Department of Software Science, Radboud University, Nijmegen, The Netherlands

Abstract. We present *SymLearn*, a method to automatically infer fault tree (FT) models from data. *SymLearn* takes as input failure data of the system components and exploits evolutionary algorithms to learn a compact FT matching the input data. *SymLearn* achieves scalability by leveraging two common phenomena in FTs: (i) We automatically identify symmetries in the failure data set, learning symmetric FT parts only once. (ii) We partition the input data into independent modules, subdividing the inference problem into smaller parts.

We validate our approach via case studies, including several truss systems, which are symmetric structures commonly found in infrastructures, such as bridges. Our experiments show that, in most cases, the exploitation of modules and symmetries accelerates the FT inference from hours to under three minutes.

1 Introduction

Fault Tree Analysis (FTA) [23,25] is one of the most prominent methods in reliability engineering, used on a daily basis by thousands of engineers. *Fault Trees (FTs)* are a graphical model describing how failures occurring in (atomic) system components propagate through a system and eventually lead to an overall system failure. The quantitative and qualitative analysis of FTs is essential for risk management of complex engineering systems.

An important challenge in FTA is the creation of faithful FT models. Therefore, inference of FTs, also known as *construction* [24], *synthesis* [8], or *induction* [16], has been investigated since the 1970s. Three categories of approaches exist: (i) *Knowledge-based* methods were investigated first, and are semi-automated approaches that derives an FT from a knowledge-based representation using heuristics [3]. These deploy techniques such as decision tables [24,29],

This research has been partially funded by NWO under the grant PrimaVera number NWA.1160.18.238 and by the ERC Consolidator grant CAESAR number 864075.

mini FTs [21,26], and Piping and Instrumentation Diagrams [26,31]. (ii) *Model-based* techniques derive an FT by translating a system model (e.g., using AADL [11,17], Digraphs [5,12], Simulink [30], or SysML [18,30]) into a FT.

(iii) Due to the increasing availability of inspection and monitoring data, *data-driven* inference methods have emerged. These automatically infer an FT closely matching a given structured data set, exploiting techniques like Bayesian networks [15] and genetic algorithms [10,14]. The resulting FTs closely match the given data set but only contain events also present in the data—and therefore may lack rare events. Nevertheless, data-driven inference can provide a good basis for fault tree creation. A key drawback of data-driven inference methods is that they still lack sufficient *scalability* for larger systems.

In this work, we tackle the scalability challenge of FT inference by exploiting two concepts commonly used in FTs: symmetries and modules. *Symmetries* between components are commonly present in real-world systems, e.g., due to structural properties or redundancies in safety-critical systems. *Modules* correspond to subsystems and allow to subdivide the inference problem into smaller, possibly independent, problems. Our approach, called *SymLearn*, automatically identifies symmetries and modules, and exploits them to reduce the solution space.

We implemented the SymLearn method in Python and numerically evaluated it in five case studies, including three truss system models, which are structural systems typically found in civil infrastructures such as roofs, transmission towers, and bridges. We compare SymLearn to the previous FT-MOEA implementation [10], which was shown to be faster than its predecessor FT-EA [14]. Our experiments show that: (1) SymLearn is orders of magnitude faster than FT-MOEA if modules and symmetries can be exploited; (2) SymLearn is in some cases slower than inference based on Boolean formulas, it yields, however, more compact FTs than Boolean methods.

Contributions. Our main contributions are:

(i) We define modules and symmetries based on the minimal cut sets (MCSs).
(ii) We present algorithms to automatically identify modules and symmetries from the MCSs.
(iii) We introduce *SymLearn*, an approach to automatically infer FTs from failure data sets by exploiting modules and symmetries.
(iv) We implemented SymLearn in Python and numerically evaluated it in several case studies.

The implementation and all data are available at zenodo.org/record/5571811.

Related Work. An early technique for *data-driven* FT inference is the *IFT* algorithm [16], which deploys Quinlan's ID3 algorithm to induce Decision Trees. Inspired by Causal Decision Trees, the *LIFT* algorithm [20] exploits the *Mantel-Haenszel* test to discover dependencies between events. While most data-driven approaches only require information about basic events, LIFT also needs information about failures of intermediate events. Both the *ILTA* [27] and *MILTA* [28] algorithms make use of *Knowledge Discovery in Data sets*, *Interpretable Logic Tree Analysis*, and *Bayesian probability rules*. The method in [15] first learns a *Bayesian Network* and then translates it into an FT model, using *blacklists* and *whitelists* to define missing or present arcs. The *DDFTA* algorithm [13] infers FTs from time series of failure data via binarization techniques and simplification of Boolean equations. Approaches based on evolutionary algorithms include our earlier work *FT-EA* [14] and *FT-MOEA* [10]. FT-MOEA uses a multi-objective cost function, which outperforms the one-dimensional cost function in FT-EA.

Since FTs encode Boolean functions, FT inference is closely related to synthesis of Boolean circuits with a minimal number of gates [9, 19]. Manual simplification of Boolean functions in the context of FT inference is considered in [13]. Common automated methods for simplifying Boolean functions are the Quine–McCluskey algorithm [4] that finds the optimal solution based on prime implicants but only works for a few variables, and the Espresso algorithm [1] that uses efficient heuristics, but does not guarantee finding the optimal solution.

Outline. Section 2 introduces FTs. Sect. 3 defines modules and symmetries. Section 4 details the SymLearn approach. In Sect. 5, we evaluate SymLearn on truss system models and discuss the results. We conclude in Sect. 6 and present future work.

2   Fault Trees

Fault Trees. A *fault tree (FT)* is a directed acyclic graph that models how system component failures occur, propagate, and can lead to a system failure [23, 25].

The leaves, called *basic events (BE)*, model (atomic) system components. The intermediate nodes are equipped with a logical *gate* and model how failures propagate through the system. Intermediate nodes with an AND-gate fail if all successor nodes fail, nodes with an OR-gate fail if at least one successor node fails. An FT $\mathcal{F}$ fails if the root node has failed. Figure 1 depicts an FT modeling a computer. *Computer* is equipped with an OR-gate, *Memory* and *Processor* with AND-gates, circles indicate BE.

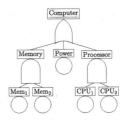

Fig. 1. Example FT.

Definition 1 (Fault tree). *A fault tree (FT) is a rooted directed acyclic graph* (V, E) *with a function* $Tp : V \rightarrow \{BE, AND, OR\}$ *satisfying* $Tp(v) = BE$ *iff* v *is a leaf. The successors of a node* v *are called the* inputs *of* v *and their set is denoted by* $I(v)$. *All nodes in* V *must be reachable from the dedicated root* Top.

We use $\text{BEs} := \{v \in V \mid Tp(v) = \text{BE}\}$ to denote all nodes of type BE. A vector $\vec{b} = \langle b_1, \ldots, b_{|\text{BEs}|} \rangle \in \{0,1\}^{|\text{BEs}|}$ is called a *status vector*. Here $b_i = 1$ indicates that the i-th BE has failed, and $b_i = 0$ that it is functioning properly, respectively. The semantics of an FT $\mathcal{F}$ is given by its *structure function* f.

Definition 2 (Semantics of FT). *Given a status vector $\vec{b}$, the structure function $f : \{0,1\}^{|BEs|} \times V \to \{0,1\}$ returns the status of node v. It is given by*

$$f(\vec{b}, v) := \begin{cases} b_i & \text{if } Tp(v) = BE \text{ and } v \text{ is the } i\text{-th } BE, \\ \bigwedge_{v' \in I(v)} f(\vec{b}, v') & \text{if } Tp(v) = AND, \\ \bigvee_{v' \in I(v)} f(\vec{b}, v') & \text{if } Tp(v) = OR. \end{cases}$$

We use the shorthand $f(\vec{b}) := f(\vec{b}, \mathsf{Top})$. We say FT $\mathcal{F}$ fails for $\vec{b}$ if $f(\vec{b}) = 1$. A status vector $\vec{b}$ can also be given as the set $C = \{b_i \in \vec{b} \mid b_i = 1\}$ of failed BE and we often write $f(C)$ instead of $f(\vec{b})$.

Minimal Cut Sets. *Minimal cut sets (MCSs)* are a common representation of the structure function f. A MCS is a minimal set of BE s.t. the FT fails.

Definition 3 ((Minimal) cut sets). *A* cut set *for FT $\mathcal{F}$ is a set $C \subseteq BEs$ with $f(C) = 1$. A minimal cut set (MCS) for $\mathcal{F}$ is a cut set C which is minimal, i.e., for all proper subsets $C' \subsetneq C$, $f(C') = 0$ holds. We denote the set of all minimal cuts sets for FT $\mathcal{F}$ by $\mathcal{C}_\mathcal{F}$.*

The FT in Fig. 1 has 3 MCSs: $\mathcal{C}_\mathcal{F} = \{\{\mathrm{Mem}_1, \mathrm{Mem}_2\}, \{\mathrm{Power}\}, \{\mathrm{CPU}_1, \mathrm{CPU}_2\}\}$.

3 Modules and Symmetries

Given a failure data set D, we want to find a compact FT $\mathcal{F}_D$ which matches D.

Failure Data Set. The failure data D is given as a labelled binary data set indicating the failure status of each component, together with the corresponding status of the overall system. Table 1 gives an example corresponding to the FT in Fig. 1 where M_1 corresponds to Mem_1, etc. We assume the data is *coherent*, i.e., once the system fails, it cannot become operational again through further component failures, and it is *noise-free*, i.e., observations with unchanged component states always yield the same system state.

Table 1. Example data.

M_1	M_2	P	C_1	C_2	Sys.
0	0	0	0	1	0
0	0	0	1	1	1
0	0	1	0	0	1
⋮	⋮	⋮	⋮	⋮	⋮

We can also identify MCSs in the failure data D. A (minimal) cut set C of D is a (minimal) set of BEs s.t. the corresponding status vector $\vec{b}$ yields a system failure in D. The set of all MCSs in D is denoted by $\mathcal{C}_D$.

Problem Statement. We want to find an FT $\mathcal{F}_D$ s.t. the structure function f of $\mathcal{F}_D$ captures failure data D as accurately as possible. To assess the quality of the resulting FT w.r.t. input data D, we use three metrics [10]:

– *Size of the FT ($|\mathcal{F}_D|$)* is the number of nodes $|\mathcal{F}_D| := |V|$ in the FT.

- *Error based on data set D (ϕ_d)* is the fraction of times where $\mathcal{F}_D$ fails and the system (according to data set D) does not, and vice versa. Let $E := \left\{ \vec{b} \in \{0,1\}^{|\mathsf{BEs}|} \mid f(\vec{b}) \neq D(\vec{b}) \right\}$ denote the status vectors which yield different results for $\mathcal{F}_D$ and D. Then the error based on D is given by $\phi_d := \frac{|E|}{|D|}$.
- *Error based on the MCSs* (ϕ_c) compares the set $\mathcal{C}_{\mathcal{F}_D}$ of MCSs of the FT $\mathcal{F}_D$ and the set of MCSs $\mathcal{C}_D$ derived from the data D. The metric ϕ_c computes the similarities between both sets of MCSs based on the RV-coefficient [22], see [10] for the details.

> **Formal Problem.** Given a failure data set D, create a (compact) FT $\mathcal{F}_D$ s.t. its BEs correspond to the atomic components in D and $f(\vec{b})$ captures the system failures in D as accurately as possible. In other words, ϕ_c and ϕ_d should be (close to) zero, and $|\mathcal{F}_D|$ should be as small as possible.

In our approach, we first create $\mathcal{C}_D$ from D and infer the FT $\mathcal{F}_{\mathcal{C}_D}$.

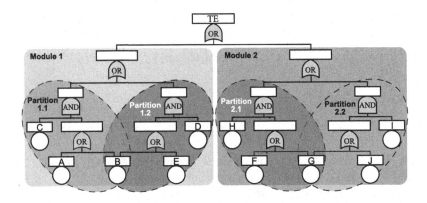

Fig. 2. FT with independent modules and further partitioning. (Color figure online)

3.1 Modules

Instead of directly inferring an FT $\mathcal{F}_{\mathcal{C}_D}$ from the MCSs $\mathcal{C}_D$, we aim to first partition $\mathcal{C}_D$ into multiple parts, infer individual FTs for each of them, and then combine the FTs into the overall FT $\mathcal{F}_{\mathcal{C}_D}$.

Definition 4 (MCS partitioning). *Let $M_1, \ldots, M_n \subseteq \mathcal{C}$ be a partitioning of the set $\mathcal{C}$ of MCSs, i.e., $M_i \cap M_j = \emptyset$ for all $i \neq j$ and $M_1 \cup \cdots \cup M_n = \mathcal{C}$. For a partition M_i, we let $\mathsf{BEs}^{M_i} := \bigcup_{C \in M_i} C$ denote the set of BE occurring in M_i. BE occurring in multiple partitions are called the* shared BE.

In the case of a large number of shared BE, the inferred FTs—which each might be optimal individually—can yield an overall FT which is sub-optimal. For example, gates with (some of the) shared BE as input might occur in multiple

FTs. Thus, the goal is to find a partitioning such that the number of shared BE is as small as possible. If no BE are shared, the resulting partitioning of BEs forms *independent modules*. In FTs, (independent) modules are independent subtrees, where only the root node is connected to other parts of the FT [7]. Modules can therefore be thought of as coherent entities in the context of the overall system, e.g., components. Modularization is used to simplify the FT analysis.

Definition 5 (Modules). *A partitioning $M_1, \ldots M_n$ of the set $\mathcal{C}$ of MCSs is called a* module partitioning *if the corresponding* $BEs^{M_1}, \ldots, BEs^{M_n}$ *form a partitioning of BEs. A subset $\mathfrak{M}$ of BEs is called an* independent module *if it is part of a module partitioning, i.e., all BE of $\mathfrak{M}$ are included in MCSs of a single M_i.*

An independent module $\mathfrak{M}$ does not share BE. Thus, the BE in $\mathfrak{M}$ are not connected to other parts of the FT and they belong to an independent subtree.

Example 1 (Modules). The partitioning for the FT in Fig. 2 is given by colored boxes. The BEs $\{A, B, C, D, E\}$ and $\{F, G, H, I, K\}$ form independent modules. The corresponding MCSs can be further subdivided. For instance, Partition 1.1 with $\{\{A, C\} \{B, C\}\}$ and Partition 1.2 with $\{\{B, D\}, \{D, E\}\}$ share BE B.

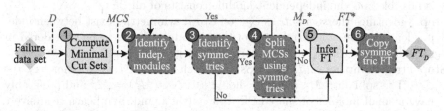

Fig. 3. *SymLearn* tool chain overview. Blue boxes indicate novel steps. (Color figure online)

3.2   Symmetries

Symmetries in an FT describe components, e.g., BE or complete subtrees, that can be swapped without changing the failure behavior of the FT. In our setting, symmetries reduce the computational effort for inferring FTs as only one of the sub-trees must be constructed; other subtree(s) can be copied from the (original) subtree because of the symmetry. We define symmetries on the MCSs. Applying a symmetry on the MCSs yields the same MCSs, i.e., swapping symmetric BE does not change the structure function of the FT.

Definition 6 (Symmetry on MCSs). *A symmetry on the set $\mathcal{C}$ of all MCSs is a permutation $\sigma : BEs \to BEs$ which preserves $\mathcal{C}$, i.e., $\sigma(\mathcal{C}) = \mathcal{C}$ where $\sigma(\mathcal{C}) := \{\sigma(C) \mid C \in \mathcal{C}\}$ and $\sigma(C) := \{\sigma(b) \mid b \in C\}$.*

We denote all possible symmetries on $\mathcal{C}$ by $\mathcal{S}_\mathcal{C}$. A *symmetry between sets* $A, B \subseteq$ BEs is a symmetry $\sigma \in \mathcal{S}_\mathcal{C}$ with $\sigma(A) \subseteq B$ and $\sigma(B) \subseteq A$. Note that we define symmetries only on BEs and not on gates. The definition is thus more general and allows symmetries even in cases where sub-trees are not isomorphic.

Lemma 1 (Necessary condition for symmetry). *If* $\sigma \in \mathcal{S}_\mathcal{C}$ *is a symmetry on the MCSs* $\mathcal{C}$, *then* $count(b) = count(\sigma(b))$ *for all* $b \in$ BEs, *where* $count(b) :=$ $|\{C \in \mathcal{C} \mid b \in C\}|$ *denotes the number of occurrences of* b *in* $\mathcal{C}$.

Example 2 (Symmetry). Consider again the FT $\mathcal{F}$ in Fig. 2. The permutation $\sigma_1 = (AF)(BG)(CH)(DI)(EJ)$ is a symmetry in $\mathcal{F}$ (between the independent modules). For example, $\sigma_1(\{A, C\}) = \{F, H\} \in \mathcal{C}_\mathcal{F}$. Symmetries within the modules are given by $\sigma_2 = (AE)(CD) \in \mathcal{S}_{\mathcal{C}_\mathcal{F}}$ and $\sigma_3 = (FJ)(HI) \in \mathcal{S}_{\mathcal{C}_\mathcal{F}}$.

4   Exploiting Modules and Symmetries in FT Inference

Our *SymLearn* approach is outlined in Fig. 3 and consists of 6 steps:

Step 1 computes the set of all *MCSs* $\mathcal{C}_D$ associated with input data set D.

Step 2 finds a partitioning $M_1, \ldots, M_n$ of $\mathcal{C}_D$ s.t. the corresponding BEs form *independent modules* $\mathfrak{M}_1, \ldots, \mathfrak{M}_n$. In the worst case, no proper partitioning is possible and the independent module consists of all BEs.

Step 3 identifies the *symmetries* $\mathcal{S}_{\mathcal{C}_D}$ on $\mathcal{C}_D$. If symmetries exist between independent modules, then only one of these modules needs to be considered in the following. Otherwise, SymLearn directly goes to Step 5.

Step 4 tries to further *split* the MCSs M_i of each module $\mathfrak{M}_i$ via a symmetry $\sigma \in \mathcal{S}_{\mathcal{C}_D}$. The split into M_i^1 and M_i^2 should satisfy $\sigma(M_i^1) = M_i^2$ and preferably have a small number of shared BE. If a split is found, SymLearn recursively starts again with Step 2 for M_i^1; otherwise it proceeds with Step 5.

Step 5 infers an FT $\mathcal{F}_M$ for each partition M of the MCSs. Several approaches can be used, e.g., *FT-MOEA* [10] or simplification of Boolean formulas [13].

Step 6 creates for each set of symmetric MCSs M_i^2 a corresponding *symmetric FT* $\mathcal{F}_{M_i^2}$ by copying the "original" FT $\mathcal{F}_{M_i^1}$ and renaming the BEs according to the symmetry σ. Last, all inferred FTs are joined under an OR-gate.

We provide details on all steps of SymLearn in the following.

Step 1: Compute Minimal Cut Sets. SymLearn starts by extracting all the MCSs $\mathcal{C}_D$ from the data D. We use the algorithm from [13], but employ an improved computation of the MCSs from the cut sets. Here, we iteratively select a cut set C with minimal cardinality and remove all cut sets that include C. The runtime complexity of the algorithm is quadratic in D, i.e., $\mathcal{O}(D^2) = \mathcal{O}(2^{2 \cdot |\text{BEs}|})$.

Algorithm 1. Identifying independent modules $\mathfrak{M}_1, \ldots, \mathfrak{M}_n$ from the MCSs $\mathcal{C}_D$.

Input: MCSs $\mathcal{C}_D$.
Output: Partitioning $M_1, \ldots, M_n$ of $\mathcal{C}_D$, corresp. independent modules $\mathfrak{M}_1, \ldots, \mathfrak{M}_n$.
  $Partitioning \leftarrow \{\{C\} \mid C \in \mathcal{C}_D\}$
  while $\exists M, M' \in Partitioning$ with M and M' sharing BE **do**
    $Partitioning \leftarrow (Partitioning \setminus \{M, M'\}) \cup \{M \cup M'\}$
  return $Partitioning = \{M_1, \ldots, M_n\}$, modules $\{\mathfrak{M}_1 = \mathsf{BEs}^{M_1}, \ldots, \mathfrak{M}_n = \mathsf{BEs}^{M_n}\}$

Step 2: Identify Independent Modules. Our aim is to partition the MCSs $\mathcal{C}_D$ s.t. an FT for each partition can be learned individually. This allows for a more efficient inference which could even be performed in parallel.

We start by trying to find independent modules from $\mathcal{C}_D$ as described in Algorithm 1. The initial partitioning uses each cut set of $\mathcal{C}_D$ as its own partition. If two partitions share BE, they must be merged to satisfy the constraint for independent modules in Definition 5. We iteratively merge partitions until their BEs are disjoint. The BEs then form the independent modules. The following Steps 3–5 are performed for each independent module and corresponding MCSs individually. The FTs created for the modules are combined by an OR-gate in the end.

Example 3 (Identify independent modules). We use the MCSs $\mathcal{C}_D = \{\{A, C\}, \{B, C\}, \{B, D\}, \{D, E\}, \{F, H\}, \{G, H\}, \{G, I\}, \{I, K\}\}$ corresponding to Fig. 2. Applying the algorithm, cut sets $\{A, C\}$ and $\{B, C\}$, for instance, are merged as they share BE C. In the end, the independent modules and partitioning are:

$$\mathfrak{M}_1 = \{A, B, C, D, E\} \qquad M_1 : \{\{A, C\} \{B, C\}, \{B, D\}, \{D, E\}\}$$
$$\mathfrak{M}_2 = \{F, G, H, I, K\} \qquad M_2 : \{\{F, H\} \{G, H\}, \{G, I\}, \{I, K\}\}$$

Extraction of BE. As an additional optimization, we automatically derive BE which occur in all minimal cut sets of a partition. In order for the partition to cause a system failure, all these BE must fail. Hence, they are excluded from all MCSs and the approach continues on the reduced MCS. In the end, the excluded BE are joined under an AND-gate with the FT resulting from the reduced MCSs.

Step 3: Identify Symmetries. Next, we identify the symmetries $\mathcal{S}_{\mathcal{C}_D}$ from $\mathcal{C}_D$ in a fully automated manner. The simplest way is a brute-force approach trying out all possible permutations and checking whether they are valid symmetries according to Definition 6. While this approach is factorial in $|\mathsf{BEs}|$, we obtain good performance in practice by exploiting two optimizations.

Symmetries Between Independent Modules. The most efficient approach is to exploit the independent modules from the previous step. Symmetries between two independent modules $\mathfrak{M}, \mathfrak{M}'$ can be quickly found by restricting the permutations to only the ones matching each BE in $\mathfrak{M}$ to one in $\mathfrak{M}'$.

Algorithm 2. Splitting of MCS M_i into two symmetric parts M_i^1 and M_i^2.

Input: MCS M_i, symmetry $\sigma \in \mathcal{S}_{\mathcal{C}_D}$
Output: Symmetric MCSs M_i^1, M_i^2 with corresponding contained BE $\mathsf{BEs}^{M_i^1}, \mathsf{BEs}^{M_i^2}$

    $M_i^1 \leftarrow \emptyset,\ M_i^2 \leftarrow \emptyset,\ \mathsf{BEs}_1 \leftarrow \emptyset,\ \mathsf{BEs}_2 \leftarrow \emptyset$
    $Q \leftarrow \mathcal{C}_D$
    while $C \in Q$ **do**
        if $C = \sigma(C)$ **then return** $M_i, \emptyset, \mathsf{BEs}^{M_i}, \emptyset$
        $Q \leftarrow Q \setminus \{C, \sigma(C)\}$
        if $|C \cap \mathsf{BEs}_1| \geq |C \cap \mathsf{BEs}_2|$ **then**
            $M_i^1 \leftarrow M_i^1 \cup \{C\},\ M_i^2 \leftarrow M_i^2 \cup \{\sigma(C)\},\ \mathsf{BEs}_1 \leftarrow \mathsf{BEs}_1 \cup C,\ \mathsf{BEs}_2 \leftarrow \mathsf{BEs}_2 \cup \sigma(C)$
        else
            $M_i^1 \leftarrow M_i^1 \cup \{\sigma(C)\},\ M_i^2 \leftarrow M_i^2 \cup \{C\},\ \mathsf{BEs}_1 \leftarrow \mathsf{BEs}_1 \cup \sigma(C),\ \mathsf{BEs}_2 \leftarrow \mathsf{BEs}_2 \cup C$
    return $M_i^1, M_i^2, \mathsf{BEs}_1, \mathsf{BEs}_2$

Fast Exclusion of Non-symmetric BEs. If only one independent module was found in Step 2, then the symmetries must be computed by an exhaustive search. However, we can exclude infeasible permutation candidates early on by using Lemma 1. Two BE with different numbers of occurrences in $\mathcal{C}_D$ cannot be symmetric and thus all permutations containing such mappings are excluded.

Example 4 (Identify symmetries). Continuing Example 3, we find the symmetry $\sigma_1 = (AF)(BG)(CH)(DI)(EK)$ between independent modules $\mathfrak{M}_1$ and $\mathfrak{M}_2$. As a result, the symmetric set M_2 of MCSs will not be considered in the remainder. We continue by searching for symmetries within $\mathfrak{M}_1$ according to M_1. Candidate permutations such as (AC) are quickly excluded, because $\mathrm{count}(A) = 1 \neq 2 = \mathrm{count}(C)$. In the end, symmetry $\sigma_2 = (AE)(CD)$ is found.

Step 4: Split MCSs Using Symmetries. A symmetry σ found in the previous step can be used to split the MCSs M_i. We restrict ourselves to splits into two parts here, but more parts work in the same manner. A successful split creates two symmetric subsets M_i^1 and M_i^2 of M_i with $\sigma(M_i^1) = M_i^2$.

Algorithm 2 describes the split of the MCSs M_i according to a symmetry $\sigma \in \mathcal{S}_{\mathcal{C}_D}$. Initially, the queue Q contains all MCSs from $\mathcal{C}_D$. For each MCS C we compute the symmetric MCS $\sigma(C)$. If C is symmetric to itself ($C = \sigma(C)$), a split would add the same MCS to both parts. As this would only increase the size of the resulting FTs, we do not proceed further. If both MCSs are distinct, we add C to the set of MCSs with which it shares the most BE. For example, we add C to M_i^1 if $|C \cap \mathsf{BEs}_1| \geq |C \cap \mathsf{BEs}_2|$. By this choice, we ensure that adding C to M_i^1 does not add too many new BE to BEs_1 and we keep the number of shared BE between BEs_1 and BEs_2 small.

Note that the split can still yield two parts which share a significant amount of BE. Composing the two resulting FTs can therefore yield an FT which is larger than the single FT inferred without the split. However, the composed FT will capture the symmetric structure present in the given MCSs.

Example 5 (Split the MCSs). We continue with symmetry $\sigma_2 = (AE)(CD)$ and MCSs $M_1 = \{\{A,C\}, \{B,C\}, \{B,D\}, \{D,E\}\}$ from Example 4. We start the algorithm with MCS $\{A,C\}$. The symmetric MCS is $\sigma(\{A,C\}) = \{D,E\}$. The first split yields $M_1^1 = \{\{A,C\}\}$ and $M_1^2 = \{\{D,E\}\}$. The next MCS $\{B,C\}$ is added to M_1^1 because they both share BE C. The final split is:

$$M_1^1 = \{\{A,C\}, \{B,C\}\} \qquad \text{BEs}_1 = \{A,B,C\},$$
$$M_1^2 = \{\{D,E\}, \{B,D\}\} \qquad \text{BEs}_2 = \{B,D,E\}.$$

The split corresponds to the purple and dark blue sub-trees in Fig. 2.

Step 5: Infer FT. If no further partitioning of the MCSs M_i w.r.t. Steps 2–4 is possible, we use existing techniques to infer an FT from the (reduced) MCSs. SymLearn is modular and supports the use of any learning approach in this step, for example, based on genetic algorithms [14] or Boolean logic [13]. In our setting, we use the multi-objective evolutionary algorithm *FT-MOEA* [10].

FT-MOEA starts in the first generation by default with two *parent* FTs: one FT consists of an AND-gate connected to all BEs, and the other one uses an OR-gate. In each generation, several *genetic operators* are applied which randomly modify the FT structure. Each FT is evaluated according to three metrics given in Sect. 3: size of the FT $|\mathcal{F}|$, error based on the failure data set (ϕ_d), and error based on the set of MCSs (ϕ_c). The aim is to minimize the multi-objective function ($|\mathcal{F}|, \phi_d, \phi_c$) by applying the *Elitist Non-dominated Sorting Genetic Algorithm* (NSGA-II) [6] and obtain the Pareto sets. Only the best candidates according to the metrics are then passed to the next generation. The algorithm stops if no improvement was made in a given number of generations and returns the FTs ordered according to the multi-objective function.

Example 6 (FT-MOEA). Given the MCS $\{\{A,C\}, \{B,C\}\}$, we use FT-MOEA to infer a FT. The resulting FT is the sub-tree indicated by purple color in Fig. 2.

Step 6: Copy Symmetric FTs. After obtaining an FT $\mathcal{F}_M$ for MCSs M, we obtain the symmetric FT $\mathcal{F}_{M'}$ for the symmetric MCSs $M' = \sigma(M)$ by copying $\mathcal{F}_M$ and replacing each BE b with its symmetric BE $\sigma(b)$. The original and the symmetric FT are then joined under an OR-gate.

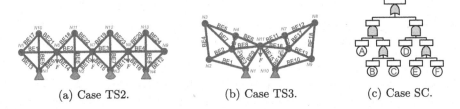

(a) Case TS2.   (b) Case TS3.   (c) Case SC.

Fig. 4. Visualization of case studies TS2, TS3 and SC.

Example 7 (Copy symmetric FT). We continue with Example 6. Copying the purple sub-tree in Fig. 2 and applying symmetry $\sigma_2 = (AE)(CD)$ yields the symmetric (dark blue) FT. Joining both FTs with an OR-gate yields *Module 1*.

5   Experimental Evaluation

We implemented the *SymLearn* methodology in a Python toolchain, available at zenodo.org/record/5571811, and evaluate our approach on five case studies, see Table 2: *Cases SC* and *SS* are two small systems, depicted in Fig. 4c (case SC) and running example of Fig. 2 (case SS). We also consider three *truss system models*.

Table 2. Overview of case studies.

Case	#BEs	$|D|$	$|\mathcal{C}_D|$
SC	6	64	4
SS	10	1024	8
TS1	10	1024	16
TS2	24	16 777 216	26
TS3	20	1 048 576	18

Truss System Cases. Truss systems are commonly used in civil infrastructures such as roofs, transmission towers, and bridges, see Fig. 5a. Truss systems are composed of elements connected by nodes, generating rigid bodies with the elements acting under tensile stresses.

Truss systems feature a high degree of symmetry and a modular structure. Moreover, as elaborated below, they allow us to obtain the failure data sets via structural analysis (similar to [2]). Therefore, we consider truss systems to be a very suitable model to evaluate *SymLearn* in a realistic setting.

We use three truss system variants: Cases TS1 (Fig. 5a) and TS2 (Fig. 4a) are typical configurations in bridges, while Case TS3 (Fig. 4b) is found in roofs. Note that Case TS1 contains no independent modules, whereas TS2 and TS3 contain four and two modules, respectively.

Generation of Failure Data Set. Based on case TS1 (Fig. 5) we explain how we use numerical truss system models to generate complete failure data sets. TS1 consists of 10 elements (interpreted as BEs), and two symmetric loads applied on the control nodes. We model damage by reducing close to zero the cross-sectional area of at least one element in the truss system model, and by determining the displacements and stresses in the components due to the applied loads at the

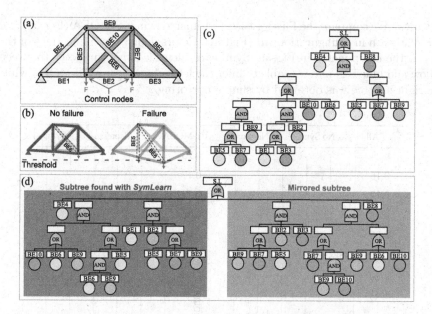

Fig. 5. Example case TS1 modeling a symmetric truss bridge system. (a) Model. (b) Depiction of failure/no-failure states. (c) FT inferred by FT-MOEA. (d) FT inferred by SymLearn. Top corresponds to the truss system instability. (Color figure online)

nodes of the numerical model. We generate a synthetic failure data set D by randomly drawing 10^6 data points for the status of elements in the truss model via Monte Carlo simulation, and evaluating *structural instability* (S.I.) based on the displacement of control nodes.

Experimental Setup. We compare the SymLearn tool with 3 different backends in Step 5, to infer the FT from data.

- *FT-MOEA* is used in 4 different settings: (1) *All* is the default setting using both modules and symmetries; (2) *No Sym* is *All* but without symmetries; (3) *No rec.* is *All* but without recursive calls for further sub-division; (4) *FT-MOEA* is the original implementation [10] without modules and symmetries.
- *Espresso* translates a set of MCSs $\mathcal{C}_D$ into a Boolean formula $\bigvee_{C \in \mathcal{C}_D} \bigwedge_{b \in C} b$ and simplifies it via the *ESPRESSO* algorithm [1] available in PYEDA[1]. The resulting formula is then translated into an FT.
- *Sympy* is similar to *Espresso* but uses the SYMPY library[2] for simplification.

We ran all case studies three times on a CPU with 2.3 GHz and 8 GB of RAM.

---

[1] https://pyeda.readthedocs.io/en/latest/2llm.html.

[2] https://docs.sympy.org/latest/modules/logic.html.

Results. We compare the FTs for case TS1 inferred via FT-MOEA (Fig. 5c) and via SymLearn in configuration *All* (Fig. 5d). Colors depict the connections of the BEs to the components in Fig. 5a. SymLearn identified the symmetry (between yellow and blue BE) and was able to infer the left subtree using FT-MOEA while the right subtree was obtained by simple mirroring.

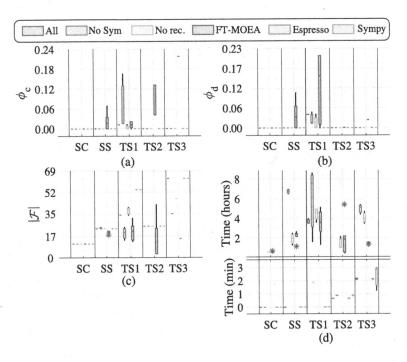

Fig. 6. Results for the case studies and different metrics: (a) error ϕ_c based on the MCSs, (b) error ϕ_d based on data set, (c) FT size $|\mathcal{F}|$, and (d) runtime.

The box charts in Fig. 6 compare the different configurations in all five cases w.r.t. the three metrics in Sect. 3: the size $|\mathcal{F}|$ of the FT, the error ϕ_d based on the failure data set, and the error ϕ_c based on the MCSs. From Fig. 6a and 6b, we see that the SymLearn configurations based on Boolean functions as a back-end (i.e., *Espresso* and *Sympy*) always yield an FT that exactly matches the input, i.e., $\phi_c = \phi_d = 0$. This is expected since the Boolean logic formula perfectly encodes all the MCSs. In contrast, the other configurations using FT-MOEA did not always yield a completely accurate FT (i.e., $\phi_c, \phi_d > 0.0$), for example, case TS1. The error stems from the multi-objective optimization which also aims to provide a small FT and the evolutionary algorithm which can fall into local optima. However, for the cases TS2 and TS3 (with independent modules), all configurations of SymLearn (*All*, *No Sym*, *No rec.*) outperformed FT-MOEA by returning an FT that accurately reflects the input ($\phi_c = \phi_d = 0.0$). This shows the clear benefit of subdividing the problem using independent modules.

Figure 6c shows the advantage of using FT-MOEA as a back-end compared to Boolean logic, since the sizes of the returned FTs can be considerably smaller. The FTs inferred using Espresso or Sympy can be twice as large as the ones resulting from FT-MOEA. The reason is that for the Boolean logic formulas, no simplifications were performed by the libraries and the resulting FTs are therefore exactly encoding all the MCSs. Notice that the original FT-MOEA yields smaller or equal FT sizes than any of the configurations of SymLearn. This smaller size can however also come at the cost of losing accuracy, as demonstrated by case TS2. The larger FTs in SymLearn mostly stem from the composition of partitions where shared BE occur in both sub-trees, see for example Fig. 5c and 5d. While explicitly capturing the symmetries can therefore increase the size of the resulting FT, it also provides more insights into the system.

Figure 6d shows that SymLearn (*All*) runs significantly faster than FT-MOEA alone. If independent modules are present (cases TS2, TS3, SC and SS), SymLearn yields an FT within at most 2 min while FT-MOEA requires at least 1 h. The benefit of exploiting symmetries and modules can also be seen when comparing configuration *All* to *No Sym* and *No. rec.* which both run longer. Note that for SymLearn nearly all computation time is spent in the FT-MOEA backend (Step 5). Computing the modules and symmetries (Steps 2–4) took 50 ms at most whereas the computation of the MCSs (Step 1) took 43 s at most (for case TS2). Configurations based on Boolean functions always yield a result within minutes, but yield significantly larger FTs.

6 Conclusions

We presented *SymLearn*, a data-driven algorithm that infers a Fault Tree model from given failure data in a fully automatic way by identifying and exploiting modules and symmetries. Our evaluation based on truss system models shows that SymLearn is significantly faster than only using evolutionary algorithms when modules and symmetries can be exploited.

In the future, we aim to further improve the scalability by *optimizing the inference process*. First, the current partitioning of the MCSs requires the top gate to be an OR-gate. We aim to support the AND-gate as well. In addition, the inference back-end can be improved by either optimizing FT-MOEA or developing new inference approaches.

We also plan to *relax restrictions on the input data*. In the current approach, the resulting FTs are only as good as the given input data, which may be incomplete, e.g., due to rare events not present in the data. Moreover, the input may not completely represent the reality due to noise in the data. Hence, we aim to extend our approach to account for missing information and noise.

Acknowledgment. We thank Milan Lopuhaä-Zwakenberg for useful comments on an earlier version of this paper.

References

1. Brayton, R.K., Hachtel, G.D., McMullen, C.T., Sangiovanni-Vincentelli, A.L.: Logic Minimization Algorithms for VLSI Synthesis. The Springer International Series in Engineering and Computer Science, vol. 2. Springer, New York (1984). https://doi.org/10.1007/978-1-4613-2821-6
2. Byun, J., Song, J.: Efficient probabilistic multi-objective optimization of complex systems using matrix-based Bayesian network. Reliab. Eng. Syst. Saf. **200**, 106899 (2020)
3. Carpignano, A., Poucet, A.: Computer assisted fault tree construction: a review of methods and concerns. RESS **44**(3), 265–278 (1994)
4. Coudert, O.: Two-level logic minimization: an overview. Integration **17**(2), 97–140 (1994)
5. De Vries, R.C.: An automated methodology for generating a fault tree. IEEE Trans. Reliab. **39**(1), 76–86 (1990)
6. Deb, K., Agrawal, S., Pratap, A., Meyarivan, T.: A fast and elitist multiobjective genetic algorithm: NSGA-II. IEEE Trans. Evol. Comput. **6**(2), 182–197 (2002)
7. Dutuit, Y., Rauzy, A.: A linear-time algorithm to find modules of fault trees. IEEE Trans. Reliab. **45**(3), 422–425 (1996)
8. Hunt, A., Kelly, B., Mullhi, J., Lees, F., Rushton, A.: The propagation of faults in process plants: 6, overview of, and modelling for, fault tree synthesis. RESS **39**(2), 173–194 (1993)
9. Jiang, J.H.R., Devadas, S.: Logic synthesis in a nutshell. In: Electronic Design Automation, pp. 299–404. Elsevier, Amsterdam (2009)
10. Jimenez-Roa, L.A., Heskes, T., Tinga, T., Stoelinga, M.: Automatic inference of fault tree models via multi-objective evolutionary algorithms. CoRR abs/2204.03743 (2022)
11. Joshi, A., Vestal, S., Binns, P.: Automatic generation of static fault trees from AADL models (2007)
12. Lapp, S.A., Powers, G.J.: Computer-aided synthesis of fault-trees. IEEE Trans. Reliab. **26**(1), 2–13 (1977)
13. Lazarova-Molnar, S., Niloofar, P., Barta, G.K.: Data-driven fault tree modeling for reliability assessment of cyber-physical systems. In: WSC. IEEE (2020)
14. Linard, A., Bucur, D., Stoelinga, M.: Fault trees from data: efficient learning with an evolutionary algorithm. In: Guan, N., Katoen, J.-P., Sun, J. (eds.) SETTA 2019. LNCS, vol. 11951, pp. 19–37. Springer, Cham (2019). https://doi.org/10.1007/978-3-030-35540-1_2
15. Linard, A., Bueno, M.L., Bucur, D., Stoelinga, M.: Induction of fault trees through Bayesian networks. In: ESREL, pp. 910–917. Research Publishing (2019)
16. Madden, M.G., Nolan, P.J.: Generation of fault trees from simulated incipient fault case data. WIT Trans. Inf. Commun. Technol. **6** (1994)
17. Mahmud, N., Mian, Z.: Automatic generation of temporal fault trees from AADL models. In: ESREL, pp. 2741–2749 (2013)
18. Mhenni, F., Nguyen, N., Choley, J.: Automatic fault tree generation from SysML system models. In: AIM, pp. 715–720. IEEE (2014)
19. Murray, C.D., Williams, R.R.: On the (non) NP-hardness of computing circuit complexity. Theory Comput. **13**(1), 1–22 (2017)
20. Nauta, M., Bucur, D., Stoelinga, M.: LIFT: learning fault trees from observational data. In: McIver, A., Horvath, A. (eds.) QEST 2018. LNCS, vol. 11024, pp. 306–322. Springer, Cham (2018). https://doi.org/10.1007/978-3-319-99154-2_19

21. Powers, G.J., Tompkins, F.C., Jr.: Fault tree synthesis for chemical processes. AIChE J. **20**(2), 376–387 (1974)
22. Robert, P., Escoufier, Y.: A unifying tool for linear multivariate statistical methods: the rv- coefficient. J. Roy. Stat. Soc. Ser. C (Appl. Stat.) **25**(3), 257–265 (1976)
23. Ruijters, E., Stoelinga, M.: Fault tree analysis: a survey of the state-of-the-art in modeling, analysis and tools. Comput. Sci. Rev. **15**, 29–62 (2015)
24. Salem, S.L., Apostolakis, G., Okrent, D.: Computer-oriented approach to fault-tree construction. Technical report, California University (1976)
25. Stamatelatos, M., Vesely, W., Dugan, J., Fragola, J., Minarick, J., Railsback, J.: Fault tree handbook with aerospace applications (2002)
26. Taylor, J.: An algorithm for fault-tree construction. IEEE Trans. Reliab. **31**(2), 137–146 (1982)
27. Waghen, K., Ouali, M.: Interpretable logic tree analysis: a data-driven fault tree methodology for causality analysis. Expert Syst. Appl. **136**, 376–391 (2019)
28. Waghen, K., Ouali, M.: Multi-level interpretable logic tree analysis: a data-driven approach for hierarchical causality analysis. Expert Syst. Appl. **178**, 115035 (2021)
29. Wang, J., Liu, T.: A component behavioural model for automatic fault tree construction. RESS **42**(1), 87–100 (1993)
30. Xiang, J., Yanoo, K., Maeno, Y., Tadano, K.: Automatic synthesis of static fault trees from system models. In: SSIRI, pp. 127–136. IEEE Computer Society (2011)
31. Xie, G., Xue, D., Xi, S.: Tree-expert: a tree-based expert system for fault tree construction. RESS **40**(3), 295–309 (1993)

Assurance Cases

ARACHNE: Automated Validation of Assurance Cases with Stochastic Contract Networks

Chanwook Oh[1]([⊠]), Nikhil Naik[1], Zamira Daw[2], Timothy E. Wang[2], and Pierluigi Nuzzo[1]

[1] University of Southern California, Los Angeles, CA, USA
{chanwooo,nikhilvn,nuzzo}@usc.edu
[2] Raytheon Technologies Research Center, Berkeley, CA, USA
{zamira.daw,timothy.wang}@rtx.com

Abstract. We present ARACHNE, a framework for the automated, compositional validation of *assurance cases* (ACs), i.e., structured arguments about the correctness or safety of a design. ARACHNE leverages assume-guarantee contracts, expressed in a stochastic logic formalism, to formally capture AC claims (guarantees) subject to their contexts (assumptions) as well as the sources of uncertainty associated with them. Given an AC, modeled as a hierarchical network of stochastic contracts, and a library of confidence models, expressed as a set of Bayesian networks, we propose a procedure that coordinates logic and Bayesian reasoning to check that the AC argument is sound and quantify its strength in terms of a confidence measure. The effectiveness of our approach is illustrated on case studies motivated by testing and validation of airborne and automotive system software.

Keywords: Assurance cases · Confidence assessment · Bayesian networks

1 Introduction

Stringent regulations govern the operation of software-controlled, engineered systems in safety-critical applications, and their deployments are the results of a lengthy certification process, where a great amount of evidence about a product and its development process is collected and presented to human evaluators to validate if the product conforms with the qualification criteria stipulated by a regulatory agency. *Design assurance* is usually advocated by arguing compliance with a set of standards such as ISO-26262 [1] in the automotive and DO-178C [2] in the aerospace industry, laying down comprehensive guidelines for system development, testing, and certification. However, enforcing regulatory compliance of complex cyber-physical systems operating in dynamic, uncertain environments remains an uphill task [3]. The high cost and low flexibility of certification processes tend to impede the timely adoptions of new technologies

M. Trapp et al. (Eds.): SAFECOMP 2022, LNCS 13414, pp. 65–81, 2022.
https://doi.org/10.1007/978-3-031-14835-4_5

and the recent rise of networked, artificial intelligence-enabled systems [4] brings another dimension of design challenge.

Assurance cases (ACs) are an emerging method for providing comprehensive and defensible arguments that a design satisfies the properties of interest [5,6]. They show the promise of bridging the gap between the body of evidence and the assessment of the safety and dependability of a system via structured argumentation that facilitates critical examination of the evidence, premises, and claims toward the fulfillment of the system requirements. By leveraging structured languages or graphical representations [7,8], ACs enable recourse for review and reuse of argumentation patterns to promote system correctness or establish safety claims [9]. However, the creation of rigorous and interpretable arguments is nontrivial, and only a number of attempts have been made toward formalisms and tools that can assist in this task [10,11].

A major challenge in the construction and validation of ACs stems from their *inductive* nature [6] and the need to combine reasoning about system properties, often formalized by logic languages, with system and process uncertainty, often captured by probabilistic formalisms. While grounding the texture of an AC to the principles of logic and *deductive* reasoning goes a long way toward enhancing their rigor [12], ACs conspicuously rely on confirmatory evidence. Their objective is to convey a persuasive argument in fulfillment of a set of desired specifications with high *confidence* as a result of the mitigation of multiple sources of uncertainty in the environment, the system, and the development process. Combining probabilistic inference with logic inference brings difficulties due to the different mathematical foundations of logic and probability. Another challenge to AC formalization lies in the highly heterogeneous nature of the evidence and the associated sources of uncertainty, ranging from aleatoric[1] to epistemic uncertainty.[2] As a result, the rendering of the argumentation involved in validating the top-level claims may be susceptible to human bias [13].

This paper aims to address the above challenges by introducing ARACHNE (Automated Rapid Assurance via Compositional and Hierarchical Net Evaluation), a formal, compositional framework for representing and validating ACs. Our contributions can be summarized as follows:

- We introduce *stochastic assume-guarantee (A/G) contracts* as a semantic unit for AC representation to capture the claims and their premises as well as the confidence associated with them. Contract operations and relations are used to represent complex argumentation structures.
- We introduce *confidence networks* as a formalism to represent and quantify the level of uncertainty and confidence associated with predicates about a system and its development process given the available evidence.

---

[1] Due to randomness in the system or process, often quantified via *objective* measures from statistics (e.g., number of heads out of n tosses of a coin).

[2] Uncertainty about the system or process (e.g., whether a coin is fair or not), often captured by *subjective* measures of belief.

– We propose a decision procedure that efficiently coordinates logic and probabilistic reasoning to check the validity of an argument and evaluate its overall strength.

To the best of our knowledge, this is the first computer-aided framework for AC validation and confidence assessment via a coordination of probabilistic reasoning for uncertainty quantification and logic reasoning for hierarchical refinement of arguments.

Related Work. Graydon *et al.* [13] surveyed multiple proposals for quantifying confidence in assurance arguments leveraging different uncertainty quantification frameworks [14–18], revealing a number of potential shortcomings in existing approaches. For example, a confidence metric may fall short of accounting for missing or contrary information which may be *masked* by the overall confidence score at the top-level claim, thus undercutting the sensitivity of the metric to critical evidence. Similarly, assigning *equal weights* to all the evidence items irrespectively of their impact on the overall system reliability may also lead to implausible results. In this paper, we adopt Bayesian reasoning [19] for quantifying confidence values. However, our method can circumvent these issues since it does not exclusively rely on probabilistic inference to determine the confidence of the top claim. It rather adopts a *hierarchical* approach where probabilistic reasoning, performed locally, is combined with logic reasoning, performed globally on the AC. Moreover, we introduce a two-stage design of the confidence assessment algorithm coupling an *uncertainty quantification* step with a *decision-making* step, offering mechanisms to appropriately weigh different evidence items and discount unreliable evidence with low confidence (high risk) levels.

Prevailing approaches to propagate probabilistic assessments through the reasoning steps of an argument either bound the uncertainty of the conclusion with the sum of the uncertainties of the premises, or assume that top-level claims always follow from the conjunction of subclaims [20]. Conversely, our confidence computation and propagation approach based on contracts can better account for the dependencies among sources of uncertainty, the logical form of the reasoning steps, and their relationship with the system architecture, components, context, and the overarching system properties.

2   Background

Assurance Cases. An *assurance case* (AC) is an argument constructed to establish that a system satisfies the requirements in its operative environment by means of hierarchical steps which map a *claim* to *evidence* via strategies and intermediary claims [6,11]. ACs are often described using a structured language [21] or graphical notations such as the Claims-Arguments-Evidence (CAE) notation [7] and the Goal Structuring Notation (GSN) [8]. An AC can then be represented as a directed acyclic graph mapping the system specification (the top-level claim) from the root node to the leaf nodes, representing the evidence.

Commercially available software tools [22, 23] implement GSN (or CAE) pattern libraries, providing a limited degree of automation for representation and validation of ACs. However, some elements of the semantics in these tools are not well-defined in their respective conventions, leaving room for an individual developer to clarify them [6]. The characterization of refinement steps between claims, whether they are inductive or deductive, often lacks rigor, opening the door for confirmation bias [11]. We address these concerns by leveraging contract operations to solidify the relationship between claims, allied with Bayesian reasoning to assess their strength.

Assume-Guarantee Contracts. A/G contracts offer effective mechanisms to analyze system requirements and behaviors in a modular way [24–27]. We use A/G contracts as a specification formalism to represent claims about the system as well as the contexts under which the claims must hold. An A/G contract C is a triple (V, A, G) where V is the set of variables, A (assumptions) is a specification for an environment over V, and G (guarantees) is a specification for an implementation over V, representing the set of promised behaviors given that the environment satisfies A. We omit V in the contract tuple, when this is clear from the context.

A contract C is *compatible* if there exists a valid environment for it, i.e., A is satisfiable, and *consistent* if there exists a valid implementation, i.e., $A \to G$ is satisfiable. We can reason about the replaceability of a contract (or a claim) by another contract at a different level of abstraction via the *refinement* relation. We say that C_2 refines C_1, written $C_2 \preceq C_1$, if and only if C_2 has weaker assumptions and stronger guarantees than C_1. We can then replace C_1 with C_2. Contracts C_1 and C_2 can also be combined using *conjunction* ($C_1 \wedge C_2$) and *composition* ($C_1 \otimes C_2$) to construct a more complex claim from two simpler claims on the same component or on different components of an argument, respectively. We refer to the literature [24, 25] for further details on the formal semantics of contracts and their algebra.

3 Assurance Cases as Contract Networks

We propose a formal model to represent ACs where A/G contracts are used as a semantic unit. First, we introduce a logic language for expressing A/G contracts, then discuss the formalization of an AC as a graph of contracts.

3.1 Stochastic Propositional Logic

We introduce *stochastic propositional logic* (StPL) as an extension of propositional logic, building on previous notions of unification between logic and probability [28–30]. Let $\mathcal{X} = \{X_1, \ldots, X_n\}$ be a set of Boolean random variables (RVs) and $(\Omega, \mathcal{F}, \mathbb{P})$ a reference *probability space*, where the set of *outcomes* $\Omega = \mathcal{A}(\mathcal{X})$ is given by the set of value assignments over $\mathcal{X}$, $\mathcal{F} = 2^\Omega$ is a set of *events*, and $\mathbb{P} : \mathcal{F} \to [0, 1]$ is the probability measure induced by the joint distribution d over

$\mathcal{X}, d : \mathcal{A}(\mathcal{X}) \to [0, 1]$, with $\sum_{a \in \mathcal{A}(\mathcal{X})} d(a) = 1$. StPL formulas are defined over the set of RVs $\mathcal{X}$ and interpreted over the probability measure $\mathbb{P}$.

Let ϕ be a propositional formula over $\mathcal{X}$, constructed by combining the Boolean RVs via logical connectives, e.g., $X_1 \to (X_2 \wedge X_3)$. We denote the Boolean values *true* and *false* by $\top$ and $\bot$, respectively. We define a probabilistic atomic predicate (AP) of the form $\phi^{[p]} := \mathbb{P}(\phi) \geq p$, where $p \in [0, 1]$ is a *probability threshold*. The truth value of $\phi^{[p]}$ is interpreted based on the satisfaction of the probabilistic constraint, i.e., $\phi^{[p]} = \top$ if and only if $\phi = \top$ holds with probability larger than or equal to p. The syntax of StPL is then defined as follows: $\psi := \phi^{[p]} \mid \neg\psi \mid \psi_1 \vee \psi_2$, where ψ, ψ_1, ψ_2 are StPL formulas. The semantics are defined recursively as: $\mathcal{X} \models \phi^{[p]} \leftrightarrow \mathbb{P}(\phi) \geq p$, $\mathcal{X} \models \neg\psi \leftrightarrow \neg(\mathcal{X} \models \psi)$, and $\mathcal{X} \models \psi_1 \vee \psi_2 \leftrightarrow (\mathcal{X} \models \psi_1) \vee (\mathcal{X} \models \psi_2)$, where $\leftrightarrow$ is the logical bi-implication.

An StPL formula ψ can be *determinized* to a propositional formula $\widetilde{\psi}$ by replacing every probabilistic AP $\phi_i^{[p_i]}$ in ψ with the propositional formula ϕ_i. For example, $\psi_1 := (X_1 \wedge X_2)^{[0.98]} \wedge (X_3 \vee X_4)^{[0.9]}$ can be determinized to $\widetilde{\psi_1} := (X_1 \wedge X_2) \wedge (X_3 \vee X_4)$.

3.2 Hierarchical Stochastic Contract Networks

We express the assumptions and guarantees of a contract using StPL formulas to specify probabilistic behaviors over $\mathcal{X}$. We denote the *stochastic contract* by $C = (\mathcal{X}, \psi_A, \psi_G)$. The main contract operators can then be mapped to logical operations and entailments between formulas [31]. Given a stochastic contract C, we define the *determinized version* of C, denoted by $\widetilde{C}$, as the contract whose assumption and guarantee formulas are determinized versions of ψ_A and ψ_G, $\widetilde{\psi}_A$ and $\widetilde{\psi}_G$, respectively. Then, we can associate a notion of *confidence* in the claim captured by a stochastic contract as follows.

Definition 1 (Contract Confidence). *Let* $C = (\mathcal{X}, \psi_A, \psi_G)$ *be a stochastic contract and* $\widetilde{C} = (\mathcal{X}, \widetilde{\psi}_A, \widetilde{\psi}_G)$ *be its determinized version. The confidence* $\mathcal{C}(C)$ *in* C *is* $\mathcal{C}(C) := \mathbb{P}(\widetilde{\psi}_A \to \widetilde{\psi}_G)$.

By extending a formal model developed largely concurrently in the context of hierarchical contract-based synthesis [32], we represent an argumentation step as a graph of interconnected stochastic contracts, termed *stochastic contract network*. Let a *connection* be a formula of the form $\gamma_i := X_1 \leftrightarrow X_2$, establishing that two RVs X_1 and X_2 are shared (or connected).

Definition 2 (Stochastic Contract Network). *A stochastic contract network (SCN)* N *is a triple* $(\mathbf{C}, \gamma, \|)$ *where* $\mathbf{C} = \{C_1, C_2, \cdots\}$ *is a finite set of stochastic contracts,* $\gamma = \{\gamma_1, \gamma_2, \cdots\}$ *is a finite set of connections, and* $\| \in \{\otimes, \wedge\}$ *is a contract operation.*

An SCN N is equivalent to a single contract $C_N = C_1 \| \cdots \| C_{|\mathbf{C}|} \| (\top, \gamma_1) \| \cdots \| (\top, \gamma_{|\gamma|})$ where $|\mathbf{C}|$ and $|\gamma|$ are the cardinality of $\mathbf{C}$ and γ, respectively. It can represent either a collection of interconnected claims on different components of the argument (via composition) or claims on the same component (via conjunction). Further, we can relate stochastic contracts and SCNs via a weaker notion of refinement, termed *conditional refinement*.

Definition 3 (Conditional Refinement). *A conditional refinement R is a tuple (C_u, φ, C_l) where C_u and C_l are stochastic contracts and φ is a propositional formula, termed* context formula. *C_l refines C_u in the context of φ, written, $C_l \preceq_\varphi C_u$ if and only if $C_l \preceq C_u$ when φ holds, i.e., $\varphi \to (C_l \preceq C_u)$.*

C_l may not refine C_u in general, but it does so under the restrictions imposed by φ. A context formula can then be used to model, for example, a "side condition" that is necessary for the correctness of an argumentation step in an AC. The third element C_l of a conditional refinement R can be represented as a contract C_N that is equivalent to an SCN N. In this case, we write $R = (C_u, \varphi, N)$ with a slight abuse of notation. Finally, stepwise refinements of higher-level claims into lower-level claims can be captured by graphs of SCNs, termed *hierarchical stochastic contract networks*.

Definition 4 (Hierarchical SCN). *A hierarchical stochastic contract network (HSCN) H is a triple $(N_0, \mathbf{N}, \mathbf{R})$, where N_0 is the top-level SCN, $\mathbf{N} = \{N_1, N_2, \cdots\}$ is a finite set of SCNs, and $\mathbf{R} = \{R_1, R_2, \cdots\}$ is a finite set of conditional refinements. Each conditional refinement in $\mathbf{R}$ connects a stochastic contract in $N_i \in \mathbf{N} \cup \{N_0\}$ with a SCN $N_j \in \mathbf{N}$ with $j \neq i$.*

N_0 in Definition 4 represents the top-level claim (contract) that is not linked by refinement relations to a contract of any SCN in $\mathbf{N}$. HSCNs are trees of contract networks that enable relating claims at different levels of the argument hierarchy to the argumentation steps that support them. For example, the HSCN $H = (N_0, \{N_1\}, \{R_0\})$ in Fig. 1a represents an AC that argues that a claim (conclusion) about a software module can be drawn from two sub-claims related to two testing activities. The contract network N_0 includes a contract, *test*, capturing the top-level claim that "the software module meets the design criterion via multiple testing activities," while N_1 includes two contracts $test_1$ and $test_2$, each capturing the sub-claim that "the software module meets the design criterion via testing activity 1 (or 2)." The conditional refinement $R_0 := (N_0, \varphi_0, N_1)$ models the fact that the claim in *test* is supported by an argument N_1 involving two contracts (sub-claims), $test_1$ and $test_2$, in a context where φ_0 holds. Within N_1, connections between contracts are denoted by shared variables, e.g., *correctSpec*. For simplicity, we represent contracts with their determinized versions. We then resort to the stochastic versions as we assign confidence values to the contract predicates, computed using confidence networks.

3.3   Confidence Networks

We use *confidence networks* to represent the sources of uncertainty in the predicates about a system, its development process, and the associated evidence. In this paper, confidence networks are implemented as Bayesian networks (BNs) which have been used in many application domains to quantitatively reason

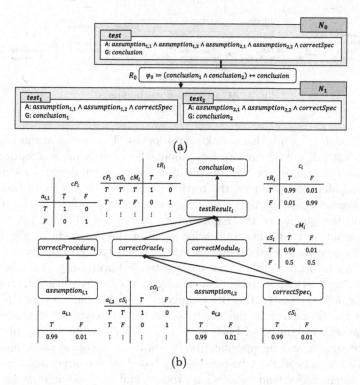

Fig. 1. A generic argumentation template for structural coverage formalized using an HSCN (a) together with the associated confidence network (b).

about the confidence in assertions affected by uncertainty [33], especially in the presence of a causal relationship between them. Models based on BNs tend to be more compact in the number of uncertain variables than in other probabilistic frameworks for uncertainty quantification [34]. Our framework can, however, be extended, as future work, to incorporate other approaches, such as the one based on Dempster-Shafer theory [15], providing confidence measures that are closely related to probability distributions.

In a BN, the sources of uncertainty are modeled using RVs. The BN itself is a graph representation of the joint probability distribution of a set of RVs, associated with the graph nodes, where the edges and the associated conditional probabilities capture the dependencies between nodes, i.e., specify whether and by which extent two variables may affect each other's distribution. For example, the BN template in Fig. 1b encapsulates notions from testing to express the key correlations between the outcome of a test and the quality of the artifacts (e.g., test procedure, test oracle) produced during the development and testing steps. The confidence in the testing result (*testResult*) can then be computed based on the beliefs in the quality of the testing procedure (*correctProcedure*), the testing oracle (*correctOracle*), and the quality of the actual software module

Fig. 2. AC validation methodology.

(*correctModule*), even if this is unknown *a priori*. The confidence in the oracle depends, instead, on the uncertainty about the underlying assumptions that support its construction or the sources of doubt that can defeat its soundness. Similar considerations hold for the testing procedure. Finally, both the quality of the software module (*correctModule*) and the test oracle (*correctOracle*) depend on the quality of the requirements (*correctSpec*). This BN template allows computing confidence values for some of the contracts in Fig. 1a, e.g., $test_1$, $test_2$, and associated predicates, e.g., $conclusion_1$, $correctSpec$.

BNs can incorporate aleatoric and epistemic uncertainty, and allow combining multiple evidence items. For example, via the conditional probability $P(conclusion|testResult)$, the BN template in Fig. 1b can capture the dependency on the confidence in the result of the test (a source of aleatoric uncertainty), as well as the belief (*subjective* probability) in the quality of the test procedure, oracle, and the specification (a source of epistemic uncertainty).

Confidence networks can be constructed based on domain expert knowledge, e.g., via an elicitation and calibration process, and can also account for lack of knowledge, using methods from Bayesian epistemology [6,35]. The objective of confidence models is not to approximate the "probability of correctness" (e.g., absence of bugs) of a design, which is difficult in practice, but rather estimate the amount by which the evidence is convincing enough to support a claim, e.g., by drawing from the knowledge base underlying testing or formal verification, to guide the construction of arguments in the direction of mitigating the underlying sources of uncertainty or doubt.

4   Assurance Case Validation

We denote a contract of the HSCN which is not linked via conditional refinement to any other SCN in the HSCN as an *evidential contract*. For example, contracts $test_1$, and $test_2$ in Fig. 1a are evidential contracts, while $test$ is not. The HSCN validation problem can be defined as follows:

Problem 1 (HSCN Validation). *Given an HSCN $H = (N_0, \mathbf{N}, \mathbf{R})$ and a library (collection) of confidence networks $\mathcal{L}$, let C_0 be the top-level contract in N_0 and $\delta^* \in [0,1]$ the minimum required confidence for C_0. Let the contracts in H be defined over a set of RVs $\mathcal{X}$ distributed according to the confidence networks in $\mathcal{L}$ and let $\phi_i \in R_i$ hold for all $i \in \{1, \dots, |\mathbf{R}|\}$. The HSCN validation problem consists in verifying that $\mathcal{C}(C_0) \geq \delta^*$ holds.*

Problem 1 simultaneously requires that: (1) the argument given by H be sound, and (2) the confidence in the evidential contracts, inferred from the confidence networks in $\mathcal{L}$, be sufficient to support the top-level claim with confidence at least δ^*. We address this problem by coordinating logic and probabilistic reasoning, as shown in Fig. 2.

4.1   Checking the Soundness of an HSCN

We evaluate the soundness of the logical argumentation steps by recursively traversing the HSCN graph using a depth-first-search approach, and by checking compatibility, consistency, and refinement between contracts hierarchically. These verification tasks are translated into satisfiability problems for satisfiability modulo theory (SMT) formulas in first order logic. When checking the soundness of an evidential contract claim based on the evidence, we assume a deterministic interpretation of the contract predicates, in which the availability of evidence, i.e., a matching node in a confidence network, is sufficient to determine whether an assertion is true or false. For example, the confidence network in Fig. 1b with $i = 1$ is a matching network for contract $test_1$ of N_1 since all the propositions in the contract, i.e., $assumption_{1,1}$, $assumption_{1,2}$, $correctSpec_1$, and $conclusion_1$ can be found in the confidence network. If such a network is found in the library, then all the propositions of $test_1$ are assumed to be true in this phase of the validation process. If at least one of the evidential contracts cannot be supported by evidence, the HSCN is marked as infeasible. Similarly, if one of the refinement relations fails to hold, we return an infeasibility certificate reporting the relation that is invalid. Otherwise, we conclude that the HSCN is logically sound and proceed with assessing its confidence level.

4.2   Confidence Assessment

Our two-stage confidence assessment algorithm couples *quantitative probabilistic reasoning* with *qualitative decision-making* strategies capable of appropriately discounting unreliable evidence with low confidence levels. We adopt a hierarchical approach that can achieve scalability by virtue of its modularity, as further detailed below.

Confidence Computation. For each evidential contract, we search for a matching confidence network in the confidence library $\mathcal{L}$, which we use to perform probabilistic inference and determine confidence values for the contract predicates. Once a confidence network is found, we assign confidence values to the evidential contract predicates $\widetilde{\psi}_A$ (assumptions) and $\widetilde{\psi}_A \to \widetilde{\psi}_G$ (guarantees in the context of the assumptions). For example, we obtain confidence values for $test_1$ in Fig. 1a using the axioms of probability and probabilistic inference on the BN in Fig. 1b. The evidential contract then turns into the following stochastic contract:

$$\psi_A := (assumption_{1,1} \land assumption_{1,2} \land correctSpec)^{[0.9703]}$$

$$\psi_G := ((assumption_{1,1} \land assumption_{1,2} \land correctSpec) \rightarrow conclusion_1)^{[0.9808]},$$

where we use the fact that $\mathbb{P}\{(assumption_{1,1} \land assumption_{1,2} \land correctSpec) \rightarrow conclusion_1\} = 1 - \mathbb{P}\{assumption_{1,1} \land assumption_{1,2} \land correctSpec \land \neg conclusion_1\}$.

Decision Making. While a confidence model is useful to perform *fine-grained comparisons and sensitivity analysis*, it is affected by inaccuracies and is, in general, not sufficient to define absolute thresholds for determining whether there is enough evidence [13]. We address this issue by combining probabilistic reasoning with a decision scheme that helps determine whether there is sufficient confidence in a claim and the claim can be used to support higher-level claims in the argumentation hierarchy.

Our decision strategy consists of the following steps: (i) *coarse-grained classification* of the previously computed confidence values in the evidential contracts according to pre-determined qualitative levels, such as `Low`, `Medium`, `High`; (ii) *rule-based decision* about the sufficiency of the evidence by combining the qualitative confidence levels above. For example, a simple rule may require that the majority of the premises must have confidence level `High` in the stochastic contract network. A more systematic procedure would analyze the evidential contract premises, to check whether the confidence in the contract assumptions is sufficient given the available evidence, or whether there is evidence that the guarantees may not hold. Similarly to the construction of confidence networks, our decision strategy is the result of an elicitation and calibration process based on expert knowledge.

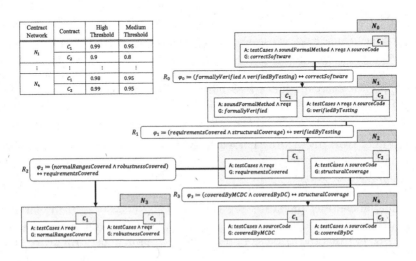

Fig. 3. HSCN for the correctness of a software module and table for classifying confidence levels.

Confidence Propagation. If a claim in the HSCN has high enough confidence level, the confidence levels associated with the contract propositions can be propagated upward in the HSCN until the root contract is reached. We propagate the confidence hierarchically from a lower-level SCN to its higher-level stochastic contract by requiring that conditional refinement hold according to the calculus of stochastic contracts and the confidence composition rules from the confidence models. Confidence propagation can be cast as an SMT problem including polynomial arithmetic constraints on the rational numbers. Otherwise, if propagation cannot occur, the algorithm returns an infeasibility certificate, listing the sources of uncertainty, the gaps, and the violated rule that have made it impossible to establish one or more claims.

5 Case Studies

We implemented ARACHNE as a Python package. SMT problems are solved using Z3 [36], while the Python package PGMPY [37] is used to capture the confidence networks and perform Bayesian inference. Experiments are executed on an Intel core i7 processor with 16-GB RAM.

5.1 Software Correctness Assurance

In this case study, we illustrate the advantages of our approach by comparing it with a confidence quantification method based on translating the entire AC into a *single BN* to perform probabilistic inference monolithically [14,38] and infer a confidence measure for the top-level claim. We validate the HSCN in Fig. 3 aiming to assess the top-level claim with a confidence level $\delta^* = 0.9$. Multiple sub-claims based on formal verification, requirement, and structural test coverage support the top-level claim that "the software module is correct," inspired by the prescriptions of the DO-178C standard [2]. We assume a library of confidence networks supporting all the evidential contracts, including the one in Fig. 4, a set of thresholds for classifying confidence levels as in Fig. 3, and a decision rule requiring that all the confidence values for the premises (or sub-claims) of a claim be High for successful confidence propagation. We place a higher weight on the outcome of *decision coverage (DC)*, C_2 of N_4, than on *modified condition/decision coverage (MCDC)*, C_1 of N_4, by using a higher threshold to determine whether the confidence for DC (0.99) is high enough. The decision to allocate higher weight on the outcome of DC follows from the fact that the criteria for DC are less restrictive than those for MCDC and a lower confidence value in the outcome of DC denotes a potential flaw in the development process.

As shown in Table 1, we introduce three scenarios assigning different confidence levels to predicates DCO and $MCDCO$ in Fig. 4, stating that "the DC (or MCDC) testing oracle is correct," due to the available evidence. In all scenarios, we check the soundness of the conditional refinements by solving SMT problems and match each evidential contract to an appropriate confidence network. For scenario 1, ARACHNE provides a confidence value of 0.9767 while inference on

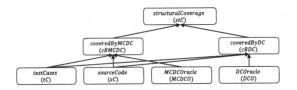

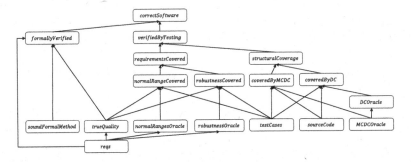

Fig. 4. Confidence network for C_1 and C_2 of N_4.

Fig. 5. A single BN used to reason about the confidence in the argument of Fig. 3.

the single BN shown in Fig. 5 yields 0.9826 for the top-level claim. In both cases, the evidence is determined as sufficient to support the claim. In scenario 2, we assume instead that the belief in DCO decreases, e.g., due to the realization that an outdated oracle has been used. ARACHNE identifies the low-confidence claim C_2 of N_4, which has now Medium confidence, and returns a failure due to the violation of the decision rule. On the other hand, a method using the single BN in Fig. 5 fails to effectively isolate the potential gap: the confidence in the top-level claim, 0.98, is still deemed as admissible (≥ 0.9), and the reduced belief in DCO gets "masked" by the overall high confidence. In scenario 3, we assume that the belief in $MCDCO$ increases while the one in DCO decreases symmetrically to scenario 1. In this case, the claim on DC (C_2 of N_4) does not pass ARACHNE's threshold for sufficient confidence. The confidence level in C_2 of N_4 is classified as Medium and the validation leads, again, to a failure due to violation of the decision rule. On the other hand, inference on the single BN fails to recognize the different weights placed on DCO and $MCDCO$. Since the confidence in the top-level claim is 0.9836, the evidence is considered as sufficient despite the different roles played by C_1 and C_2 of N_4 in the decision-making process. Overall, ARACHNE can circumvent the limitations of monolithic inference, including the "masking" of weak premises (as shown in scenario 2) and the equal weighing of evidence (as shown in scenario 3) by virtue of its hierarchical approach and propagation strategy.

Table 1. Results for the case study on software correctness.

Scenario	P(MCDCO)	P(DCO)	Confidence level on C_1 of N_4	Confidence level on C_2 of N_4	Top-claim confidence (or failure reason)	
					ARACHNE	Single BN
1	0.99	0.995	High (0.9900)	High (0.9950)	0.9767	0.9826
2	0.99	0.97	High (0.9900)	Medium (0.9701)	Rule violation	0.9800
3	0.995	0.99	High (0.9950)	Medium (0.9900)	Rule violation	0.9836

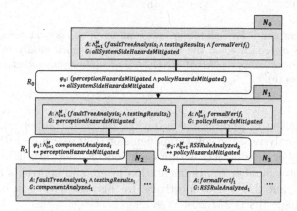

Fig. 6. HSCN for an autonomous vehicle.

5.2   Scalable Assurance for Autonomous Driving Systems

We assess the scalability of the proposed framework by constructing an HSCN for an autonomous vehicle, as shown in Fig. 6, inspired by some of the criteria proposed in the literature [39,40] to assess safety and reliability. We again compare our approach with a method using monolithic inference on a single BN.

In the proposed AC, system hazards are mitigated via a divide-and-conquer approach by mitigating the hazards associated with the perception sub-system and the driving policy sub-system. The overall confidence in the performance of the system is then computed by combining the confidence in these two legs of the arguments. Each component in the perception sub-system operates independently from the other components and is subject to testing methods to assess the performance as well as fault-tree analysis against specific hazards. The driving policy is, instead, specified by a set of rules, derived from the responsibility-sensitive safety (RSS) model [39] to guarantee that accidents will never be caused by the autonomous vehicle in control. We assume that each RSS-derived rule can be independently verified by a set of formal methods.

We expand the AC in Fig. 6 horizontally or vertically. In the horizontal case, we fix the number of argumentation layers, and increase the number of components and RSS rules to M, which results in an increased number of contracts in N_2 and N_3. The total number of contracts in the HSCN is $2M + 3$. Since each evidential contract is supported by a BN with k_c nodes, a single BN modeling the same argument has $2M(k_c + 1) + 3$ nodes. In the vertical case, we assume

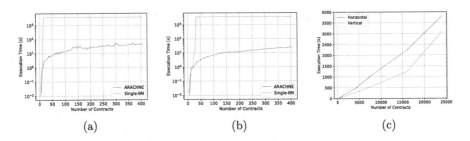

Fig. 7. Execution times for validation and confidence assessment using ARACHNE and a single-BN approach when the HSCN is expanded horizontally (a) or vertically (b). Runtime performance of ARACHNE for horizontally-expanded and vertically-expanded HSCNs (c).

that the mitigation of undesirable behaviors for each component or RSS rule hinges on the analysis of the sub-components or their associated RSS rules. The maximum number of contracts within each contract network is now limited to 2, while the total number of argumentation layers and contracts in the HSCN is $2 + \lceil \log_2 M \rceil$ and $4M + 1$, respectively. In this case, the total number of the nodes in the single BN is $2M(k_c + 2) + 1$.

As reported in Fig. 7a and 7b, our approach scales well with an increasing number of components and RSS rules. Computing the confidence in the top-level claim for up to 400 contracts takes less than 100 s. On the other hand, inference on the single BN reaches a timeout threshold of 1 h for less than 50 contracts. This result is consistent with the asymptotic complexity of Bayesian inference, which is exponential in the width of the elimination order w, a measure of the maximum number of neighbors of a BN node [41]. For example, the complexity of variable elimination for exact Bayesian inference is $O(k^2 e^w)$, where k is the number of BN nodes and w is the width of the elimination order. By virtue of our compositional approach, confidence computations require $2M$ inference tasks on BNs with a small number of nodes, bounded by k_c, and a constant width w_c, which amounts to linear complexity ($O(k_c^2 M e^{w_c})$). On the other hand, the single BNs with $2M(k_c + 1) + 3$ and $2M(k_c + 2) + 1$ nodes and maximum widths of M and 2, respectively, for horizontally and vertically expanded arguments, lead to the observable exponential and quadratic explosions of execution time for inference tasks, with complexity $O(k_c^2 M^2 e^M)$ and $O(k_c^2 M^2 e^2)$, respectively.

As shown in Fig. 7c, validating HSCNs with more than 15,000 contracts incurs additional overhead due to the cost for finding a matching confidence network for each evidential contract, currently based on linear search, which becomes inefficient for large confidence libraries. Moreover, validating vertically-expanded HSCNs takes less time than horizontally-expanded HSCNs due to the different size of the associated SMT problems. Solving multiple smaller SMT instances in a vertically-expanded HSCN is less expensive than solving just a few, but larger, SMT instances in a horizontally-expanded HSCN. Overall, HSCNs with more than 24,000 contracts, organized in 3 layers and 18 layers in the horizontally and vertically expanded cases, respectively, and using a library of 24,000 confidence networks, can be validated in less than an hour.

6 Conclusions

We presented ARACHNE, a validation framework for assurance cases represented as networks of stochastic assume-guarantee contracts. By coordinating logic and probabilistic reasoning, ARACHNE can circumvent the limitations of previous approaches, such as the "masking" of low-confidence premises and the equal weighting of claims, and shows superior scalability on case studies motivated by safety-critical avionic and automotive applications. Future work includes extending the framework to richer stochastic logics with temporal modalities and exploring the relationship between confidence and costs to achieve cost-effective arguments.

Acknowledgments. Distribution statement "A" (approved for public release, distribution unlimited). This research was developed with funding from the Defense Advanced Research Projects Agency (DARPA), contract FA875020C0508. The views, opinions, or findings expressed are those of the authors and should not be interpreted as representing the official views or policies of the Department of Defense or the U.S. Government. The authors wish to also acknowledge the partial support by the National Science Foundation (NSF) under Awards 1839842, 1846524, and 2139982, the Office of Naval Research (ONR) under Award N00014-20-1-2258, and the Defense Advanced Research Projects Agency (DARPA) under Award HR00112010003.

References

1. ISO 26262:2018: Road vehicles - Functional safety. International Organization for Standardization, Standard (2018)
2. DO-178C: Software considerations in airborne systems and equipment certification. RTCA Inc., Standard (2011)
3. Brunner, M., Huber, M., et al.: Towards an integrated model for safety and security requirements of cyber-physical systems. In: International Conference on Software Quality, Reliability and Security Companion (QRS-C) (2017)
4. Lee, J., Davari, H., et al.: Industrial artificial intelligence for industry 4.0-based manufacturing systems. Manuf. Lett. **18**, 20–23 (2018)
5. Bloomfield, R., Bishop, P.: Safety and assurance cases: past, present and possible future-an Adelard perspective. In: Dale, C., Anderson, T. (eds.) Making Systems Safer, pp. 51–67. Springer, London (2010). https://doi.org/10.1007/978-1-84996-086-1_4
6. Rushby, J.: The interpretation and evaluation of assurance cases. Technical report, Computer Science Laboratory, SRI International (2015)
7. Adelard LLP: Claims, Arguments and Evidence (CAE) (2019). https://www.adelard.com/asce/choosing-asce/cae.html
8. The Assurance Case Working Group: Goal Structuring Notation Community Standard (Version 3) (2021). https://scsc.uk/r141C

9. Hawkins, R., Habli, I., et al.: Assurance cases and prescriptive software safety certification: a comparative study. Saf. Sci. **59**, 55–71 (2013)

10. Hawkins, R., Habli, I., et al.: Weaving an assurance case from design: a model-based approach. In: International Symposium on High Assurance Systems Engineering (2015)

11. Bloomfield, R., Rushby, J.: Assurance 2.0, arXiv preprint arXiv:2004.10474 (2020)

12. Denney, E., Pai, G., Pohl, J.: Heterogeneous aviation safety cases: integrating the formal and the non-formal. In: International Conference on Engineering of Complex Computer Systems (2012)

13. Graydon, P.J., Holloway, C.M.: An investigation of proposed techniques for quantifying confidence in assurance arguments. Saf. Sci. **92**, 53–65 (2017)

14. Denney, E., Pai, G., Habli, I.: Towards measurement of confidence in safety cases. In: 2011 International Symposium on Empirical Software Engineering and Measurement (2011)

15. Dempster, A.P.: Upper and lower probabilities induced by a multivalued mapping. Ann. Math. Stat. **38**(2), 325–339 (1967)

16. Jøsang, A.: A logic for uncertain probabilities. Int. J. Uncertain. Fuzziness Knowl. Based Syst. **9**(03), 279–311 (2001)

17. Yamamoto, S.: Assuring security through attribute GSN. In: International Conference on IT Convergence and Security (ICITCS) (2015)

18. Nair, S., Walkinshaw, N., Kelly, T.: Quantifying uncertainty in safety cases using evidential reasoning. In: Bondavalli, A., Ceccarelli, A., Ortmeier, F. (eds.) SAFECOMP 2014. LNCS, vol. 8696, pp. 413–418. Springer, Cham (2014). https://doi.org/10.1007/978-3-319-10557-4_45

19. Neapolitan, R., Neapolitan, R.: Learning Bayesian Networks. Pearson Prentice Hall, Hoboken (2004)

20. Adams, E.W.: A Primer of Probability Logic. Center for the Study of Language and Information (1996)

21. Holloway, C.M.: Explicate'78: uncovering the implicit assurance case in DO-178C. In: Safety-Critical Systems Symposium 2015 (SSS 2015) (2015)

22. Denney, E., Pai, G., Pohl, J.: AdvoCATE: an assurance case automation toolset. In: Ortmeier, F., Daniel, P. (eds.) SAFECOMP 2012. LNCS, vol. 7613, pp. 8–21. Springer, Heidelberg (2012). https://doi.org/10.1007/978-3-642-33675-1_2

23. Fujita, H., Matsuno, Y., et al.: DS-bench toolset: tools for dependability benchmarking with simulation and assurance. In: IEEE/IFIP International Conference on Dependable Systems and Networks (DSN) (2012)

24. Benveniste, A., Caillaud, B., et al.: Contracts for system design. Found. Trends Electron. Des. Autom. **12**(2–3), 124–400 (2018)

25. Bauer, S.S., et al.: Moving from specifications to contracts in component-based design. In: de Lara, J., Zisman, A. (eds.) FASE 2012. LNCS, vol. 7212, pp. 43–58. Springer, Heidelberg (2012). https://doi.org/10.1007/978-3-642-28872-2_3

26. Sangiovanni-Vincentelli, A., Damm, W., Passerone, R.: Taming Dr. Frankenstein: contract-based design for cyber-physical systems. Eur. J. Control. **18**(3), 217–238 (2012)

27. Nuzzo, P., Sangiovanni-Vincentelli, A.L., et al.: A platform-based design methodology with contracts and related tools for the design of cyber-physical systems. In: Proceedings of the IEEE (2015)

28. Gaifman, H.: Concerning measures in first order calculi. Israel J. Math. **2**(1), 1–18 (1964)

29. Hailperin, T.: Probability logic. Notre Dame J. Formal Logic **25**(3), 198–212 (1984)

30. Nilsson, N.J.: Probabilistic logic. Artif. Intell. **28**(1), 71–87 (1986)
31. Nuzzo, P., Li, J., et al.: Stochastic assume-guarantee contracts for cyber-physical system design. ACM Trans. Embed. Comput. Syst. **18**(1), 1–26 (2019)
32. Wang, T.E., Daw, Z., Nuzzo, P., Pinto, A.: Hierarchical contract-based synthesis for assurance cases. In: Deshmukh, J.V., Havelund, K., Perez, I. (eds.) NASA Formal Methods, pp. 175–192. Springer, Cham (2022). https://doi.org/10.1007/978-3-031-06773-0_9
33. Hobbs, C., Lloyd, M.: The application of Bayesian belief networks to assurance case preparation. In: Dale, C., Anderson, T. (eds.) Achieving Systems Safety, pp. 159–176. Springer, London (2012). https://doi.org/10.1007/978-1-4471-2494-8_12
34. Verbert, K., Babuška, R., De Schutter, B.: Bayesian and Dempster-Shafer reasoning for knowledge-based fault diagnosis-a comparative study. Eng. Appl. Artif. Intell. **60**, 136–150 (2017)
35. Bovens, L., Hartmann, S.: Bayesian Epistemology. Oxford University Press, Oxford (2003)
36. De Moura, L., Bjørner, N.: Z3: An efficient SMT solver (2008)
37. Ankan, A., Panda, A.: pgmpy: probabilistic graphical models using python. In: Proceedings of the 14th Python in Science Conference (SCIPY 2015). Citeseer (2015)
38. Zhao, X., Zhang, D., Lu, M., Zeng, F.: A new approach to assessment of confidence in assurance cases. In: Ortmeier, F., Daniel, P. (eds.) SAFECOMP 2012. LNCS, vol. 7613, pp. 79–91. Springer, Heidelberg (2012). https://doi.org/10.1007/978-3-642-33675-1_7
39. Shalev-Shwartz, S., Shammah, S., Shashua, A.: On a formal model of safe and scalable self-driving cars, arXiv preprint arXiv:1708.06374 (2017)
40. Mobileye: The Mobileye safety methodology (2021). https://www.mobileye.com/safety-methodology/
41. Darwiche, A.: Modeling and Reasoning with Bayesian Networks. Cambridge University Press, Cambridge (2009)

Automating Pattern Selection for Assurance Case Development for Cyber-Physical Systems

Shreyas Ramakrishna[1]([✉]), Hyunjee Jin[2], Abhishek Dubey[1],
and Arun Ramamurthy[2]

[1] Institute for Software Integrated Systems, Vanderbilt University, Nashville, USA
{shreyas.ramakrishna,abhishek.dubey}@vanderbilt.edu
[2] Siemens Corporation, Technology, Princeton, NJ, USA
{hyunjee.jin,arun.ramamurthy}@siemens.com

Abstract. Assurance Cases are increasingly being required for regulatory acceptance of Cyber-Physical Systems. However, the ever-increasing complexity of these systems has made the assurance cases development complex, labor-intensive and time-consuming. Assurance case fragments called patterns are used to handle the complexity. The state-of-the-art approach has been to manually select generic patterns from online catalogs, instantiate them with system-specific information, and assemble them into an assurance case. While there has been some work in automating the instantiation and assembly, a less researched area is the automation of the pattern selection process, which takes a considerable amount of the assurance case development time. To close this automation gap, we have developed an automated pattern selection workflow that handles the selection problem as a coverage problem, intending to find the smallest set of patterns that can cover the available system artifacts. For this, we utilize the ontology graphs of the system artifacts and the patterns and perform graph analytics. The selected patterns are fed into an external instantiation function to develop an assurance case. Then, they are evaluated for coverage using two coverage metrics. An illustrative autonomous vehicle example is provided, demonstrating the utility of the proposed workflow in developing an assurance case with reduced efforts and time compared to the manual development alternative.

Keywords: Cyber physical systems · Assurance case · Patterns · GSN · Optimization · Ontology · Graph isomorphism · Coverage metrics

1 Introduction

Assurance Cases (ACs) are increasingly being required for regulatory acceptance of Cyber-Physical Systems (CPSs) in several safety-critical applications, such as automotive [19], aviation [8] and medical devices [9]. For example, the development of a safety case (AC with a focus on safety) is a requirement for compliance

© The Author(s), under exclusive license to Springer Nature Switzerland AG 2022
M. Trapp et al. (Eds.): SAFECOMP 2022, LNCS 13414, pp. 82–96, 2022.
https://doi.org/10.1007/978-3-031-14835-4_6

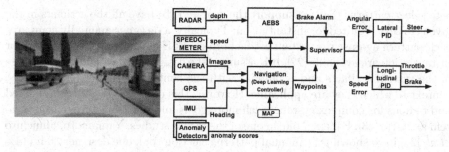

Fig. 1. (left) Image from the forward-looking camera of an autonomous vehicle in CARLA simulation. (right) The system model of the autonomous vehicle.

with the ISO 26262 safety standard in the automotive domain [19]. An AC is a structured argument, supported by evidence, intended to demonstrate that the system satisfies its assurance guarantees under a particular context and under a given set of assumptions about the behavior of the system's components and its operating environment [1]. Goal Structuring Notation (GSN) [15] has been a widely used graphical modeling language used to represent an AC.

However, the increasing complexity of CPS has made the assurance process complex, labor-intensive, and time-consuming because of the activities that involve managing numerous requirements, curating a large number of artifacts and evidence, developing and managing huge ACs, among others [18]. These problems can be alleviated with an adequate tool that can partially automate some of these activities. In this regard, several tools like Advocate [6], Resolute [11], Isabelle [10], AMASS [23], among others [17] have been developed in the recent years. In addition to managing the requirements and artifacts, these tools utilize modular assurance arguments called assurance case patterns[1] [16] to handle the size and complexity of AC being developed. Patterns are argument fragments that provide a partial solution for one aspect of the overall AC. They provide a reusable structure through parameter placeholders that can be instantiated with system-specific artifacts and assembled with other patterns into an AC.

While these tools specialize in data management and automation of the instantiation and assembly algorithm, an activity that has not been researched is the automation of the pattern selection process. To contextualize the selection process, consider the Autonomous Vehicle (AV) example in Fig. 1. Assume we want to develop an AC with the goal that the "Automatic Emergency Braking System (AEBS) will function satisfactorily in applying the emergency brake", given that the operating context is a clear day. For this, we are given an artifact database with system architecture, component decomposition, component testing results (from different contexts like a clear day, rainy day, night, etc.), and a pattern database with patterns related to requirement decomposition, component decomposition, and failures, functional decomposition, hazard decomposition, etc. The problem

---

[1] In the rest of this paper, we will refer to "AC patterns" as "patterns".

is to select patterns that (a) support the goal and (b) have all the artifacts in the given context required for instantiation. Typically, a designer manually compares each pattern against the system artifacts to check if all the artifacts required for instantiation are available [22]. It is assumed the designer has complete knowledge of the system artifacts and is familiar with the content of the patterns and the context to which they are applicable. However, this comparison gets complicated and tedious for complex systems with more goals and diverse heterogeneous system artifacts [23]. For example, in one of the recent studies, Yamamoto, Shuichiro *et al.* [24] have shown that manual pattern selection took one designer 30 h (14% of the development time) and required significant understanding about the available artifacts and patterns. Therefore, automating the selection process can aid the assurance process.

Contributions: To close this automation gap, we have developed a workflow that handles the selection problem as a coverage problem, intending to find the smallest set of patterns that can cover the system artifacts. For this, we leverage the ontology graph of the system artifacts and patterns and perform graph analytics. We address the coverage problem using an optimization problem setup, which is assisted by a data preparation function that utilizes a weaving model[2] [3] to generate data files, a mapping file, and an ontology graph of the artifacts. A selection function uses the processed files and a database of patterns to select a set of patterns, which are then plugged into an instantiation function to develop an AC. Finally, the AC is evaluated for coverage, and a report with information about unused artifacts and patterns is generated to aid the developer with future refinement. To evaluate the workflow, we have integrated it with a newly developed tool called ACCELERATE to automatically construct an AC for an Autonomous Vehicle[3] example within a CARLA simulation [7].

Outline: The rest of this paper is organized as follows. In Sect. 2, we formalize assurance case patterns. In Sect. 3, we present the proposed workflow that includes the data preparation, pattern selection, and evaluation functions to automate the development and evaluation of an AC. In Sect. 4, we demonstrate the utility of our workflow by an AV example in a CARLA simulation. Finally, we present the related research in Sect. 5 followed by our conclusion in Sect. 6.

2   Assurance Case Patterns

Goal Structuring Notation uses an iterative decomposition strategy to decompose the top-level system goal(s) to be proved to lower-level component goals, often supported by evidence. Although this notation has simplified the documentation of ACs, it is challenging to design monolithic GSNs for complex systems. Patterns [16] are argument fragments that provide a partial solution for one aspect of the overall AC. They capture common repeated argument structures

---

[2] Captures the fine-grained relationships between different system artifacts.

[3] For the CARLA AV setup, visit https://github.com/scope-lab-vu/AV-Assurance.

and abstract system-specific argument details as placeholders with free parameters to be instantiated. Patterns typically include information like name, intent, motivation, structure, applicability, related patterns, description of the decomposition strategy, and implementation details. In addition, Kelly has introduced several structural and entity abstractions to the GSN modeling language for describing a pattern [16]. Currently, there are several online catalogs [16,21,22] with patterns in GSN format that can be readily used to design an AC.

2.1   Pattern Formalization

We adapt the formal definition of patterns as presented by Denney *et al.* [4] with slight modifications, including a metadata field that holds additional information about the pattern and a modifier function that specifies the operations that need to be performed on the nodes. We provide a formal definition below:

Definition 1 (Pattern). *A pattern $\mathcal{P}$ is a tuple $\langle \mathcal{M}, \mathcal{N}, l, t, i, mul, c, mod, \rightarrow \rangle$, where $\langle \mathcal{N}, \rightarrow \rangle$ is a finite, directed hypergraph in which each edge has a single source and possibly several destination targets. $\rightarrow : \langle \mathcal{N}, \mathcal{N} \rangle$ is the connector relation between nodes, $\mathcal{M}$ is the pattern metadata, and the functions l, t, p, mul, and mod are defined below:*

- $\mathcal{M}$ is the pattern metadata tuple $\langle N, R, pl \rangle$, where N is the name of the pattern, R is a set of relevant patterns that share the same intent as this pattern or patterns that can be composed with this pattern for further growing the assurance case, and pl is a dictionary that maps a system artifact label (key) to a placeholder variable (value) that requires instantiation. The artifact label is of the type string. An illustrative placeholder dictionary is of the form {"system" : SM, "top-level-goals : TG", "requirements" : SR}.
- l and t are labeling functions, where $l : \mathcal{N} \rightarrow \{g, s, c, a, j, e\}$ maps each node onto its type, namely on g (goal), s (decomposition strategy), c (context), a (assumption), j (justification), or e (evidence).
- i is the id label of each node, $i : \mathcal{N} \rightarrow id \times class$, which returns the identifier and the type of each node, i.e. $class = \{g, s, c, a, j, e\}$.
- *mul* provides a multiplicity label for each outgoing connector. For the example shown in Fig. 2, $mul = n : RC$ represents a one-to-many relationship, where n is an integer value determined by placeholder RC, such that each instance of node $S2$ is related to n instances of node $G4$. The relationship is one-to-one if not explicitly stated otherwise.
- *mod* indicates the modifying operation to be performed on a given node: no-operation, instantiate, or develop.

In addition to the pattern entities, there are several structural rules required:

- The root node of a pattern is always a goal.
- The connectors can only go out of the goal and the strategy nodes: $n_a \rightarrow n_b$ $\Rightarrow l(n_a) \in \{g, s\}$.

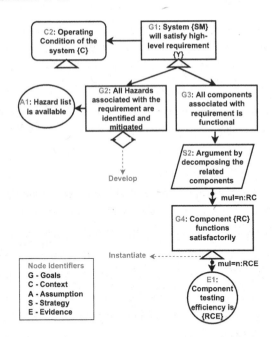

Fig. 2. An example pattern based on requirements decomposition arguments.

– A strategy node cannot directly connect to another strategy node or an evidence node: $(n_a \rightarrow n_b) \wedge [\mathrm{l}(n_a){=}\mathrm{s}] \Rightarrow \mathrm{l}(n_b) \in \{g, a, c, j\}$.

Figure 2 illustrates an example requirements decomposition pattern based on the formalization in Definition 1. This pattern argues for the satisfaction of the system's high-level requirements through the requirements decomposition of all the associated components. A node in this pattern is represented by its labels (e.g., G1, G2) and content with placeholders (e.g., SM, C) that can be replaced by system-specific information. The node multiplicity (mul) is marked on the graph edges, representing how one node is related to another. Further, "instantiate" and "develop" are the two modifier (mod) operations that can be performed on the nodes.

3   Pattern Selection Workflow

We present the proposed workflow that leverages an ontology graph of the system artifacts and patterns to automatically select patterns that can be instantiated to construct an AC. The workflow is composed of several functions that work as follows: First, the $prepare(\mathcal{AD}, WM)$ function uses a weaving model (WM) to map artifact files from the artifact database ($\mathcal{AD}$) onto several data files (F_D) and a mapping file F_M. Then, the function $select(\mathcal{AD}, \mathcal{PD})$ selects a set of patterns $\mathcal{P}_S$ from the pattern database ($\mathcal{PD}$). The selected patterns are instantiated and assembled into an AC using an external $instantiate$ function. Finally, the

---

Algorithm 1. Data Preparation

1: **function** PREPARE($\mathcal{AD}$:Artifact Database,WM:weaving model)
2:     $F_D \leftarrow \{\}$, $F_M \leftarrow \{\}$, $temp \leftarrow \{\}$
3:     **for** each $file$ in $\mathcal{AD}$ **do**
4:         processed file $\leftarrow$ process($file$)
5:         $temp \leftarrow temp \bigcup \{$processed file$\}$
6:     **end for**
7:     $accepted\_files \leftarrow manual\_check(temp)$
8:     **for** each $file$ in $accepted\_files$ **do**
9:         data file $\leftarrow$ arrange($file$,WM)
10:        $F_D \leftarrow F_D \bigcup \{$data file$\}$
11:    **end for**
12:    $place \leftarrow \{\}$, $depend \leftarrow \{\}$, $source \leftarrow \{\}$
13:    **for** each $file$ in F_D **do**
14:        $source \leftarrow get\_source\_query(file)$
15:        $place \leftarrow extract(header)$
16:        **for** each $entry$ in $header$ **do**
17:            $result \leftarrow search(entry, F_D)$
18:            $depend \leftarrow result$
19:        **end for**
20:        $F_M \leftarrow \{place, depend, source\}$
21:        $\mathcal{G}_A \leftarrow make\_graph(place,depend)$
22:    **end for**
23:    $\mathcal{AD} \leftarrow F_M, F_D, \mathcal{G}_A$
24:    **return** F_M, F_D
25: **end function**

$evaluate(AC, F_D, F_M)$ function generates a report with the coverage score (CS) and additional information to aid the evaluation and further refinement of the AC. We discuss these functions in the rest of this section.

3.1   Data Preparation

The artifacts (e.g., goals, requirements, system models) for the assurance process are typically curated using several engineering activities and stored in a database $\mathcal{AD}$. These activities include requirements engineering, system analysis, hazard analysis and risk assessment, and evidence generation. The artifacts generated from these activities are usually in heterogeneous file formats like PDF, Text, Architecture Analysis and Design Language (AADL) and System Modeling Language (SysML). The *prepare* function takes these raw artifact files to prepare the processed files required for the pattern selection discussed in the next section. The function performs two operations as shown in Algorithm 1.

The first operation processes relevant artifacts required for the AC into processed data files stored in tabular format (CSV file). The function can currently process AADL files. We are working towards automatically processing other file formats. Then, the processed files are checked for completeness, correctness, and relevance. The check is to ensure that only complete and essential artifacts necessary for the development of the AC are retained while discarding the non-essential artifacts. Non-essential artifacts bloat the $\mathcal{AD}$, which slows the selection process and impacts the evaluation metrics (discussed later in Sect. 4). In the current implementation, the checking is manually performed by a designer. We assume the designer has complete knowledge of the system for which the AC is being developed. The accepted files are passed through an arrange function to generate a set of data files F_D. To generate the file, we use a weaving model WM that weaves the different artifacts and transforms them into a single model file. The model is developed based on our domain knowledge and previous experience with CPSs. Each data file is a table where the column headers represent the name of the artifacts, and the rows capture the content of these artifacts. Also, each column in the data file is related to the other columns, with the relationship derived using the weaving model. Finally, these accepted files are manually tagged with labels required for the selection process. For example, the context in which particular artifacts and evidence are applicable is one label that we currently include.

The second operation generates a mapping file F_M, which is a lookup table of system artifacts and their ontology required to bridge the data files for the pattern selection algorithm discussed in Sect. 3. F_M holds the physical link to the data file location obtained using a simple query to the database. It also holds the placeholder and dependency mapping derived from an *extract* function, which reads the header of each data file to create an intra-file dependency mapping between them. For example, one entry capturing the relationship between a cause and a hazard in the dependency mapping file looks like $[cause, cause\_table, hazard]$. If there are multiple causes for the same hazard, they will be stored as separate entries. Next, to capture the inter-file dependencies, each header (e.g., cause) is searched across every data file using a *search* function. The search result is used for placeholder mapping, required for pattern selection. For example, the search result for the cause header is $\{[mitigation\_table, cause], [cause\_table, cause], [risk\_table, cause]\}$, which shows all the other files in which the entry is present. Finally, the ontology captured in F_M is also stored as an artifact graph $\mathcal{G}_A$ as shown in Fig. 3.

Then, we curate $\mathcal{PD}$ for which we gather patterns from online catalogs [16, 22] and manually re-design them using the formalization and rules discussed in Sect. 2. While re-designing, a designer checks the language consistency across data in the nodes. These patterns are stored in textual format (JSON) and as a graph $\mathcal{G}_P$ with placeholders as nodes (See Fig. 3).

3.2 Pattern Selection

As discussed earlier, the goal of the selection algorithm is to select a smallest set of patterns $\mathcal{P}_S$ from the database $\mathcal{PD} = \{\mathcal{P}_1, \mathcal{P}_2, \cdots, \mathcal{P}_n\}$ that maximizes the artifact coverage. We formulate the selection as a two-objective optimization problem: (a) maximizing the coverage such that the placeholders of every selected pattern have the corresponding artifact for instantiation and (b) minimizing the

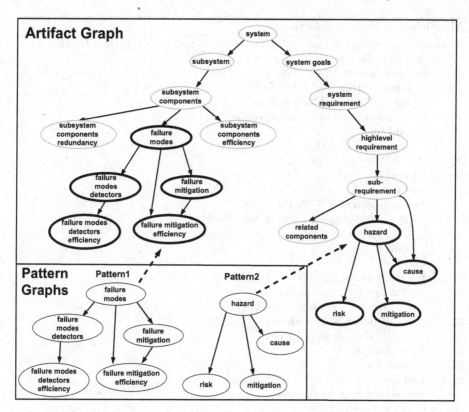

Fig. 3. The artifact and pattern ontology extracted for pattern selection. The selected patterns are highlighted by thick outlines in the artifact graph.

number of patterns selected by iteratively comparing the pattern graph to the artifact graph (See Fig. 3).

The optimization is realized using the $select(\mathcal{PD}, F_M, F_D)$ function shown in Algorithm 2. It takes the patterns from $\mathcal{PD}$, the mapping file and the data files as inputs to select $\mathcal{P}_S$. The selection is performed using the *findmatch*, the *findconflict* and the *findsubgraph* functions. The selected patterns are then instantiated and assembled into an AC using an external *instantiate* function. An existing algorithm [12,13] can be used for instantiation and assembly.

Next, the $findcomplete(\mathcal{P}, F_M)$ function in Definition 2 checks if the place-holders in the patterns have a matching entry in F_M. If all the placeholders have corresponding entries, the pattern is said to be complete, and it is added to $\mathcal{P}_S$. Otherwise, the pattern is discarded from the selection process.

Definition 2 (Pattern Completeness). *We say a pattern is complete if each placeholder has a corresponding entry in F_M. We define a function $findmatch(pl)$ that determines if a given placeholder has a corresponding entry.*

Algorithm 2. Pattern Selection

```
1: function SELECT(PD:Pattern Database,F_M:Mapping File,F_D:Data Files)
2:     P_S ← {}, dups ← {}
3:     for each pattern P ∈ PD do
4:         temp ← True
5:         for each placeholder p ∈ P do
6:             temp ← temp ∧ findmatch(p)
7:         end for
8:         if temp is True then
9:             P_S ← P_S ∪ {P}
10:        end if
11:    end for
12:    for each pattern P ∈ P_S do
13:        if findsubgraph(G_A, G_P) is False then
14:            P_S.remove(G_P)
15:        end if
16:    end for
17:    for i ← 1 to len(P_S) do
18:        for j ← i + 1 to len(P_S) do
19:            match ← findconflict(P_i, P_j)
20:            if match is True then
21:                dups ← dups ∪ {P_j}
22:            end if
23:        end for
24:    end for
25:    for each entry E in dups do
26:        P_S.remove(E)
27:    end for
28:    AC ← instantiate(P_S,F_M,F_D)
29:    return AC
30: end function
```

Once P_S has been selected, the *findsubgraph* and the *findconflict* functions are used to minimize the cardinality of P_S and remove duplicate patterns. First, the $findsubgraph(G_A, G_{Pi})$ function checks whether the artifact graph G_A contains a subgraph that is isomorphic to G_{Pi}, the graph of the ith pattern. Two graphs are isomorphic (or equivalent) if their structures preserve a one-to-one correspondence between their vertices and between their edges. For example, in Fig. 3, pattern1 and pattern2 are isomorphic to subgraphs of G_A. The non-isomorphic patterns are removed from P_S.

Next, the $findconflict(P_1, P_2)$ function checks P_S for redundant patterns. For this, it performs the following steps: (a) duplication checking checks if the patterns have the same set of placeholders requiring instantiation (see Definition 3). (b) graph checking checks if the graphs of the two patterns are isomorphic. While performing this, we also require data on corresponding nodes of the patterns to be equivalent. Only if the duplication checking fails, the function performs graph checking. On the whole, the function $findconflict$ returns true if steps (a) or (b) return true, i.e., if the patterns are redundant.

Definition 3 (Duplication Checking). *We say two patterns* $\mathcal{P}_1 = \langle \mathcal{M}_1, \mathcal{N}_1, l_1, t_1, i_1, m_1, s_1, \rightarrow_1 \rangle$ *and* $\mathcal{P}_2 = \langle \mathcal{M}_2, \mathcal{N}_2, l_2, t_2, i_2, m_2, s_2, \rightarrow_2 \rangle$ *are duplicates if they contain exactly the same placeholders.*

3.3   Coverage Evaluation

As discussed previously, automating different activities of the assurance process reduces the development time and manual efforts. However, this gain is at the expense of increased effort and time required to review and evaluate the quality and correctness of the generated AC. To aid the evaluation process, the $evaluate(AC, F_D, F_M)$ function takes the AC and generates a report to provide qualitative insights which is not available in the generated AC graphical structure. We believe this information can aid the designer in further refinement. The report includes the coverage score, the selected and unused patterns, and the unused artifacts. The coverage score is a tuple $\langle \mathcal{A}, \mathcal{S} \rangle$ of the artifact coverage ($\mathcal{A}$) and the problem coverage ($\mathcal{S}$).

1) Artifact Coverage ($\mathcal{A}$): The artifact coverage metric measures the proportion of the artifacts available in $\mathcal{AD}$ that have been included in the AC. Also, a relevance check (discussed in Sect. 3.1) on the artifact is essential for this metric to be accurate. Besides the score itself, this metric can also be used to derive a list of unused artifacts.

$$\mathcal{A} = \frac{\text{\# Artifacts used in the AC}}{\text{\# Artifacts available in } \mathcal{AD}} \tag{1}$$

2) Problem Coverage ($\mathcal{S}$): The problem coverage metric quantifies the coverage of all the known problems affecting a system's property (e.g., safety, availability). Problem coverage is a tuple $\mathcal{S} = (C_{\mathcal{P}_1}, C_{\mathcal{P}_2}, \cdots, C_{\mathcal{P}_n})$ consisting of coverage measures $C_{\mathcal{P}_i}$ related to different problem classes $\mathcal{P}_i$. The coverage measure is shown in Eq. (2), and it is computed as the percentage of problems within a given problem class which are addressed by an AC.

$$C_{\mathcal{P}_i} = \frac{\text{\# Problems from } \mathcal{P}_i \text{ addressed by the AC}}{\text{\# Problems in } \mathcal{P}_i \text{ identified during analysis}} \tag{2}$$

While coverage metrics and the report can aid the refinement process by providing insights into the missing patterns or artifacts, they do not fully quantify the quality of artifacts (e.g., evidence) required for AC selection. So, the coverage metrics cannot solely rely on measuring the quality of the AC. A combination of coverage and confidence metrics is needed for robust quantitative assessment. We are therefore working towards integrating a confidence metric.

4   Illustrative Example

In this section, we provide an illustrative example by applying the proposed workflow to develop an AC for an AV in the CARLA simulator [7]. In this example, the AV is required to navigate a town while avoiding collisions with obstacles in its travel path. We integrate our workflow with the ACCELERATE tool[4] for pattern instantiation and assembly as shown in Fig. 4.

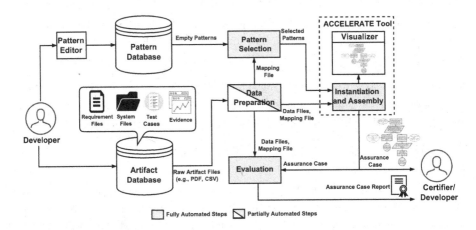

Fig. 4. The proposed pattern selection workflow integrated with the ACCELERATE tool for AC development.

Artifacts and Patterns Preparation: We performed the analysis steps listed in Sect. 3.1 to curate $\mathcal{AD}$. We first performed a requirement and system analysis using the given requirements document. The vehicle has three goals associated with two system requirements and three high-level requirements, each associated with several sub-requirements. We then designed the AV system model shown in Fig. 1. It has a navigation component that uses three cameras, a global positioning system (GPS), an inertial measurement unit (IMU), a speedometer, and a route planner to compute the vehicle's next position. Then a velocity planner calculates the average velocity needed to traverse from the current position to the next position. The velocity and the camera images are fed to a deep-learning controller to predict the waypoints, which are passed to a motion estimator to compute throttle, brake, and steer errors. In addition, it has an AEBS controller that uses two radars to raise a brake alarm on detecting obstacles. We then performed fault analysis of the system model to identify 14 component faults and analyzed the possible mitigation strategies. Further, we performed hazard analysis to identify eight operational and functional hazards associated with the

---

[4] Tool is being built as part of the DARPA ARCOS program. Check our GitHub for release information.

different system components. Finally, we curated $\mathcal{PD}$ for which we gathered several patterns from online catalogs [16, 22] and re-designed them using the formalization discussed in Sect. 3.2.

Results: We applied the integrated tool to develop an AC for the vehicle. We summarize the key results in terms of the coverage metrics and the size of the AC (computed in terms of GSN nodes) in two revisions. We used the AC report[5] from "revision1" to refine the AC in "revision2". The pattern database had seven patterns for the selection process to choose from in these revisions. The analysis of the revisions is: In "revision1", four patterns were selected to develop an AC (see Footnote 5) with 805 nodes. The evaluation function returned a coverage score with artifact coverage of 76%, a problem coverage of $[C_H : 60\%, C_F : 100\%]$ with five unused artifacts. Here, C_H represents the percentage of known hazards that are covered, and C_F represents the percentage of known system faults that are covered. From the report, we analyzed the artifacts relating to failure decomposition that was unused. So, we designed a new failure decomposition pattern that was added to $\mathcal{PD}$. Further, some of the sub-requirements associated with the hazards were missing, which we included. In "revision2", the selection mechanism selected five patterns, including the new pattern to develop an AC with 909 nodes. The refined AC had a higher coverage with an artifact coverage of 90%, a problem coverage of $[C_H : 85\%, C_F : 100\%]$ with unused artifacts reduced by two. We performed several iterations until all the artifacts were included in the AC.

To estimate the time saved by the workflow, the data preparation and selection steps were first performed manually by a developer who performed the following tasks: re-design of patterns into the defined formalization, which took approximately one hour, processing the artifact files, extracting the artifact dependencies to generate an ontology file, and instantiation and assembly of the patterns using the ACCELERATE tool. While instantiation and assembly were performed in less than a minute, the manual selection and data curation process took approximately three hours. Next, for comparison, we fed the manually re-designed patterns and the artifacts to the integrated tool (See Fig. 4), which only took close to one minute for data preparation, pattern selection, instantiation, and assembly. Finally, to stress test the integration, we increased the artifacts and patterns in the database. Our workflow took less than five minutes, even for large ACs with 1500 to 3000 nodes. Significantly less manual processing was needed when the artifact files were changed or updated. We expect the time saving to get even more significant as the size of the artifact database grows. However, the manual steps involved in the data preparation step are a bottleneck for scaling the workflow, which we want to address in the future.

---

[5] For a bird's eye view of the "revision1" assurance case and the report, visit https:// github.com/scope-lab-vu/AV-Assurance.

5   Related Work

The last decade has seen several tools with automation capabilities to support different activities of the AC development process. A comprehensive survey on these tools is available in [17]. We discuss a few of these tools that support automation. Advocate [6] is one such tool that provides an editor for designing system architectures, patterns, and automated development of ACs from patterns. A pattern formalization and the instantiation algorithm is built into the tool for automating pattern instantiation [4]. Here, a pattern dataset and a parameter table are manually created to assist the instantiation algorithm. Resolute [11] is another tool that automatically synthesizes an AC from AADL models. Isabelle [10] is a recently developed tool with integrated formal methods for evidence generation. Assurance language and automated document processing are a few tool features that support the development process. AMASS tool [23] provides a partially automated heterogeneous collaborative environment that supports activities such as requirement management, artifacts and evidence generation, pattern composition, and AC construction.

There are several independent efforts. For example, Ramakrishna et al. [20] have presented a methodology to partially automate AC construction directly from system models and graphs. Hawkins et al. [13] utilize the concept of model weaving to automatically learn the artifact files from system models and use them for instantiating patterns. The authors of [12] provide an automated mechanism for instantiation and composition of patterns, where the artifacts are heterogeneous system models that are linked to represent the cross-domain relationship. While these tools and approaches automate the instantiation and assembly of patterns, their selection largely remains manual.

Further, evaluation is key to automating AC development. Confidence metrics are often used to represent the assurance deficit [14]. However, there has been minimal work in coverage evaluation. Denney et al. [5] have presented several coverage metrics for different system artifacts like hazards and requirements. These metrics measure the proportion of the system artifacts used in the AC to those available in the database. Chindamaikul et al. [2] have presented two coverage metrics: a claim coverage that is similar to those in [5], and an argument coverage metric that measures the arguments and evidence covered in the AC. We build on prior work to provide additional coverage metrics.

6   Conclusion and Future Work

In this paper, we have presented a workflow that can automate the pattern selection process. We formulate the selection problem as a coverage problem that selects the smallest set of patterns that can maximally cover the available system artifacts. The coverage problem is realized using an optimization problem that leverages the ontology graphs of the artifacts and patterns and performs graph analytics. The optimization is aided by an array of functions that perform data preparation, pattern selection, and AC evaluation. These functions collectively reduce the manual effort and time required in selecting the necessary patterns.

We plan to move this research in several directions. First, fully automating the data processing function using natural language processing (NLP). Second, design a translator to convert textual patterns into our format. Third, automate the language check using NLP and relevance check using topic modeling [2]. Finally, include confidence metrics for AC evaluation.

Acknowledgement. The authors would like to thank Sarah C. Helble and Dennis M. Volpano for helpful discussions and feedback. This work was supported by the DARPA ARCOS project under Contract FA8750-20-C-0515 (ACCELERATE) and the DARPA Assured Autonomy project. The views, opinions, and/or findings expressed are those of the author(s) and do not necessarily reflect the views of DARPA. We would like to thank the reviewers and editors for taking the time and effort necessary to review the manuscript. We appreciate the valuable feedback, which helped us to improve the quality of the manuscript.

References

1. Bishop, P., Bloomfield, R.: A methodology for safety case development. In: Safety and Reliability, vol. 20, pp. 34–42. Taylor & Francis (2000)
2. Chindamaikul, K., Toshinori, T., Port, D., Hajimu, I.: Automatic approach to prepare information for constructing an assurance case. In: International Conference of Product Focused Software Development and Process Improvement (2014)
3. Del Fabro, M.D., et al.: Applying generic model management to data mapping. In: BDA (2005)
4. Denney, E., Pai, G.: A formal basis for safety case patterns. In: Bitsch, F., Guiochet, J., Kaâniche, M. (eds.) SAFECOMP 2013. LNCS, vol. 8153, pp. 21–32. Springer, Heidelberg (2013). https://doi.org/10.1007/978-3-642-40793-2_3
5. Denney, E., Pai, G.: Automating the assembly of aviation safety cases. IEEE Trans. Reliab. **63**(4), 830–849 (2014)
6. Denney, E., Pai, G., Pohl, J.: AdvoCATE: an assurance case automation toolset. In: Ortmeier, F., Daniel, P. (eds.) SAFECOMP 2012. LNCS, vol. 7613, pp. 8–21. Springer, Heidelberg (2012). https://doi.org/10.1007/978-3-642-33675-1_2
7. Dosovitskiy, A., Ros, G., Codevilla, F., Lopez, A., Koltun, V.: Carla: an open urban driving simulator. arXiv:1711.03938 (2017)
8. European Organisation for the Safety of Air Navigation: Safety case development manual, version 2.2 (2006)
9. FDA: Introduction of assurance case method and its application in regulatory science (2019). https://www.fda.gov/media/125182/download
10. Foster, S., Nemouchi, Y., O'Halloran, C., Stephenson, K., Tudor, N.: Formal model-based assurance cases in Isabelle/SACM (2020)
11. Gacek, A., Backes, J., Cofer, D., Slind, K., Whalen, M.: Resolute: an assurance case language for architecture models. ACM SIGAda Ada Lett. **34**(3), 19–28 (2014)
12. Hartsell, C., Mahadevan, N., Dubey, A., Karsai, G.: Automated method for assurance case construction from system design models. In: 2021 5th International Conference on System Reliability and Safety (ICSRS), pp. 230–239 (2021)
13. Hawkins, R., Habli, I., Kolovos, D., Paige, R., Kelly, T.: Weaving an assurance case from design: a model-based approach. In: 2015 IEEE 16th International Symposium on High Assurance Systems Engineering, pp. 110–117. IEEE (2015)

14. Hawkins, R., Kelly, T., Knight, J., Graydon, P.: A new approach to creating clear safety arguments. In: Dale, C., Anderson, T. (eds) Advances in Systems Safety, pp. 3–23. Springer, London (2011). https://doi.org/10.1007/978-0-85729-133-2_1

15. Kelly, T., Weaver, R.: The goal structuring notation-a safety argument notation. In: Proceedings of the Dependable Systems and Networks Workshop on Assurance Cases, p. 6. Citeseer (2004)

16. Kelly, T.P.: Arguing safety: a systematic approach to managing safety cases. Ph.D. thesis, University of York, York (1999)

17. Maksimov, M., Fung, N.L.S., Kokaly, S., Chechik, M.: Two decades of assurance case tools: a survey. In: Gallina, B., Skavhaug, A., Schoitsch, E., Bitsch, F. (eds.) SAFECOMP 2018. LNCS, vol. 11094, pp. 49–59. Springer, Cham (2018). https://doi.org/10.1007/978-3-319-99229-7_6

18. Nair, S., de la Vara, J.L., Sabetzadeh, M., Falessi, D.: Evidence management for compliance of critical systems with safety standards: a survey on the state of practice. Inf. Softw. Technol. **60**, 1–15 (2015)

19. Palin, R., Ward, D., Habli, I., Rivett, R.: Iso 26262 safety cases: compliance and assurance (2011)

20. Ramakrishna, S., Hartsell, C., Dubey, A., Pal, P., Karsai, G.: A methodology for automating assurance case generation. arXiv preprint arXiv:2003.05388 (2020)

21. Safety-Critical Systems Club: Tiered pattern catalogue (2022). https://scsc.uk/gsn?page=gsn%205Library%20Patterns

22. Szczygielska, M., Jarzkebowicz, A.: Assurance case patterns on-line catalogue. In: Advances in Dependability Engineering of Complex Systems, pp. 407–417 (2017)

23. de la Vara, J.L., Parra, E., Ruiz, A., Gallina, B.: The amass tool platform: an innovative solution for assurance and certification of cyber-physical systems. In: REFSQ Workshops (2020)

24. Yamamoto, S., Matsuno, Y.: An evaluation of argument patterns to reduce pitfalls of applying assurance case. In: 2013 1st International Workshop on Assurance Cases for Software-Intensive Systems (ASSURE), pp. 12–17. IEEE (2013)

Generating Assurance Cases Using Workflow$^+$ Models

Nicholas Annable(✉), Thomas Chiang, Mark Lawford,
Richard F. Paige, and Alan Wassyng

McMaster Centre for Software Certification, McMaster University, Hamilton, Canada
{annablnm,chiangte,lawford,paigeri,wassyng}@mcmaster.ca

Abstract. The increasing complexity and scale of safety-critical systems makes it challenging to perform necessary safety analyses and document them convincingly in an assurance case. In previous work we introduced Workflow$^+$, a model-based framework for modelling the processes and work products in both the development and safety assurance life cycles. WF$^+$ metamodels not only serve as templates that guide the development of a safe system, they also facilitate generation of an assurance case. In this paper, we explain the fundamentals of generating assurance cases from WF$^+$ models as well as the advantages of doing this. We also discuss an initial evaluation of the application of WF$^+$ in practice.

Keywords: Assurance case · Model driven assurance · Safety

1 Introduction

Increasingly, safety assessments are documented in (safety) assurance cases, e.g. using Goal Structuring Notation (GSN) [13]. In [1,2,5], we proposed a safety assurance development framework, Workflow$^+$ (WF$^+$), that is capable of formally modelling the processes and associated data (work products) in a Safety Engineering Process (SEP). The purpose of this framework is to plan the development of safety-related products and to facilitate the systematic generation of a safety assurance argument for products produced by that SEP, by use of GSN, for example.

Motivation for the development of the WF$^+$ framework came from identifying a number of limitations associated with current assurance case methods, as exemplified by GSN. Our primary concerns were:

- There is a lack of a systematic method for structuring assurance cases. Notations like GSN rely heavily on the experience and knowledge of the practitioner. This can result in many different argument structures, even for similar systems.

Partially supported by the Natural Sciences and Engineering Research Council of Canada.

- The assurance case and the SEP are separate entities. They are connected through references, but they are not integrated. This has a negative consequence in terms of traceability between the developed system and the assurance case.
- The arguments in assurance cases leave information implicit. The fact that they are developed top-down makes it difficult to check the argument, which logically starts from the evidence and proceeds bottom-up.
- The evidence used to support claims is of very coarse granularity. Practitioners often use complete documents, or sections of documents, to support a constrained claim. This is not required by the method, but is an indirect consequence of determining a claim and then finding evidence to support it.

This paper shows how it is possible to counter these difficulties using WF^+ while achieving additional benefits. One crucial benefit is that the enhanced traceability between process, data and argument artifacts facilitates change impact analysis that works seamlessly throughout the process, its work products and the assurance case. We regard this as a prerequisite for many forms of incremental assurance.

To illustrate how WF^+ can be used to systematically generate assurance arguments we first present a segment of a safety assurance case in a GSN-like format. To make it realistic, the segment is based on a portion of the Hazard Analysis and Risk Assessment (HARA) requirements in the automotive functional safety standard, ISO 26262 [12]. We then show a (simplified) WF^+ meta-model for that process and illustrate how the safety argument can be generated from the WF^+ model. We highlight the advantages that this approach has over traditional assurance methods. Finally, we briefly describe our initial evaluation of the use of WF^+ in practice, and summarize our contributions.

2   An Example in GSN

Consider Fig. 1 which shows a GSN example involving a claim regarding finding all relevant hazards at the vehicle level. This example is based on the Hazard Analysis and Risk Assessment (HARA) in ISO 26262-3. GSN decomposition is typically based on experience and published patterns, but is surprisingly ad hoc. This results in many different plausible decompositions even for similar systems. The evidence nodes in this example are all labelled "?" to emphasize that GSN is developed top-down and there are various ways in which evidence to support each terminal claim can be selected [15].

The argument in the assurance case is bottom-up. Even if the assurance case structure is developed top-down by decomposing claims into sub-claims eventually grounded in evidence, the logical structure of the argument starts with the evidence as premises for terminal claims. Then terminal claims act as premises for their parent claims, and so on. So, what we should be doing if we use GSN or similar, is to develop the argument top-down, and then "verify" the soundness of the argument bottom-up. This is a daunting task, made even more

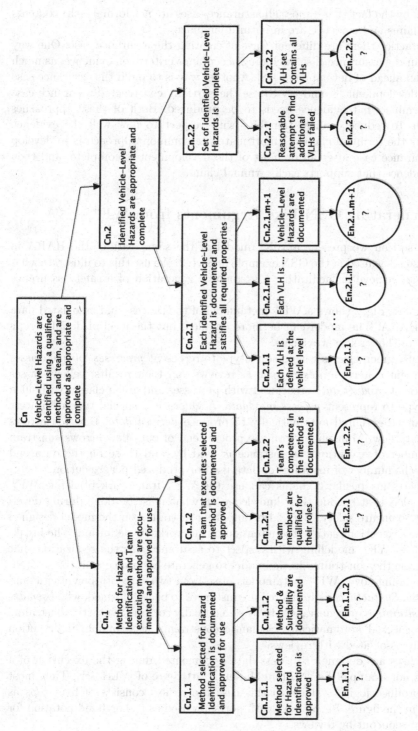

Fig. 1. GSN example of vehicle-level hazard identification

complex by the fact that almost all assurance cases are not formal – the contents of the claims and evidence are in natural language.

In practice there are different ways of creating the assurance case. One way is to plan the assurance case, including acceptance criteria on evidence, as much as we can ahead of development [18]. Another way is to build the assurance case during development [8] and try to use the partially constructed assurance case to determine what evidence needs to be produced. Both of these approaches can help to reduce confirmation bias with respect to how well the evidence supports the terminal claims. Unfortunately, a common approach is to develop the assurance case after all or most of the development is complete, and then find evidence that supports each terminal claim.

3   Generating GSN-Like Arguments from WF$^+$

In this section we present a WF$^+$ model of the same part of the HARA in ISO 26262-3 as used in the GSN example in Sect. 2. We use this to illustrate what WF$^+$ can achieve in facilitating a systematic generation of a safety assurance case.

To start, Fig. 2 shows a WF$^+$ metamodel of the process and associated data of the HARA. The model can be more detailed, but the level of detail here is enough to show relevant aspects.

We use green classes with a stereotype to represent *processes*, purple classes to represent *generic processes* such as reviews and their results, yellow classes to represent *product data* associated with processes and green classes without a stereotype to represent *process metadata*. A *Query* is a special type of process that can be executed automatically to produce *derived data*. Directed arrows show data flow. Multiplicities on the process end of data flow arrows constrain the number of executions an instance is used by, and those on the data end specify the number of instances of data used or produced per execution.

Experts in specific domains can use the WF$^+$ framework to define WF$^+$ metamodels that encode their knowledge on what must be done during development to ensure safety. WF$^+$ also supports constraints on the model designed to ensure executions satisfy the intention of the workflow definition. The breakthrough in WF$^+$ modelling with respect to assurance was the realization that we can use the constraints in the model to generate assurance claims.

Constraints over WF$^+$ metamodels arise from two categories: syntactic and semantic. *Syntactic constraints* require instances to be well formed, while *semantic constraints* require instances to be semantically correct. Syntactic constraints can be checked automatically. Semantic constraints need human intervention typically associated with reviews.

Reviews are designed to assess data documented during the execution of a process, for example the "NothingMissing?" attribute of [VLH Set]. They most often produce logical values. In this case the review consists of five steps as shown in the figure. Purple text with ports are used as a shorthand notation for attributes output by reviews.

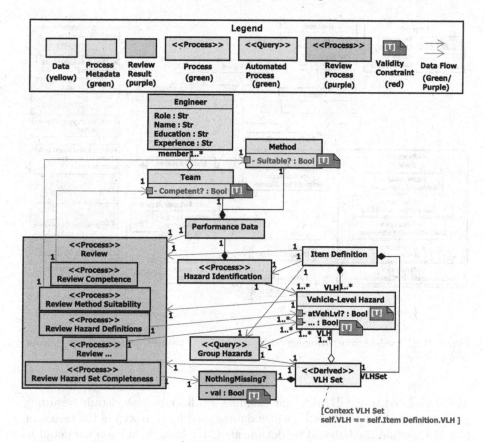

Fig. 2. WF⁺ model of process and data for the HARA (Colour figure online)

[VLH Set] is necessary as a modelling artefact if we want to say anything about the aggregated hazards, which are otherwise dealt with individually in the model. In this case it is important to include argumentation as to why we believe the set to be "complete". The task of adding each [Vehicle-Level Hazard] to a set can be easily automated with appropriate tooling by creating a new instance of [VLH Set] and a reference to each [Vehicle-Level Hazard] belonging to [Item Definition].

We also include *validity constraints* in the model shown as red "notes" with the label "T" for True. These enable us to check that reviews produced the desired results. They also indicate that the assurance will fail if any one of these is recorded as False rather than True. This is illustrated in Fig. 5.

Figure 3 shows how the lowest level claims (terminal claims in a GSN-like assurance case) are constructed systematically from the WF⁺ model using the same hazard identification example we used for GSN in Sect. 2.

Note that we have not included all available detail in the WF⁺ model in order to make the model more readable and to focus on the argumentation

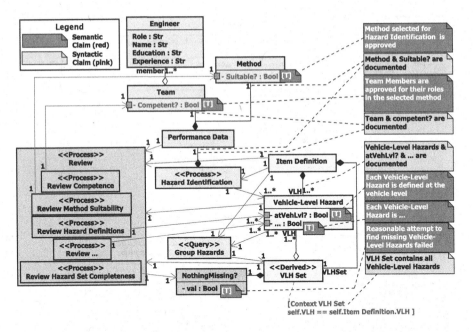

Fig. 3. WF⁺ model – generating lowest level (terminal) claims from constraints (Colour figure online)

directly related to the HARA. For example we did not show details regarding the expertise of the reviewer(s), which data is used by each step in the review or how the method used should be documented. We have included some detail in the reviews specifically to illustrate how the lowest level claims in the argument tree are systematically generated from the evidence that supports them. The sections on syntactic and semantic constraints (Sects. 3.1 and 3.2) describe how the constraints lead to those lowest level claims. The evidence associated with a syntactic constraint is typically tightly linked to a multiplicity constraint. There is also (syntactic) evidence associated with more complex constraints as indicated by the syntactic check on the completeness of the [VLH Set] in Fig. 3. The evidence associated with a semantic constraint is the result of a review.

3.1   Syntactic Constraints

The goal of syntactic constraints is to ensure the information being reviewed is structurally correct. They can be either multiplicity constraints or complex constraints (e.g., OCL-specified), both of which are used in the metamodels above. Figure 3 shows each syntactic claim as a pink "note" connected by a dashed line to the relevant constraint.

Starting with the 1..* multiplicity on the association from [Item Definition] to [Vehicle-Level Hazard], we can generate a syntactic claim that there are vehicle-level hazards documented in a valid instance. An important benefit of syntactic constraints is that they are automatically verifiable with appropriate tooling. A more interesting argument is related to the constraint on [VLH Set] where we express that the set of vehicle-level hazards being evaluated for completeness actually consists of all hazards that were identified.

On the surface, these syntactic arguments may seem redundant: it is not possible for an instance of [Vehicle-Level Hazard] to satisfy some semantic property if it is not defined in the first place. They are, however, still useful to be included. Syntactic errors in complex documentation are inevitable in practice, and these syntactic arguments provide additional confidence in the quality of documentation. Additionally, it is common in practice for reviewers to have to spend time working through syntactic errors in documentation or traceability when trying to identify safety concerns. Applying these automatic checks before documentation reaches the reviewing stage would be useful in practice. The syntactic claims in this example are all direct translations of syntactic constraints over the metamodel. In the case of multiplicities, it is easy to imagine how an argument could be automatically generated by simply looking at associations and making a statement based on the multiplicities and classes on either end. To improve readability not all arguments related to multiplicities are included, but in a more complete example each multiplicity would have a corresponding argument. When it comes to more complex OCL-style constraints, fully automatic-generation of arguments may be difficult. We are exploring if these can be automated based on patterns, or if suggestions could be made to analysts.

3.2 Semantic Constraints

Semantic claims are based on semantic constraints in the metamodel. They are defined over the results of verification/validation processes such as reviews and testing to ensure their output is acceptable.

There are several semantic checks within the definition of HARA itself. In addition, ISO 26262 specifies several verification checks that ensure the work product is semantically correct. For the sake of readability, we model only a limited number of semantic constraints over the hazard identification process. We chose these to illustrate how product, process and people aspects related to assurance cases can be modelled in WF$^+$. They are shown in Fig. 3 as the validity constraints we saw in Fig. 2, but are now connected by dashed-lines to *semantic claims* shown as red "notes".

3.3 Deriving Higher-Level Argumentation

We can now demonstrate how the syntactic and semantic lowest level claims are used to generate a (blue) higher-level argument about the contribution of hazard identification to system safety. When defining constraints/claims in the previous sections, we made an effort to ensure that related syntactic and semantic claims always appeared alongside each other. That way, we can use the fact that the data in the model is constrained to only allow instances that are well-formed and semantically correct, allowing us to derive higher-level arguments about what

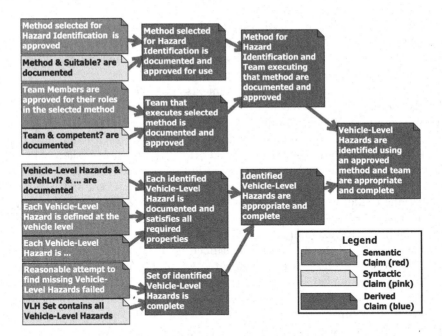

Fig. 4. GSN-like argument segment generated from a WF$^+$ model (Colour figure online)

those instances guarantee. This derivation is often straightforward, as is the case for the arguments related to [Method], where they are simply combined. In other cases the derivation can be nontrivial, such as the derivation from arguments related to [VLH Set], where we derive that reviewing a set of all identified vehicle-level hazards and failing to find additional ones can indicate that the set of hazards is complete. These nontrivial derivations depend on greater detail being included in the model. We are exploring semi-automation of the higher level argument. The resulting safety argument for this example is shown in Fig. 4. The "generation" in this example was done manually, but we were careful to do this systematically, using quite simple rules. It is also important to note that although we have shown the "argument" separately from the WF$^+$ model, in reality Fig. 4 is simply an extension of Fig. 3 and retains the comprehensive traceable links in the model. Thus, traceability is comprehensive and extends throughout the processes, data and argument.

Comparing Figs. 1 and 4 we see that the GSN-like argument is structured in precisely the same way in both figures. This is not surprising since we structured the GSN assurance in Fig. 1 knowing what we had generated using WF$^+$. The point here was that the structure of that GSN assurance probably seemed quite acceptable to most readers. Wording is sometimes manually changed if our rules generate argumentation that reads in an unusual way. For example, the generated version says "Team Members are *approved...*", whereas the GSN version was worded in the more usual way as "Team members are *qualified...*".

3.4   Integrating Assurance Segments

We have illustrated how a WF⁺ metamodel for a particular process can be used to generate an assurance argument. The same pattern can be followed to create WF⁺ metamodels of other processes and derive arguments as to how each part contributes to the safety of the system being developed. We then have multiple WF⁺ metamodels that have to be integrated so that the overall assurance case is cohesive and convincing. This requires model management techniques, but also direction on how they should fit together. Direction in our case is provided by common safety practice: i) requirements will result in a safe system; ii) the manufactured system complies with its requirements; and iii) the manufactured system does not include "additional" behaviours that have not been justified. The resulting process is then iterative. We start with the bottom-up results of two or more processes and examine their top-most claims and how they can be related, bearing in mind the overall argument. Sometimes those top-level claims have to be "adjusted", and this adjustment has then to be propagated down the tree. This does not negate the advantage of the lowest level claims being "fixed" to a large extent by the syntactic and semantic constraints in the metamodels.

3.5   Instantiating WF⁺ Models

When a workflow is executed, its metamodel is instantiated. Since our arguments are based on constraints in the metamodel, arguments hold in instances as long as the constraints they are based on are satisfied.

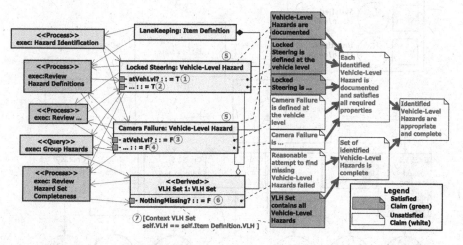

Fig. 5. A simplified view of an instance of the hazard identification process (Colour figure online)

Figure 5 shows a simplified illustrative instance documenting a [Hazard Identification] process execution. We omitted most of the instance for simplicity.

[Lane Keeping] is used for an execution of [Hazard Identification], and two hazards, [Locked Steering] and [Camera Failure], are found. The hazard definitions are reviewed, and it is determined that [Locked Steering] satisfies the required properties, but [Camera Failure] does not. The completeness of the set is also reviewed, and the reviewer found that the set is not complete. The syntactic constraint on the association from [Item Definition] to [Vehicle-Level Hazard] in the metamodel is satisfied, so the related claim holds in this instance and is coloured in green. The constraints requiring the properties to be True are satisfied for [Locked Steering], so its related claims are also coloured green. For [Camera Failure] and [VLH Set 1] the constraints are not satisfied, so the corresponding claims are not satisfied. Finally, since the OCL-style syntactic constraint on [VLH Set] in the metamodel is satisfied, the related claim holds in this instance and is coloured in green. Since some claims supporting the derived claims are not satisfied, the higher-level claims are not true in this instance. Figure 6 shows the same argument as in Fig. 5, but is presented now in GSN format. The references in evidence nodes point to encircled numbers in Fig. 5.

This example also illustrates how the impact of changes can be made more precise using detailed traceability. If [Lane Keeping] is changed, this change could be propagated to other affected processes and data, and all related claims could be marked as affected using the traceability links. Engineers could then be directed to the processes or reviews that may need to be re-executed to resolve issues introduced by the change.

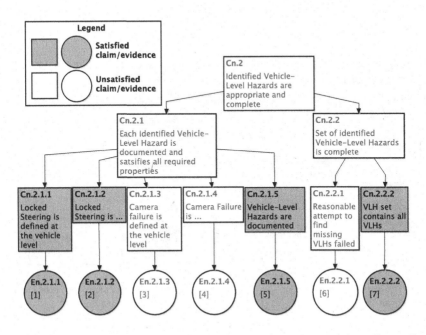

Fig. 6. GSN version of example in Fig. 5. Numbers in evidence nodes refer to Fig. 5 (Colour figure online)

4   Related Work

There is substantial literature on approaches for developing assurance cases. By far the most common notation is the Goal Structuring Notation (GSN) [13]. There are other similar notations like Claims Arguments Evidence (CAE) [6], but GSN is the most common in published literature [15]. A comprehensive report on assurance cases was compiled by John Rushby, et al. [16].

While GSN and CAE offer well-defined notations for documenting assurance cases, they provide little guidance on what claims should be included and how they should be structured. Several papers have questioned the foundations of assurance cases built in these notations and have aimed to mitigate their lack of a systematic development method [18–20]. The use of patterns and templates has helped make developing assurance cases more systematic, but in many cases the problem has just been moved to the definition of the template itself. Our work aims to make the entire process of creating argumentation more systematic by basing argumentation on constraints in WF$^+$ models. There have also been attempts to promote the use of formal methods in assurance cases, e.g., [17]. Our work is philosophically inspired by some of this research, but takes into account limitations at the foundational and methodological level.

Several other papers have presented approaches for generating assurance cases from model-based product data. AdvoCATE provides support for automated argument creation [4]. In [14] the authors discuss an approach for automated instantiation of argument patterns. A generic approach is proposed in [9] where a weaving model is used to connect argumentation patterns to reference information so they may be automatically instantiated. This approach is demonstrated in [10] and [11]. There has also been work on generating argumentation based on model-based process artefacts [7]. In these works templates or patterns are created manually and automatically instantiated. Our work differs in that we are investigating how templates can be generated in addition to their instances. Discussion on the state of the art of model-based safety case generation can be found in [21]. In this context, we aim to automate steps 2–5 of the generic approach defined in Section III-B of [21].

5   Evaluation

5.1   Collaboration with an Industrial Partner

WF$^+$ was developed during a multi-year collaborative project with an automotive OEM. We have developed many metamodels based on ISO 26262 as well as for safety engineering processes of our industrial partner. However, the models related to their engineering processes are proprietary. The models created span the entire safety engineering process, from early hazard analyses to V&V. Evaluation by the OEM focusing on accuracy of the metamodels, fidelity of the models (in terms of accurately capturing the OEM's safety processes), and completeness (in terms of being able to support the OEM's modeling requirements) is very promising, especially with regard to enabling incremental assurance using the detailed traceability inherent in WF$^+$. One question raised by our industrial collaborator was how those doing the everyday safety engineering work would use WF$^+$ models and if they would be too complex. To address this we created mechanisms to transform WF$^+$ models to and from familiar formats, such as tabular representations, with the detailed traceability in the WF$^+$ model maintained behind the scenes. Another question was related to the effort required to create WF$^+$ models. The models created can be reused for different systems, and will be useful in the context of product lines. We already demonstrated how successful WF$^+$ can be in implementing change impact analyses.

5.2 Comparison with Other Approaches

The assurance case in WF$^+$ is generated directly from the syntactic and semantic checks that are based on the processes, associated data and constraints in the WF$^+$ metamodel – supplemented by well-known safety engineering principles. The argument structure is calculated from the metamodel, and we build the assurance case bottom-up, starting with the evidence. There are advantages in doing this:

- The evidence directly supports the associated claim.
- The evidence is used to determine the claim, not the other way around, and this reduces the potential for confirmation bias in constructing the argument.
- In all GSN-like assurance arguments the logical structure of the argument is bottom-up – but the development of the argument is top-down. This is part of the reason why GSN-like argumentation is so variable.

6 Conclusion

We have demonstrated how WF$^+$ is used to model development and safety engineering processes. The WF$^+$ models use UML class diagrams that define data and safety processes that operate over these data. WF$^+$ modelling is rigorous with well-defined semantics; admittedly, the fact that we can develop metamodels and their instantiations, together with their associated data, is not conceptually new. However, the fact that these models can be used to generate GSN-like assurance arguments is new and we believe that this way of generating safety assurance has advantages:

- Our assurance argument splits the lowest level claims into those that arise from syntactic checks and those from semantic checks. Syntactic checks are numerous, expensive, yet important in the documentation of evidence. Model management can automate and record compliance with these checks.
- Traceability is extensive. It is pervasive throughout the integrated metamodels which link processes and their input and output data – and lead directly to terminal claims in the assurance argument.
- The metamodel acts as a template; it is created once (at significant effort) but is instantiated as often as needed.

- The extensive traceability support and the reusable template facilitate incremental assurance. It is this particular challenge that we have been working on in our industrial collaboration.
- Model management techniques hold the promise of significant automation; modelling tools ease the task of developing a WF$^+$ metamodel and its necessary constraints; in addition, they can check that an instance is compliant with the metamodel.
- We have started developing initial tool support for WF$^+$ [3]. It allows for the development of the automated steps required for constraint checking, model conformance, syntactic validation and more. The tooling uses the Eclipse Modelling Framework (EMF), specifically the Ecore and Sirius technologies available within that framework, and the Epsilon Object Language (EOL), part of Epsilon, for implementing queries.

Future Work. As mentioned in Sect. 3.4, as a WF$^+$ metamodel is developed incrementally it requires the use of different model management techniques to manage how the different pieces fit together. Tool support will enable us to enforce conventions and modelling strategies to ensure that users develop valid models from which rigorous assurance cases can be generated. Furthermore, the ability to write formal constraints within the metamodel will further strengthen both the usability of WF$^+$ and the argumentation built from the constraints. Finally, it would be ideal to be able to manage incremental assurance and change propagation automatically through the model when changes are made in either the metamodel level or its instance. This would further enhance the maintainability of WF$^+$, addressing reservations our industry collaborators voiced concerning the cost of its use.

We intend to implement model management using Epsilon, for example by using EOL to implement various change impact analysis algorithms and the Epsilon Transformation Language to project the results of the analysis onto the target model. Future work for tool support also includes integration with existing engineering technologies such as Simulink, and with those used for documentation, such as Microsoft Excel.

Acknowledgment. WF$^+$ was primarily the idea of Zinovy Diskin who led its initial development. We also want to thank Joseph D'Ambrosio, Mehrnoosh Askarpour, Sahar Kokaly, Lucian Patcas, Galen Ressler, Ramesh S, Sigrid Wagner, Marsha Chechik and Alessio Disandro for their invaluable comments and suggestions.

References

1. Annable, N.: A Model-Based Approach to Formal Assurance Cases. Master's thesis, McSCert, Department of Computing and Software, McMaster University (2020)
2. Annable, N., Bayzat, A., Diskin, Z., Lawford, M., Paige, R., Wassyng, A.: Model-driven safety of autonomous vehicles. In: proceedings of CSER (2020)

3. Chiang, T.: Creating An Editor For The Implementation of WorkFlow+: A Framework for Developing Assurance Cases. Master's thesis, McSCert, Department of Computing and Software, McMaster University (2021)
4. Denney, E., Pai, G.: Tool support for assurance case development. Autom. Softw. Eng. **25**(3), 435–499 (2018)
5. Diskin, Z., Annable, N., Wassyng, A., Lawford, M.: Assurance via workflow+ modelling and conformance. CoRR abs/1912.09912 (2019)
6. Emmet, L.: Using claims, arguments and evidence: a pragmatic view—and tool support in ASCE. Accessible from www.adelard.com
7. Gallina, B.: A model-driven safety certification method for process compliance. In: 2014 IEEE International Symposium on Software Reliability Engineering Workshops, pp. 204–209 (2014). https://doi.org/10.1109/ISSREW.2014.30
8. Graydon, P.J., Knight, J.C., Strunk, E.A.: Assurance based development of critical systems. In: Proceedings of DSN 2007, pp. 347–357 (2007). https://doi.org/10.1109/DSN.2007.17
9. Hawkins, R., Habli, I., Kolovos, D., Paige, R., Kelly, T.: Weaving an assurance case from design: a model-based approach. In: IEEE HASE, pp. 110–117 (2015)
10. Hawkins, R., Kelly, T., Habli, I.: Developing assurance cases for D-MILS systems. In: MILS@ HiPEAC (2015)
11. Hawkins, R., Richardson, T., Kelly, T.: Using process models in system assurance. In: Skavhaug, A., Guiochet, J., Bitsch, F. (eds.) SAFECOMP 2016. LNCS, vol. 9922, pp. 27–38. Springer, Cham (2016). https://doi.org/10.1007/978-3-319-45477-1_3
12. ISO 26262: Road vehicles - Functional safety. International Organization for Standardization, Geneva, Switzerland (2018)
13. Kelly, T., Weaver, R.: The goal structuring notation-a safety argument notation. In: Proceedings of the Dependable Systems and Networks Workshop on Assurance Cases, p. 6. Citeseer (2004)
14. Meng, B., Paul, S., Moitra, A., Siu, K., Durling, M.: Automating the assembly of security assurance case fragments. In: Habli, I., Sujan, M., Bitsch, F. (eds.) SAFECOMP 2021. LNCS, vol. 12852, pp. 101–114. Springer, Cham (2021). https://doi.org/10.1007/978-3-030-83903-1_7
15. Nair, S., de la Vara, J.L., Sabetzadeh, M., Briand, L.C.: An extended systematic literature review on provision of evidence for safety certification. Inf. Softw. Technol. **56**(7), 689–717 (2014)
16. Rushby, J., Xu, X., Rangarajan, M., Weaver, T.L.: Understanding and evaluating assurance cases. Technical report, SRI International (2015)
17. Rushby, J.M.: Formalism in safety cases. In: Dale, C., Anderson, T. (eds.) In: Dale, C., Anderson, T. (eds) Making Systems Safer, pp. 3–17. Springer, London (2010). https://doi.org/10.1007/978-1-84996-086-1_1
18. Wassyng, A., et al.: Can product-specific assurance case templates be used as medical device standards? IEEE Des. Test **32**(5), 45–55 (2015)
19. Wassyng, A., Maibaum, T.S.E., Lawford, M., Bherer, H.: Software certification: is there a case against safety cases? In: 16th Monterey Workshop, pp. 206–227 (2010)
20. Wei, R., Kelly, T.P., Dai, X., Zhao, S., Hawkins, R.: Model based system assurance using the structured assurance case metamodel. J. Syst. Softw. **154**, 211–233 (2019)
21. Yan, F., Foster, S., Habli, I.: Safety case generation by model-based engineering: state of the art and a proposal. In: Proceedings of The Eleventh International Conference on Performance, Safety and Robustness in Complex Systems and Applications, International Academy, Research, and Industry Association (2021)

Uncertainty Elicitation and Propagation in GSN Models of Assurance Cases

Yassir Idmessaoud[1(✉)], Didier Dubois[2], and Jérémie Guiochet[1]

[1] LAAS-CNRS, University of Toulouse, Toulouse, France
{yassir.id-messaoud,jeremie.guiochet}@laas.fr
[2] IRIT, University of Toulouse, Toulouse, France
dubois@irit.fr

Abstract. Goal structuring notation (GSN) is commonly proposed as a structuring tool for arguing about the high-level properties (e.g. safety) of a system. However, this approach does not include the representation of uncertainties that may affect arguments. Several works extend this framework using uncertainty propagation methods. The ones based on Dempster-Shafer Theory (DST) are of interest as DST can model incomplete information. However, few works relate this approach with a logical representation of relations between elements of GSN, which is actually required to justify the chosen uncertainty propagation schemes. In this paper, we improve previous proposals including a logical formalism added to GSN, and an elicitation procedure for obtaining uncertainty information from expert judgements. We briefly present an application to a case study to validate our uncertainty propagation model in GSN that takes into account both incomplete and conflicting information.

Keywords: Uncertainty propagation · Belief elicitation · Goal structuring notation · Dempster-Shafer application · Safety cases

1 Introduction

Due to its expressiveness, the goal structuring notation (GSN) has became a de-facto standard for graphical documentation of argument structures. It is notably used to argue about the safety of critical systems. However, even a well-designed GSN may include uncertainties that may question the final statement of the GSN. There is a lack of consensus about how to model these uncertainties in the argument structure. An interesting proposal [19] is to use Dempster-Shafer Theory (DST), since incomplete information can be explicitly modeled and calculated with. Several research works are investigating its use, but as presented in [7], the proposed uncertainty propagation schemes are often not clearly justified. This is mainly due to a lack of a clear definition of the logical relations between GSN elements. We investigate this issue in this paper, using DST and logical representations of arguments with new propagation models. We do not

© The Author(s), under exclusive license to Springer Nature Switzerland AG 2022
M. Trapp et al. (Eds.): SAFECOMP 2022, LNCS 13414, pp. 111–125, 2022.
https://doi.org/10.1007/978-3-031-14835-4_8

replace GSN informal notation, but build a formal model on top of it to propagate uncertainties. We also study how expert judgments can be elicited to feed our models.

The paper is structured as follows. Section 2 presents background and some related works. Sections 3 and 4 present the uncertainty propagation and elicitation methods respectively. Finally, Sect. 5 presents some experimental results gained by the proposed approach.

2   Background and Related Work

Goal structuring notation (GSN) is a graphical notation/language which represents argument structures (i.e., safety and assurance cases) in form of directed acyclic graphs (directed trees or arborescences). It breaks down a top claim, called "goal", into elementary sub-goals following a specific strategy and in accordance with a particular context. Each sub-goal is associated with pieces of evidence, called solutions, which support the conclusion. Figure 1 represents a typical hazard avoidance GSN pattern. To be considered as *"acceptably safe"* (G_1) all hazards (G_2 to G_n) of the system (X), listed in the context box (C_1), should be provably handled (Sn_1, Sn_2, ...) following the strategy (S_1). However, this symbol-based language does not specify the nature of the logical links between $G_1, G_2, \ldots G_n$, nor does it capture the uncertainty that may exist in the argument structure. Previous works [5,7] stated and discussed proposals that deal with the issue of uncertainty. An important part of these studies use probability theory to address it [4,8]. For instance, some authors [15] transform GSN into a Bayesian network (BBN) and propagate probabilities accordingly. Due to the limited expressiveness of the probabilistic framework when information is lacking, such approaches can properly deal with uncertainties due to aleatory phenomena, but they poorly represent epistemic uncertainties due to incomplete information. In addition, these methods are also very greedy in terms of data, which requires much time to collect and process.

As a generalization of probability theory, Dempster-Shafer theory [16] (DST) offers tools to model and propagate both aleatory and epistemic uncertainty. A mass function, or basic belief assignment (BBA), is a probability distribution over the power set of the universe of possibilities (Ω), known as the *frame of discernment*. Formally, a mass function $m : 2^\Omega \to [0,1]$ is such that $\sum_{E \subseteq \Omega} m(E) = 1$, and $m(\emptyset) = 0$. Any subset E of Ω such that $m(E) > 0$ is called a focal set of m. $m(E)$ quantifies the probability that we only know that the truth lies in E; in particular $m(\Omega)$ quantifies the amount of ignorance. A mass assignment induces a so-called belief function $Bel : 2^\Omega \to [0,1]$, defined by: $Bel(A) = \sum_{E \subseteq A} m(E)$. It represents the sum of all the masses supporting a statement A. Belief in the negation $\neg A$ of the statement A is represented by: $Disb(A) = Bel(\neg A)$; the value $Uncer(A) = 1 - Bel(A) - Disb(A)$ quantifies the lack of information about A. In this paper, a *conjunctive rule of combination* is used for uncertainty propagation. This rule combines multiple pieces of evidence (represented by mass functions m_i, with $i = 1, 2, ..., n$)

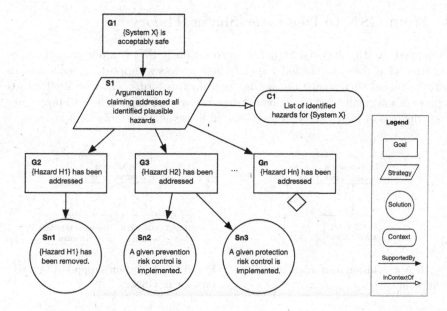

Fig. 1. GSN example adapted from the Hazard Avoidance Pattern [14]

coming from independent sources of information: $m_\cap = m_1 \otimes m_2$ such that $m_\cap(A) = \sum_{E_1 \cap E_2 = A} m_1(E_1) \cdot m_2(E_2)$. In DST, an additional step eliminates conflicts that may exist by means of a normalization factor (dividing $m_\cap$ by $1 - m_\cap(\emptyset)$). This is Dempster rule of combination [16]. This step is omitted here to indicate the presence of possibly conflicting pieces of information.

Our approach builds on some previous works (mainly [2,19]) that define a number of argument types and associate to each of them an uncertainty propagation formula in the setting of DST. However, in [2], no logical framework is provided, which prevents a formal justification of uncertainty propagation formulas. An implicit logical setting is offered in [19]. But it remains questionable since, for instance, rules that represent the relations between premises and the top-goal are modelled by equivalences. In our work we explicitly build propagation rules on a logical framework and we adopt a more flexible format using implications. A second issue is the elicitation process that collects information from experts and transforms it into belief and disbelief pairs in DST. For that, the method proposed in [2] and taken over in [19] is *ad hoc*. This transformation between expert information and (belief, disbelief) pairs is not *one to one* when the expert expresses no information. It yields some anomalous cases as discussed in [9]. Finally, no proposal was given in [2] to elicit belief on rules, while in [19] negative beliefs can be obtained, which is not acceptable. In this paper, we propose a new better-behaved elicitation approach based on the pignistic transform proposed in [17] that solves the two last issues.

3   From GSN to Dempster-Shafer Theory

As defined by [13,14], Goal Structuring Notation (GSN) is a non-formal representation that does not formally specify how premises support a conclusion. In order to model such a relation, we use logical expressions. Then we shall attach degrees of uncertainty to these logical expressions and explain how to propagate these degrees of uncertainty in the GSN, in agreement with classical logic.

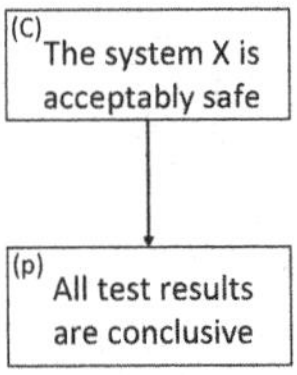

Fig. 2. A conclusion supported by one premise in GSN.

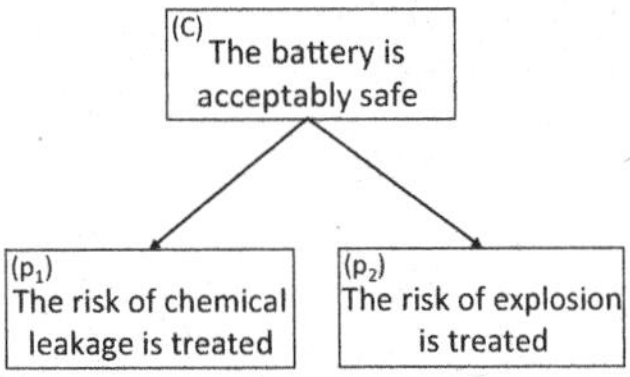

Fig. 3. A conclusion supported by two premise in GSN.

3.1   Logical Modeling of GSN

Figure 2 represents a conclusion (C) supported by a single premise (p). It describes the situation in which the conclusion (C) is true if the premise (p) supporting it is also true. This statement can be expressed using a logical implication connective: $p \Rightarrow C$ standing for $\neg p \vee C$, using negation $\neg$ and disjunction $\vee$. It is obvious that such an expression can only assert the validity of the conclusion (in case p holds), i.e., whether C is provably true, not whether it is provably false. Note that even if C can only be true or false, we may fail to know it. So we work in a three-state universe (belief, disbelief and ignorance). To establish disbelief in C, we need to add an implication of the form $\neg p \Rightarrow \neg C$. It describes the situation where the conclusion (C) would be false, when the premise (p) is false. We call such logical expressions "rules". Those that induce belief in C are called *direct rules* and those that induce disbelief are called *reverse rules*.

With complex systems, it is more likely to find claims supported by more than one piece of evidence. In these cases, it is necessary to consider the relationship between the premises that support the same claim. On the other hand, logical implications remain the only connective that links the evidence domain to the conclusion. Through the different GSN patterns encountered in the literature, we can identify three types:

– **Conjunctive (C-Arg):** It describes the case when all premises are needed to support the conclusion. The direct rule is obtained by translating this definition into a logical expression: $(\wedge_i^n p_i) \Rightarrow C$. On the other hand, the reverse one is obtained by reversing the direct one: $\neg(\wedge_i^n p_i) \Rightarrow \neg C$, which is equivalent to $\wedge_i^n(\neg p_i \Rightarrow \neg C)$, a conjunction of simple rules.

- **Disjunctive (D-Arg):** It describes the case when one premise is enough to support the whole conclusion. The corresponding rules are: $\wedge_i^n(p_i \Rightarrow C)$ (direct), and $(\wedge_i^n \neg p_i) \Rightarrow \neg C$ (reverse).
- **Hybrid (H-Arg):** It describes the case where each premise supports the conclusion to some extent, but their conjunction does it to a larger extent. This rule type could be considered as a general type which includes the two previous ones. In fact, conjunctive and disjunctive types correspond to limit cases of the hybrid one.

Figure 3 represents an example of the conjunctive type. To assert that the battery is acceptably safe, all risks of chemical leakage and explosion should be treated. It gives the expression: $(p_1 \wedge p_2) \Rightarrow C$. On the other hand, if one of the risks remains present we may assert that the battery is unsafe, which gives the expressions: $\neg p_1 \Rightarrow \neg C$ and $\neg p_2 \Rightarrow \neg C$.

All rules defined above will be used to build our uncertainty propagation model. Since the conjunctive and disjunctive types represent a special case of the hybrid one, we will only present the last one. However, it is simple to deduce their expressions from the general formula.

3.2 Uncertainty Propagation Model

In order to build our uncertainty propagation model, we define two kinds of parameters:

- Uncertainty on premises: It is modeled as a mass function on each premise of the argument: $<m_p^1, ..., m_p^n>$. m_p^i assigns a mass to the premise p_i, one on its negation $(\neg p_i)$ and one on the tautology $(\Omega$, representing ignorance) summing to 1.
- Uncertainty on rules: It is used to evaluate the impact of premises on a conclusion. We associate a simple support function [16] to each rule r of the argument type. Each simple support function consists in assigning a mass $m_r(r) = s$ to the rule and another one $m_r(\Omega) = 1 - s$ to the tautology, these weights summing to 1. The set of mass functions is formally defined as: $<m_\Rightarrow, m_\Rightarrow^i, m_\Leftarrow, m_\Leftarrow^i>$, where:
$m_\Rightarrow$ and $m_\Leftarrow$ represent, respectively, direct and reverse conjunctive mass functions that assign support to rules $(\wedge_i^n p_i) \Rightarrow C$ and $(\wedge_i^n \neg p_i) \Rightarrow \neg C$, respectively.
$m_\Rightarrow^i$, and $m_\Leftarrow^i$ respectively, assign support to elementary rules $p_i \Rightarrow C$ and $\neg p_i \Rightarrow \neg C$ occurring in the disjunctive type.

Using the conjunctive rule of combination presented in Sect. 2, to merge the masses on the rules (conjunctive and disjunctive ones) with the masses on premises $(m_\cap = m_\Rightarrow \otimes m_\Leftarrow \otimes m_\Rightarrow^i \otimes m_\Leftarrow^i \otimes m_p^i)$, we quantify the uncertainty on the conclusion C [1]. Since we work on a two-state frame of discernment for both premises $\Omega_p = \{p_i, \neg p_i\}$ and conclusion $\Omega_C = \{C, \neg C\}$, masses and (dis-)belief degrees on premises, rules and the conclusion are equal. For instance,

$m_C(C) = Bel_C(C)$ and $m_C(\neg C) = Bel_C(\neg C) = Disb_C(C)$. We can prove the following results, by projecting $m_\cap$ on the universe $\Omega_C = \{C, \neg C\}$:

$$Bel_C(C) = Bel_\Rightarrow([\wedge_{i=1}^n p_i] \Rightarrow C) \cdot \prod_{i=1}^n \{Bel_p^i(p_i) \cdot [1 - Bel_\Rightarrow^i(p_i \Rightarrow C)]\}$$

$$+ \{1 - \prod_{i=1}^n [1 - Bel_p^i(p_i) \cdot Bel_\Rightarrow^i(p_i \Rightarrow C)]\} \tag{1}$$

$$Disb_C(C) = Bel_\Leftarrow([\wedge_{i=1}^n \neg p_i] \Rightarrow \neg C) \cdot \prod_{i=1}^n \{Disb_p^i(p_i) \cdot [1 - Bel_\Leftarrow^i(\neg p_i \Rightarrow \neg C)]\}$$

$$+ \{1 - \prod_{i=1}^n [1 - Disb_p^i(p_i) \cdot Bel_\Leftarrow^i(\neg p_i \Rightarrow \neg C)]\} \tag{2}$$

where:

- $Bel_C(C)$ (resp. $Disb_C(C)$): the degree of belief (resp. disbelief) in the conclusion C obtained by projection of $m_\cap$ on Ω_C.
- $Bel_p^i(p_i)$ (resp. $Disb_p^i(p_i)$): the degree of belief (resp. disbelief) in the ith premise.
- $Bel_\Rightarrow([\wedge_{i=1}^n p_i] \Rightarrow C)$ (resp. $Bel_\Leftarrow^i(\neg p_i \Rightarrow \neg C)$): the degree of belief in the direct conjunctive rule (resp. i^{th} reverse rule).

We can notice that each formula (1) and (2) is the result of the summation of two terms. The first part expresses a generalized conjunction (the product), and the second part reflects a generalized disjunction (the probabilistic sum $1 - (1 - a)(1 - b)$). To extract propagation formulas for the pure conjunctive type (C-Arg), it is enough to set to zero the masses on the direct rules ($Bel_\Rightarrow^i(p_i \Rightarrow C)$) and the mass on the conjunctive reverse rule ($Bel_\Leftarrow([\wedge_i^n \neg p_i] \Rightarrow \neg C)$). Similarly, to derive the pure disjunctive formulas (D-Arg), we set to zero the mass on the conjunctive direct rule ($Bel_\Rightarrow([\wedge_{i=1}^n p_i] \Rightarrow C)$) and the masses on the reverse rules ($Bel_\Leftarrow^i(\neg p_i \Rightarrow \neg C)$). We obtain:

$$\text{C-Arg}: \begin{cases} Bel_C(C) = Bel_\Rightarrow([\wedge_{i=1}^n p_i] \Rightarrow C) \cdot \prod_{i=1}^n Bel_p(p_i) \\ Disb_C(C) = 1 - \prod_{i=1}^n [1 - Disb_p^i(p_i) \cdot Bel_\Leftarrow^i(\neg p_i \Rightarrow \neg C)] \end{cases}$$

$$\text{D-Arg}: \begin{cases} Bel_C(C) = 1 - \prod_{i=1}^n [1 - Bel_p^i(p_i) \cdot Bel_\Rightarrow^i(p_i \Rightarrow C)] \\ Disb_C(C) = Bel_\Leftarrow([\wedge_{i=1}^n \neg p_i] \Rightarrow \neg C) \cdot \prod_{i=1}^n Disb_p^i(p_i) \end{cases}$$

Note that the belief (resp. disbelief) degree of the conclusion ($Bel_C(C)$) only depends on the belief (resp. disbelief) degree of premises ($Bel_p^i(p_i)$) and of the corresponding direct (reverse) rules ($Bel_\Rightarrow$ and $Bel_\Rightarrow^i$).

However, we observe in some cases that the sum of belief and disbelief of the conclusion, as calculated above, is greater than 1 which is not coherent.

This is when the mass $m_\cap(\emptyset) > 0$. It is then counted in both sums defining the degrees of belief and disbelief. It indicates the presence of conflict between premises and rules. The coherence property $Bel_C(C) + Disb_C(C) \leq 1$ always hold if $m_\cap(\emptyset) = 0$. If it is not null, the conflict mass (3) should be subtracted from both belief and disbelief values, in order to get genuine contradiction-free degrees of belief and disbelief that respect the coherence property.

In [10], we provided a recursive equation to compute $m_\cap^n(\emptyset)$ for n premises when we know $m_\cap^{n-1}(\emptyset)$:

$$m_\cap^n(\emptyset) = Bel_C^{n-1}(C) \cdot m_n(\neg p_n \wedge \neg C) + Disb_C^{n-1}(C) \cdot m_n(p_n \wedge C) + m_\cap^{n-1}(\emptyset) \quad (3)$$

where:

- $Bel_C^{n-1}(C) = \{1 - \prod_{i=1}^{n-1}[1 - Bel_p^i(p_i) \cdot Bel_\Rightarrow^i(p_i \Rightarrow C)]\} - m_\cap^{n-1}(\emptyset)$
- $Disb_C^{n-1}(C) = \{1 - \prod_{i=1}^{n-1}[1 - Disb_p^i(p_i) \cdot Bel_\Leftarrow^i(\neg p_i \Rightarrow \neg C)]\} - m_\cap^{n-1}(\emptyset)$
- $m_i(p_i \wedge C) = Bel_p^i(p_i) \cdot Bel_\Rightarrow^i(p_i \Rightarrow C)$
- $m_i(\neg p_i \wedge \neg C) = Disb_p^i(p_i) \cdot Bel_\Leftarrow^i(\neg p_i \Rightarrow \neg C)$

Remark: D-Arg and C-Arg are conflict-free. Assuming that rule masses are maximal (= 1), for $n = 2$ we get: $Bel_C(C) = Bel_p^1(p_1) \cdot Bel_p^2(p_2)$ (for C-Arg) and $Bel_C(C) = Bel_p^1(p_1) + Bel_p^2(p_2) - Bel_p^1(p_1) \cdot Bel_p^2(p_2)$ (for D-Arg).

3.3   Belief and Disbelief Elicitation

The model of uncertainty propagation presented above requires two types of inputs in order to compute belief and disbelief degrees of a conclusion: Belief/Disbelief on the rules and on the premises. These two information items will be directly collected from experts. To give their assessment about a premise or a rule, experts are asked to fill in an evaluation matrix, presented in Fig. 4. Each point of this matrix corresponds to a strength of decision, denoted by $Dec(A)$, and a degree of confidence in this decision, denoted by $Conf(A)$

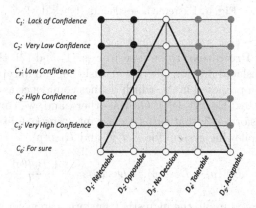

Fig. 4. Evaluation matrix

attached to a proposition A. In a scale of 5 equidistant items, decision describes which side the expert leans towards: From the rejection $(Dec(A) = 0)$ of a claim A, to its acceptance $(Dec(A) = 1)$. It is formally the same as a degree of probability. On the other hand, confidence reflects the amount of information an expert possesses that can justify a decision. There are 6 equidistant levels of the confidence scale, from "Lack of confidence" $Conf(A) = 0$ to "For sure" $Conf(A) = 1$.

In Fig. 5, we present four extreme expert assessments (see the black dot). The upper matrices represent the case of total confidence. The assessor rejects (resp. accepts) the claim in Fig. 5a (resp. 5b). It corresponds to a maximal disbelief (resp. belief) degree. In contrast, the lower matrices represent resp. the cases of total conflict (Fig. 5c) and ignorance (Fig. 5d). In both cases, the expert cannot make a clear decision either because he has as a lot of information both to support and reject the claim $(Conf(A) = 1)$, or because he has no information $(Conf(A) = 0)$. In contrast to other works [2, 18], we allow the assessor to use a midpoint value $(Dec(A) = 1/2)$ to show full hesitancy.

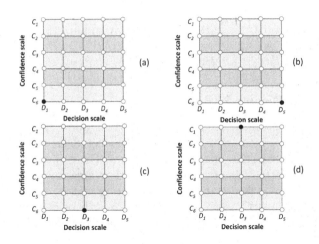

Fig. 5. Extreme assessments (black dot)

Uncertainty on Premises: To be used in Eqs. (1) and (2), the pair (decision, confidence) is translated into a triple (belief, disbelief and uncertainty). To do so, we use the formula proposed in [2], which defines confidence as the sum of belief and disbelief degrees (Eq. (4), left). On the other hand, we consider decision as the pignistic transform [17] that turns a mass into a probability (Eq. (4), right). So, we solve the following system for $Bel(p)$ and $Disb(p)$:

$$Conf(p) = Bel(p) + Disb(p); \quad Dec(p) = \frac{1 + Bel(p) - Disb(p)}{2} \qquad (4)$$

However, as indicated in [9], the pignistic transform can generate negative belief and disbelief values when the pair $(Dec, Conf)$ given by an expert lies outside the triangle shown in Fig. 4. Known as "Josang Triangle" [12], it represents a constraint that brackets decision $Dec(p)$ between two values:

$$\frac{1 - Conf(p)}{2} \leq Dec(p) \leq \frac{1 + Conf(p)}{2} \tag{5}$$

It guarantees that all clear-cut decisions (rejection or acceptance) are made only when the confidence level is maximal. To avoid negative belief and disbelief values, we must adjust the decision value to respect constraint (5). Therefore, when $Dec(p) < \frac{1-Conf(p)}{2}$ (rejection: black dots in Fig. 4), we set $Dec(p) = \frac{1-Conf(p)}{2}$. On the other hand, when $Dec(p) > \frac{1+Conf(p)}{2}$ (acceptance: grey dots in Fig. 4), we set $Dec(p) = \frac{1+Conf(p)}{2}$.

Example 1. Suppose we get the following assessments on two goals (p_1) and (p_2):

- p_1: Opposable with high confidence $(Dec(p_1) = 0.25, Conf(p_1) = 0.6)$.
- p_2: Acceptable with very high confidence $(Dec(p_2) = 1, Conf(p_2) = 0.8)$.

To calculate $Bel(p_i)$ and $Disb(p_i)$, we write them in terms of $Dec(p_i)$ and $Conf(p_i)$, from (4): $Bel(p) = \frac{Conf(p)-1}{2} + Dec(p)$, $Disb(p) = \frac{Conf(p)+1}{2} - Dec(p)$.

We can notice that the assessment for p_1 is inside the triangle in the matrix (Fig. 4). Hence, there is no need to adjust the values: $Bel(p_1) = \frac{0.6-1}{2} + 0.25 = 0.05$, $Disb(p_1) = \frac{0.6+1}{2} - 0.25 = 0.55$ and $Uncer(p_1) = 1 - Bel(p_1) - Disb(p_1) = 0.4$ for the amount of ignorance.

On the other hand, the assessment for p_2 is situated outside the triangle. In this case, we can be sure that the decision degree must be adjusted in accordance with the confidence value to get correct inputs. Before adjustment, we find a negative value of disbelief, which does not make sense: $Bel(p_2) = \frac{0.8-1}{2} + 1 = 0.9$ and $Disb(p_2) = \frac{0.8+1}{2} - 1 = -0.1$. Following the description above, we set $Dec(p_2) = \frac{1+Conf(p_2)}{2} = \frac{1+0.8}{2} = 0.9$. Then we find that $Bel(p_2) = 0.8$, $Disb(p_2) = 0$ and $Uncer(p_2) = 1 - Bel(p_2) - Disb(p_2) = 0.2$.

Uncertainty on Rules: Assuming clear-cut knowledge about some (or all) premises $(Bel_p^i(p_i), Disb_p^i(p_i)) \in \{0,1\}$ and total ignorance about the others $(Uncer_p^i(p_i) = 1)$, we notice that $Bel_C(C)$ and $Disb_C(C)$ in (1) and (2) are equal to rule masses. For instance, in the case of a conclusion C supported by two premises p_1 and p_2, assuming total acceptance of these two premises with maximal confidence, we get: $Bel_C(C) = Bel_{\Rightarrow}([p_1 \wedge p_2] \Rightarrow C)$. While assuming total rejection with maximal confidence of p_1, and total ignorance about p_2, we get: $Disb_C(C) = Bel_{\Leftarrow}(\neg p_1 \Rightarrow \neg C)$.

In order to collect masses on rules, under the assumption mentioned above (sure truth, sure falsity or ignorance on premises) we use the same approach as for eliciting uncertainty on premises. First, using the evaluation matrix (Fig. 4), we take the expert opinions about the conclusion (which corresponds to the rules masses under those assumptions). Then, we change them to belief values using transformation formulas (4).

Moreover, we assume that a rule is either accepted or discarded, but not negated. In fact, for any rule $R : p \Rightarrow C$ we do not consider a positive disbelief because this would imply a belief in $\neg(p \Rightarrow C) = p \wedge \neg C$, i.e., $\neg R$ which is not a rule. So we only assign mass to a rule or to the tautology; the latter is the extent to which a rule is discarded. This constraint impacts the allowed pairs (Dec, Conf) for the expert. The latter is constrained to choose only a decision on the positive side (from "No decision" to "acceptable") for direct rules. On the contrary, (s)he can only choose a negative decision (from "rejectable" to "No decision") for the reverse rules. Formulas in (4) are used to derive the degrees of belief on rules.

Example 2. Consider the case of Fig. 2:

- Direct rule ($R_1 : p \Rightarrow C$): Assuming $Dec(p) = 1$, expert assigns "Tolerable with high confidence" to C: $Dec(C) = 0.75$, $Conf(C) = 0.6$
- Reverse rule ($R_2 : \neg p \Rightarrow \neg C$): Assuming $Dec(p) = 0$, expert assigns "Opposable with very high confidence" to C: $Dec(C) = 0.25$, $Conf(C) = 0.8$

We can notice in this example that both cases respect the Josang constraint (5). Hence, there is no need to adjust the decision value. Using (4) for the direct rule R_1: $Bel_{\Rightarrow}(R_1) = Bel_C(C) = \frac{(0.6)-1}{2} + (0.75) = 0.55$ and we set $Bel_{\Rightarrow}(\neg R_1) = 0$. In the same way, for the reverse rule R_2: $Bel_{\Leftarrow}(R_2) = Disb_C(C) = \frac{(0.8)+1}{2} - (0.25) = 0.65$ and we set $Bel_{\Leftarrow}(\neg R_2) = 0$.

4   Uncertainty Assessment Procedure

In this section, we present our approach to uncertainty propagation from premises to the top goal of a GSN. As illustrated on Fig. 6, this procedure is structured in two phases.

The first one, called *modeling phase*, collects expert opinions on rules, expressed with qualitative scores $(Dec, Conf)$, and translates them into numerical mass assignments to rules. It will be conducted by asking $(2n+2)$ questions to the assessor using the evaluation matrices, n being the number of premises. The first $(2n)$ questions concern masses on elementary rules (direct and reverse). For instance, to get, respectively, the values of $Bel^i_{\Leftarrow}(\neg p_i \Rightarrow \neg C)$ and $Bel^i_{\Rightarrow}(p_i \Rightarrow C)$ the expert will be asked the following questions (in case $n = 2$):

1. Supposing no knowledge about premise p_1 (resp. p_2) : $(Dec = 0.5, Conf = 0)$ and minimal Dec value (rejectable for sure) in premise p_2 (resp. p_1): $(Dec = 0, Conf = 1)$, what is your Decision/Confidence in the conclusion?
2. Supposing no knowledge about premise p_1 (resp. p_2): $(Dec = 0.5, Conf = 0)$ and a maximal Dec value (acceptable for sure) concerning premise p_2 (resp. p_1) : $(Dec = 1, Conf = 1)$, what is your Decision/Confidence in the conclusion? The additional two questions concern the conjunctive rules (resp. reverse and direct):

3. Supposing minimal *Dec* value (rejectable for sure) concerning both premises $p_1, p_2 : (Dec = 0, Conf = 1)$, what is your Decision/Confidence in the conclusion?

4. Supposing maximal *Dec* value (acceptable for sure) concerning both premises $p_1, p_2 : (Dec = 1, Conf = 1)$, what is your Decision/Confidence in the conclusion?

We assume that once these masses on rules are evaluated, they can be used for the considered system using the second phase explained below.

The second phase, called *application phase*, concerns the collection of expert data on premises. One question per premise is then formulated to the experts: considering the knowledge on the pieces of evidence (also called *solutions* in GSN), what is your "Decision" and "Confidence" concerning premise p_i?

Grouped in a questionnaire, these $(3n + 2)$ questions will be asked in form of matrices to be filled in by the assessor (for rules, some matrices may be pre-filled, see Fig. 6). Then, these values (on rules and premises) are used to calculate the belief/disbelief in the conclusion (Eqs. (1) and (2)). Finally, we may transform the resulting triple (Belief, Disbelief, Uncertainty) concerning the conclusion, to a pair (Decision, Confidence) using formulas (4) and approximate them by qualitative values.

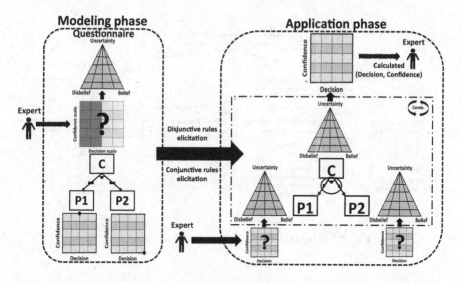

Fig. 6. Schema of the assessment framework for safety argument

5   Case Study

In this section, we use a portion of GSN proposed in [3] to test and validate our uncertainty propagation approach. That study proposed a hybrid architecture of a collision avoidance system for drones, Urban Air Mobility and Air Taxis with horizontal automatic resolution. It is named ACAS-X (Next-Generation Airborne Collision Avoidance System). It replaces a set of lookup tables (LUTs) (that provide anti-collision maneuvering guidance according to the speed of the two aircrafts, their relative positions, and the time until the loss of vertical separation occurs) by a neural network (NN) of much smaller size. In addition to the NN-based controller, this architecture includes a safety net which contains a portion of LUTs (already established as safe) for unsafe areas (where the NN may give results different from those of the LUTs), and a check module which controls the switch between these two sub-systems (NN and LUTs). The GSN section (Fig. 7) in which we are interested, argues that "G_1: *Real world situations where MLM*[1] *is not robust are identified and mitigated*". To demonstrate this statement, the top goal (G_1) is broken down into two sub-goals (G_2) and (G_3). (G_2) ensures that the property was correctly defined to identify all unsafe situations (G_4) and formally checked (G_6) in each of the areas (called p-boxes) into which the input space was correctly decomposed (G_5). (G_3) ensures that unsafe situations were properly mitigated via an appropriate architecture (G_7).

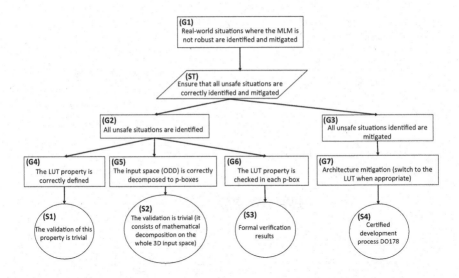

Fig. 7. Assurance Case - ML subsystem robustness [3]

Table 1 groups the degrees of belief on the rules involved in this case. Following the assessment procedure above, these values are the result of a questionnaire[2] answered by a safety expert about this system. We can notice that all direct conjunctive rules receive maximal weights and the elementary rule weights for (G_1) and (G_2) are null. Thus, we deduce that this GSN represent a conjunctive type where all sub-goals are needed to support (G_1). As seen in [10],

---

[1] Machine learning Model.

[2] The questionnaire is available in [11].

C-Arg tends to propagate the premises that support the conclusion with the least weight, increasing along with it the uncertainty level. Thus, we can explain why we go from acceptable premises with very high confidence (G_6, G_7), high confidence (G_5) and for sure (G_4) to a tolerable top goal (G_1) with low confidence $(Dec = 0.692, Conf = 0.384)$. Graphs in Figs. 8 and 9 present, respectively, the sensitivity of decision and confidence degrees of the conclusion (G_1) to the sub-goals (G_4), (G_5), (G_6) and (G_7). To determine the latter, we vary the value of a premise from its minimal to its maximal value, while we keep the values of the other premises to their base values. We can notice that all values, are indeed included in the interval $[0,1]$. We can also notice that the pair (decision, confidence) on the goal (G_1) varies from *"Rejectable for sure"* $(Dec = 0, Conf = 1)$ to *"Tolerable with high confidence"* $(Dec = 0.82, Conf = 0.64)$. The sub-goal (G_4) has the lowest influence on decision and the highest influence on confidence; the opposite applies for sub-goal (G_5).

Table 1. Elicited belief degrees on rules

Goal (G_i)	Belief degree on rules
G_1 ($i = 2, n = 3$)	$Bel_\Rightarrow([\wedge_i^n G_i] \Rightarrow G_1) = 1$ $Bel_\Leftarrow([\wedge_i^n \neg G_i] \Rightarrow \neg G_1) = 1$ $Bel_\Rightarrow(G_i \Rightarrow G_1) = 0$ $Bel_\Leftarrow(\neg G_i \Rightarrow \neg G_1) = 1$
G_2 ($i = 4, n = 6$)	$Bel_\Rightarrow([\wedge_i^n G_i] \Rightarrow G_2) = 1$ $Bel_\Leftarrow([\wedge_i^n \neg G_i] \Rightarrow \neg G_2) = 1$ $Bel_\Rightarrow(G_i \Rightarrow G_2) = 0$ $Bel_\Leftarrow(\neg G_i \Rightarrow \neg G_2) = 1$
G_3	$Bel_\Rightarrow(G_7 \Rightarrow G_3) = 1$ $Bel_\Leftarrow(\neg G_7 \Rightarrow \neg G_3) = 1$

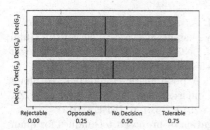

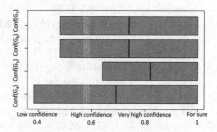

Fig. 8. Decision sensitivity on the top goal G_1

Fig. 9. Confidence sensitivity on the top goal G_1

124   Y. Idmessaoud et al.

6 Conclusion

In this paper, we propose an extensive approach to the elicitation and propagation of uncertainty in a logical GSN model and report on a preliminary case study for testing our approach. However, some issues still need to be addressed. First of all, our propagation model does not consider all GSN components (such as Justification, Assumption, etc.). In addition, our elicitation model seems to encourage experts to give extreme values of (decision, confidence) so that we often end up with a conjunctive or disjunctive type. But these two types are not the only types that exist in literature. Finally, the transformation of expert opinion from quantitative to qualitative values is also a source of uncertainty. In a future work, we plan to develop a purely qualitative approach to information fusion based on [6], and compare it to the quantitative one.

Acknowledgement. A special thanks to the authors of [3], especially to Christophe GABREAU for answering the questionnaire concerning the assessment of the GSN presented in our case study.

References

1. Chatalic, P., Dubois, D., Prade, H.: An approach to approximate reasoning based on Dempster rule of combination. Int. J. Expert Syst. Res. Appl. **1**, 67–85 (1987)
2. Cyra, L., Górski, J.: Support for argument structures review and assessment. Reliab. Eng. Syst. Saf. **96**(1), 26–37 (2011)
3. Damour, M., et al.: Towards certification of a reduced footprint ACAS-Xu system: a hybrid ML-based solution. In: Habli, I., Sujan, M., Bitsch, F. (eds.) SAFECOMP 2021. LNCS, vol. 12852, pp. 34–48. Springer, Cham (2021). https://doi.org/10.1007/978-3-030-83903-1_3
4. Denney, E., Pai, G., Habli, I.: Towards measurement of confidence in safety cases. In: 2011 International Symposium on Empirical Software Engineering and Measurement, pp. 380–383. IEEE (2011)
5. Duan, L., Rayadurgam, S., Heimdahl, M.P.E., Ayoub, A., Sokolsky, O., Lee, I.: Reasoning about confidence and uncertainty in assurance cases: a survey. In: Huhn, M., Williams, L. (eds.) FHIES/SEHC -2014. LNCS, vol. 9062, pp. 64–80. Springer, Cham (2017). https://doi.org/10.1007/978-3-319-63194-3_5
6. Dubois, D., Faux, F., Prade, H., Rico, A.: A possibilistic counterpart to Shafer evidence theory. In: IEEE International Conference on Fuzzy Systems (FUZZ-IEEE), New Orleans, LA, USA, 23–26 June 2019, pp. 1–6. IEEE (2019)
7. Graydon, P.J., Holloway, C.M.: An investigation of proposed techniques for quantifying confidence in assurance arguments. Saf. Sci. **92**, 53–65 (2017)
8. Guiochet, J., Do Hoang, Q.A., Kaaniche, M.: A model for safety case confidence assessment. In: Koornneef, F., van Gulijk, C. (eds.) SAFECOMP 2015. LNCS, vol. 9337, pp. 313–327. Springer, Cham (2015). https://doi.org/10.1007/978-3-319-24255-2_23
9. Idmessaoud, Y., Dubois, D., Guiochet, J.: Belief functions for safety arguments confidence estimation: a comparative study. In: Davis, J., Tabia, K. (eds.) SUM 2020. LNCS (LNAI), vol. 12322, pp. 141–155. Springer, Cham (2020). https://doi.org/10.1007/978-3-030-58449-8_10

10. Idmessaoud, Y., Dubois, D., Guiochet, J.: Quantifying confidence of safety cases with belief functions. In: Denœux, T., Lefèvre, E., Liu, Z., Pichon, F. (eds.) BELIEF 2021. LNCS (LNAI), vol. 12915, pp. 269–278. Springer, Cham (2021). https://doi.org/10.1007/978-3-030-88601-1_27
11. Idmessaoud, Y., Guiochet, J., Dubois, D.: Questionnaire for estimating uncertainties in assurance cases, April 2022. https://hal.laas.fr/hal-03649068
12. Jøsang, A.: Subjective Logic. Springer, Cham (2016). https://doi.org/10.1007/978-3-319-42337-1
13. Kelly, T.: Arguing safety - a systematic approach to safety case management. Ph.D. thesis, Department of Computer Science, University of York, UK (1998)
14. Kelly, T.P., McDermid, J.A.: Safety case construction and reuse using patterns. In: Daniel, P. (ed.) Safe Comp 1997, pp. 55–69. Springer, London (1997). https://doi.org/10.1007/978-1-4471-0997-6_5
15. Nešić, D., Nyberg, M., Gallina, B.: A probabilistic model of belief in safety cases. Saf. Sci. **138**, 105187 (2021)
16. Shafer, G.: A Mathematical Theory of Evidence. Princeton University Press, Princeton (1976)
17. Smets, P.: Decision making in the TBM: the necessity of the pignistic transformation. Int. J. Approximate Reasoning **38**, 133–147 (2005)
18. Wang, R., Guiochet, J., Motet, G.: Confidence assessment framework for safety arguments. In: Tonetta, S., Schoitsch, E., Bitsch, F. (eds.) SAFECOMP 2017. LNCS, vol. 10488, pp. 55–68. Springer, Cham (2017). https://doi.org/10.1007/978-3-319-66266-4_4
19. Wang, R., Guiochet, J., Motet, G., Schön, W.: Safety case confidence propagation based on Dempster-Shafer theory. Int. J. Approximate Reasoning **107**, 46–64 (2019)

Fault Detection, Monitoring
and Tolerance

Impact of Machine Learning on Safety Monitors

Francesco Terrosi[1]([✉]), Lorenzo Strigini[2], and Andrea Bondavalli[1]

[1] Università degli Studi di Firenze, Firenze, Italy
{francesco.terrosi,andrea.bondavalli}@unifi.it
[2] City, University of London, London, UK
strigini@csr.city.ac.uk

Abstract. Machine Learning components in safety-critical applications can perform some complex tasks that would be unfeasible otherwise. However, they are also a weak point concerning safety assurance. An aspect requiring study is how the interactions between machine-learning components and other non-ML components evolve with training of the former. It is theoretically possible that learning by Neural Networks may reduce the effectiveness of error checkers or safety monitors, creating a major complication for safety assurance. We present an initial exploration of this problem focused on automated driving, where machine learning is heavily used. We simulated operational testing of a standard vehicle architecture, where a machine learning-based Controller is responsible for driving the vehicle and a separate Safety Monitor is provided to detect hazardous situations and trigger emergency action to avoid accidents. Among the results, we observed that indeed improving the Controller could make the Safety Monitor less effective; it is even possible for a training increment to make the Controller's own behaviour safer but the vehicle's less safe. We discuss implications for practice and for research.

Keywords: Safety · Autonomous vehicles · Automotive · Machine-learning

1 Introduction

Machine Learning (ML) is bringing great changes in many embedded computing applications. In many applications, Neural Networks (NNs) generalize well from situations encountered during training to those it will encounter during subsequent testing and, with luck, to those it will encounter during operation. However, neural networks also represent a weak point from the viewpoint of safety assurance. The lack of an explicit design derived from a specification undermines the very basis of established verification activities for critical systems: verifying with confidence that the implementation satisfies its specifications, and the specified safety properties. An additional concern is that established practice requires a safety-critical system to change as little as possible, and changes to be clearly documented, to support verification towards their acceptance. Machine learning, by contrast, encourages a development culture in which frequent change (additional "learning") is accepted and, due to the nature of ML, there is no documentation of the changes that could directly support verification. Manufacturers of autonomous vehicles are known to collect data from their fleets of vehicles under test, and even in commercial operation, to incrementally train and improve the ML "driver" [1–3]. Last but not least, some self-driving vehicles must satisfy extreme safety requirements (accident rates comparable to, or substantially better than, those of human drivers), such that simple statistical demonstration of their satisfaction through road resting is not feasible [9–12].

Given that we cannot trust these control systems ("Controllers", for brevity) to be safe enough, it is natural to apply independent safety subsystems ("Safety Monitors" SMs, hereafter) that can detect hazardous situations, e.g., approaching collisions, and command remedial actions such as braking, as an additional line of defense [4–7].

Ideally, a safety monitor is much simpler than a Controller, so that, once verified, it gives strong confidence that it will perform to the level of reliability (and hence of vehicle safety) that has been assessed. This may seem to offer a solution for the assurance problem: aim for strong confidence in the safety system even if there will be uncertainties on the safety of the Controller by itself. Although a real safety monitor does not have 100% coverage (probability of detecting and mitigating a hazard situation, conditional on its arising), the coverage could be assessed by extensive simulation testing. The goal is a high enough coverage value that if one multiplies (1-coverage) times the estimate of the rate at which the Controller allows hazardous situations to arise, the result is a low enough rate of accidents. Even if the Controller is frequently changed, this form of reasoning will remain valid. Estimating the two multiplicands separately through testing would require substantially less testing than estimating the rate of accidents directly.

This solution to the assessment difficulties is – however – illusory. The coverage of the Safety Monitor depends on the Controller that it monitors [8]. It is possible that, as a vehicle's Controller improves, and even if this improvement includes its safety (i.e., if without the help of the Safety Monitor each new version would cause fewer accidents than the previous one), the coverage of the Safety Monitor becomes worse, because the fewer hazard situations allowed by the Controller are increasingly of kinds with which the Safety Monitor cannot cope. So, the *whole system* must be tested enough to demonstrate that the rate of accidents would not exceed the required bound. In theory the coverage may decrease so much that *improving* the Controller makes the vehicle as a whole *less safe*. It would be very desirable to have a strong argument that this will not happen [9], since this would support a sound and simple form of safety argument based on operational testing of the vehicle.

A first step to study this possibility is the empirical study that we present here, to answer these research questions:

1. Can one observe in practice these "unwelcome surprises" in which improving a Controller reduces the monitor's coverage, or even increases the vehicle's accident rate?
2. If so, can we derive insights on what factors in the Controller's training, the operating environment or the safety subsystem's design contribute to such surprises?

Our study applies these questions to a primitive simulated vehicle and its environment. The goal of this paper is to share with the community i) *the methodology*, so that it can be used and improved, ii) *a proof of existence* of the "unwelcome surprises", and iii) initial insights on what contributes to them.

2 Related Work

Research on machine learning techniques in many diverse applications, some of them safety-critical, has proliferated in recent years [26–30]. Concerns about machine learning in safety-critical systems have led to research to develop techniques for safety and/or explainability of ML components [32–34]. A common approach in safety-critical systems is to pair the main system Controller, which may use ML, with a Safety Monitor which may be a human or, more commonly, a dedicated hardware-software subsystem [13, 20, 31, 33]. Another approach, hardening and verifying the safety properties of neural networks by developing new training algorithms and network architectures, has proved effective in some studies [35, 38]. Unfortunately, improving ML components is not enough by itself to prove valid safety arguments for such systems [19, 36]. Thus, effort is also applied on how to provide sound and reasonable safety arguments of such systems. These research efforts aim at improving the explainability of the decisions of the ML components and at designing and providing guidelines for safety/assurance cases [19, 33, 34, 36–38].

In this rich research corpus, however, we found no studies of our topic, i.e., how improving ML components affects the efficacy of Safety Monitors that monitor them.

3 Problem Statement

Verifying that "ultra-high" dependability requirements are satisfied is known to be a hard problem [9–12] and the use of ML makes it even harder. The challenge of assuring the safety properties of autonomous vehicles is, as of now, one of the main concerns delaying their deployment [13, 14]: because it is hard to collect enough evidence to prove that one system is "safe enough", and because it is difficult to understand the inner process that made a neural network take a specific decision [15]. Simulation proved effective for training a neural network to drive, and it is one of the first steps in the development of automated, unmanned vehicles [16–18]. However, testing an autonomous vehicle is a hard task even with the aid of a simulated environment because i) neural networks cannot generalize their function to every possible event, ii) it is not possible to test every possible event and iii) designing an end-to-end design and deployment process for such complex systems is hard [19].

In this work we are interested in studying the effects of "additional learning" of a Controller on the coverage of the Safety Monitor (probability of detecting a hazard situation, conditional on its arising: true positive rate of the hazard detection – and mitigation – function). Since the probability of the SM preventing an accident depends on the relative frequencies with which the Controller generates various types of demands on the SM (hazardous situations for which coverage is high vs those for which coverage is low) [8], the Controller may significantly change these probabilities as it "learns". So, *every change* in the Controller will invalidate the coverage estimate and thus any safety argument that assumes i) unchanging coverage of the Safety Monitor or even just ii) that more learning by the Controller implies improving system safety.

4 System Model and Terminology

Here we describe the system model and the terminology used and define and discuss the metrics used to measure the performance of the Safety Monitor when applied to a learning Controller. We simulated the architecture depicted in Fig. 1, where an end-to-end learning Controller is paired with a Safety Monitor to make the car move safely.

The *Controller* is the main component of the system. Its task is to drive the car from a starting position to a destination, obeying traffic laws and other internal rules such as ensuring a "smooth" ride or acceptable fuel consumption. A Controller is often built as a set of specialized modules which implement the required functions of perception, planning, etc. This allows run-time monitoring of the operation of each module. We used a simpler, monolithic design: the whole process from perception to motion control is encoded into a single deep learning architecture (end-to-end learning [20]). The Controller is thus a "black box": the Safety Monitor can only react to hazardous actions of the Controller, not to internal errors of the Controller that might lead to such actions.

Our *Safety Monitor* uses data from other sensors (a LiDAR) than those used by the Controller, as recommended by good practice, to sense objects and obstacles near the car. If the action of the Controller would cause a safety hazard (i.e., potential for a crash: e.g., not braking when crossing the minimum safe distance from an obstacle in front), the SM triggers emergency braking.

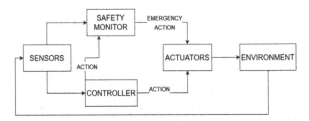

Fig. 1. System architecture

4.1 Terminology

Neural networks can be trained over long periods, using multiple data sets to improve their performance. Their evolution is described by the changes in their internal parameters, i.e., weights of the prediction function. We define a *checkpoint* as the set of weights of the NN's function after a series of training steps. We say: checkpoint$_i$ < checkpoint$_j$ if checkpoint j is obtained from checkpoint i after a number of training steps. We define C_i as "the Controller obtained at checkpoint i" and will refer to it just as "Controller" when the level of training is irrelevant. Note that $j > i$ only means that C_j had more training than C_i, not necessarily that it performs better.

The Controller's task is to drive the car efficiently and safely, while obeying traffic laws. In practice in our simulation, since the car's training was stopped at a comparatively immature stage, we allowed all simulated trips to continue until a crash occurred. Since we are only interested, at this stage of the work, in safety, we define a failure of the Controller as:

"Any action taken by the Controller that would result in a crash", i.e., the output of the Controller will trigger a transition from inside to outside the space of safe states. The safety performance of the Controller can be evaluated as a rate of accidents per km, or per unit of time in operation, or per trip.

Whenever the Controller fails, the SM has to detect this situation and intervene as soon as possible to prevent the imminent crash. The SM may respond correctly, which will in some cases avert the accident and lead the system to a safe state. Obviously, the SM can fail as well, in one of these two ways:

- It does not detect the problem (obstacle).
- It detects the obstacle and takes action, but the car still crashes.

The Safety Monitor can thus be seen as an "extended binary classifier" that classifies the system's state as safe or unsafe, based on the Controller's actions and sensor data, and takes action accordingly. Its performance can be described via a matrix, akin to the Confusion Matrix for a classifier, but related to results of actions (e.g., success or failure of a safety intervention) rather than just classification decisions.

4.2   Description of the State Space

We divide the state space of the system (Controller plus Safety Monitor) into:

- *Safe States*: all the states in which the Controller does not need the intervention of the Safety Monitor, and the Monitor does not intervene.
- *Mitigation States*, in which the Controller behavior would lead to a system failure (accident), but the Monitor correctly prevents the crash.
- *False Alert States*: the states in which the Controller does not need the intervention of the Safety Monitor, but the Monitor wrongly intervenes.
- *Accident States*: all the states in which the Controller's behavior leads to a crash which *are not* solved by the Monitor.

The actions of the Controller cause transitions between the system states. Figure 2 is a Venn diagram representing the events "transitions from the safe state". Areas represent event probabilities, determined by the system and its environment, and which will normally change if the system components change (e.g., through machine learning). For reasonably safe systems, transitions to *safe states* and *mitigation states* will be much more likely than the others. For good availability, performance, comfort, transitions to *false alert states* should also be rare.

Any further training of the Controller will change its behavior and thus the probabilities associated to each transition. If the probabilities of transitions to both *safe states* and *mitigation states* increase, system safety improves. However, it is also possible that, even if the Controller learned to drive very safely (i.e., the probability of transitions to *safe states* gets very large), transitions to *accident states* also become more frequent, at the expenses of transitions to the *mitigation states*. These two possible effects of training *that makes the Controller safer* are shown in Fig. 3. Starting from the diagram in Fig. 2, additional training may produce, among others, either one of these two Venn diagrams.

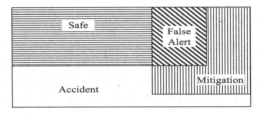

Fig. 2. "Safe" + "False Alerts" indicates probability of the Controller continuing safe operation; the squarish rectangle on the right, "False Alerts" + "Mitigation", represents the SM's interventions. The remaining white area rep resents initiation of accidents.

5   Study Method

To test the Controller at different stages of its training, we generated m checkpoints, resulting in m Controllers $C_1...C_m$. We tested all these on the same predefined set of scenarios, to observe how well the ML component handles the same task (i.e., reaching a target destination, via specified waypoints, given a starting position, in the same environmental conditions) at different stages of its training. A "scenario" is defined by the initial conditions of the environment in which the system is tested. This includes the starting point, seeds for random number generators, a target destination and intermediate waypoints, and environmental conditions such as weather and traffic density. Scenarios can be made more difficult by manipulating conditions, e.g., by increasing the traffic present in the environment or by simulating adverse weather. We call the difficulty levels h_0, h_1, etc. A higher subscript represents greater difficulty: if $x < y$, h_y is designed to be harder than h_x. We note that a level that is harder for the Controller may not be harder for the SM monitoring *that* Controller in *that* environment.

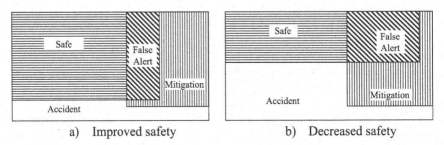

a)   Improved safety   b)   Decreased safety

Fig. 3. Examples of training that improves the Controller's safety shown in Fig. 2. In case a) this improvement reduces hazards that the SM could not mitigate; in case b) it reduces hazards that the SM would mitigate, while adding some that the SM cannot mitigate.

5.1   Paired Tests with and Without Safety Monitor

The Controllers were first tested without the Safety Monitor in every scenario, until the car reached the target destination, or crashed. Our setup also allows a test to be stopped earlier, but we did not use this option.

For every such trip, we recorded the initial conditions and the sequence of actions chosen by the Controller; then "replayed" the run exactly, but activating the SM, to observe whether it intervenes correctly to interrupt the specific accident sequences that ended SM-less runs.

This setup allows one not only to observe "how good" the SM is in preventing failures, but also, in some cases, to understand which situations are difficult for the Controller, and which ones are difficult for the Safety Monitor.

In more detail: in the run with the Safety Monitor, we record all the alerts it raises in each simulation step, but with safety braking *disabled* until it becomes necessary to prevent the collision that ended a specific SM-less run. To this end, we computed by what earlier time t the hazard must be detected so that braking may prevent the accident. We assumed that any alert raised by the Safety Monitor before time t is not necessary and thus a *false alarm*. After time t, that is, during the series of simulation frames that directly resulted in a crash, we enable emergency braking by the SM. If the imminent collision is avoided, we terminate the run and log a successful SM intervention.

These precautions are needed because if we simply re-ran each SM-less run, from the same initial conditions but with the SM active, the sequence of events that led to a crash might not happen again: e.g., a false alert by the SM could slow down the car so that it would not encounter the same hazard.

In the present study, we enabled emergency braking 2 seconds before the accident happened; this interval was chosen based on the maximum speed (50 km/h) the car can reach, the reaction time needed to respond to the hazard, and the distance required for braking. In the last 2 seconds of the simulation, an alert raised by the SM will now effectively make the car brake.

We note that with this setup our test of the Safety Monitor will omit some events of potential interest: in reality, false alarms may cause accidents, e.g., if hard braking causes the vehicle to be hit from behind. This risk complicates the task of specifying safety monitors. This potential for the SM to cause accidents is also one way that improving the Controller may make the vehicle less safe, e.g., if the Controller learns "bold" maneuvers that it would complete safely but that prompt a SM to apply potentially risky emergency actions. We left the simulation of these more complex effects to future research; the focus of this study was to demonstrate subtle problems in safety arguments even with a safety monitor whose interventions are always beneficial.

5.2 Evaluation of the Components and the System (Vehicle) Safety

We define the event "a crash would occur without the SM" as "C_crash" (Controller crash). We define classes of correct and wrong actions of the SM as follows:

- *Successful Intervention (SI)*. Every crash prevented by the SM: the safety response of the SM triggers a transition from a *safe* state to a *mitigation* state.
- *False Alarm (FA)*. Each alert raised by the SM when the system is in a *safe state*.
- *True Negative (TN)*. The system is in a *safe state* and the SM does not raise an alert.
- *Crash (CR)*. Every crash not prevented by the Safety Monitor, i.e., there is a transition from a *safe* state to an *accident* state.

From the recorded counts of these events, we derived safety measures of interest. First, we computed the Coverage (COV) of the SM, the ratio between the number of crashes avoided by the SM and the number of crashes that the Controller would cause if the SM were not present, that is:

$$COV = \frac{number\ of\ SIs}{number\ of\ C\_crashes} \tag{1}$$

We also compare the rate of occurrence of accidents per kilometer caused by the Controller without a Safety Monitor:

$$P(C\_crash) = \frac{number\ of\ C\_crashes}{kilometers\ driven} \tag{2}$$

with the rate when the SM is active:

$$P(crash) = \frac{number\ of\ Crashes}{kilometers\ driven} \tag{3}$$

We also measure (but did not analyze in detail) the False Alarm Rate:

$$FAR = \frac{number\ of\ FAs}{number\ of\ FAs\ +\ number\ of\ TNs} \tag{4}$$

The SM may raise a false alarm at any time during a simulation run, while the Coverage is measured on the number of crashes, which happen once per run at most.

These measures are sufficient for answering the immediate questions of this study. This simulation setup allows one also to assess, for instance, Mean Distance Between Accidents, Mean Time Between Accidents and Reliability Functions related to accidents and False Alarms.

Another study of interest would consider the severity of accidents. For example, a crash at 10 km/h against a fence may be flagged as a less serious failure than hitting a group of pedestrians at 50 km/h. These data can be used to observe correlations between failure modes and difficulty levels that may be counterintuitive, such as a Controller that crashes more frequently with *vehicles* when the number of *pedestrians* is increased.

6   Details of the Simulation

6.1   CARLA Simulator

We used CARLA 0.8.4 [21], an open-source simulator, sponsored by Intel and Toyota among others. It provides a realistic urban environment and was developed specifically to train and test autonomous vehicles controlled by ML components. It allows full customization and control over vehicles, pedestrians, weather, and sensors. In this version of CARLA there are four sensors:

- *Scene Final Camera:* provides a view of the scene like that produced by ordinary cameras

- *Depth Map Camera:* provides a depth mapping of the objects in the environment.
- *Semantic Segmentation Camera:* it paints object pertaining to different classes (e.g., vehicles and pedestrians) with different colors.
- *LiDAR sensor:* Light Detection and Ranging creating a 3D map of the surroundings.

The Depth Map Camera and the Semantic Segmentation Camera provide ground truth values for depth mapping and object classification. The ray-cast based LiDAR provided by CARLA was tuned to simulate a slightly modified version of the HDL-64E Velodyne LiDAR. The modifications were necessary because of the computational cost required to simulate a real LiDAR.

6.2 Implementation of the Controller and Safety Monitor

The Controller was implemented using the implementation of the Deep Deterministic Policy Gradient (DDPG) algorithm [22], provided by Coach, a framework for reinforcement learning developed by Intel's AI Labs [23]. The DDPG algorithm was chosen because it is specifically designed for environments with a continuous action space, such as the one we study, and it proved to perform well in driving tasks.

The Safety Monitor, implemented using the Point Cloud Library [24], is based in part on E. Bozkurt's project "Lidar Obstacle Detection", available on GitHub [25]. It implements a safety braking function using non-ML processing of data from the LiDAR sensor to map the environment. Using two consecutive measurements, it can track objects in the environment and estimate the relative speed of objects in front of the car. Thus, it is possible to implement a safety routine based on the braking distance between the car and the object detected, and their relative speed. To test the efficacy of the whole safety routine (not only the ability of the SM to raise an alert) the runs previously recorded without the SM are repeated with it, rather than just replaying the LiDAR data from them to the Safety Monitor to record the alerts raised.

6.3 Structure of the Study

We collected 5 checkpoints from the training activity: Controllers C_1 to C_5. CARLA offers 150 predefined locations in the city. For each one of these, we created a trip specification that started from it and had to travel through a randomly selected sequence of 15 other locations (the latest one being the destination of that trip). Each trip specification was then combined with 4 different traffic conditions, or "difficulty levels", h_0, h_1, h_2, h_3, to vary the difficulty of the Controller's task:

h0) *Default*: the map is generated with 30 pedestrians and 15 vehicles.
h1) *Pedestrians:* the number of pedestrians in the map is doubled.
h2) *Vehicles:* the number of vehicles in the map is twice that in h0.
h3) *Pedestrians and Vehicles:* both pedestrians and vehicles are twice as many as in h0.

From each combination of trip specification and difficulty levels we created 4 scenarios by applying different Random Number Generator seeds in CARLA. We thus had $4 \times 150 \times 4 = 2400$ test scenarios, on which each Controller C_i was tested with and without the Safety Monitor. A SM-less run ends when a collision happens, or the car reaches its destination (passing by the intermediate waypoints). The paired run with SM is ended at the same point, as explained in Sect. 5.1.

The simulation runs at a fixed time step of 10 Frames Per Second, so the number of simulation steps created per second of simulated time is an invariant. This avoids potential accuracy problems with timing and measurements and gives a reference time-base to compute time-dependent metrics.

7   Results of the Simulation

7.1   Controller

Table 1 shows the rates of occurrence of crashes of Controllers C_1 to C_5, operating, *without* the SM, at the four levels of environment difficulty.

One sees that there is safety improvement from C_1 to C_5: e.g., the rate at difficulty h_0 improved from 0.95 for C_1 to 0.29 for C_5, although the improvement is non-monotonic (e.g., C_3 is less safe than C_2). Moreover, the way we manipulated difficulty from h_0 to h_3 appears effective: it actually makes the environment more difficult for the Controller, as $P(C\_crash)_{hi} < P(C\_crash)_{hj}$ if $j > i$, for all Controllers (except for C_2 performing slightly better in h_1 than in h_0).

7.2   Safety Monitor

The Safety Monitor was tested with the procedure described in Sect. 5.2.

Table 2 shows the COV, and FAR of the SM combined with each Controller, for each difficulty level. We observe that as the Controller was trained, the coverage of the SM remained almost unchanged between C_1 and C_2, decreased for C_3, increased again a bit with C_4 and drastically dropped with C_5. Decreased coverage of the SM represents the fact that among the hazardous situations created by the Controller, a larger fraction is harder for the SM to mitigate successfully.

These data confirm that the efficacy of an unchanging SM may depend heavily on the behavior of the Controller, that is, for a ML component, on its training level. With training, the Controller learns to handle by itself some or most of the situations that previously required the SM to intervene; but the fewer hazardous situations it now creates may be too hard for the SM to handle, reducing its effectiveness.

7.3   Whole-Vehicle Evaluation

Table 3 shows the following measures: the rate of occurrence (per km) of crashes if Controller is operating without SM, $P(C\_crash)$ (from Table 1), the coverage of the SM (from Table 2), and the rate of occurrence (per km) of crashes with the SM active, $P(crash)$. These three rows are repeated for each difficulty level, $h_0,...,h_3$.

Table 1. Rate of occurrence P(C_crash), per kilometer, of crashes caused by the Controller, in each difficulty level.

	C_1	C_2	C_3	C_4	C_5
h_0	0.95	0.5	0.66	0.54	0.29
h_1	0.95	0.48	0.68	0.64	0.32
h_2	0.96	0.69	0.76	0.79	0.51
h_3	0.97	0.74	0.79	0.8	0.55

Table 2. Coverage and false alarm rate of the SM paired with each Controller

		C_1	C_2	C_3	C_4	C_5
h_0	COV	0.76	0.76	0.69	0.72	0.57
	FAR	0.005	0.007	0.007	0.008	0.006
h_1	COV	0.73	0.73	0.7	0.66	0.54
	FAR	0.005	0.007	0.007	0.008	0.005
h_2	COV	0.71	0.75	0.71	0.73	0.6
	FAR	0.004	0.009	0.009	0.01	0.008
h_3	COV	0.73	0.74	0.7	0.7	0.6
	FAR	0.004	0.009	0.008	0.01	0.008

Looking at the first two rows, P(C_crash) and COV, for any difficulty level, we see that between the worst and best Controller C_1 and C_5, both decrease: as the Controller learned to cause fewer accidents, it reduced the ability of the SM to *prevent* an accident. Such patterns of contrasting changes appear repeatedly in the table. For example, between the two best Controllers, C_2 and C_5, we observe that for any difficulty level, P(C_crash) improved but COV became worse: $P_{C5}(C\_crash) < P_{C2}(C\_crash)$ but $COV_{C2} > COV_{C5}$. E.g., at difficulty h_0, the additional training that resulted in a 42% improvement of the Controller ($P_{C2}(C\_crash) = 0.5$ but $P_{C5}(C\_crash) = 0.29$) caused a reduction of almost 25% in the coverage of the SM ($COV_{C2} = 0.76 > COV_{C5} = 0.57$). Thus, using the coverage measured on a version of the Controller to estimate the accident rate for a different version may err on the side of optimism.

Table 3. Essential measures of vehicle safety and SM efficacy at different stages of training of the Controller

		C_1	C_2	C_3	C_4	C_5
	P(C_crash)	0.95	0.5	0.66	0.54	0.29
h_0	COV	0.76	0.76	0.69	0.72	0.57
	P(crash)	**0.228**	**0.12**	**0.2046**	**0.1512**	**0.1247**
	P(C_crash)	0.95	0.48	0.68	0.64	0.32
h_1	COV	0.73	0.73	0.7	0.66	0.54
	P(crash)	**0.2565**	**0.1296**	**0.204**	**0.2176**	**0.1472**
	P(C_crash)	0.96	0.69	0.76	0.79	0.51
h_2	COV	0.71	0.75	0.71	0.73	0.6
	P(crash)	**0.2784**	**0.1725**	**0.2204**	**0.2133**	**0.204**
	P(C_crash)	0.97	0.74	0.79	0.8	0.55
h_3	COV	0.73	0.74	0.7	0.7	0.6
	P(crash)	**0.2619**	**0.1924**	**0.237**	**0.24**	**0.22**

Next, we can compare the first and third rows for each difficulty level: the rate of occurrence of crashes without the SM, P(C_crash), against the rate of occurrence of crashes for the complete vehicle (C plus SM), P(crash):

1. adding our SM ·to *any* version of the Controller reduces the probability of crash if compared to that of the Controller alone.
2. This confirms that our SM is effective. Indeed, this simulation setup is such that it allows the SM to prevent crashes but not cause them, as explained in Sect. 5.1.
3. but making the Controller safer has in certain cases made the vehicle *less* safe.

E.g., Controller C_5 without SM is safer than C_2, but with the SM, the vehicle with Controller C_5 crashes more often that with Controller C_2. The worst case is for difficulty h2: C_5 by itself would cause 26% fewer crashes than C_2, but C_5 with the SM causes 18% crashes more than C_2 with SM. The system was safer with C_2 thanks to the greater efficacy of SM with that Controller, that is, thanks to C_2's flaws "favouring" those accidents that the SM can prevent. Point 2 above indeed proves that, in certain situations, the decreased coverage of the SM may outstrip the Controller improvement and reduce overall vehicle safety. Table 4 highlights this by showing accident rates obtained for the vehicle with C_2, with C_5, and in a hypothetical calculation for C_5 under the wrong assumption of unchanging coverage, i.e., multiplying the SM coverage measured with C_2 by $P_{C5}(C\_crash)$. The wrong assumption would lead to an underestimation of the accident rate by 39%.

Table 4. Accident rates (per km, averaged over difficulty levels) of the system for different configurations: $C_2 + SM$, $C_5 + SM$ (observed values), and for the system under the wrong assumption of unchanging coverage of the SM.

	$C_2 + SM$	$C_5 + SM$	C_5 with COV_2
P(crash)=P(C_crash)(1-COV)	0.154	0.174	0.1066

8 Concluding Remarks

We have shown an empirical example of how an error checker's (our SM's) efficacy may change when the system that it monitors changes ("learns"). The essential conclusions are that:

1. In this study the safety monitor made *safer every* version of the monitored system, yet it may be *less effective* on an improved version of the monitored system (one that is *safer* than the previous version, *without* the safety monitor).
2. this reduction of coverage may be so large that the new, improved version of the monitored system may be *less safe*, when paired with the safety monitor, than the earlier, worse version was, when paired with the same safety monitor.

With the frequent, hard-to-analyze changes typical in the development of machine learning systems, the implication is that architectures that pair ML components with safety monitors need joint quantitative assessment of the entire architecture at every change of the ML component, a much more onerous process than separate assessment of the ML-based part alone and of the safety monitor, as is often advocated.

Our very basic experiment does not prove that such "unwelcome surprises" will be common in real-life systems, or in autonomous cars in particular; nor that they will be rare. It proves instead that safety arguments cannot assume them to be rare or impossible. We ran the simulations on an "immature" simulated car, allowing us to count large numbers of events that in a real, mature products would very rare. Thus, the car was unsafe from the start, improved very quickly and yet was still unrealistically unsafe at the point where we took the final set of measurements. We do not propose the numbers we report as generalizable to any real-world situation, but rather as a *proof of existence* of the phenomena of concern, lest they be thought possible "only in theory".

These early observations suggest directions for future work including: applying this methodology to more thoroughly trained Controllers, with repeated training, to study the likelihoods of the various possible trends in how improvements to the Controller affect SM coverage; studying how variations in training strategy affect these likelihoods (e.g., would using SM alerts as input in the training, to make the Controller safer, exacerbate the reduction in SM coverage?); a more complete simulation design that allows for SM-caused accidents; more detailed measurement to study various trade-offs involving severity of accident, ride comfort, energy efficiency.

Acknowledgements. Strigini's work was supported in part by ICRI-SAVe, the Intel Collaborative Research Institute on Safe Automated Vehicles. The authors are grateful to Peter Bishop for his insightful comments on the results.

References

1. WAYMO: Technology. https://waymo.com/tech/. Accessed 23 Dec 2021
2. NVIDIA: Training AI for Self-Driving Vehicles: the challenge of scale. https://developer.nvidia.com. Accessed 23 Dec 2021
3. Drago Anguelov (Waymo): MIT Self-Driving Cars (2019)
4. WAYMO: Waymo Safety Report (2021)
5. UNECE: UN Regulation on Advanced Emergency Braking Systems for cars to significantly reduce crashes (2019)
6. EU: Road safety: commission welcomes agreement on new EU rules to help save lives (2019)
7. American Safety Council – Should Autonomous Emergency Braking be Mandatory?
8. Popov, P., Strigini, L.: Assessing asymmetric fault-tolerant software. ISSRE, IEEE (2010)
9. Zhao, X. et al.: Assessing safety-critical systems from operational testing: a study on autonomous vehicles. Inform. Software Technol. **128**, 106393 (2020)
10. Littlewood, B., Strigini, L.: Validation of ultrahigh dependability for software-based systems. Commun. ACM **36**, 69–80 (1993)
11. Butler, R.W., Finelli, G.B.: The infeasibility of quantifying the reliability of life-critical real-time software. IEEE Trans. Software Eng. **19**(1), 3–12 (1993)

12. Kalra, N., Paddock, S.M.: Driving to safety: how many miles of driving would it take to demonstrate autonomous vehicle reliability? Transportation Research Part A: Policy and Practice (2016)

13. Koopman, P., Wagner, M.: Autonomous vehicle safety: an interdisciplinary challenge. IEEE Intell. Transp. Syst. Magaz. **9**, 90–96 (2017)

14. Varshney, K.R.: Engineering safety in machine learning. IEEE ITA (2016)

15. Nguyen, A., Yosinski, J., Clune, J.: Deep neural networks are easily fooled: High confidence predictions for unrecognizable images. CVPR, IEEE, pp. 427–436 (2015)

16. Zhao, D., et al.: Autonomous driving simulation for unmanned vehicles. In: IEEE Winter Conference on Applications of Computer Vision, pp. 185–190 (2015)

17. Baltodano, S., et al.: The RRADS platform: a real road autonomous driving simulator. In: Proceedings of AUTOUI, pp. 281–288 (2015)

18. Osiński, B., et al.: Simulation-based reinforcement learning for real-world autonomous driving. IEEE ICRA, pp. 6411–6418 (2020)

19. Koopman, P., Wagner, M.: Challenges in autonomous vehicle testing and validation. SAE Int. J. Transp. Saf. **4**(1), 15–24 (2016)

20. Grigorescu, S., et al.: A survey of deep learning techniques for autonomous driving. J. Field Robot. **37**(3), 362–386 (2020)

21. Dosovitskiy, A., et al.: CARLA: an open urban driving simulator. CoRL, pp. 1–16 (2017)

22. Lillicrap, T.P., et al.: Continuous Control with Reinforcement Learning. arXiv:150902971 (2015)

23. Caspi, I., Leibovich, G., Novik, G., Endrawis, S.: Reinforcement Learning Coach (2017)

24. Rusu, R.B., Cousins, S.: 3d is here: Point cloud library (pcl). IEEE ICRA, pp. 1–4 (2011)

25. Bozkurt, E.: LidarObstacleDetection (2019). https://github.com/enginBozkurt/

26. Greengard, S.: Gaming machine learning. Commun. ACM **60.12** (2017)

27. Singh, N., et al.: Facial recognition using deep learning. In: Jain, V., Chaudhary, G., Taplamacioglu, M., Agarwal, M. (eds.) Advances in Data Sciences, Security and Applications, LNEE, vol. 612, pp. 375–382. Springer, Singapore (2020). https://doi.org/10.1007/978-981-15-0372-6_30

28. Rao, Q., Jelena F.: Deep learning for self-driving cars: Chances and challenges. SEFAIS 2018

29. Ravi, M., Kantheti, S.C.: Application of artificial intelligence in healthcare: chances and challenges. Curr. J. Appl. Sci. Technol. (2021)

30. Hoang, D.-T., Kang, H.-J.: A survey on deep learning based bearing fault diagnosis. Neurocomputing **335**, 327–335 (2019)

31. Jesse, L., et al.: Towards fully autonomous driving: Systems and algorithms. In: 2011 IEEE Intelligent Vehicles Symposium (IV). IEEE (2011)

32. Koorosh, A., et al.: SafeML: Safety monitoring of machine learning classifiers through statistical difference measures. In: Zeller, M., Höfig, K. (eds.) IMBSA, LNPSE, vol. 12297. Springer, Cham (2020). https://doi.org/10.1007/978-3-030-58920-2_13

33. Kurd, Z., Kelly, T., Austin, J.: Developing artificial neural networks for safety critical systems. Neural Comput. Appl. **16**(1), 11–19 (2007)

34. Randy, G., et al.: Explainable AI: the new 42? In: Holzinger, A., Kieseberg, P., Tjoa, A., Weippl, E. (eds.) CD-MAKE, LNISA, vol. 11015. Springer, Cham (2018). https://doi.org/10.1007/978-3-319-99740-7_21

35. Cheng, C.-H.: Safety-aware hardening of 3D object detection neural network systems. In: Casimiro, A., Ortmeier, F., Bitsch, F., Ferreira, P. (eds.) SAFECOMP, LNPSE, vol. 12234. Springer, Cham, 2020. https://doi.org/10.1007/978-3-030-54549-9_14

36. Koopman, P., et al.: Credible autonomy safety argumentation. SCSC, UK (2019)

37. Gauerhof, L., Munk, P., Burton, S.: Structuring validation targets of a machine learning function applied to automated driving. In: Gallina, B., Skavhaug, A., Bitsch, F. (eds.) SAFECOMP 2018. LNCS, vol. 11093, pp. 45–58. Springer, Cham (2018). https://doi.org/10.1007/978-3-319-99130-6_4
38. Huang, X., et al.: A survey of safety and trustworthiness of deep neural networks: verification, testing, adversarial attack and defence, and interpretability. Comput. Sci. Rev. **37**, 100270 (2020)

Comprehensive Analysis of Software-Based Fault Tolerance with Arithmetic Coding for Performant Encoding of Integer Calculations

Marc Fischer[(⊠)] , Oliver Riedel , and Armin Lechler

Institute for Control Engineering of Machine Tools and Manufacturing Units, University of Stuttgart, 70174 Stuttgart, Germany
marc.fischer@isw.uni-stuttgart.de

Abstract. Safety-critical systems are becoming more complex with use cases like autonomous driving or human-robot collaboration. Therefore, the performance impact of software-based fault-tolerance methods is challenging. Using software-based fault tolerance is an attractive approach because commercial off-the-shelf hardware can be used. One possibility to implement software-based fault tolerance are arithmetic codes, already used in safety-critical products. Recently, AN codes have received particular attention; however, they have a significant performance impact in complex safety applications that require 64-bit wide integer calculations. Therefore, we comprehensively analyze different arithmetic codes in this work to identify the best suitable 64-bit integer support. We identify the ones' complement as the best matching encoding strategy through new code metrics, fault simulations, and performance analysis. We validate our results by applying ones' complement coding to a sample algorithm. Performance measurements and fault injection simulation confirm our results.

Keywords: Arithmetic coding · Fault tolerance · Ones' complement

1 Introduction

Unreliability of hardware is an ever-increasing problem for systems depending on hardware. Not only do safety-critical systems face the challenge of dealing with unreliability, but others like Google's cloud farms face this issue as well, according to a new report [14]. One reason for hardware unreliability are hardware faults caused by various impacts in the lifetime of hardware from specification and implementation over fabrication to the run-time [4]. The faults can manifest in form of errors, e.g., a flipped bit. Therefore, typically, bit-flip or stuck-at fault models are used to describe the impact of a hardware fault on gate-level [4]. The errors can further lead to system failure. Hardware faults are typically classified by their duration into permanent, transient, and intermittent faults [2].

© The Author(s), under exclusive license to Springer Nature Switzerland AG 2022
M. Trapp et al. (Eds.): SAFECOMP 2022, LNCS 13414, pp. 144–157, 2022.
https://doi.org/10.1007/978-3-031-14835-4_10

Permanent faults continuously affect the system and can be caused by physical impacts during the operation phase of hardware like electromigration, gate oxide breakdown, shorts, or broken interconnections. Furthermore, permanent faults can be induced during chip fabrication due to the difficulties with decreasing structure sizes [4, 24]. Transient faults occur for a short time only and are caused, for example, by radiation, extreme temperatures, noisy power supply, and electrostatic discharge [24]. Intermittent faults also occur for a short time but periodically [4, 24].

1.1   Fault Tolerance

In safety-critical systems, the handling of hardware faults, also called fault tolerance, is required by standards like IEC-61508 as a system failure leads to injury or death of humans or the damage to machines or the environment. Fault tolerance is always based on redundancy [12]. Koren *et al.* [12] distinguishes between Hardware, Software, Time, and Information redundancy. In domains like manufacturing, aerospace, or automotive the use of hardware redundancy is common. Multiple physical copies of the hardware are provided, which requires the development of specialized hardware, introducing high costs and reducing flexibility [20]. Therefore, the use of commercial off-the-shelf (COTS) hardware in safety-critical systems is favored but requires other types of redundancy [17, 21].

We now provide a more profound insight into requirements and other redundancy methods enabling fault tolerance with COTS. First, the requirement of handling permanent, transient, and intermittent faults must be considered. Moreover, the redundancy method must be easily applicable for the end-user, in the best case automatically, and the implementation effort should be low. Moreover, use cases like collision detection within human-robot collaboration [10], cable-driven parallel robot simulators [6], or autonomous driving require complex safety functions with high computational cost and precision. Therefore, an essential requirement is the performant support of high precision, e.g., 64-bit processing of integers.

Time redundancy is defined as the repeated computation of software. Thus, only transient faults are detectable because permanent faults influence each computation equally, rendering detection impossible. Nevertheless, time redundancy can be used if combined with other redundancy forms. *Software redundancy* is often divided into single and multi-version [4, 12]. Single-version methods extend the functionality of the software to detect hardware faults like time checking, reasonableness checks, reversal checks, or structural checks [4]. The multi-version method uses multiple but different software versions where different teams, different languages, or different algorithms achieve the diversity [4]. The multi-version method can detect transient, permanent, and intermittent faults, but the effort for developing independent versions is high. *Information redundancy* adds information to a given value v by encoding it to the codeword v_c. Many coding techniques are available and used, e.g., in storage systems or communication. One group of codes are arithmetic codes which preserve the codes after arithmetic operations [4]. This feature enables performant and automated encoding of any algorithms consisting of arithmetic operations, such as shown in, e.g., [13,24,27].

1.2 Arithmetic Coding

Different codes exist within the arithmetic codes, which differ in the detection rate of hardware faults and the performance overhead. In the last few years mainly AN codes were analyzed in literature [8,9,13,16,22,23,27]. AN codes are successfully applied in safety-critical products of SIListra Systems [27]. The usage of AN codes requires more bits. In general a doubling of the used integer width is performed. A high-performance overhead follows when 64-bit integers are doubled to 128-bit on a 64-bit hardware platform because 128-bit calculations are realized in software with multiple 64-bit operations on such platforms. The literature does not address this problem adequately and no viable AN codes with performant support of 64-bit integer calculations can be found. The Residue and Inverse-Residual-Codes are named as an alternative to AN codes in the literature. However, no details about detection capabilities and performance overhead are given when using them for the encoding of a whole software [1,4,12,15,24]. Another possibility for arithmetic codes is the use of the complement [19, p. 21].

1.3 Contribution

Therefore, this paper makes a detailed comparison of arithmetic codings. First, a general strategy is presented in Sect. 2 to develop and analyze arithmetic codes. This strategy also gives other researchers guidance to evaluate works in this field. Next, we give insight into the implementation of every arithmetic coding in Sect. 3 and give the most performant alternatives where operations are not supported. In Sect. 4 the detection capabilities of the encodings are analyzed with the code distance and fault simulation. To the best of our knowledge, we are the first to analyze metrics for the combination of redundant execution and information diversity with arithmetic codings. Furthermore, in Sect. 5, we give a consistent comparison of the performance overhead of the different codings. The ones' complement has outstanding detection capabilities and generally lower performance overhead. Especially the 64-bit calculations have a lower performance impact. Hence, we experimentally validate the usage of the ones' complement with example algorithms in Sect. 6.

2   Encoding Strategy

Identifying the best suitable encoding for a specific use case requires a strategy. Therefore, we want to give guidance in identifying encoding methods by the following steps:

1. **Identify arithmetic coding requirements:** Arithmetic codes have advantages when used on arithmetic operations. If only data elements need to be encoded, other codes such as cyclic codes are a better option [4]. Thus, the necessity of arithmetic coding must be checked first.

2. **Identifying hardware fault types:** Next, the types of hardware faults must be identified to evaluate the behavior on upper system levels. Typically, permanent, intermittent, and transient faults are assumed in the literature. The faults can propagate through the systems, which lead to bit-flips and stuck-at faults on gate-level [4]. In this paper, we consider permanent, intermittent, and transient faults, too.

3. **Identifying a software-level error model:** When hardware faults are propagated through the system, they can cause software-level errors. An error model on the software level simplifies the application of codings. The encoding must cover all software-level errors. In literature, the errors *exchanged operand, exchanged operator, faulty operation, lost update*, and *modified operand* are often used and are introduced by Forin [8]. In this paper, we assume this error model, too. The model does not cover control-flow errors. Therefore, additional methods must be used to detect control-flow errors, e.g., [25], but this is not considered in our work.

4. **Determining detection rate of hardware faults:** In safety-critical systems, a minimum detection rate or availability is required. For example, in the IEC 61508 standard, a minimum safe failure fraction of 99% is demanded when using non-redundant hardware [11]. The detection rate can be analyzed theoretically with metrics like the hamming distance or code distance [4], or by residual error estimation like in [7]. We suggest a theoretical analysis of the coding method before the implementation. Furthermore, experimental fault injection experiments are often used in literature, for example, in [13,24] and should be used as an overall validation for the encoding approach.

5. **Implementation and application:** Implementing and applying the coding on programs must be evaluated together. The arithmetic code can be applied in different development stages and software levels. We distinguish compile-time and run-time for the development stages and instruction, function, and program-level for the software levels [20,24]. In the rest of the paper, we focus on compile-time approaches because the performance overhead of run-time using an interpreter is higher [24]. Furthermore, we use the program-level and apply the encoding on the source code because the human readability is high. Implementing an encoding requires a careful analysis of edge cases like overflow behavior or edge values and analysis for adapting the arithmetic operation due to particular behavior of the chosen coding like the required division by A in the multiplication of the AN-Coding. Special handling of edge cases or adaption of arithmetic operations increases the performance overhead. On some operations, the arithmetic codings cannot be applied in general, e.g., for the bitwise AND and OR. In this case, alternatives must be found, like replacing them with other operations or doing a reversal check. Safety-critical systems must meet real-time constraints with short response times. Thus, low-performance impact is needed. In a previous work, a procedure to identify the most performant implementation for floating-point operations is presented [6], which can be used similarly for integer operations.

6. **Developing a check mechanism:** Every encoding strategy needs a check mechanism to detect errors in the software execution. For AN codes, one

method is the usage of an accumulator where the result of an operation is added to the accumulator [13,24]. The accumulator can be checked for divisibility by the encoding constant A. Others like [9,27] check only the output values at the end of the program execution, which reduces the performance impact.

7. **Performance evaluation:** The performance overhead is an essential metric for selecting an arithmetic code. Comparing single instructions gives fundamental insight into the overhead, but realistic algorithms must be used for realistic results.

3   Comparison of Arithmetic Codes and Their Implementations

Before we analyze the detection capabilities and the performance overhead, we give a detailed overview over each encoding and their implementation. If an operation is not supported, we give an alternative method. Arithmetic codes are divided into separate and non-separate codes [1].

3.1   AN Codes

AN codes belong to the non-separate codes and are formed by multiplying a value $v \in \mathbb{N}$ by the constant $A \in \mathbb{N}$. The encoded value is denoted by v_c. Due to the multiplication, the encoded value is longer than the original value. In practice, this means doubling the integer width, e.g., from 32-bit integer to 64-bit integer. Schiffel states that AN codes cannot detect all types of faults and suggests the extension by ANB- or ANBD-codes [24]. In contrast to that, others solve the problem by using a duplicated execution where both channels are encoded differently [13,27]. The former method has better performance than the suggested ANBD-Codes from Schiffel. We call AN codes with duplicated execution separate AN codes. Schiffel [24] provides a good overview of implementing AN codes. Bitwise and logic operations cannot be encoded directly. For our tests, we replace the bitwise logic operations with De Morgan's laws, which are equivalent expressions for logical operations. The shift operations are replaced with multiplication and division and the logic operations are replaced with multiplication or division [24]. The comparison operators work on encoded values directly but must be adapt to return an encoded result. The division is adapted by the multiplication with A. The multiplication requires adaption due to the overflow behavior and the constant A. We remove A by decoding the second operand and use the same overflow correction as Schiffel.

$$\text{mul}(x_c, y_c)_c = x_c \cdot y - \frac{x \cdot y}{2^{\text{bitwidth}}} \cdot (2^{\text{bitwidth}} \cdot A) \tag{1}$$

The subtraction must handle underflow behavior, but the addition and the modulo can be used directly.

3.2   Residue-Codes

The residue code forms the residuum of a value for encoding values so that $v_c = v \bmod A$. The inverse residue code from [1] is formed by $v_c = A - (v \bmod A)$. The residuum is a surjective function and, therefore, we cannot decode values uniquely. Thus, decoding values is not possible. Some arithmetic operations on encoded values require over- and underflow handling, which can be handled solely with the uncoded values. Thus, the implementation must process a tuple (v, v_c) of the uncoded and coded values. Therefore, two independent channels cannot be realized. Bitwise and logic operators are not supported and can be replaced similar to the AN codes. The rest of the operations must be adapted, or the overflow and underflow behavior must be handled.

3.3   Complement-Codes

The idea behind the complement is to use the signed representation to encode values. The most common way of representing signed numbers is the two's complement because the same unsigned circuits for addition and subtraction can be used, and for the multiplication, only minor changes are needed [19]. Two other major systems are the ones' complement and the magnitude. Standard hardware does not support arithmetic operations in the magnitude system. Therefore, we do not consider it further.

A signed number is formed in the ones' complement by inverting each bit of the corresponding positive number. The two's complement is defined by adding 1 to the ones' complement.

The two's complement can be used for encoding values on standard systems with two's complement support. Similar to the other codes, adaption is required. For the signed multiplication and division, the sign of the result must be changed. The unsigned division and the unsigned modulo are not supported, and therefore, we use reversal checks instead. The comparisons and logic operations can operate directly with the encoded values, however the result is uncoded and hence must be encoded. The bitwise AND, OR, and XOR are not supported but can be replaced with De Morgan's laws. The XOR can be replaced with a reversal check. The left shift can be used directly on encoded values, but the right shift is not supported. We replace the right shift with division.

The ones' complement can also be used on standard systems but needs more adaption. A correction by $+1$ respectively -1 is required for addition and subtraction. Multiplication, division, and modulo are not supported. Therefore, we transfer the encoded values in the two's complement. After calculating, the values are transferred back in the ones' complement. As stated previously, the transfer is given by adding 1 to the ones' complement. The comparisons operations can operate directly on the encoded values, but require an encoding of the results similarly to the two's complement, and the logic operations are transformed in the two's complement. The bitwise AND and OR are modified based on De Morgan's laws so that $v_1 \wedge v_2$ operates on encoded values with $v_{1,c} \vee v_{2,c}$ because $v_c = \overline{v}$. The XOR operation only needs changed sign. The NOT operation works directly on encoded values, whereas the shift operations are not supported. Therefore, the shift operations are transformed in the two's complement.

3.4 Comparison

In Table 1, an overview of arithmetic codes and their encoding capability of all operations is given. We distinguish the signedness because there are differences for some operations.

Table 1. Overview over all operations and their encoding capability

	1's Complement		2's Complement		AN		Residual	
	Unsign.	Sign.	Unsign.	Sign.	Unsign.	Sign.	Unsign.	Sign.
Arith.								
+	Adapt.	Adapt.	Direct	Direct	Direct	Direct	OF corr.	OF corr.
-	Adapt.	Adapt.	Direct	Direct	UF corr.	Direct	UF corr.	UF corr.
×	No	No	Adapt.	Adapt.	Adapt.	Adapt.	OF corr.	OF corr.
/	No	No	No	Adapt.	Adapt.	Adapt.	No	No
mod	No	No	No	Direct	Direct	Direct	No	No
Comp.								
==	Adapt.	Adapt.	Adapt.	Adapt.	Adapt.	Adapt.	Adapt.	Adapt.
!=	Adapt.	Adapt.	Adapt.	Adapt.	Adapt.	Adapt.	Adapt.	Adapt.
<	Adapt.	Adapt.	Adapt.	Adapt.	Adapt.	Adapt.	No	No
>	Adapt.	Adapt.	Adapt.	Adapt.	Adapt.	Adapt.	No	No
<=	Adapt.	Adapt.	Adapt.	Adapt.	Adapt.	Adapt.	No	No
>=	Adapt.	Adapt.	Adapt.	Adapt.	Adapt.	Adapt.	No	No
Bitwise								
AND	No	No	No	No	No	No	No	No
OR	No	No	No	No	No	No	No	No
XOR	Adapt.	Adapt.	No	No	No	No	No	No
NOT	Direct	Direct	Adaption	Adaption	No	No	No	No
<<	No	No	Direct	Direct	No	No	No	No
>>	No	-	No	-	No	-	No	-
Logic								
LAND	Adapt.	Adapt.	Adapt.	Adapt.	No	No	No	No
LOR	Adapt.	Adapt.	Adapt.	Adapt.	No	No	No	No
LNOT	Adapt.	Adapt.	Adapt.	Adapt.	No	No	No	No

4 Fault Detection Capabilities

In this section, we analyze the fault detection capability of each arithmetic coding[1]. Transient, intermittent, and permanent faults must be detected. Thereby, the detection capability depends on the encoding constant A. Schiffel [24] and Ulbrich [28] state that traditional metrics like the code distance cannot be used directly to identify the fault detection capability of a non-separate code.

---

[1] The source code of all analyses and measurements in this paper can be found at https://github.com/iswunistuttgart/arithmetic-coding-int.

They use experimental fault simulation to identify the best constant A. The code distance $C_{d,n}$ of non-separate codes is the minimum hamming distance between any two distinct pairs of encoded values [4].

The code distance cannot be used with the definition above for separate codes. Instead, we define the code distance for separate codes $C_{d,s}$ as the minimum hamming distance of each tuple (v, v_c). Further, we use the average Hamming distance $\overline{H_d}$ and the quotient $\frac{\overline{H_d}}{\max H_d}$ as another metric. This allows us to select the best A when multiple code distances with the same value exist. In Table 2 the metrics are evaluated for each coding.

Table 2. Metrics for the different codings on 8 bit integers

Coding	1's comp.	2's comp.	AN sep.	Residue	Inv. residue
A	–	–	255	1	255
C_d	8	0	7	0	0
$\overline{H_d}$	8.00	6.01	10.02	4.00	7.97
$\frac{\overline{H_d}}{\max H_d}$	1	0.75	0.62	0.5	0.996

We use 8 bit width integers for calculating the metrics. We argue that the results can be generalized to wider integers. The ones' complement has the best detection capabilities where each tuple has a $C_{d,s} = 8$. The two's complement has a code distance $C_{d,n} = 0$ because the value 0 and the signed maximum value have the same binary representation. The other values have a higher code distance with an average of 6. The separate AN codes are calculated on 16-bit integers because the AN-Coding requires an up-scaling to 16-bit while encoding. The best results are given for $A = 255$, the maximum value of 8 bit wide integers. The results for the residue and inverse reside codes confirm Avizienis [1] statement that the inverse residue code has better detection capabilities.

Next, we simulate transient and permanent faults on the codes and count the undetected faults, also called silent data corruption (SDC). With the results, we want to validate the significance of the metrics for separate codes. Table 3 shows the results. We flip all possible bit patterns on each encoded and unencoded value for transient fault simulation and count the SDCs. With separate codes, transient faults can always be detected if the coding is an injective function. This is because only one duplication can be corrupted independent of the number of flipped bits. The residuum is a surjective function and cannot detect all transient faults. We stuck all possible bit patterns on each encoded and unencoded pair for permanent fault simulation and counted the SDCs. The simulation shows that the highest possible C_d and $\overline{H_d}$ for the one's complement can detect all permanent fault types. Furthermore, it can be seen that a quotient $\frac{\overline{H_d}}{\max H_d}$ closer to 1 has fewer undetected permanent faults.

Table 3. Fault simulation for the different codings on 8 bit integers

	Trans. SDCs	Perm. SDCs
1's comp.	0	0
2's comp.	0	$6.31 \cdot 10^3$
AN sep.	0	$1.77 \cdot 10^5$ (A = 255)
Residue	$6.53 \cdot 10^4$ (A = 1) 2 (A = 255)	$1.29 \cdot 10^6$ (A = 1) $1.50 \cdot 10^7$ (A = 255)
Inv. residue	2 (A = 255)	255 (A = 255)

5   Performance Overhead

In this section, we analyze the performance impact of the different codings. First, we compare the performance impact on single operations. We use a real-time Linux system with an Intel i7-4790K CPU @ 4.00 GHz and 16 GB RAM and execute each operation $2.5 \cdot 10^5$ times on an isolated core with real-time priorities.

The time for execution is measured, and the median of multiple runs is calculated. With these results, the slowdown S is calculated as $S = \frac{t_{encoded}}{t_{native}}$. In Fig. 1 the slowdown of the AN-Coding, Complement-Coding, and Residue-Coding is shown. The $t_{encoded}$ is the time for executing the operation in the encoded channel and native channel.

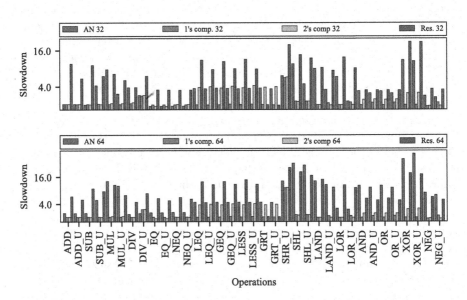

Fig. 1. Slowdown of each operation of different arithmetic codings

The overhead for 64-bit AN-Coding and Residue-Coding is higher than the 64-bit Complement-Coding because the AN-Coding requires a doubling of the integer width to 128-bit, which has lower performance. Furthermore, the mean slowdown of the ones' complement is with 2.2 for 32-bit and 2.3 for 64-bit lower compared to the two's complement with 2.7 and 2.8. The Residue-Coding requires complex overflow correction, so the performance overhead is higher than the AN-Coding. The slowdown of our codings is also lower than the ANB-Coding of Schiffel [24, p. 73].

For more realistic comparison, real-world algorithms must be used as stated in Sect. 2. The results depend on the algorithm. Therefore, in the next Section, matrix multiplication is used as a real-world algorithm.

6   Evaluation and Experimental Validation of the Ones' Complement

The comparison of the different arithmetic codings is now followed by an experimental evaluation.

6.1   Evaluation

We identified the ones' complement as the best suiting arithmetic coding with performant coding of 64-bit integers for the following reasons:

- In contrast to the other codings, it can detect all permanent faults if the faults are manifested as stuck-at errors on data values. This is due to the inversion of the bit pattern.
- The performance overhead is significantly lower compared to the AN-Coding and Residue-Coding for 64-bit, but also for 32-bit. This is because AN-Coding and Residue-Coding require more overflow and underflow corrections, and AN-Coding requires a doubling of the integer width. Furthermore, the mean overhead is slightly lower than the two's complement.
- The calculation of the redundant channels can be independently compared to the residue codes.

In the next section, we experimentally validate the ones' complement by applying it on an example algorithm. The performance overhead is measured and a fault injection simulation shows the fault detection capabilities.

6.2   Experimental Validation

We use a matrix multiplication of 64-bit integer values with dimensions of 100 × 100 as an example algorithm. We encode the algorithm with an automatic source-to-source approach based on the python library pycparser[2], which was already used in our previous work [6]. We use the same procedure as in

---

[2] https://github.com/eliben/pycparser.

Sect. 5 to measure the performance impact. In Table 4 the performance impact is shown. The slowdown of 6.34 for an 64-bit calculation is even lower compared to the 32-bit AN and ANBD-Coding of Schiffel [24], and comparable to the 32-bit Delta-Encoding of Kuvaiskii [13]. To the best of our knowledge, no performance measurements for 64-bit calculations can be found.

Table 4. Performance comparison of native execution and encoding with the ones' complement

	Native	1's complement
Median execution time	2.67 ms	16.9 ms
Slowdown	1	6.34

Moreover, we test the fault detection rate with stimulative fault injection. The Intel Pin-Tool[3] and the bit-flip injector (BFI) plug-in[4] is used, which is already applied in [6,7,13]. In Fig. 2 the results of the fault injection simulation are shown.

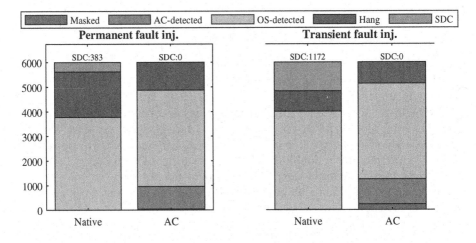

Fig. 2. Results of the fault injection simulation

We conducted 6000 experiments with randomly injected faults. For permanent faults random bits were either stucked at 0 or 1. For transient faults random bits were flipped. The results of the fault injections are divided into the following categories: masked, hang up the program (Hang), detected by the operating system (OS), detected by the arithmetic coding (AC), and not detected but

---

[3] https://software.intel.com/en-us/articles/pintool.
[4] https://bitbucket.org/db7/bfi.

influences the result (SDC). All injected faults are detected by the encoded program, which confirms our analysis in Sect. 4. Although the statement of an experimental validation is limited to the tested inputs and errors, it gives a good indication of the general detection capability. Comparing the results with similar experimental validations in the literature [13,22,24] our detection capability is better.

6.3   Outlook for Future Validation

To enable the usage in safety-certified products a formal validation must be used. In particular, the fault detection capability must be formally determined. Due to the complexity of electronic systems, a formal validation could be based on an error model like the model in Sect. 2. For each encoded operation, evidence must be given for the rate of SDCs over all possible input values and error possibilities.

7   Related Works

Works like [8,9,13,22,23,27] do not take the performance impact of 64-bit integers into account. Oh *et al.* [16] names the non-doubling of the integer width instead of checking for overflows during compile time. But this only works for small As. We close this gap and make a comprehensive analysis with different codings of the performance impact for 64-bit integers processing.

In current literature related to fault-tolerance like [4,12,15], the usage of the complement as arithmetic coding is not known. Surveys like [20,26] also focus on redundancy on different architectural layers but do not take the complement into account. Only Engel [5] gives a detailed analysis on using the ones' and two's complement by diversified redundancy on assembler and C-Level. Engel gives only some basic assumptions on the detection capabilities. In contrast to Engel, we calculate metrics and do fault simulation to determine the detection capabilities. Oh *et al.* [16] show weak points for the two's complement on stuck-at faults, which is why they suggest separate AN codes. A comprehensive and comparable analysis of the performance overhead cannot be found in the literature. Only non-comparable experiments are given for single arithmetic codes like in [13,24].

The selection of the best constant A is addressed in many works for non-separate AN-Coding like [3,24,28]. These works use metrics, e.g., the code distance for estimating the detection capabilities for each constant A. Also, for residue codes, the selection of A is analyzed [18]. For separate codings, no general comparison on the detection capabilities is given in the literature. In contrast, in this work we introduce an adapted code distance for separate codings and make a general comparison.

8   Conclusion

The rise in complexity of safety-critical systems requires performant fault tolerance methods. For software-based arithmetic coding, the current commonly used

AN-Coding lack performant support of 64-bit integer calculations. Therefore, a comprehensive analysis of arithmetic coding as a fault-tolerance method is made in this work. First, a general encoding strategy is introduced to enable a structured analysis and development of arithmetic codes. Based on this strategy, AN, Residue, and Complement-Codes are analyzed according to their implementation possibilities, their fault detection capabilities, and their performance overhead. We identified the ones' complement as the best suiting strategy for arithmetic coding because the performance overhead is lower and the detection capabilities are higher compared for the other methods. The effectiveness of the ones' complement is validated with an automatically encoded example algorithm. The slowdown of 6.34 for 64-bit integer calculations is even better than the results in the literature for AN-Coding. A fault injection simulation showed that every fault could be detected.

References

1. Avizienis, A.: Arithmetic error codes: cost and effectiveness studies for application in digital system design. IEEE Trans. Comput. **C-20**(11), 1322–1331 (1971)
2. Aviziens, A.: Fault-tolerant systems. IEEE Trans. Comput. **C-25**(12), 1304–1312 (1976)
3. Braun, J., Mottok, J.: The myths of coded processing. In: 17th International Conference on High Performance Computing and Communications, pp. 1637–1644. IEEE (2015)
4. Dubrova, E.: Fault-Tolerant Design. Springer, New York (2013). https://doi.org/10.1007/978-1-4614-2113-9
5. Engel, H.: Data flow transformations to detect results which are corrupted by hardware faults. In: IEEE High-Assurance Systems Engineering Workshop, pp. 279–285. IEEE Computer Society Press (1997)
6. Fischer, M., Riedel, O., Lechler, A.: Arithmetic coding for floating-points and elementary mathematical functions. In: 5th International Conference on System Reliability and Safety (ICSRS), pp. 270–275. IEEE (2021)
7. Fischer, M., Riedel, O., Lechler, A., Verl, A.: Arithmetic coding for floating-point numbers. In: IEEE Conference on Dependable and Secure Computing (DSC), pp. 01–08. IEEE (2021)
8. Forin, P.: Vital coded microprocessor principles and application for various transit systems. IFAC Proc. Vol. **23**(2), 79–84 (1990)
9. Früchtl, M.: Sicherheit eingebetteter Systeme auf Basis arithmetischer Codierungen. Ph.D. thesis, Universität Kassel, Kassel (2014)
10. Haddadin, S., de Luca, A., Albu-Schäffer, A.: Robot collisions: a survey on detection, isolation, and identification. IEEE Trans. Robot. **33**(6), 1292–1312 (2017)
11. ISO/IEC: IEC 61508-2 functional safety of electrical/electronic/programmable electronic safety-related systems - part 2: requirements for electrical/electronic/programmable electronic safety-related systems
12. Koren, I., Krishna, C.M.: Fault-Tolerant Systems. Elsevier Morgan Kaufmann, Amsterdam (2007)
13. Kuvaiskii, D., Fetzer, C.: Delta-encoding: practical encoded processing. In: 2015 45th Annual IEEE/IFIP International Conference on Dependable Systems and Networks (DSN 2014), pp. 13–24. IEEE Computer Society (2015)

14. Kwan, D., Shtoyk, K., Serebryany, K., Lifantsev, M.L., Hochschild, P.: SiliFuzz: fuzzing CPUs by proxy. Technical report, Google (2021)
15. Mukherjee, S.: Architecture Design for Soft Errors. Elsevier, Burlington (2008)
16. Oh, N., Mitra, S., McCluskey, E.J.: ED4I: error detection by diverse data and duplicated instructions. IEEE Trans. Comput. 51(2), 180–199 (2002)
17. O'Halloran, M., Hall, J.G., Rapanotti, L.: Safety engineering with COTS components. Reliab. Eng. Syst. Saf. 160, 54–66 (2017)
18. Omidi, R., Towhidy, A., Mohammadi, K.: A survey on the best choice for modulus of residue code. Indones. J. Electr. Eng. Inform. (IJEEI) 7(4), 734–741 (2020)
19. Omondi, A.R.: Cryptography Arithmetic: Algorithms and Hardware Architectures. Advances in Information Security, vol. 77. Springer, Cham (2020). https://doi.org/10.1007/978-3-030-34142-8
20. Osinski, L., Langer, T., Mottok, J.: A survey of fault tolerance approaches at different architecture levels. In: Trinitis, C., Pionteck, T. (eds.) ARCS 2017. VDE Verlag GmbH (2017)
21. Profeta, J.A., et al.: Safety-critical systems built with COTS. Computer 29(11), 54–60 (1996)
22. Reis, G.A., Chang, J., August, D.I.: Automatic instruction-level software-only recovery. In: International Conference on Dependable Systems and Networks, pp. 83–92. IEEE Computer Society (2006)
23. Reis, G.A., Chang, J., Vachharajani, N., Rangan, R., August, D.I.: SWIFT: software implemented fault tolerance. In: International Symposium on Code Generation and Optimization, pp. 243–254. IEEE Computer Society (2005)
24. Schiffel, U.: Hardware error detection using AN-codes. Ph.D. thesis, Technischen Universität Dresden, Dresden (2011)
25. Schuster, S., Ulbrich, P., Stilkerich, I., Dietrich, C., Schröder-Preikschat, W.: Demystifying soft-error mitigation by control-flow checking - a new perspective on its effectiveness. ACM Trans. Embed. Comput. Syst. 16(5s), 1–19 (2017)
26. Srikanth, S., Deng, B., Conte, T.M.: A brief survey of non-residue based computational error correction (2016)
27. Süßkraut, M., Schmitt, A., Kaienburg, J.: Safe program execution with diversified encoding. In: Proceedings of the 13th Embedded World Conference (2015)
28. Ulbrich, P.: Ganzheitliche Fehlertoleranz in eingebetteten Softwaresystemen. Ph.D. thesis, Friedrich-Alexander-Universität Erlangen-Nürnberg (FAU) (2014)

STPA-Driven Multilevel Runtime Monitoring for In-Time Hazard Detection

Smitha Gautham[1]([✉]), Georgios Bakirtzis[2], Alexander Will[1], Athira Varma Jayakumar[1], and Carl R. Elks[1]

[1] Virginia Commonwealth University, Richmond, VA, USA
{gauthamsm,willar,jayakumarar,crelks}@vcu.edu
[2] The University of Texas at Austin, Austin, TX, USA
bakirtzis@utexas.edu

Abstract. Runtime verification or runtime monitoring equips safety-critical cyber-physical systems to augment design assurance measures and ensure operational safety and security. Cyber-physical systems have interaction failures, attack surfaces, and attack vectors resulting in unanticipated hazards and loss scenarios. These interaction failures pose challenges to runtime verification regarding monitoring specifications and monitoring placements for in-time detection of hazards. We develop a well-formed workflow model that connects system theoretic process analysis, commonly referred to as STPA, hazard causation information to lower-level runtime monitoring to detect hazards at the operational phase. Specifically, our model follows the DepDevOps paradigm to provide evidence and insights to runtime monitoring on what to monitor, where to monitor, and the monitoring context. We demonstrate and evaluate the value of multilevel monitors by injecting hazards on an autonomous emergency braking system model.

Keywords: Dynamic safety management · Cyber-physical systems · STPA · Runtime verification · Runtime monitors · Hazard analysis

1 Introduction

Cyber-physical systems (CPS) are increasingly challenging to assess at design time with respect to system errors or hazards that could pose unacceptable safety risks during operation [16]. These challenges lead to the need for new methods allowing for a continuum between design time and runtime or operational assurance [7]. Safety and security assurance at design level must be extendable to the runtime domain, creating a shared responsibility for reducing the risk during deployment. These emerging methods include dynamic safety management [22], DepDevOps (dependable development operations continuum) [3], systematic safety and security assessment processes such as STPA (system-theoretic process analysis) and STAMP (systems-theoretic accident model and processes), and MissionAware [2].

M. Trapp et al. (Eds.): SAFECOMP 2022, LNCS 13414, pp. 158–172, 2022.
https://doi.org/10.1007/978-3-031-14835-4_11

One emerging solution to help with the DepDevOps continuum is runtime monitoring or verification that observes system behavior and provides assurance of safety and security during the operational phase [3,12]. Runtime verification uses a monitor that observes the execution behavior of a target system. A monitor is concerned with detecting violations or satisfactions of properties (e.g., safety, security, functional, timeliness, to name a few) during the operation phase of a CPS. Execution trace information (i.e., states, function variables, decision predicates, etc.) is extracted directly from the CPS and forwarded to the monitor, where temporal logic expressions, called critical properties, are elaborated with this trace data for an on-the-fly verification of system behavior.

To have effective runtime monitors, identifying critical properties to detect hazards (*what* to monitor) and efficiently placing monitors where hazards may originate (*where* to monitor) is crucial. However, most runtime monitoring frameworks for CPS emphasize *how to monitor* [18]. That is, runtime monitoring languages and tools primarily focus on (1) the expressiveness of the runtime verification language to capture complex properties, and (2) instrumenting a system to extract traces for monitoring, assuming the *what to monitor* comes from some higher-level safety analysis process or methodology. Integrating system-level hazard analysis processes with runtime monitor design is essential for "end-to-end" functional safety assessment standards such as IEC-61508 and ISO 26262 that require traceable safety assurance evidence from requirements to design to implementation.

Contributions. Our paper develops a well-formed workflow model which connects STPA hazard analysis information to lower level runtime monitoring used to detect hazards at the operational phase. Specifically, our model follows the DepDevOps paradigm to provide evidence and insights to runtime monitoring on: (1) what to monitor, (2) where to monitor, and (3) the context of the monitoring. Our work addresses the gap between safety analysis and runtime monitor formulation.

In particular, we simulate hazard scenarios specified by STPA using model-based design and engineering (MBDE) tools, in our case MathWorks Simulink, to understand the boundary where a system can transition from a safe into an unsafe state. During hazard analysis, simulating hazard scenarios can reveal losses and their causal factors. We can thereby design well-informed context-aware runtime monitors to augment verification and validation (V&V) performed at design time.

Related Work. STPA has been used extensively in avionics and automotive applications to study unsafe interactions among system components and how such interactions can result in unsafe control actions (UCAs) that may lead to system failures [13]. STPA indicates that a UCA may result from multiple causal factors at different layers in a CPS. For efficient detection of these causal factors, we developed a multilevel runtime monitoring framework to support *in-time anomaly detection*. In-time detection is the ability to detect hazard states before they lead to an accident and provide time for mitigation of the hazard. Multilevel monitoring was inspired by the fact that there is no single monitor type to solve in-time hazard detection problems of CPS. Instead, several types of monitors are usually needed to address this challenge [9].

STPA-driven runtime monitor design to ensure safety (and security) during the operational phase is an important and emerging research area. STPA is used to analyze unsafe system contexts in medical CPS to develop runtime safety monitors [1,24]. In addition, work in the runtime monitoring domain emphasizes accuracy and integration over formal property development, whether by monitoring CPS [19] or by adding safety checking to a pre-existing system, such as monitoring distributed algorithms [14]. Properties for autonomous vehicle monitoring are derived from analyzing prior test results rather than being developed during the design process [23]. We, instead, integrate runtime verification into CPS by creating properties through hazard analysis built into system design.

Service-oriented component fault trees are used for property derivation for runtime monitors with safety in mind [17]. Runtime monitors focus on the fault-tolerant qualities [10] rather than emphasizing property generation, whereas property generation is our primary focus. Design-time safety measures that use STPA and model-based system engineering similar to our autonomous emergency braking (AEB) case study could incorporate our methods for runtime assurance [6]. Attacks occur in hardware, communication, and processing levels within complex systems [4], and using monitors at multiple system levels can increase causal factor awareness [5,8].

2   STPA-Driven Runtime Monitor Design

An important motivation for this work is to explore an integrative approach to in-time hazard detection and informed risk that incorporates system level analysis into the design of monitoring architectures. Accordingly, we develop a STPA-driven model-based process for identifying and simulating hazard scenarios for designing multilevel runtime monitors (Fig. 1).

2.1   Losses, Hazards and Unsafe Control Actions

A CPS consists of multiple coordinating components, continuously sensing and processing inputs from the physical domain and human users, and performing software-intensive tasks to produce time-critical outputs. This complex interaction among system components at specific system states increases the possibility of transitioning a system from a safe operating region $\mathcal{G}$ into an unsafe hazard space $\bar{\mathcal{G}}$. We denote all the identified hazards as $H = \{H_1, H_2, H_3 \cdots H_n\}$. Such hazards can result in losses $L = \{L_1, L_2, L_3 \cdots L_m\}$ that include loss of life, damage to property, to name a couple. Higher-level safety constraints (system constraints) φ_s are derived from hazard analysis. These safety constraints result in safety requirements R_s that inform the system development stage.

We denote the finite set of all possible control actions as Σ. Σ is continuously influenced by the vehicle, environmental and operational context $\mathcal{CO}$ of the system. The context $\mathcal{CO}$ is a critical element in determining if a control action

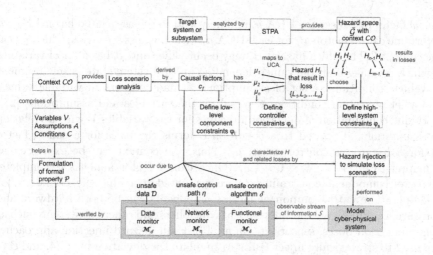

Fig. 1. STPA-driven runtime monitor generation.

is safe or unsafe. For example, consider a scenario where the road conditions must be considered to determine the time at which braking should be applied to avoid a collision. A braking action applied at a given time t may be safe to avoid a collision. Whereas if there are snowy road conditions, braking action applied at the same time t may be unable to avoid a collision. An earlier braking action or a collection of actions may be needed for it to be safe in a particular scenario. Therefore, in this context of snowy road conditions, the time when braking is applied determines if the braking action was safe or unsafe. Thus, we denote $\Sigma(\mathcal{CO}) = \mu(\mathcal{CO}) \cup \alpha(\mathcal{CO})$ where μ is the set of unsafe and α the set of safe control actions. UCAs from μ can drive the system to a hazardous state $\bar{\mathcal{G}}$. Every specific hazard H_i can be related to a finite subset of UCAs denoted by u_k, where $u_k \subseteq \mu$.

Safety constraints φ_c (sometimes called controller constraints) and safety requirements R_c are defined at the controller level. Although φ_c are typically incorporated into a design to prevent a hazard, there can be faults/attacks during operation that can violate the safety requirements R_c imposed by the designer. Furthermore, in some scenarios, φ_c cannot be enforced in a system. Runtime safety assurance via monitors is important for promptly detecting safety constraints and requirements violations to prevent a hazard.

2.2 Causal Factors and Relation to Multilevel Monitoring

Finding the possible causes for a specific UCA $\mu_i \in u_i$ is an essential step in preventing a hazard H_i. When a violation is detected, providing a timely safe control action α_i can prevent a system from transitioning into the unsafe operating region $\bar{\mathcal{G}}$, consequently avoiding a hazard.

We denote the causes for a UCA μ_i as a causal factor c_f. Causal factors c_f are directly related to a given UCA $\mu_i \in u_i$ (Fig. 1), where in a given context $\mathcal{CO}$ a causal factor c_f causes the UCA μ_i and may lead to the associated hazard H_i. To determine causal factors c_f for each UCA μ_i we define loss scenarios, which reveal the context $\mathcal{CO}$ in which hazard H_i may occur. The context has a set of variables $\mathcal{V}$ which can take multiple values depending on the system state or environment or vehicle conditions, a set of assumptions $\mathcal{A}$ made on certain variable values, and a set of system conditions $\mathcal{C}$ based on the variables and assumptions [21]. A unique combination of deviation in values for the variables $\mathcal{V}$ with a violation of assumptions $\mathcal{A}$ related to a condition $\mathcal{C}$ forms the basis for a causal factor c_f for a hazardous control action μ_i. Thus, the context can be expressed as a mapping $\mathcal{CO} \colon \mathcal{V} \times \mathcal{A} \times \mathcal{C} \to c_f$. Once causal factor analysis is complete, low-level component constraints φ_l are generated to define the boundary for safe operation at the component level. Components can be both hardware and software, i.e. functional modules such as controllers and other subsystems such as communication buses, sensors etc. in a CPS. Fault/hazard injection approaches are used to strategically inject faults to simulate the deviation in $\mathcal{V}$, $\mathcal{A}$, and $\mathcal{C}$ to create loss scenarios and test the boundaries of these constraints.

Further, the causal factors can specifically be related to one of the levels or layers in a multilevel view of the system. STPA provides suggestions for classification of causal factors for hazards that can occur at multiple levels, including controller-based (inadequate control algorithm, flawed control algorithm), input-based (unsafe data from other controllers, failure of sensor inputs), and control path-based (network delays, flaws in data process algorithm in a controller) [13]. For our multilevel monitoring structure, we define the following levels: unsafe data $\mathcal{D}$, unsafe processing δ, and unsafe behavior in the communication path η. The causal factors related to unsafe inputs to a controller from sensors, user inputs, or input from another controller as well as unexpected/incorrect data patterns are $\mathcal{D} = \{d_1, d_2, \cdots, d_n\}$, where $\mathcal{D} \in \mathcal{V} \times \mathcal{A}$. The causal factors related to flaws in the control algorithm and incorrect functional behavior in the controller are $\delta = \{\delta_1, \delta_2, \cdots, \delta_n\}$, where $\delta \in \mathcal{V} \times \mathcal{A} \times \mathcal{C}$. The causal factors related to flaws in the control path through which inputs/outputs are communicated between the subsystems are $\eta = \{\eta_1, \eta_2, \cdots, \eta_n\}$, where $\eta \in \mathcal{V} \times \mathcal{A} \times \mathcal{C}$. For timely detection of such causal factors before they result in a UCA μ_i, we believe that a viable approach is to employ monitors at these various levels of processing and integration where the vulnerabilities originate.

2.3   Multilevel Runtime Monitoring Framework

Multi-level monitoring extends traditional runtime verification or monitoring by providing a monitor classification or organization schema that maps monitor types to various functions or components in distributed real-time architectures [9]. In this work, we augment a multi-level monitoring framework [8] as it directly addresses monitoring CPS from multiple layer perspectives. A monitor $\mathcal{M}_a$ observes streams of time stamped information from a target CPS. A *stream*, denoted as $\mathcal{S}_a = \mathcal{S}_a(t-m), \cdots, \mathcal{S}_a(t-2), \mathcal{S}_a(t-1), \mathcal{S}_a(t)$, where $\mathcal{S}_a$ is a sequence of time-stamped information, from the past m instances starting with $\mathcal{S}_a(t-m)$ and ending at the current instance $\mathcal{S}_a(t)$. The a subscript denotes a stream associated with a specific part of the system. We denote the set of all streams from different parts of a CPS as $\mathcal{S}$, in particular, $\mathcal{S}_a \in \mathcal{S}$ for all streams $\mathcal{S}_a$.

The streams of information that we want to verify as being compliant to safe operation requirements can be represented as a monitorable property $\mathcal{P}$ derived from component constraints φ_l. The property $\mathcal{P}$, also referred to as a monitor specification, is a checking condition that represents the conditions given by a context $\mathcal{CO} \subseteq \mathcal{V} \times \mathcal{A} \times \mathcal{C}$ (Fig. 1), and is most often expressed in temporal logic. Thus, in multi-level monitoring, a monitor of a specific type placed at a specified level detects unsafe or hazardous conditions for the stream it is observing. We classify monitors (and their associated properties) as data, network, or functional monitor types depending on the causal factors c_f and the possible location of emerging hazard states given by STPA. We consider the following three types of monitoring for CPS: input-output (I/O) data-oriented monitors of type M_d, network-oriented monitors of type M_η, functional monitors of type M_δ.

- **Data Monitor** $\mathcal{M}_d$ observes streams of data from sensors and actuators that provide an interface to the physical environment, signals behavior of a controller and verifies the data integrity. The causal factors related to $\mathcal{D}$, i.e. unsafe input from sensors or from other controllers are verified by $\mathcal{M}_d$.
- **Network Monitor** $\mathcal{M}_\eta$ verifies the integrity of the data received by the communication layer by observing streams of information from the network layer. They check for signal faults, incorrect signaling protocol, timing delays etc. They observe the causal factors related to η, i.e. unsafe control path.
- **Functional Monitor** $\mathcal{M}_\delta$ verifies properties for the system's functional behavior. For example, the relation between input and output of a controller is verified by a functional correctness property. In particular, $\mathcal{M}_\delta$ observe the causal factors related to δ, i.e., an unsafe control algorithm, by observing streams of information consisting of system states, internal variables, memory read/writes, and event counts.

3   Monitoring an AEB Controller

A simplified AEB system model [15] is a representative system for studying the methodology for STPA-driven runtime monitor design (Fig. 2). The output of the AEB controller determines the braking state that decelerates the ego car, which is a car with autonomous features.

A model of the vehicle dynamics module was considered whose output—together with the scenario under consideration—determines the inputs to the radar and vision sensors. The outputs of these sensors are fused to estimate the relative distance and relative velocity between the ego car and the "most important object" (MIO). The MIO is not always the lead car. For example, if a pedestrian comes in front of the ego car, this would be the MIO. Based on these inputs (distance and velocity relative to the MIO), the AEB controller estimates the braking state (Fig. 2). When the ego car is at a safe distance but gets closer

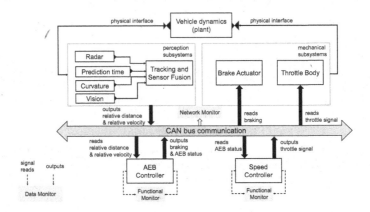

Fig. 2. Schematic of an autonomous emergency braking (AEB) system.

than required for safe operation, an alert, forward collision warning, is issued. If the driver does not brake or the braking is insufficient, then the AEB engages the "stage I" partial braking (PB1) at a certain critical relative distance. If this does not suffice, "stage II" partial braking (PB2) is applied at a closer relative distance, and then full braking (FB) is engaged. This action decelerates the car to avoid a collision characterized by a minimum headway distance when the velocity of the ego car reaches zero. Runtime monitors of data, network and functional types are placed at different levels in a CPS (Fig. 2).

3.1 STPA for AEB

Losses and Hazards. From our analysis, we consider the losses L that must not occur, and the hazards H related to the losses L are described below. These form the foundation for producing UCAs (Fig. 6). For some of the hazards, we mention sub-hazards to cover different cases. Some illustrative subsets of losses and hazards:

L-1 Loss of life or injury due to collision
L-2 Loss via damage to the vehicle or property (repair, fines etc.)
L-3 Loss of reputation

H-1 Unsafe headway distance to the MIO [L-1, L-2, L-3]
H-1.1 Unsafe headway distance to vehicles, pedestrians [L-1, L-2, L-3]
H-1.2 Unsafe headway distance to sidewalks, curb etc. [L-2, L-3]
H-2 Vehicle is traveling at an inappropriate speed. [L-1, L-2, L-3]

Higher-level system constraints φ_s are derived from rephrasing of the hazard statements as a binding mandatory requirement. For example, the system constraint for the hazard H-1 is: "SC^1_{system} (φ_s) The Ego car must always maintain a safe distance to the MIO."

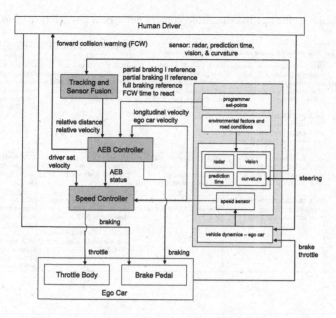

Fig. 3. STPA control structure diagram for AEB system.

Control Structure Diagram. The STPA control structure diagram shows all the components in the AEB system along with vehicle dynamics and environmental factors. It is a hierarchical control structure with a human driver at the top, brake and throttle controllers in the middle, and mechanical components such as the throttle body and brake pedal at the bottom of the diagram.

Next, we identify UCAs from μ that can occur in the AEB system. This step occurs after loss and hazard determination because UCAs from μ directly cause hazards (Fig. 6). The AEB controller provides a *braking* signal to the brake pedal, an `AEBstatus` signal to the speed controller, and forward collision warning (FCW) to the driver (Fig. 3). *Braking* is a deceleration signal with different braking levels PB1, PB2, and FB (Sect. 3). Whenever the AEB controller activates the brakes, the `AEBstatus` signal indicates to the speed controller the braking level applied. `AEBstatus` 1 indicates "Partial Braking I", `AEBstatus` 2 indicates "Partial Braking II", and `AEBstatus` 3 indicates "Full Braking", all as applied by the AEB. Based on the `AEBstatus`, the speed controller provides or ceases to provide an acceleration signal to the throttle.

Identifying Unsafe Control Actions (UCAs). Based on the control structure diagram analysis, we illustrate a subset of UCAs (Table 1). As an example, we state the controller constraint φ_c for UCA 1: "$SC^1_{controller}$ (φ_c) AEB must provide a *braking* signal when MIO is approaching the Ego car and AEB detects an imminent collision [UCA 1]." Here, *braking* and *detection of imminent collision* are AEB's control actions. Finding incorrect or untimely control actions

Table 1. Partial list of unsafe control actions in the AEB system.

Control Action	Not providing causes hazard	Providing causes hazard	Too early, too late, out of order	Stopped too soon, applied too long
Braking (AEB controller)	UCA 1—AEB does not provide braking signal when MIO is approaching the ego car and AEB detects an imminent collision. [H-2] UCA 2—AEB provides insufficient *braking* signal when MIO is approaching the ego car and there is an imminent collision. [H-2]	UCA 3—AEB provides unexpected *braking* signal when there is no imminent collision, and the MIO is at a safe distance from the Ego car during operation. [H-2]	UCA 4—AEB provides delayed *braking* signal when the distance from the MIO is less than safe ego car distance. [H-1, H-2]	UCA 5—AEB provides *braking* signal for insufficient duration when there is an imminent collision. [H-1,H-2]
AEB Status (AEB controller)	UCA 6—AEBstatus is not updated to the Speed Controller when the AEB controller is activated. [H-2]	UCA 7—Incorrect *AEB Status* is provided to the Speed Controller when the AEB provides *braking* signal. [H-1]	UCA 8 - Delayed update in AEBstatus after the AEB has provided *braking* signal. [H-1]	UCA 9—AEBstatus changes before it is read by the Speed controller. [H-1]
Throttle (Speed controller)	UCA 10—ThrottleRelease false unexpectedly resulting in slowing down of the vehicle. [H-2]	UCA 11—ThrottleRelease false when AEB is activated. [H-1, H-2]	UCA 12—*Throttle* is not applied when AEB is deactivated. [H-2] UCA 13—ThrottleRelease late when AEB is activated. [H-1, H-2]	UCA 14—*Throttle* is applied for too long and vehicle exceeds safe speed limit. [H-1] UCA 15—*Throttle* is released too soon and the vehicle operates at below safe driving speed [H-2]

can guide designers towards finding comprehensive loss scenarios and low-level safety requirements for *braking* and correct *detection of imminent collision*.

3.2   Loss Scenarios and Causal Factors as Design Guides for Multilevel Runtime Monitoring

Causal factors for a UCA μ_i provide insights on complex subsystem interactions and failure patterns that are critical in developing component-level safety constraints φ_l. These low-level component constraints φ_l are vital for detection of fault/attack and possible isolation of the causal factors. As a case study, we identify the potential causal factors that result in unsafe *braking* by the AEB controller and unsafe throttle action by the speed controller. Causal factors for UCAs could be due to a) failures related to the controller, b) inadequate control algorithm, c) unsafe control inputs, and d) inadequate process model as described in the STPA handbook [13]. To determine the causal factors, Fig. 6 explains that we must describe loss scenarios based on each UCA in μ as to both realize the context CO and formulate each of the different causal factors c_f. For the AEB system, we describe two scenarios which describe the context CO for unsafe *braking* UCA. In each scenario we identify the component level safety constraints φ_l based on the illustrated causal factor c_f along with the runtime verification properties used to detect the causal factor c_f. We express the monitor properties using event calculus temporal formal language [20].

Scenario 1: Safe Braking Distance. The vehicle is operating and begins approaching an MIO. The AEB applies *braking* in accordance with its control algorithm and updates the AEBstatus to a non-zero number corresponding to the level of *braking* applied. The speed controller applies throttle and ignores

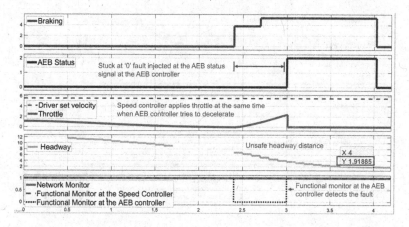

Fig. 4. Localized monitors at each level are beneficial (Scenario 1).

the change in AEBstatus. If the speed controller continues acceleration while *braking* is occurring, the braking components experience undue strain and may fail, leading to potential unsafe headway [H-2] and collision [L-1]. The rationale for simultaneous *braking* and acceleration from the speed controller's perspective varies depending on the context $\mathcal{CO}$ in the scenarios. Potential causes include:

Scenario 1a. The speed controller has an inadequate control algorithm and does not release the throttle when the AEBstatus is non-zero.

Scenario 1b. The communication between the AEB and the speed controller is delayed. Thus, the speed controller is not aware of the change in AEBstatus, and it keeps the throttle on when the AEBstatus is non-zero.

Scenario 1c. The AEB does not properly update AEBstatus signal, even after beginning braking [UCA-6,7]. Thus, the speed controller believes the AEB is not *braking* and keeps the throttle on when the AEBstatus is non-zero.

The context in the scenario can be expressed as a function of $\mathcal{V}$, $\mathcal{A}$ and $\mathcal{C}$ [21]. For example in scenario 1, throttle and AEBstatus are the variables $\mathcal{V}$, the assumption $\mathcal{A}$ is that the input AEBstatus is accurate and the vehicle is in motion. "Release throttle when AEBstatus is non-zero" is the condition $\mathcal{C}$. The component-level safety constraints and their corresponding properties are listed below:

$SC^1_{\text{component}}$ (φ_l). The Speed Controller should release the throttle when the AEBstatus is non-zero.

Property 1 (Detects inadequate control algorithm in speed controller (Scenario 1a)). "If AEBstatus is equal to 1, 2, or 3, the throttle should be released." This ensures that the car throttle is not engaged when the brake is engaged by the AEB,

$$\text{Happens}(\text{AEBstatus} = 1 \vee 2 \vee 3, T) \Rightarrow \text{HoldsAt}(\text{ThrottleRelease}, T).$$

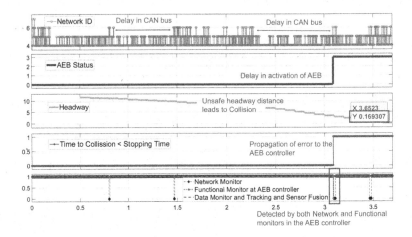

Fig. 5. Multilevel monitoring for in-time detection (Scenario 2).

$SC^2_{\text{component}}$ (φ_l). The data packet's arrival rate via the CAN bus should have an acceptable delay.

Property 2 (Detects flaw in control path to speed controller (Scenario 1b)). "The time interval between two successive packet arrival via the CAN bus should be less than T_{safe}." This condition ensures that the consecutive packets Packet_A and Packet_B should arrive at time T_a and T_b respectively, where $T_d = T_b - T_a$ should satisfy the condition $T_d < T_{\text{safe}}$, $\text{Happens}(\text{Packet}_A, T_a) \wedge \text{Happens}(\text{Packet}_B, T_b)$.

$SC^3_{\text{component}}$ (φ_l). When the AEB controller begins the *braking* action, the `AEBstatus` should be updated accordingly.

Property 3 (Detects inadequate control algorithm in AEB (Scenario 1c)). "If deceleration is greater than D_{safe} m/s^2, the `AEBstatus` should be non-zero." This property ensures that the `AEBstatus` corresponds to the AEB controller's current braking signal, $\text{Happens}(\text{Deceleration} > D_{\text{safe}}, T) \Rightarrow \text{HoldsAt}(\text{AEBstatus} \neq 0, T)$.

Scenario 2: Communication Delay. The vehicle is operating and begins to approach an MIO. There is a communication delay in sending the relative distance and relative velocity signals from the Tracking and Sensor Fusion module to the AEB controller resulting in delayed calculation of Time To Collision (TTC). Because of this, sufficient and timely braking is not applied. The component level safety constraints and runtime property based on this scenario were formulated similar to Scenario 1b to detect delay in communication in the CAN bus.

Hazard Injection and Monitor Detection. Using a model-based fault injection toolbox [11], faults and attacks were injected strategically to simulate the loss scenarios 1 and 2. STPA provides a systematic method to analyze the system and identify loss scenarios. After identifying loss scenarios, we explore the adequacy of the causal factor analysis by property-based hazard injection [11].

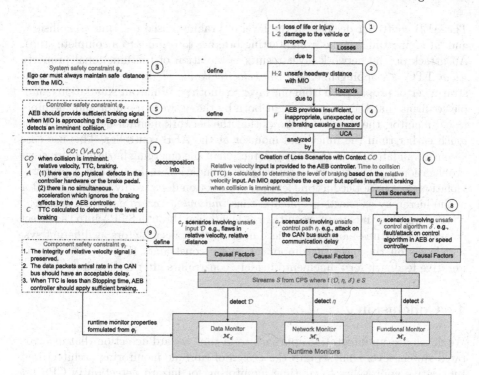

Fig. 6. Deriving multilevel runtime monitor properties from STPA for AEB system (numbers denote the order of the workflow).

For the first scenario, faults were injected on the AEBstatus signal in the AEB controller (Scenario 1c). Although the AEB controller provides braking action, the speed controller is unaware of the braking and continues to apply throttle due to the fault. This results in simultaneous braking and acceleration of the vehicle, thus causing the unsafe headway distance hazard [H-1]. The headway reduces to 1.9 m at 4 s (Fig. 4) (safe headway distance should be at least 2.4 m). The functional monitor at the AEB controller detects the fault much earlier than the occurrence of the hazard. This error is detectable only by having a localized monitor at the AEB controller. The functional monitor at the speed controller and the network monitor do not detect such a fault, as a fault on AEBstatus neither changes the functionality of the speed controller nor the network behavior. Thus, having local monitors at each level is beneficial in *early detection* and *isolation of faults/attacks*.

For the second scenario, we emulate a malicious node attack where sporadic messages on the CAN bus causes delay in the communication of packets between the tracking and sensor fusion module and the AEB controller. The network-level monitor detects this scenario (Fig. 5). A message injection attack at the network layer also results in violation of a functional property in the AEB controller which verifies the control algorithm at the AEB controller level.

The AEB controller decides on the level of braking based on "time to collision" and "stopping time" (time from starting braking to coming to a complete stop). An attack on the network layer results in violation of the functional property *when* TTC < stoppingtime, *ego car velocity should be decreasing,* thus demonstrating error propagation from one layer to another. While our simulation example confirms that the error is caught both by the network monitor and the functional monitor, the simulation shows that the network monitor detects the error much earlier than the functional monitor at the AEB controller. This use case scenario validates the in-time early detection of the emerging hazard before error propagation reaches the system's output boundaries. In fact, when a property violation goes unnoticed at one level, they are often detected by another monitor in the hierarchy as effects propagate, thus *improving hazard detection coverage.*

The workflow integrates requirement elicitation through STPA into the direct creation of runtime monitors by decomposing the causal factors at different system levels on the basis of component safety constraints (Fig. 6). There is an iterative feedback for refinement of safety constraints after hazard injection.

4   Conclusion

We developed an integrative approach to in-time hazard detection that incorporates system-level analysis into the design of runtime monitoring architectures. Integrative approaches to runtime monitoring for hazard detection in CPS are needed to augment the technical basis for DepDevOps style methods. We demonstrated that the systematic nature of STPA hazard analysis is beneficial in deriving and refining multilevel monitoring properties related to causal factors. By developing monitors across multiple system levels, we can accurately detect the origin of a hazard even when it propagates errors across different CPS levels.

In other words, when faults go undetected at their original location, monitors at other system levels can detect propagated errors, thus increasing hazard detection coverage. We also found that MBDE methods and tools significantly improve the productivity of STPA and assist in evaluating runtime monitoring schemes for hazard coverage and refinement.

References

1. Ahmed, B.: Synthesis of a Context-Aware Safety Monitor for an Artificial Pancreas System. Master's thesis, University of Virginia (2019)
2. Bakirtzis, G., Carter, B.T., Fleming, C.H., Elks, C.R.: MISSION AWARE: evidence-based, mission-centric cybersecurity analysis. arXiv:1712.01448 [cs.CR] (2017)
3. Combemale, B., Wimmer, M.: Towards a model-based DevOps for cyber-physical systems. In: Bruel, J.-M., Mazzara, M., Meyer, B. (eds.) DEVOPS 2019. LNCS, vol. 12055, pp. 84–94. Springer, Cham (2020). https://doi.org/10.1007/978-3-030-39306-9_6

4. Cui, J., Liew, L.S., Sabaliauskaite, G., Zhou, F.: A review on safety failures, security attacks, and available countermeasures for autonomous vehicles. Ad Hoc Netw. (2019). https://doi.org/10.1016/j.adhoc.2018.12.006

5. Daian, P., Shiraishi, S., Iwai, A., Manja, B., Rosu, G.: RV-ECU: maximum assurance in-vehicle safety monitoring. SAE Techn. Paper Ser. (2016). https://doi.org/10.4271/2016-01-0126

6. Duan, J.: Improved systemic hazard analysis integrating with systems engineering approach for vehicle autonomous emergency braking system. ASME J. Risk Uncertain. Part B (2022). https://doi.org/10.1115/1.4051780

7. Fremont, D.J., Sangiovanni-Vincentelli, A.L., Seshia, S.A.: Safety in autonomous driving: can tools offer guarantees? In: Proceedings of the 58th ACM/IEEE Design Automation Conference (DAC 2021). IEEE (2021). https://doi.org/10.1109/DAC18074.2021.9586292

8. Gautham, S., Jayakumar, A.V., Elks, C.: Multilevel runtime security and safety monitoring for cyber physical systems using model-based engineering. In: Casimiro, A., Ortmeier, F., Schoitsch, E., Bitsch, F., Ferreira, P. (eds.) SAFECOMP 2020. LNCS, vol. 12235, pp. 193–204. Springer, Cham (2020). https://doi.org/10.1007/978-3-030-55583-2_14

9. Goodloe, A.E., Pike, L.: Monitoring distributed real-time systems: a survey and future directions. Technical report CR-2010-216724, NASA (2010)

10. Haupt, N.B., Liggesmeyer, P.: A runtime safety monitoring approach for adaptable autonomous systems. In: Romanovsky, A., Troubitsyna, E., Gashi, I., Schoitsch, E., Bitsch, F. (eds.) SAFECOMP 2019. LNCS, vol. 11699, pp. 166–177. Springer, Cham (2019). https://doi.org/10.1007/978-3-030-26250-1_13

11. Jayakumar, A.V., Elks, C.: Property-based fault injection: a novel approach to model-based fault injection for safety critical systems. In: Zeller, M., Höfig, K. (eds.) IMBSA 2020. LNCS, vol. 12297, pp. 115–129. Springer, Cham (2020). https://doi.org/10.1007/978-3-030-58920-2_8

12. Leucker, M., Schallhart, C.: A brief account of runtime verification. J. Log. Algebraic Methods Program. (2009). https://doi.org/10.1016/j.jlap.2008.08.004

13. Leveson, N., Thomas, J.P.: STPA handbook (2018)

14. Liu, Y.A., Stoller, S.D.: Assurance of distributed algorithms and systems: runtime checking of safety and liveness. In: Deshmukh, J., Ničković, D. (eds.) RV 2020. LNCS, vol. 12399, pp. 47–66. Springer, Cham (2020). https://doi.org/10.1007/978-3-030-60508-7_3

15. Mathworks: Autonomous emergency braking with sensor fusion (2021). https://www.mathworks.com/help/driving/ug/autonomous-emergency-braking-with-sensor-fusion.html

16. Redfield, S.A., Seto, M.L.: Verification challenges for autonomous systems. In: Lawless, W.F., Mittu, R., Sofge, D., Russell, S. (eds.) Autonomy and Artificial Intelligence: A Threat or Savior?, pp. 103–127. Springer, Cham (2017). https://doi.org/10.1007/978-3-319-59719-5_5

17. Reich, J., et al.: Engineering of runtime safety monitors for cyber-physical systems with digital dependability identities. In: Casimiro, A., Ortmeier, F., Bitsch, F., Ferreira, P. (eds.) SAFECOMP 2020. LNCS, vol. 12234, pp. 3–17. Springer, Cham (2020). https://doi.org/10.1007/978-3-030-54549-9_1

18. Sánchez, C., et al.: A survey of challenges for runtime verification from advanced application domains (beyond software). Form. Methods Syst. Des. 1–57 (2019). https://doi.org/10.1007/s10703-019-00337-w

19. Schwenger, M.: Monitoring cyber-physical systems: from design to integration. In: Deshmukh, J., Ničković, D. (eds.) RV 2020. LNCS, vol. 12399, pp. 87–106. Springer, Cham (2020). https://doi.org/10.1007/978-3-030-60508-7_5

20. Shanahan, M.: The event calculus explained. In: Wooldridge, M.J., Veloso, M. (eds.) Artificial Intelligence Today. LNCS (LNAI), vol. 1600, pp. 409–430. Springer, Heidelberg (1999). https://doi.org/10.1007/3-540-48317-9_17

21. Thomas, J.: Extending and automating a systems-theoretic hazard analysis for requirements generation and analysis. Ph.D. thesis, MIT (2013)

22. Trapp, M., Schneider, D., Weiss, G.: Towards safety-awareness and dynamic safety management. In: Proceedings of the 14th European Dependable Computing Conference (EDCC 2018) (2018). https://doi.org/10.1109/EDCC.2018.00027

23. Zapridou, E., Bartocci, E., Katsaros, P.: Runtime verification of autonomous driving systems in CARLA. In: Deshmukh, J., Ničković, D. (eds.) RV 2020. LNCS, vol. 12399, pp. 172–183. Springer, Cham (2020). https://doi.org/10.1007/978-3-030-60508-7_9

24. Zhou, X., Ahmed, B., Aylor, J.H., Asare, P., Alemzadeh, H.: Data-driven design of context-aware monitors for hazard prediction in artificial pancreas systems. In: Proceedings of the 51st Annual IEEE/IFIP International Conference on Dependable Systems and Networks, (DSN 2021). IEEE (2021). https://doi.org/10.1109/DSN48987.2021.00058

Security and Safety

Proposal of Cybersecurity and Safety Co-engineering Approaches on Cyber-Physical Systems

Pierre-Marie Bajan$^{(\boxtimes)}$, Martin Boyer, Anouk Dubois, Jérôme Letailleur,
Kevin Mantissa, Jeremy Sobieraj, and Mohamed Tlig

Institute of Research Technology SystemX, Palaiseau, France
{pierre-marie.bajan,martin.boyer,anouk.dubois,jerome.letailleur,
kevin.mantissa,jeremy.sobieraj,mohamed.tlig}@irt-systemx.fr
https://www.irt-systemx.fr/en/

Abstract. Cybersecurity and Safety co-engineering is at the heart of various ongoing works for the industry and deals with highly complex and connected systems. However, as this topic grows, few shared methodologies, standards and organizations exist to enable this co-engineering process. In this context, we had the opportunity to bring together both a Safety and a Cybersecurity team to work on methods of collaboration. This resulted in mutually sharing methods and tools between both teams, as well as experiencing the challenges of co-engineering. In this article, we suggest two types of approaches encouraging Cybersecurity and Safety co-engineering and interactions. In the first approach, a Safety team contributes to Cybersecurity activities as defined by EBIOS RM methodology. In the second approach, a Cybersecurity team contributes to Safety inputs for the Safety demonstration. Those approaches are mainly based on the ISO 26262 automotive standard and the EBIOS RM methodology, but they can be extended to any type of context. Alongside the proposed approaches, we suggest orientations and perspectives for future works.

Keywords: Cyber-Physical Systems · Safety · Cybersecurity · Co-engineering · EBIOS RM

1 Introduction

Cyber-Physical Systems (CPS) are an integral part of domains that have a strong impact on society, the economy and the environment. In order to guarantee the robustness of such systems, they must respect two main criteria: Safety and Security. We define these concepts as follows: Safety aims at protecting people against accidental and involuntary acts (failures, misuses, etc.), Security aims at protecting people and assets against malicious and voluntary acts (attacks).

This research work has been carried out within the framework of IRT SystemX, Paris-Saclay, France, and therefore granted with public funds within the scope of the French Program "Investissements d'Avenir". Authors are listed alphabetically by last name.

While today's industries are well aware of the need of co-engineering and look for initiatives, Safety and Security have historically been carried out separately. Indeed, Safety is essential for risky systems in sensitive fields like aeronautics, aerospace, automotive, nuclear, etc. As for Security, it evolved over time with the notion of Cybersecurity threats appearing shortly after the arrival of Internet. Today, the *Safe-by-design* mindset is the norm in aeronautic and automotive fields. However, the concept of *Secure-by-design* is not as widespread. The hack of the Jeep Cherokee [18] and the recent Log4Shell vulnerability affecting the Java Log4j utility [1] show the need to improve the application of Cybersecurity best practices and to consider Cybersecurity issues starting from the concept phase. The idea of proposing a secure and safe system appeared as the correct path forward, but the implementation encountered some difficulties due to the differences in approaches.

The objective of this article is to highlight the possible links between Cybersecurity and Safety activities and to propose a co-engineering process. First, we present the state of the art of the Cybersecurity/Safety co-engineering approaches as well as the positioning of standards on such approaches (Sect. 2). Then, we study several ways to improve Cybersecurity/Safety co-engineering, based on observations from previous works that used the Cybersecurity risk analysis method EBIOS RM. We explain in detail its concepts and mechanisms (Sect. 3). Afterwards, we present our two approaches of Cybersecurity/Safety co-engineering (Sect. 4). Finally, we conclude with considerations on the relevance of these approaches and present the remaining challenges (Sect. 5).

2   State of the Art

The question of Cybersecurity/Safety co-engineering is an ongoing issue to address by using different means.

2.1   Standards

The article [14] lists several standards regarding co-engineering in various fields (automotive, aviation, space, railway, medical, and nuclear) and highlights that several standards for Safety and Cybersecurity have been developed while keeping each domain independent.

However, the boundaries between Safety and Cybersecurity in the normative environment are fading away. The authors of [5] pinpoint this evolution and the progressive emergence of overlaps in Safety and Cybersecurity activities in the context of CPS. In this particular context, they consider that the conventional Safety domain should evolve to include "Security for Safety" considerations in its scope. "Security for Safety" consists in identifying and dealing with Cybersecurity threats that can lead to Safety issues.

For example, concerning Safety, the 2010 version of the IEC 61508 [8] standard addresses the inclusion of scenarios with malicious intent in the Safety risk analysis (including cyberattacks). The 2018 update of the automotive Safety standard ISO 26262 [9] includes an annex regarding potential collaboration with Cybersecurity. While these standards do not provide practical processes to integrate Cybersecurity with Safety, they reveal a gradual evolution regarding the need for coordination between the two domains.

In the railway field, from the Cybersecurity viewpoint, the TS 50701:2021 standard [4] represents a significant step towards facilitating Cybersecurity/Safety co-engineering: it relies on the EN 50126 [6] lifecycle used in railway Safety to establish the activities in railway Cybersecurity. Among the propositions, it suggests hints on how to handle Cybersecurity activities in regard to Safety. It also defines a Cybersecurity Case according to the model of the Safety Case in EN 50129 [7], which takes into account safety-related high-level objectives. The TS 50701 views co-engineering as the proper coordination of lifecycles, activities and establishing proper interfaces, rather than fully integrating Safety with Cybersecurity. Indeed, integration can negatively impact the two domains and their approval process, with a risk of higher costs in resources and re-certification.

2.2 Co-engineering Methods

Beyond standards, independent initiatives and methods have been developed. The authors of [11] deliver the most detailed and complete co-engineering method classification to date. In 2020, nearly 70 methods have been studied and classified according to different categories (application fields, method type, scalability, etc.). Among those methods, some apply a "Security for Safety" approach, while others combine Safety and Cybersecurity results at specific development stages [3]. This is the case for the following methods:

- SAHARA [12]: a risk analysis tool based on the Hazard Analysis and Risk Assessment (HARA) method (Safety) and the STRIDE method (Cybersecurity).
- Six-Step-Model [16]: a risk modeling method where the Safety and Cybersecurity teams define links between several aspects of the system (functions, structure, failures, attacks, countermeasures) in order to solve conflicts.
- KAOS [15]: a definition of system requirements based on GORE (Goal-Oriented Requirements Engineering), applicable in the context of a Cybersecurity/Safety approach.

2.3 Positioning

From the standards and methods discussed previously, we make the following observations:

- *Position of standards*: more and more standards in Safety and Cybersecurity identify synergies between these two aspects. While some initiatives propose tangible co-engineering processes in standards like the SAE J3061 [17], the transition into international standards is not always done or built upon. The

ISO/SAE 21434 [10], which today supersedes and abandons the aspects of co-engineering of SAE J3061, is an example of this phenomenon: Safety and Cybersecurity are still kept independent in the normative environment.

– *Absence of a universal methodology*: we lack a generic methodology applicable to every field.
– *Teams interactions*: few methods consider the different interactions between the Cybersecurity and the Safety teams. The AQUAS project, concluded in 2020, explores and details the methods first proposed by the SAE J3061 in the deliverable [2].
– *Verification & Validation* (V&V) *activities*: most of the contributions deal with the co-engineering activities in the design phase. The AQUAS project is among the ones to also explore the potential synergies of Cybersecurity and Safety in V&V.

The first three observations pinpoint the challenge to find a complete Cybersecurity/Safety methodology that improves communication and interactions between both teams. Regarding the V&V treatment in Cybersecurity/Safety co-engineering, the authors of [19] indicate that there are more potential synergies during the V&V phase (right side of the V-Model) than during the design phase (left side of the V-Model), as shown in Fig. 1. However, we think it is crucial to properly identify the synergies in the design phase, in order to be more robust during the V&V phase. Thus, we focus strictly on the design phase with two approaches for Cybersecurity/Safety co-engineering, as described in Sect. 4 of this article.

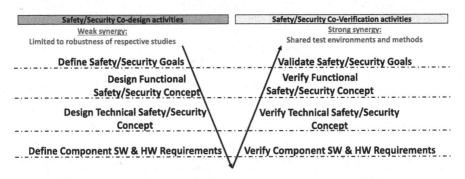

Fig. 1. Cybersecurity and safety synergies in simplified V-model (from [19])

3   EBIOS RM Method

We assume in this paper that ISO 26262 standard is well known worldwide, which is not the case for EBIOS RM. Thus in this section, we introduce this methodology which is essential for the understanding of our propositions.

3.1   Introduction

To study the possible convergences and divergences of Safety and Cybersecurity risk analysis methods, we choose a Cybersecurity method as a starting point. We select EBIOS Risk Manager, or EBIOS RM [13], as a Cybersecurity risk analysis method for two reasons. We are familiar with this method from its use in various projects, thus providing us with feedback and use cases to draw inspiration for improvements upon. Besides, EBIOS RM is useful to identify key issues and is adaptable to various contexts.

EBIOS RM is a risk analysis method created by the French Cybersecurity national agency, ANSSI, in 1995. This methodology, first known as EBIOS, had major updates in 2004 and 2010 before finally changing to EBIOS RM in 2018. It is actively recommended by ANSSI to French companies to raise awareness of the Cybersecurity threats. It is also indicated as a potential method for Cybersecurity risks management in the TS 50701 standard.

3.2   Five Workshops of EBIOS RM

EBIOS RM is divided into five consecutive workshops and proposes alternative methods for some specific steps to match the need of the contributors. EBIOS RM does not prohibit the use of custom methods as long as they reach the intended goals.

Scope and Cybersecurity Baseline. The first workshop consists in the definition of the scope of the analysis, the norms and the regulations constraining the object of the study. This workshop is divided into four steps:

1. We identify the goals of the analysis, the scope of the object of study, the contributors responsible for each workshop and the overall planning.
2. We identify the most important functions and/or components of the system. The goal is to identify five to ten items that would be the targets of attackers and are vital to the system. Those items are called *business assets*. We identify the contributors responsible for each *business asset*.
3. For each *business asset*, we identify *feared events* (defined in EBIOS RM). They are adverse consequences to a *business asset* due to the violation of one of its Cybersecurity criteria (availability, integrity, confidentiality, etc.). For example, a *feared event* for a given *business asset* could be its temporary unavailability (violation of availability) and the resulting consequence.
4. Finally, we determine the *security baseline* in which we identify all of the Cybersecurity reference standards applicable to the system. We then determine for each standard their implementation status (*applied without restrictions*, *applied with restrictions*, and *not applied*) along with justifications.

Risk Origins. The second workshop consists in the identification of attackers' profile and motivation for targeting the system. This workshop is divided into three steps:

1. We identify the *risk origins* (*RO*) and the *target objectives* (*TO*) of the potential attackers of the system. EBIOS RM provides a reference list of *RO* and *TO* which the workshop contributors can choose from.
2. We create pairs of *RO/TO* (e.g., organized crime / lucrative goal) and we evaluate the relevance of each pair to the system. The recommended criteria are: the motivation of the *RO/TO pair*, its resources, and how active it is in the industry.
3. Based on the previous evaluation, we select a few *RO/TO pairs* for the rest of the analysis. The recommended number is three to six pairs.

Strategic Scenarios. The third workshop consists in the elaboration of high-level attack scenarios known as *strategic scenarios*. The *strategic scenarios* are used to determine the severity of an attack. This workshop also identifies *critical stakeholders* and suggests measures to reduce their criticality. This workshop is divided in three steps:

1. We list all the stakeholders of the system and identify those that are deemed critical. A *critical stakeholder* is a stakeholder likely to be used as a vector for an attack. EBIOS RM proposes a set of criteria and a methodology to establish a *threat level* for each stakeholder. The stakeholders with the highest *threat level* are deemed *critical stakeholders*.
2. We identify *strategic scenarios*. For each *RO/TO pair*, we determine which *business assets* would be targeted and if specific *critical stakeholders* may be considered to do so. Each of those constitute a simplified attack path and thus a *strategic scenario*. We then evaluate the severity of each *strategic scenario*.
3. We propose Cybersecurity measures to reduce the *threat level* of each *critical stakeholders* to a level considered as acceptable by the workshop contributors.

Operational Scenarios. The fourth workshop consists in the elaboration of detailed attack scenarios called *operational scenarios* and in the evaluation of the likelihood of success of each *operational scenario*. This workshop is divided in two steps:

1. We identify *operational scenarios*, i.e. attack paths elaborated from the previous *strategic scenarios*. An *operational scenario* uses the same attack vector and targets the same *business asset* as the reference *strategic scenario* but provides additional information on the *supporting assets* targeted, the techniques used, etc. *Operational scenarios* can be represented by graphs or attack diagrams.
2. We evaluate the likelihood of success of each *operational scenario*. It identifies how likely an *operational scenario* can succeed if it actually happened. EBIOS RM suggests three different methods with various degrees of complexity.

Risk Treatment. The fifth and last workshop consists in the synthesis of the risks scenarios, establishing a risk treatment strategy and setting up the framework to monitor risks. This workshop is divided in four steps:

1. We first validate an initial risk mapping consensus among all evaluators. A *risk scenario* score is the combination of the severity of its *strategic scenario* and the likelihood of its *operational scenario*. We establish the risk score of all identified *risk scenarios*.
2. We establish a *risk treatment strategy* so that each *risk scenario* is covered to reach an acceptable level of risk.
3. We verify that the *risk treatment strategy* can meet our goal. We deduce the residual risk scores by assessing the risk score of each *risk scenario* if the corresponding *risk treatment strategy* is applied.
4. We establish a *steering committee* and *steering indicators* to periodically verify that the *risk treatment strategy* is correctly applied and documented.

4   Cybersecurity/Safety Co-engineering: Two Approaches

The following section presents the results of activities we conducted regarding Cybersecurity/Safety co-engineering. We had an initial exchange where both Safety and Cybersecurity teams presented their respective methods, standards and tools. The idea is to improve the understanding of one another's concepts in order to identify and deal with potential misconceptions. Following this exchange, we identified opportunities of co-engineering collaborations. We synthetize the results of our co-engineering workshops in the approaches presented in this paper.

Based on the current state of the art, and the existing EBIOS RM methodology presented in Sect. 3, we propose two approaches of Cybersecurity/Safety co-engineering. The first approach presents how the Safety team can contribute to EBIOS RM workshops, while the second approach presents how the Cybersecurity team can contribute to building the Safety demonstration.

4.1   First Approach: Safety Contributions to Cybersecurity EBIOS RM Workshops

Our approach is not limited to simple exchanges of work products between the teams. Through our own experience, it is essential that both teams educate each other on their respective work processes and issues. This can be done through close interactions between teams, like in-person workshops.

For each of the five workshops of EBIOS RM, we identify safety-related activities that can be conducted in parallel to the regular activities of EBIOS RM.

First Workshop: Scope and Cybersecurity Baseline. In the first workshop of EBIOS RM, we identify four potential Safety contributions as illustrated in Fig. 2:

1. The Safety team provides their Safety Management Plan to help the Cybersecurity team specify the technical perimeter of the study. The Safety team also helps to identify the safety-related functions and stakeholders in the scope shared by both teams.

2. The Safety team performs a Safety Risk criteria analysis to identify additional Cybersecurity criteria (e.g., traceability, performance, quality of service, etc.) that are safety-relevant.
3. The Safety team advises on missing *feared events* from their own list of *hazardous events* and Safety Goals.
4. The Safety team identifies *supporting assets* associated to Safety functions in the technical perimeter of the Cybersecurity team.

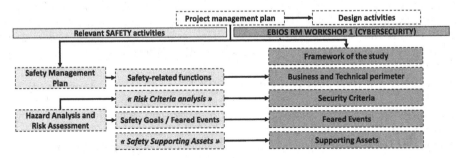

Fig. 2. Safety contributions to workshop 1 of EBIOS RM

Second Workshop: Risk Origins. In the second workshop of EBIOS RM, we identify three potential Safety contributions illustrated in Fig. 3:

– The Safety team is an active contributor to the discussion of the *risk origins* (*RO*) and their *target objectives* (*TO*).
– The Safety team also provides insights during the evaluation of the *RO/TO pairs*. They can contest or confirm individual scores of *RO/TO pairs* like their motivation or activity in the sector based on their own experience.
– The Safety team can be informed on the selected *RO/TO pairs*.

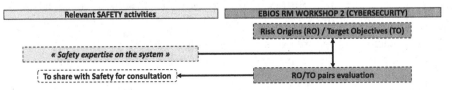

Fig. 3. Safety contributions to workshop 2 of EBIOS RM

Third Workshop: Strategic Scenarios. In the third workshop of EBIOS RM, we identify four potential Safety contributions, as illustrated in Fig. 4:

– The Safety team provides their list of stakeholders for the shared study perimeter.
– The Safety team can be informed on the list of *strategic scenarios*.
– The Safety team includes and traces the Cybersecurity measures that impact its perimeter.
– The Safety team can be informed on receiving the list of *critical stakeholders* and their *residual threat levels*.

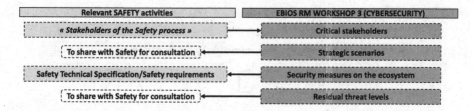

Fig. 4. Safety contributions to workshop 3 of EBIOS RM

Fourth Workshop: Operational Scenarios. The fourth workshop is dedicated to the identification and evaluation of operational scenarios. We identify synergies with the fault tree analysis in Safety. The interactions between Safety and Cybersecurity are described in Fig. 5: *operational scenarios* can serve as support for devising "Cybersecurity-related branches" in the fault tree. Additionally, the *likelihood* assessment of *operational scenarios* can be used as a qualitative metric to assess if those Cybersecurity-related branches need to be considered in the fault tree.

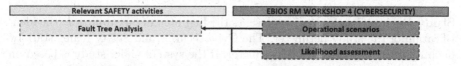

Fig. 5. Safety contributions to workshop 4 of EBIOS RM

Fifth Workshop: Risk Treatment. In the fifth and last workshop of EBIOS RM, we identify three potential Safety contributions, as illustrated in Fig. 6:

- The Safety team lists the Cybersecurity measures impacting its perimeter.
- The Safety team can be informed on potential *residual risks* identified by the Cybersecurity team.
- The *Security Continuous Improvement Plan* of the Cybersecurity team ensures that collaboration between the Safety and Cybersecurity teams continues during the development and exploitation phases. Indeed, new Cybersecurity threats are likely to emerge and present Safety stakes. Thus, the Safety team must systematically analyse the impacts of those Cybersecurity risks with a dedicated Safety Impact Analysis and a Risk Action Plan when needed.

4.2 Second Approach: Contributions of Cybersecurity to the Safety Demonstration

Prior to recent standards like TS 50701:2021 and EN 50129:2018, the Safety methodology would not consider Cybersecurity threats in the context of the Safety demonstration. Indeed, in Safety scenarios, the human actor is supposed

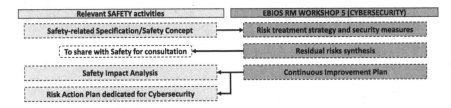

Fig. 6. Safety contributions to workshop 5 of EBIOS RM

to act in good faith. Thus, intentional attacks are not considered. However, with more and more connected systems, a change of paradigm is necessary. Consequently, in an approach coherent with the aforementioned standard, we propose to integrate Cybersecurity in the Safety demonstration while detailing how Cybersecurity and Safety work products could interact.

We identify three steps, each one corresponding to a key stage of the V-Model, where interactions between Safety and Cybersecurity can occur. We focus strictly on the design phase of the V-Model, which is covered by these steps.

Study Perimeter. Figure 7 represents the first step of our approach: the identification of the study perimeter. The Cybersecurity and Safety teams start by defining their respective study perimeter. If the system under study is based on a similar project, we can perform an impact analysis to deduce the elements that can be reused. Otherwise, such an impact analysis can be skipped. The Safety team defines the Safety Management Plan, which summarizes the global Safety organization, system perimeter and stakeholders of the study. Meanwhile, the Cybersecurity team defines a technical perimeter and identifies *business assets* relevant to that perimeter. Both teams then agree on a mutual study perimeter for future activities and select from that perimeter the *business assets* with Safety impacts.

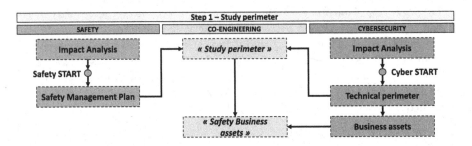

Fig. 7. Cybersecurity and safety interrelations for safety demonstration: study perimeter

Risk Analysis. Figure 8 presents our co-engineering approach during the life cycle of Safety and Cybersecurity risk analyses. To illustrate those exchanges (e.g. discussions, sharing of work products), we consider for instance a Safety risk analysis based on HARA and a Cybersecurity risk analysis based on EBIOS RM. Based on an initial input from the Safety team, the Cybersecurity team submits relevant elements from their risk analysis (*feared events, strategic scenarios*, etc.). The Safety team reviews those elements and integrates the impacting elements to the Safety risk analysis. This is done through eight steps:

1. The Safety team produces a list of *hazardous events* for the Cybersecurity team.
2. The Cybersecurity team identifies a list of *Cybersecurity Feared Events (CFE)* that are relevant to the *hazardous events*.
3. The Safety team identifies the *CFE* that are not traced in the *hazardous events*.
4. The Cybersecurity team also proposes a list of *strategic scenarios* based on the *CFE* selected in step 2.
5. The Safety team verifies the *strategic scenarios* likely to pose a Safety threat.
6. The Cybersecurity team proposes a list of *operational scenarios* based on the *strategic scenarios* selected in step 4.
7. The Cybersecurity team also provides the list of Cybersecurity measures associated to *operational scenarios* of step 6.
8. The Safety team analyses and gives their feedback on the Cybersecurity contributions resulted in steps 6 and 7.

These co-engineering exchanges are crucial for the Safety team to improve the robustness of their risk analysis. They must take place before the conclusion of the Safety risk analysis. With this approach, we want to highlight the added value of Cybersecurity experts' feedback to the Safety risk analysis.

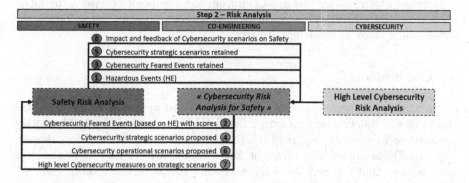

Fig. 8. Cybersecurity and safety interrelations for safety demonstration: risk analysis

Specification and Requirements Implementation. After identifying relevant risk scenarios, we present our approach for the treatment of Safety requirements and Cybersecurity measures in Fig. 9. The Safety team identifies Safety Goals that are high-level requirements that ensure the Safety of the system. From these Safety Goals, the Safety team provides the initial Safety requirements. The Cybersecurity and Safety teams select from the initial Cybersecurity measures those that are related to Safety issues. Those measures may entail conflicts, for which Safety and Cybersecurity must define best practices and a reactive treatment process. The resolution of conflicts and the potential addition of new elements lead to an update of Cybersecurity measures and Safety requirements. Additional Cybersecurity requirements can be traced to Safety requirements. The implementation of these requirements and measures are key issues for a safe and secure system.

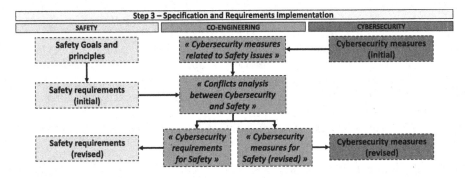

Fig. 9. Cybersecurity and safety interrelations for safety demonstration: requirements specification and implementation

Although we consider this approach from the viewpoint of Safety, the introduction of TS 50701 in Cybersecurity also makes it possible to integrate the Cybersecurity case in these activities.

5   Conclusion

In this paper, we presented two approaches: (i) an approach to integrate the inputs of the Safety team into an EBIOS RM risk analysis and (ii) another approach to include the inputs of the Cybersecurity team into a Safety demonstration. Those approaches highlight key Cybersecurity/Safety co-engineering contributions that can provide richer and more robust inputs to both Cybersecurity and Safety risk analyses. The step-by-step application of those approaches, mainly based on ISO 26262 and EBIOS RM, are compatible with other standards and are a good start for discussions between the Safety and Cybersecurity teams. Developing these approaches helped us to identify some key challenges and open questions that can guide future works on the topic.

Indeed, we observe that both teams need to be familiar with their respective vocabulary and concepts. Several key concepts like the *security criteria* (availability, traceability, etc.) or *the hazardous and feared events* can be interpreted differently by each team. The need for common language enabling proper understanding is also identified by the UK Code of Practice of Cyber Security and Safety [20] as a key challenge.

Besides, it is important to consider if we should unify similar concepts or keep them separated. Should hazardous events take into account the harm caused by malicious actors? Should Fault trees integrate dedicated branches for Cybersecurity-related Base events with malicious actors?

Finally, we keep in mind that these approaches, deduced from use cases, still need to be confronted with practical industrial contexts. We expect that Cybersecurity/Safety co-engineering can function properly only if industrial actors are willing to integrate the efforts of Safety and Cybersecurity teams. European initiatives, like the AQUAS project, along with others funded by the EU ARTEMIS/ECSEL JU, managed to achieve positive results on this topic. We also observe a rapid development of the normative environment, with the TS 50701:2021 Cybersecurity standard and the EN 50129:2018 Safety standard used in railway, which represent a significant step towards this goal.

References

1. Critical java flaw puts millions of organisations at risk. Netw. Secur. **2021**(12), 1–2 (2021)
2. Aggregated Quality Assurance in Systems (AQUAS) Project: D3.2 combined safety, security and performance analysis and assessment techniques - preliminary. Technical report (2019)
3. Boyer, M., Chelim, T., Sobieraj, J.: Hybridization of safety and security for the design and validation of autonomous vehicles: where are we? In: ESREL 2021–31st European Safety and Reliability Conference (2021)
4. BSI: Pd clc/ts 50701: Railway applications - cybersecurity. En (2021)
5. Carreras Guzman, N.H., Kozine, I., Lundteigen, M.A.: An integrated safety and security analysis for cyber-physical harm scenarios. Saf. Sci. **144**, 105458 (2021)
6. CENELEC: NF EN 50126-1: Railway applications - the specification and demonstration of reliability, availability, maintainability and safety (RAMS) - part 1: Generic RAMS process. En (2017)
7. CENELEC: Nf en 50129: Railway applications - communication, signalling and processing systems - safety related electronic systems for signalling. En (2018)
8. IEC: IEC 61508:2010 functional safety of electrical/electronic/programmable electronic safety-related systems. IEC (2010)
9. ISO 26262–1:2018: Road vehicles - functional safety. Standard, International Organization for Standardization, Geneva, CH (2018)
10. ISO/SAE 21434:2021: Road vehicles - cybersecurity engineering. Standard, International Organization for Standardization, Geneva, CH (2021)
11. Kavallieratos, G., Katsikas, S., Gkioulos, V.: Cybersecurity and safety co-engineering of cyberphysical systems - a comprehensive survey. Future Internet **12**, 65 (2020)

12. Macher, G., Höller, A., Sporer, H., Armengaud, E., Kreiner, C.: A combined safety-hazards and security-threat analysis method for automotive systems. In: Koornneef, F., van Gulijk, C. (eds.) SAFECOMP 2015. LNCS, vol. 9338, pp. 237–250. Springer, Cham (2015). https://doi.org/10.1007/978-3-319-24249-1_21

13. National Cybersecurity Agency of France (ANSSI): EBIOS Risk Manager - The method, https://www.ssi.gouv.fr/en/guide/ebios-risk-manager-the-method/

14. Paul, S., et al.: Recommendations for security and safety co-engineering (release n°3) - part a. Technical report (2016)

15. Ponsard, C., Dallons, G., Massonet, P.: Goal-oriented co-engineering of security and safety requirements in cyber-physical systems. In: Skavhaug, A., Guiochet, J., Schoitsch, E., Bitsch, F. (eds.) SAFECOMP 2016. LNCS, vol. 9923, pp. 334–345. Springer, Cham (2016). https://doi.org/10.1007/978-3-319-45480-1_27

16. Sabaliauskaite, G., Adepu, S., Mathur, A.: A six-step model for safety and security analysis of cyber-physical systems. In: Havarneanu, G., Setola, R., Nassopoulos, H., Wolthusen, S. (eds.) CRITIS 2016. LNCS, vol. 10242, pp. 189–200. Springer, Cham (2017). https://doi.org/10.1007/978-3-319-71368-7_16

17. SAE International: Cybersecurity guidebook for cyber-physical vehicle systems (stabilized December 2021). Technical report (2021)

18. Sengupta, J., Ruj, S., Bit, S.D.: A comprehensive survey on attacks, security issues and blockchain solutions for IoT and IIoT. J. Netw. Comput. App. **149**, 102481 (2020)

19. Skoglund, M., Warg, F., Sangchoolie, B.: In search of synergies in a multi-concern development lifecycle: safety and cybersecurity. In: Gallina, B., Skavhaug, A., Schoitsch, E., Bitsch, F. (eds.) SAFECOMP 2018. LNCS, vol. 11094, pp. 302–313. Springer, Cham (2018). https://doi.org/10.1007/978-3-319-99229-7_26

20. The Institution of Engineering and Technology: Code of practice: Cyber security and safety. Technical report (2020)

On the Feasibility and Performance of Secure OPC UA Communication with IIoT Devices

Florian Kohnhäuser[1(✉)], Nicolas Coppik[1], Francisco Mendoza[1], and Ankita Kumari[2]

[1] ABB Corporate Research Center, 68526 Ladenburg, Germany
{florian.kohnhaeuser,nicolas.coppik,francisco.mendoza}@de.abb.com
[2] Department of Informatics, Technical University of Munich, Munich, Germany

Abstract. OPC UA is an evolving communication protocol for industrial automation and the Industrial Internet of Things (IIoT). To protect against network attacks, OPC UA has built-in security mechanisms that can ensure the communication authenticity, integrity, and confidentiality. Since IIoT devices may be battery-powered, built into tiny chassis, or operate in hazardous environments, OPC UA must be suited for resource-constrained devices with limited power consumption and computational resources. However, secure OPC UA communication with such resource-constrained devices has not been investigated so far. This practical experience report analyzes the feasibility and performance of secure OPC UA communication with IIoT devices. To this end, an OPC UA server is implemented on an exemplifying resource-constrained industrial device. The implementation process presented several challenges, including adapting a lightweight cryptographic library to the peculiarities of OPC UA. To investigate under which conditions secure OPC UA communication is realizable, the runtime overhead, memory footprint, and power consumption are evaluated and discussed for various usage scenarios. The evaluation reveals certain bottlenecks, such as long connection times, low number of parallel sessions, limited concurrency, and high memory demands. Based on the evaluation, recommendations on the software, hardware, and usage scenarios are given.

Keywords: Industrial Internet of Things · Secure communication · OPC UA · Resource-constrained · Embedded systems · Performance

1 Introduction

The industrial automation sector is facing a digital transformation, in which the communication capabilities of industrial devices, such as sensors and actuators, are being greatly expanded [13]. A key technology for communication between such devices is the Open Platform Communications Unified Architecture (OPC UA) [8]. OPC UA is a comparatively new industrial protocol for machine-to-machine (M2M) communication, which is currently becoming an integral part of industrial automation systems. To face the increasing risk of cyberattacks on industrial systems, OPC UA has been specifically designed with security in mind. With its built-in security mechanisms, OPC UA can protect the authenticity, integrity, and confidentiality of communication between devices. Nevertheless, these security mechanisms introduce additional computational and memory overhead. Commodity computers have enough resources to deal with this overhead, but IIoT devices are typically small embedded systems with limited computing resources, memory, and power consumption. This is because IIoT devices are often limited in size, need to operate in hazardous environments, or are battery-powered. As OPC UA should, in particular, be suited for the IIoT, it is crucial that its security mechanisms can also be applied to such devices. However, the feasibility, bottlenecks, and implications of secure OPC UA communication with resource-constrained devices have not been investigated so far.

Contribution. In this practical experience report, we analyze the feasibility and implications of secure OPC UA communication on resource-constrained industrial devices. As a target evaluation platform, we use a typical IIoT device with an 80 MHz ARM Cortex-M4 CPU, 2 MB Flash memory, 640 KB RAM, and an Ethernet-APL interface, which serves as power supply and communication interface. On this device, we implement an OPC UA server based on the High Performance SDK from Unified Automation [20]. To implement security, we replace the original cryptographic library with the lightweight MbedTLS library [1]. As MbedTLS is not adapted to the peculiarities of OPC UA security, this involves a challenging adaption process. In our evaluation, we analyze the runtime overhead, memory usage, and power consumption of secure OPC UA communication between a PC client and the IIoT device. In addition, we investigate different usage scenarios, such as connecting to the device, reading values, or subscribing to multiple values, both for single connections and multiple parallel connections to the device. Our evaluation shows that secure OPC UA communication with resource-constrained industrial devices is feasible and the power consumption is low enough to allow for a certification in hazardous environments. However, we also identify several bottlenecks and limitations that need to be considered. Finally, we provide recommendations on the software, hardware, and usage scenarios for secure OPC UA communication with IIoT devices.

Outline. This report is organized as follows. Section 2 explains the basics of OPC UA security. Section 3 summarizes related works. Section 4 describes the implementation and evaluation platform. Section 5 shows the performance measurements, which are discussed in Sect. 6. Section 7 concludes the report.

2 Background

The Open Platform Communications Unified Architecture (OPC UA) [8] is a platform-independent and service-oriented standard for M2M communication. It aims at addressing all sorts of industrial components, from smallest sensors

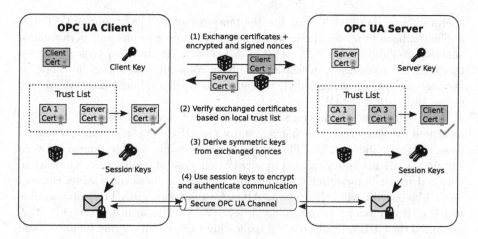

Fig. 1. Establishing a secure OPC UA connection between a client and server [12]

and actuators up to cloud applications. OPC UA is the first widely-deployed industrial protocol with built-in and attested security [6]. It specifies three security modes for secure communication between OPC UA devices: None (unprotected), Sign (authenticated), and SignAndEncrypt (authenticated and confidential communication) [16]. When establishing connections, clients and servers use *OPC UA Application Instance Certificates* for mutual authentication, which are X.509 compliant digital certificates. To verify received certificates, devices maintain a *Trust List* of trustworthy certificates. A client trusts a server if the server can authenticate itself with a certificate that the client can verify based on its Trust List, and vice versa. During the initial handshake, client and server derive symmetric keys that are used to authenticate (Sign), or to authenticate and encrypt (SignAndEncrypt) messages. This process is shown in Fig. 1.

The specific cryptographic algorithms used to realize the security modes are defined by security policies and negotiated during the initial handshake. In the current specification (Version 1.4), there are four policies: None, Aes128-Sha256-RsaOaep, Basic256Sha256, and Aes256-Sha256-RsaPss. Accordingly, OPC UA uses RSA to authenticate communication partners and exchange cryptographic nonces and SHA-based HMACs to derive symmetric keys. The symmetric keys are subsequently used by AES in CBC-mode and SHA-based HMACs to protect the communication confidentiality, integrity, and authenticity.

Note that, while OPC UA also defines alternative transport protocols and offers an additional publish/subscribe mode with different security mechanisms, this report focuses on the client/server mode over binary TCP, which is the most established OPC UA communication paradigm.

3   Related Works

The performance of OPC UA has been analyzed in several studies. Most studies focus on the client/server mode [3–5, 7, 15, 22], which is the most established operational mode for OPC UA. For the more recent and less common OPC UA publish/subscribe mode, there are are fewer implementations and performance analyses available [2,14,18,19]. OPC UA performance analyses typically investigate CPU and network utilization, memory consumption, and cycle times for varying amounts of connected clients, subscribed values, query intervals, device types, and OPC UA SDKs.

Few performance studies regard secure OPC UA communication. Vazquez [22] measured the times for retrieving values from an OPC UA server implemented on two different Windows PCs. The cycle time for reading a value ranged between 1.9 ms and 4.1 ms and increased by circa 8% in case of secured communication. Cho and Jeong [5] measured the times for retrieving values from a server running on a Cubieboard6, which features an ARM A9 quad core CPU. The response time increased from circa 1.2 ms without security to 2.4 ms with security. Burger et al. [2] measured the CPU utilization when requesting values with varying frequency and security profiles from a Raspberry Pi Zero OPC UA server. On this server, the CPU utilization only slightly increases in case of activated security, e.g., from 50% to 60% with 10 clients and 10,000 signals per second.

Among the performance studies regarding OPC UA security, none specifically focuses on the performance evaluation of secured communication. Existing works only measure a single aspect like response time [5,22] or CPU utilization [2], such that a comparison of multiple parameters is missing. Furthermore, important performance values like connection time, memory footprint, power consumption, or key and certificate generation time have not been investigated so far. In addition, none of the existing works implemented and evaluated OPC UA security on resource-constrained embedded devices. The most constrained device for measurements regarding security has been a Raspberry Pi Zero [2], with a 1 GHz single-core ARM11 CPU and 512 MB RAM, while the most constrained device for measurements without security has been a WAGO-750-860 fieldbus controller [7], which provides a 44-MHz ARM7 CPU and 16 MB of RAM.

4   Evaluation Platform

In this section, we first describe the hardware of our evaluation platform, including the measurement setup, and then explain our software implementation.

4.1   Hardware and Measurement Setup

As an exemplifying industrial IoT device, we use a prototype development board, which is henceforth referred to as "APL board". It is an Ethernet-APL prototype device based on an early version of the IEEE 802.3cg-2019 (10BASE-T1L) standard [10], an emerging communication technology for industrial automation that supplies power and a 10 Mbps Ethernet communication channel over a 2-wire physical layer. The APL board includes an STM32L4S5QII3P MCU from STMicroelectronics as the main computing unit. The MCU features a 32-bit ARM Cortex-M4 CPU clocked at 80 MHz with 640 KB RAM and 2 MB Flash memory. Although the MCU provides a hardware accelerator for AES-128, AES-256, and SHA-256 operations, we implement all security mechanisms in software. We decided against using the hardware accelerator, as neither AES nor SHA operations were performance bottlenecks in our evaluation. In addition, the APL board has a built-in 32 MB data Flash, on which we implemented a filesystem for OPC UA certificate storage. Please note that with these resources, the APL board falls into the category of a resource-constrained embedded system, according to RFC 7228.

We implemented an OPC UA server on the APL board, as described in the next section. The APL board is connected to a prototype APL switch, which in turn is connected to a server over a 1 Gbps Ethernet connection. The server runs Windows Server 2019 on an Intel Core i9-7940X with 64 GB RAM and uses the UaExpert OPC UA client from Unified Automation [21]. For our power measurements, we additionally put a N6705B Power Analyzer from Keysight Technologies between the APL switch and our evaluation platform, the APL board. Figure 2 illustrates our measurement setup.

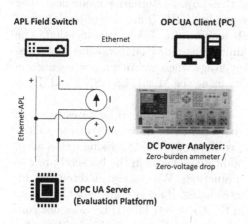

Fig. 2. Measurement setup

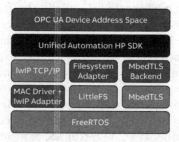

Fig. 3. Software components

4.2 Software Implementation

Software Components. Our implementation uses the software components shown in Fig. 3. The main open-source software (OSS) components are the FreeRTOS real-time operating system, the lwIP TCP/IP stack, the littleFS file system, and the MbedTLS cryptographic library. We implemented the OPC UA server based on the Unified Automation High Performance SDK in Version 1.5.1 [20], which is henceforth referred to as HP SDK. We chose the HP SDK, as it is specifically designed for smallest devices and the IoT. Implementing the server required several changes to the OSS components and a new implementation of the OPC UA device address space. Most challenging was the implementation of an MbedTLS backend for the HP SDK, which is needed to implement all OPC UA security mechanisms on the APL board, as described below.

MbedTLS Backend Implementation. To support secure OPC UA communication, the HP SDK relies on third-party libraries that provide cryptographic operations as well as certificate parsing and validation. The SDK allows the use of different backends to interface with different cryptographic libraries, but only OpenSSL is fully supported. Unfortunately, OpenSSL turned out to be too big for our APL board. Therefore, we chose the lightweight MbedTLS library [1], which offers a much smaller resource footprint than OpenSSL. This decision entailed several changes to the MbedTLS backend of the HP SDK.

First, missing functionality in the HP SDK MbedTLS backend had to be implemented, primarily related to certificate validation, such as checking extended key usage attributes or verifying signatures in self-signed certificates.

Second, numerous changes were required to work around limitations of the MbedTLS library related to certificate parsing and validation. For instance, MbedTLS does not provide access to certain certificate fields, such as the subject and authority key identifiers or parts of the subject alternative name field. The latter is particularly problematic, since parsing URIs from the subject alternative name field is necessary to establish secure OPC UA communication. The certificate creation APIs have similar limitations. For example, MbedTLS does not provide a way to set the extended key usage when creating a new certificate. We implemented the missing functionality using the MbedTLS ASN.1 and X.509 parsing and generation functions.

Finally, workarounds and additional checks were required for cases in which MbedTLS does not behave as expected by the SDK during certificate validation. For instance, MbedTLS cannot be configured to treat missing CRLs as an error. For such cases, we implemented additional checks in the backend prior to invoking MbedTLS certificate validation functions. We also encountered difficulties related to the verification of certificate chains. If an intermediate Certificate Authority (CA) certificate is included in the trust list, MbedTLS does not construct a full chain to the root certificate. We worked around this by detecting cases in which the first certificate in the chain built by MbedTLS is not self-signed (and therefore not a root certificate), temporarily modifying the trust list to omit this certificate, and starting a second validation from the intermediary certificate.

We were able to implement all our adaptions in the MbedTLS backend of the HP SDK, without modifying MbedTLS itself. Our implementation passes the HP SDK test suite and was provided to Unified Automation, who intend to release it as an official part of the upcoming HP SDK (Version 1.6).

5   Evaluation

In this section, we present the results of measuring the runtime overhead, memory footprint, and power consumption for various security-related operations in OPC UA: the key & certificate generation, connect operation, read operation, and multiple subscriptions for connections to a single client or multiple clients.

5.1   Key and Certificate Generation

The RSA key length determines the security level. Today a key length of at least 2048-bit is recommended and in the next decades (or for very high security) 4096-bit is expected to become the standard [11]. Generating keys and certificates is a one-time effort. They are stored in the certificate store, and not regenerated on subsequent server starts. We measured the time required to generate keys and certificates for three different RSA key lengths: 1024, 2048, and 4096 bit. For each key length, we performed 100 measurements.

Table 1. Key and certificate generation times for different RSA key sizes

Key length	Mean	Standard deviation	Median	MAD
1024	4.76 s	2.33 s	4.21 s	1.52 s
2048	49.75 s	34.62 s	40.11 s	20.59 s
4096	608.10 s	383.48 s	542.83 s	221.80 s

As reported in Table 1, the time required to generate keys and certificates increases substantially with increasing key sizes, with each doubling of the key size increasing the mean key generation time more than tenfold. While the times for 1024- and 2048-bit keys are below one minute, generating keys and certificates using a 4096-bit key length takes, on average, over ten minutes. We can also observe substantial variations between runs. For 4096-bit keys, this results in runtimes differing by tens of minutes.

5.2   Connect

We measured the time it took for a client to connect to the server and be ready to receive values. Table 2 and Fig. 4 show the connection time for different security policies as well as for different client and server key sizes (generated individually upfront). Each of the nine measurements was averaged based on a set of 8 runs. As opposed to the key & certificate generation times, the connection times varied very little over the runs, which is to protect against timing attacks.

Our measurements reveal a huge difference between disabled security, where clients could connect in less than 70 ms, and enabled security, where clients needed multiple seconds to connect to the server. Interestingly, increasing the server key size had higher impact on the connection times than increasing the client key size. This is because the server, or client, key size determines the key length with which the server, or client, executes the slow RSA encrypt and RSA verify operations during connect. Since the APL board (server) is significantly slower than the PC (client), the server key size thus impacts connection times most. Moreover, even with disabled security, certificates are exchanged during a connect and have an impact on connection times depending on the key sizes.

Table 2. Average connection time for different key sizes with and w/o security

Server key size	Security policy	Client key size		
		1024	2048	4096
1024	Basic256Sha256	1.47 s	1.74 s	3.28 s
2048	Basic256Sha256	3.82 s	4.17 s	5.41 s
4096	Basic256Sha256	12.36 s	12.67 s	18.04 s
1024	None	0.06 s	0.06 s	0.06 s
2048	None	0.06 s	0.06 s	0.06 s
4096	None	0.07 s	0.07 s	0.07 s

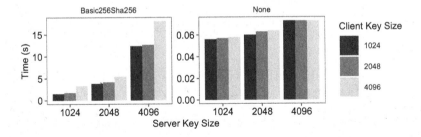

Fig. 4. Time to connect to the server with increasing server and client key size

5.3   Read Operations

We measured the time for reading a value of type float for 1000 cycles with the UaExpert Performance View. Table 3 shows the average, minimum, and maximum read time for different security modes. Compared with disabled security, the additional overhead for reading a value when protecting authenticity (Sign) amounts to 46.7%, and reaches 60.3% when protecting authenticity and confidentiality (SignAndEncrypt). Although this may seem significant percentagewise, it amounts to a runtime overhead of just 1.5 ms (Sign) and 1.9 ms (SignAndEncrypt). In addition, minimum and maximum values show that there are only small variations and few outliers between individual read operations.

Writing values to the server showed similar runtimes. Thus, reading and writing values is more than 3 orders of magnitude faster than connecting to the device.

Furthermore, we measured read times with multiple clients. In Fig. 5, a second client starts reading values from the server at around cycle 250. As shown, the read time directly jumps from circa 5.1 ms to 9.0 ms, but then remains relatively constant. This surprised us, as we expected the read time to double, as opposed to the actual increase of only 76.5%.

Table 3. Reading a value 1000 times with different security policies and modes

Security policy	Mode	Avg read	Min read	Max read
None	-	3.17 ms	2.78 ms	5.14 ms
Basic256SHA256	Sign	4.65 ms	4.21 ms	6.26 ms
Basic256SHA256	SignAndEncrypt	5.08 ms	4.75 ms	8.93 ms

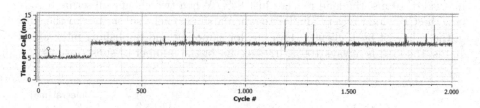

Fig. 5. Two clients reading values from the server at the same time

Finally, we investigated scenarios, in which a client connects to the server while another client is requesting values from it. As illustrated in Fig. 6, we observed that during the connect operation, the read operation is blocked for multiple seconds on two occasions: first for circa 3.5 s and shortly afterwards again for 0.7 s. This is due to the high computational load that a connect operation entails and the limited concurrency that the HP SDK provides. For certain industrial use cases, these blocking times are unacceptable. Furthermore, they allow an attacker to perform fake connects to maliciously block the device, resulting in a denial of service of the device. In Sect. 6, we analyze the underlying issue that leads to the blocking and describe measures to solve it. Once the second client has connected, reading values is as fast as before. Thus, the average read time for all 2000 cycles increases only slightly from 5.5 ms to 9.7 ms.

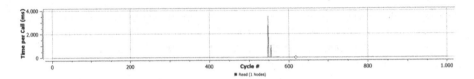

Fig. 6. Connecting while another client is reading from the server

5.4 Subscriptions

We assessed the performance of subscriptions by measuring the CPU load with different numbers of subscriptions per client. In addition, we varied the sampling and publishing intervals. As shown in Fig. 7, the CPU load is highly dependent on these factors. With enabled security, the load reaches 100% in case the sampling interval is reduced to 10 ms in case of 40 subscriptions. With so many subscriptions, the server fails to deliver all of them within time to the client and instead only provides updates for a subset of circa 10 subscriptions. In case security is disabled, the CPU load is significantly lower. Even with a publishing interval of 10 ms, the load reaches just 85%. When two clients subscribe to values, the CPU load is very similar to when a single client subscribes to the sum of the values of both clients. However, for sampling and publishing intervals of 10 ms, the load is always 100%, irrespective of the number of subscriptions.

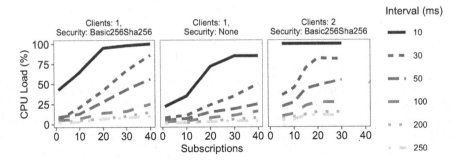

Fig. 7. Comparison of CPU load with increasing number of subscriptions

5.5 Memory Footprint

We measured the memory footprint of our implementation in two dimension: static and dynamic memory consumption. The static memory comprises all data allocated before runtime, such as the text, data, and BSS segment. It is obtained from Atollic TrueStudio for STM32 using the static stack and build analyzer. Figure 8 shows that security mechanisms in our implementation increase the Flash memory consumption by 400 KB and the static RAM consumption by 20 KB. The additional memory consumption can be attributed to the MbedTLS library [1] and the file system for certificate storage.

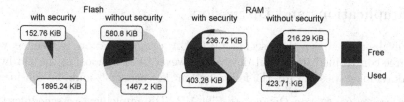

Fig. 8. Static Flash and RAM consumption with and without security

The dynamic memory contains all data allocated at runtime, i.e., stack and heap. As opposed to the static memory consumption, the dynamic memory consumption is much harder to measure, since it is determined by the usage scenario and time of measurement. To assess the maximum memory consumption at runtime, we limited the stack and heap size and investigated out-of-memory errors. We observed that the dynamic memory consumption is highly dependent on the number of connected clients. For three clients, we estimate the total dynamic memory consumption at roughly 270 KB.

5.6 Power Consumption

The peak power consumption we measured for the APL board is 395 mW. This value is well below the 500 mW required for a certification according to IEC 60079-47 [10], which allows the usage in hazardous areas with explosive atmospheres. In fact, with this power consumption, even a more powerful MCU or crypto accelerator could be used on the APL board while still achieving the certification. The peak power consumption of 395 mW is reached when clients connect to the APL board and the MCU is operating at full load. Interestingly, communication does not impact the power consumption as much as computational load. For instance, when clients repeatedly request values from the APL board over a secure connection, the power consumption peaks at 390 mW. In idle mode the power consumption is slightly lower and oscillates between 350 mW and 372 mW, with an average at 361 mW. As shown in Fig. 9, the MCU consumes only a small fraction of the total power budget (<7%). Since all security mechanisms are implemented in software and processed by the MCU, this is why security entails a small overhead on the power consumption.

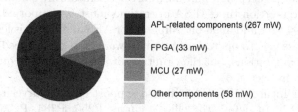

Fig. 9. Power budget distribution of the APL board (100% = 395 mW)

6 Implications and Discussion

Our evaluation shows that secure OPC UA communication is feasible with resource-constrained industrial devices. However, when choosing the hardware and developing its software, the following four key aspects should be considered:

Concurrency for Crypto Operations. The HP SDK implements a scheduler that performs context switches to achieve asynchronous operations, required to handle connections for multiple OPC UA clients. The lowest granularity of scheduling happens on a function call level, so the scheduler cannot perform a context switch before the currently executing function has returned. If functions consume large amounts of computing time, this can be problematic. This is the case for asymmetric crypto operations, which are performed when establishing a new connection with an OPC UA client. For instance, an RSA-2048-bit sign operation consumes multiple seconds on our evaluation system, during which the HP SDK is blocked. This leads to issues when a client performs an operation on the server, such as reading a value, while a second client attempts to connect to the server. In this case, the connection of the first client freezes until the necessary cryptographic operations for connecting the second client have finished.

To fix this issue, it would be necessary to improve concurrency for cryptographic operations. Long-running operations would need to be paused and continued later. This way, the HP SDK could serve other clients while a client is connecting. According to the documentation, the HP SDK already has the necessary foundation to implement this[1].

Hardware Acceleration for Asymmetric Crypto Operations. While implementing concurrency for crypto operations would prevent connection attempts blocking all other operations on the server, it would not resolve the underlying issue, namely the fact that connecting to the server requires several seconds. On the contrary, pausing crypto operations to serve other clients would further increase connection times.

Long connection times can be addressed with a hardware accelerator for cryptographic operations, to which the HP SDK could delegate cryptographic computations while continung OPC UA communication. To this end, the crypto backend of the HP SDK would need to be modified by replacing function calls to the MbedTLS library with commands to the hardware chip.

However, not all cryptographic hardware accelerators are suited for OPC UA. To speed-up connection times, RSA operations must be supported, ideally with a key size of 2048-bit and 4096-bit. Support for AES and SHA2 is less important. Delegating these crypto operations to a hardware chip could speed-up OPC UA read and write operations, but their runtime overhead is already quite low (circa 2 ms as shown in Sect. 5.3).

In the near future, OPC UA will also support elliptic curves as an alternative to RSA [17]. In detail, the elliptic curves P256, P384, P256R1, P384R1, Curve25519, and Curve448 will be supported. ECC algorithms are typically

---

[1] See "Asynchronous Crypto and PKI APIs" in [20]

faster than RSA, which will make establishing connections faster. Nevertheless, even with ECC crypto, we expect connection times to constitute the bottleneck in OPC UA communication. For this reason, choosing a cryptographic hardware accelerator that supports a broad range of the above-mentioned ECC algorithms will make the OPC UA server future-ready.

Sufficient Flash Memory and RAM. Beyond sufficient computational power, memory demands constitute another concern. Our evaluation shows that 2 MB Flash memory turned out to be just enough to store an OPC UA server with security mechanisms, with only 153 KB being left on Flash. However, industrial devices often support multiple protocols like PROFINET or Ethernet/IP. Thus, Flash memory must be dimensioned to store further protocol implementations.

In addition, we also reached the limit of the available RAM on our evaluation platform. As each connected client consumed a significant amount of heap memory, we were unable to connect more than a handful of clients with the available 640 KB of RAM. Depending on the use case, additional RAM may be needed to support more concurrent client connections.

Secure Hardware Storage for OPC UA Keys. Our implementation saves OPC UA keys in the file system. This is not ideal for security, since an adversary who gets access to the file system can exfiltrate the private OPC UA key. In addition, industrial standards, e.g., IEC 62443 [9], may mandate the secure storage of keys to fulfill a certain target security level.

A more secure way would be storing OPC UA keys in a secure hardware storage like a Trusted Platform Module (TPM). The HP SDK would utilize the key by using the API of the hardware storage. The required changes would be realizable with minor effort due to the modular architecture of the HP SDK.

7 Conclusion

In this practical experience report, we investigated under which conditions secure OPC UA communication is realizable on resource-constrained industrial devices. We implemented an OPC UA server on an 80 MHz ARM Cortex-M4 CPU with 2 MB Flash and 640 KB RAM. This required several changes to the underlying OPC UA SDK, especially for realizing OPC UA security mechanisms with the constrained resources. Our evaluation showed that secure OPC UA communication on such a resource-constrained device is feasible. The latency introduced by security in typical use cases is revealed as acceptable, since read and write operations increased from circa 3 ms to 5 ms in our experiments. The power consumption overhead for security is minimal, which enables a certification for use in hazardous environments. However, other findings also raise concerns, primarily the lack of concurrency and large delays for establishing secure connections. We identified two ways to fix this issue. First, modifying the OPC UA SDK to support pausing cryptographic operations, which would prevent connection attempts from blocking the device. Second, employing a hardware accelerator for RSA (today) and ECC (near future), which would reduce connection times.

Another concern is the memory consumption. The 2 MB Flash memory and 640 KB RAM were just enough to achieve secure OPC UA connections with a handful of connected clients. Thus, more Flash and RAM are needed, if additional concurrent client connections or additional communication protocols (e.g., PROFINET or Ethernet/IP) must be supported.

References

1. ARM Limited: Mbed TLS (previously PolarSSL) (2022). https://tls.mbed.org/
2. Burger, A., Koziolek, H., Rückert, J., Platenius-Mohr, M., Stomberg, G.: Bottleneck identification and performance modeling of OPC UA communication models. In: ACM/SPEC International Conference on Performance Engineering (2019)
3. Cavalieri, S., Cutuli, G.: Performance evaluation of OPC UA. In: 2010 IEEE 15th conference on emerging technologies & factory automation (ETFA). IEEE (2010)
4. Cenedese, A., Frodella, M., Tramarin, F., Vitturi, S.: Comparative assessment of different OPC UA open-source stacks for embedded systems. In: 2019 24th IEEE International Conference on Emerging Technologies and Factory Automation (ETFA), pp. 1127–1134. IEEE (2019)
5. Cho, H., Jeong, J.: Implementation and performance analysis of power and cost-reduced OPC UA gateway for industrial IoT platforms. In: 2018 28th International Telecommunication Networks and Applications Conference (ITNAC). IEEE (2018)
6. Federal Office for Information Security (BSI): OPC UA Security Analysis. Germany, Bonn, Germany, April 2017
7. Grüner, S., Pfrommer, J., Palm, F.: Restful industrial communication with OPC UA. IEEE Trans. Ind. Inform. **12**(5), 1832–1841 (2016)
8. International Electrotechnical Commission (IEC): IEC TR 62541 (2016)
9. International Electrotechnical Commission (IEC): IEC 62443 (2018)
10. International Electrotechnical Commission (IEC): IEC 60079-47 Explosive atmospheres - Part 47: Equipment protection by 2-Wire Intrinsically Safe Ethernet concept (2-WISE) (2021)
11. Kiviharju, M.: On the fog of RSA key lengths: verifying public key cryptography strength recommendations. In: 2017 International Conference on Military Communications and Information Systems (ICMCIS), pp. 1–8. IEEE (2017)
12. Kohnhäuser, F., Meier, D., Patzer, F., Finster, S.: On the security of IIoT deployments: an investigation of secure provisioning solutions for OPC UA. IEEE Access **9**, 99299–99311 (2021)
13. Lasi, H., Fettke, P., Kemper, H.-G., Feld, T., Hoffmann, M.: Industry 4.0. Bus. Inf. Syst. Eng. **6**(4), 239–242 (2014). https://doi.org/10.1007/s12599-014-0334-4
14. Morato, A., Vitturi, S., Tramarin, F., Cenedese, A.: Assessment of different OPC UA implementations for industrial IoT-based measurement applications. IEEE Trans. Instrum. Measur. **70**, 1–11 (2020)
15. Mühlbauer, N., Kirdan, E., Pahl, M.O., Carle, G.: Open-source OPC UA security and scalability. In: 2020 25th IEEE International Conference on Emerging Technologies and Factory Automation (ETFA), vol. 1, pp. 262–269. IEEE (2020)
16. OPC Foundation: OPC 10000-2 Unified Architecture Part 2 Security Model (2015)
17. OPC Foundation: OPC 10001-4 Unified Architecture Amendment 4 ECC (2020)
18. Pfrommer, J., Ebner, A., Ravikumar, S., Karunakaran, B.: Open source OPC UA PubSub over TSN for realtime industrial communication. In: 2018 IEEE 23rd International Conference on Emerging Technologies and Factory Automation (ETFA), vol. 1, pp. 1087–1090. IEEE (2018)

19. Profanter, S., Tekat, A., Dorofeev, K., Rickert, M., Knoll, A.: OPC UA versus ROS, DDS, and MQTT: performance evaluation of industry 4.0 protocols. In: 2019 IEEE International Conference on Industrial Technology (ICIT), pp. 955–962. IEEE (2019)
20. Unified Automation: High Performance OPC UA Server SDK (2022). https://unified-automation.com/products/server-sdk/highperf-ua-server-sdk.html
21. Unified Automation: UaExpert - A Full-Featured OPC UA Client (2022). https://unified-automation.com/products/development-tools/uaexpert.html
22. Vázquez, F.G.: Test platform for the performance evaluation of opc-ua servers for fast data transfer between intelligent equipment. In: The fourth international conference on intelligent systems and applications. p. 193 (2015)

Fault Injection

SAILFAIL: Model-Derived Simulation-Assisted ISA-Level Fault-Injection Platforms

Christian Dietrich[1]([✉]), Malte Bargholz[2], Yannick Loeck[1], Marcel Budoj[2], Luca Nedaskowskij[2], and Daniel Lohmann[2]

[1] Technische Universität Hamburg, Hamburg, Germany
christian.dietrich@tuhh.de
[2] Leibniz Universität Hannover, Hanover, Germany

Abstract. For systematic *f*ault injection (FI), we deterministically re-execute a program, introduce faults, and observe the program outcome to assess its resilience in the presence of transient hardware faults. For this, simulation-assisted ISA-level FI provides a good trade-off between result quality and the required time to execute the FI campaign. However, for each architecture, this requires a specialized ISA simulator with tracing, injection, and error observation capabilities; a dependency that not only increases the bar for the exploration of ISA-level hardening mechanisms, but which can also deviate from the behavior of the actual hardware, especially when an error propagates through the system and triggers semantic edge cases.

With SAILFAIL, we propose a model-driven approach to derive FI platforms from Sail models, which formally describe the ISA semantics. Based on two existing (RISC-V, CHERI RISC-V) and one newly introduced (AVR) Sail models, we use the Sail toolchain to derive emulators that we combine with the FAIL* framework into multiple new FI platforms. Furthermore, we extend Sail to automatically introduce bit-wise dynamic register tracing into the emulator, which enables us to harvest bit-wise access information that we use to improve the well-known def-use pruning technique. Thereby, we further reduce the number of necessary injections by up to 19%.

Keywords: ISA-level fault injection · Transient hardware faults · Simulation-assisted fault injection

1 Introduction

Shrinking transistor sizes and lowering operating voltages make transient hardware faults, where bits in a machine's dynamic state randomly flip, not only a challenge for safety-critical systems [5,7,18] but, increasingly, also for cloud providers [13]. Functional safety standards (e.g., ISO 26262 [15]) already reflect this and recommend explicit measures to assess (and possibly mitigate) the

© The Author(s), under exclusive license to Springer Nature Switzerland AG 2022
M. Trapp et al. (Eds.): SAFECOMP 2022, LNCS 13414, pp. 207–221, 2022.
https://doi.org/10.1007/978-3-031-14835-4_14

effects of *single-event upsets (SEUs)* causing transient hardware faults (soft errors) [16] on the functional safety of the system. One possibility to assess a system's resilience is a systematic *f*ault injection (FI) campaign [23] of the program-under-test (PUT), where many (or even all) of the possible faults for a single execution are injected into different program re-runs, while the injection platform classifies the subsequent behavior (e.g., benign fault, *s*ilent-data corruption (SDC)). Such precise failure classification does not only quantify the program resilience, but also guides the introduction of mitigation techniques [14].

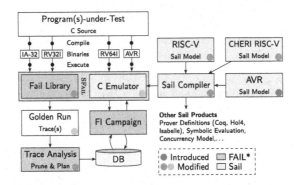

Fig. 1. Overview of SAILFAIL

For the injection platform, three solution classes emerged: (1) *Software-Implemented FI* (SWIFI) [3,24] runs a pre-injected version of the program on the final target platform, leveraging high injection speeds. (2) *Simulation-Assisted FI* (SAFI) [10,12,23] uses a low-level architecture simulator (e.g., ISA- or flip-flop level) to inject and observe the executing program "from beneath", which eases parallelization of the campaign. (3) *Hardware-Assisted FI* (HAFI) [6,9] is similar to SAFI, but loads an instrumented netlist of the target platform loaded into an FPGAs, which allows for gate-level FI at reasonable speeds. While *Software-Implemented FI (SWIFI)*'s pre-injected programs only behave similar (e.g., different code and data layout) to the PUT and HAFI can be parallelized only up to the number of available FPGAs/LUTs, SAFI provides a compromise between campaign run time and result quality.

Still, SAFI requires an instrumented simulator that provides hooks and callbacks for tracing, fault injection, and behavior observation. Often, SAFI platforms extend existing simulators, like Bochs [23] or gem5 [26], which shortens development times but bears the risk that the used simulator differs in subtle details from the actual target platform, which can skew the FI results.

Therefore, with SAILFAIL, we propose (see Fig. 1) to derive SAFI platforms from a formal description of the ISA semantic, which allows for easier validation and verification. We chose Sail [1], since Sail models cannot only be translated to theorem prover definitions, but the Sail toolchain can already compile a model to a sequential C emulator. Furthermore, we leverage the existing FAIL* toolchain and combine the generated emulator with FAIL*'s injection and experiment infrastructure. Due to our model-driven approach, we can automatically introduce callbacks during this compilation process, which not only limits the required model modifications but also allows for a fine-grained observation of the PUT down to the bit level. All in all, we are able to provide five new FAIL* backends for RISC-V (32/64 bits), CHERI RISC-V (32/64 bits), and AVR 8-bit microcontrollers.

The contributions of this paper are as follows:

- We derive ISA-level FI platforms from two existing and one newly developed Sail ISA models. In total, we provide five new FI backends.
- We extend the Sail toolchain to provide for automatically instrumented bit-precise register access tracing.
- We propose bit-wise def-use fault space pruning for partially interpreted register accesses.

The rest of the paper is structured as follows: In Sect. 2, we provide the necessary background on FAIL* and Sail, before we describe the SailFAIL approach in Sect. 3. In Sect. 4, we perform an evaluation of the resulting FI platforms against the existing FAIL* backend for IA-32 and quantify the benefits of our automatic register-tracing transformation, before we conclude in Sect. 5.

2   Background

SailFAIL integrates formal models of the ISA semantic with the existing SAFI framework FAIL* to provide different systematic FI platforms. As our ISA-modeling language, we chose Sail [1], whose toolchain provides versatile backends, including the automatic derivation of ISA-level emulators. Furthermore, different high-quality ISA models (e.g., ARMv8.5, RISC-V, MIPS) with and without the HW-enabled capability extension CHERI [4], which inspired ARM's Morrello CPU extension, are available.

2.1   Systematic Fault Injection

For the systematic FI of transient hardware faults in the volatile machine state, we execute three steps (see Fig. 1, left): (1) *trace* a fault-free program execution as the *golden run*, which spans up the *fault space (FS)* of all potential faults (one fault per time and bit, uniformly distributed). (2) *prune* the FS [11,20,25] to plan a representative subset of faults as *pilot injections*. (3) re-execute the program deterministically, *inject* the planned pilots, and classify the following program behavior. While this results in a precise (and even complete) picture of a program's resilience on the chosen level, it is not only time-consuming, but it also requires a specially-instrumented *execution platform* for steps 1 and 3, which must be able to record the program state, inject faults into the executing program, and observe the continued behavior.

For the result interpretation, we have to use metrics that incorporate not only failure counts but also the fault-space size [22]. Otherwise, the results, especially from software-level FI, can deviate substantially from the actual failure behavior [5, 19, 21] of the hardware. However, it was shown [21] that ISA-level injection, if interpreted correctly, is well suited to select the most resilient algorithm variant.

2.2 Sail: ISA Modeling Language

Sail is a special-purpose modeling language for ISA-semantic description, that comes with a toolchain to analyze and translate models to different representations. In its core, the Sail language is a dependently-typed and statically-checked first-order imperative language with strong pattern-matching capabilities that mimics existing industry ISA pseudocode. Sail's main design goal was to create a language that is expressive enough to densely describe ISA semantics but also limited enough to allow for easy translation. For example, Sail does not support higher-order functions.

```
1 register PC      : bits(22) // Program Counter
2 register nextPC : bits(22) // PC in the next cycle
3 register SP      : bits(16) // Stack Pointer
4
5 function clause decode 0b1101 @ offset : bits(12)
6    = Some(BRTYPE(AVR_RCALL, offset))
7
8 function clause execute (BRTYPE(AVR_RCALL, offset)) = {
9    // Push return address onto Stack
10   let ret = write_dmem(SP,      nextPC[7..0]);
11   let ret = write_dmem(SP - 1, nextPC[15..8]);
12   SP = SP - 2;
13
14   // Relative jump with a scaling of 2 byte.
15   let roffset = signed(offset) * 2;
16   nextPC = nextPC + roffset;
17 }
```

Fig. 2. Sail Fragment of the `rcall` Instruction in our AVR model

In a Sail model, *registers*, which are essentially global variables, contain the model state. Sail supports enums, bit vectors, bit fields, and arbitrary-precision integers as scalar types, while complex types like dynamic lists, vectors, structs and tagged unions are also available. However, most complex and nested types, beyond a simple vector of bitvectors, are quite unusual for typing registers, as the model resembles a hardware implementation. In Fig. 2, we present the relative-call instruction from our own AVR model. PC and nextPC are 22-bit registers and hold the current and the subsequently following program counter, while SP holds the stack pointer and is 16 bits wide.

Sail allows for scattered function definitions that use pattern matching on their argument values. In the example, we show one *clause* of the decode()

function that decodes `rcall` instructions. When the opcode starts with the pattern 1101, this clause captures the remaining 12 argument bits in `offset` and returns the decoded instruction. In the corresponding `execute()` clause, we push the return address onto the stack, and perform a PC-relative jump. Sail also supports slicing of bit vectors and has a built-in abstraction for memory, which is accessed through `write_dmem()`.

For generating a sequential C emulator, the Sail toolchain maps registers to global variables and collects all clauses for a function before translating it to a C function. Scalar types and bitvectors, if smaller than 128 bits, are mapped to C integers; bitfields and other complex type become specialized structs with generated accessor functions.

2.3   FAIL*: Fault Injection Leveraged

FAIL* [23] is a versatile FI platform for the injection of transient hardware faults on the ISA level that is designed to support multiple, simulator- and hardware-debugger–based, injection backends (see Fig. 1). At the moment, FAIL* already has support for Bochs (IA-32), Gem5 (ARM), and OpenOCD (ARM HW) and some experimental and less mature backends (Qemu, Trace32 Tri-Core simulator). Furthermore, FAIL* not only handles the FI itself, but also provides the necessary tooling to record the golden-run trace, plan injections, and to run and distribute the FI campaign onto multiple workers.

For providing high-speed tracing and FI, FAIL* directly links its *client* library into the simulator binary: FAIL* creates a second *co-routine* within the simulator process, which alternates its execution with the simulator's control-flow thread. On specific events, the (modified) simulator switches to the co-routine, which is able to inspect and manipulate the machine state before handing back control. Furthermore, to speed up injections [2], back ends can also support saving and restoring the machine state.

For its functionality, FAIL* relies on callbacks within the simulator to inform the client library about events, provide access to the machine state, and for (re-)storing the machine state. For the existing backends, this hand-crafted connection between FAIL* and the simulator is often rather brittle, which increases the burden of updating the simulator. FAIL*, for example, still ships with a rather ancient version of Bochs 2.4.6 (2011), while 2.7 (August 2021) is already available.

While FAIL* records memory accesses for the golden run, it uses a different route to plan CPU-register injections: FAIL* disassembles (with LLVM or libcapstone) the program binary, and inspects the list of read and written registers for each traced instruction. While such detailed instruction summaries are consistently available for COTS architectures, a hardware developer interested in resilient ISA design would have to maintain, both, the ISA-extension and the FI platform and keep them in sync. Therefore, dynamic register-access tracing, where the FI platform itself records which registers are read, would be beneficial for exploring alternative designs.

3   The SAILFAIL Approach

To speed up FI-platform development, we propose SAILFAIL, a methodology to derive FI platforms from Sail models. Thereby, we not only provide more faithful ISA-level execution platforms for SAFI, but become able to modify the Sail compiler to unleash dynamic *register tracing*: The SAILFAIL-derived simulators dynamically report register reads and writes, down to individual bit-field members, which allows for *bit-wise* def-use pruning of partially interpreted registers (e.g., status registers). Furthermore, we extend FAIL* to systematically support backends with multiple types of memory throughout the complete FI toolchain.

3.1   Connecting Sail and FAIL*

Although Sail is designed as an ISA modeling language, it has no built-in notion of traps, executed instructions, or the current program counter, and does not distinguish between ISA-defined and model-specific registers. While this leaves more room for model designers, it requires SAILFAIL to use manually inserted callbacks to indicate the current progress of the execution. Table 1 gives an overview about the necessary state-transition callbacks. However, since these callbacks are directly inserted into the ISA model, they can co-evolve with the model instead of being managed separately, as currently done in FAIL*.

Table 1. Callbacks that the emulator calls to inform FAIL* about the execution progress.

`willExecute(PC)`	Indicate the next program counter to execute
`executeRequests()`	Give FAIL* the chance to save and restore the machine state
`setIF({true, false})`	Indicate that following memory-accesses stem from the instruction fetch
`onTrap(num)`	A synchronous trap occured
`onInterrupt(num, nmi)`	An (non-maskable) interrupt occured
`didExecute(PC, opcode)`	Execution of instruction did finish

For memory accesses, we also rely on explicitly inserted callbacks (`onMemory Read()`, `onMemoryWrite()`) to report to FAIL*. While a generic modification of Sail's memory abstraction would have been possible, explicit hooks allow us to gather additional information, like the type of accessed memory (i.e., RAM or flash), that is only available within the model.

For register FI, we must have read/write access to all ISA-visible registers (e.g., general-purpose registers, program counter...). For this, we manually curate a register mapping with one line for each register to connect the global variables in the C emulator with the FAIL* machinery. From these mappings, we automatically derive the register-access functions and generate the machine-state checkpointing functionality.

We also explored the possibility of automatically exporting such mappings from the Sail compiler. However, since Sail does not distinguish between model-internal and ISA-visible registers, we decided to stick with the curated variant for now. This also has the benefit of making it easier to support registers whose ISA-level format does not match the format within the model. For example, the CHERI RISC-V model stores capabilities in a decoded form, whereby we have to en-/decode them on access.

3.2 Systematic Register Access Tracing

While deriving emulators from formal ISA models, which are easier to validate, already increases the faith in the FI platform, we can harvest more benefits from this model-driven approach. Since registers are a core concept of Sail, SAILFAIL is able to use a modified Sail compiler that inserts fine-grained register access tracing into the emulator. Thereby, we no longer require a disassembler, but also gain access to dynamic and more fine-grained tracing information: Even if an instruction statically depends on a register, it does not necessarily interpret all bits or read it in a specific context. For example, some instructions interpret/update only some bits of the machine status word and the exception table base register is only of interest in case of a trap.

To provide detailed access information, including a bit mask of potentially interpreted bits, we modified the C backend of the Sail compiler to insert code at every variable access, which covers all (global) register and (local) variable accesses. However, since Sail supports references to registers and nested data types, correlating an access back to a register definition is not straight-forward. To solve this, we search, before each access, for the memory addresses of accessed values in the previously mentioned register mapping (see Sect. 3.1), which also stores pointers to the mapped global variables. On match, SAILFAIL reports the dynamically occurred access to FAIL*, whereby we can cover all ISA registers and report only those accesses that actually occurred.

Nevertheless, there are several challenging patterns in Sail's generated emulators: For accesses to nested register (e.g., within a struct), the emulator creates a temporary copy (with a different address), performs the access, and writes back the result. To catch these accesses, we let the emulator create temporary mappings for the life-time of the copy. Furthermore, we precisely track bit field accesses, which the emulator implements in specialized accessor functions that extract and update specific bits: For each accessor, we calculate an access mask, let the accessor identify the accessed register through the register mapping, and report register and access mask to FAIL*. Thereby, SAILFAIL is able to provide precise access information for bit fields, which we subsequently use to reduce the number of necessary FIs.

3.3 Bit-Wise Def-Use Pruning

FS size is a major problem for systematic FI that aims for a high, or even complete, coverage of all faults in the FS. Naively, we would have to inject every bit of information in every cycle, which quickly becomes infeasible for realistic programs. Therefore, *fault-pruning methods*, which form sets of *equivalent faults* that all show the same erroneous behavior on injection, are used. For each equivalence set, one pilot injection is performed as a representative.

Of these methods, *def-use-pruning* [11,25] is the most established one. For a specific fault location, we partition the time axis at read and write events into compact intervals. As faulty information only becomes active on access, every fault within the interval can act as a representative injection, whose failure classification can be projected onto all members of the interval. Even more, intervals that are closed by a write event are surely benign and require no injection. For example, Fig. 3a shows a 4-bit, 10 cycle FS for a processor's status register SREG (40 faults). As there are 4 read events (after cycle 0, 2, 4, 8), def-use pruning would schedule 16 injections for complete FS coverage. In a recent work [20], we also made def-use-pruning aware of the program's data-flow to form two-dimensional equivalence intervals.

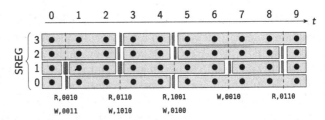

(a) Example fault space with 4-bit **Read** and **Write** masks.

```
1  def bit_wise_prune(events):
2      # Initialize Access Stacks and iterate over all events in
3      # chronological order
4      access_stacks = {loc: Event(time=0,mask=0xffff)
5                       for loc in all_locs])
6      for event in events:
7          access_mask  = event.mask # Copy mask!
8          # Iterate over previous events in reverse
9          access_stack = access_stacks[event.loc]
10         for prev in reversed(access_stack):
11             # Has previous event touched the same bits
12             overlap = access_mask & prev.mask
13             if overlap != 0:
14                 # New equiv. interval: (prev.time, event.time)
15                 new_interval(prev.time, event.time,
16                              event,    overlap)
17                 # Clear bits in both masks '
18                 prev.mask ^= overlap
19                 access_mask  ^= overlap
20             # Pop Empty events from Stack
21             if prev.mask == 0: ...
22         # Push current event onto the Stack
23         access_stack.push(event)
```

(b) Algorithm in Python Pseudocode

Fig. 3. Bit-Wise Def-Use Pruning. For Sail bit fields, SAILFAIL records access bit-masks for each read/write event, whereby a more precise def-use pruning is possible.

However, as touched on before, instructions do not necessarily access or over-write all bits of a register. For example, the first access to SREG in Fig. 3a, only reads bit 1 and writes bits 0 and 1; bits 2 and 3 remain untouched, whereby no injection for these bits is necessary at cycle 0. For bit 3, no injection is even necessary at all, as it is overwritten after cycle 2. In total, with the recorded access-mask information, only 7 injections are really required to cover the pre-sented FS.

To incorporate the access masks, we extend the byte-granular def-use pruning of FAIL* (see Fig. 3b): For each coarse-grained fault location, we keep a FIFO stack that holds previous read/write events with a bit-mask of still *open* equiv-alence intervals. For each access in the golden run, we search the access history backwards for masks that `overlap` with the current access mask. On match, we report an interval (`new_interval()`) between the previous (`prev.time`) and the current access (`event.time`) with the overlapping bit mask. Since we close those reported intervals in previous accesses, we can drop old events (not shown) such that the stack for a register never grows larger than the register width.

3.4   Virtual Fault Spaces

With the flexibility of SAILFAIL's model-driven approach, the FI platform has the chance to support a wide range of processors. However, this also requires uni-fied support for the different state holding elements (i.e., registers, RAM, EEP-ROM, flash. . .). Therefore, we introduce the *virtual fault space*, which maps the different kinds of memory into a unified FS abstraction, on which we can carry out FS analyses, the fault pruning and the campaign management. Thereby, SAILFAIL is able to handle different architectures, even with experimental ISA extensions, with the same toolchain and the same database schema.

In essence, the virtual fault space maps different fault locations within the target architecture into a linear address space for which we use 64-bit-wide addresses. While recording the golden run, we translate accesses into this unified FS, let FAIL* work on this representation, and only map the FS address back to the actual emulator register (and its corresponding global variable) at injec-tion time. In this translation step, we are also able to provide a dense encoding for unusual kinds of memory. For example, the CHERI RISC-V 32-bit architec-ture stores one out-of-band tag bit for every 64 bits of memory to ensure the "unforgeable" attribute of capabilities. With the virtual fault space, we are able to densely store those tag bits in a separate FS region instead of supporting 65-bit memory throughout the whole FI toolchain.

4   Evaluation

We used SAILFAIL with three Sail models (RISC-V, CHERI RISC-V, AVR), whereof the two RISC-V models were built by the Sail developers [1] and the AVR model was developed by us. Since the RISC-V models have configurable bit widths (32/64 bits), we provide five new backends for FAIL*. After developing

SAILFAIL for the RISC-V FI platforms, it took one developer day to derive the AVR FI platform. In the following, we will quantify the efficiency of these backends, report on the coverage of the dynamic register tracing, and show the potential saving of bit-wise pruning for bit-packed CPU registers.

4.1   Simulation Overheads

For systematic SAFI, the simulation platform executes the same program, over and over again, potentially millions of times. Thereby, the run-time-overheads for checkpointing and instruction simulation become critical properties for SAIL-FAIL's applicability. Therefore, we quantify these overheads by comparing the existing IA-32 backend (Bochs), which is FAIL*'s most mature platform, with our backends for RISC-V 32-bit, which comes closest to IA-32, and AVR. Furthermore, we perform golden-run tracing with Spike[1], the reference ISA simulator for RISC-V. We executed all benchmarks on a 48-core (96 HW threads) Intel Xeon Gold 6262 CPU with 2.10 GHz and 373 GiB of RAM, within a Debian 11.0 Docker container, which we made publicly available [8] to ease the reproduction of our results.

For the benchmark, we execute the golden run trace step, which includes starting the simulator, saving a machine state checkpoint, and performing a fault-free execution of the program, while recording *program counter (PC)* and memory accesses. We focus on the tracing step here, since fault-injected executions are all purposefully different from each other. However, since each FI run consists of checkpoint restoration and program execution, we believe that the results are transferable.

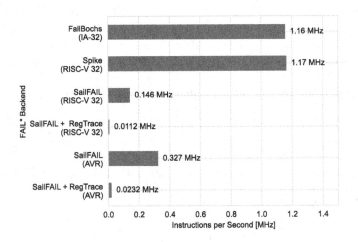

Fig. 4. Simulation performance

---

[1] https://github.com/riscv-software-src/riscv-isa-sim.

Our PUT calculates the CRC32 checksum over the first 8000 iteratively calculated Fibonacci numbers (overflowed at 32 bits). This program requires almost the same number of instructions on RISC-V and IA-32 (488K instr.). For the single-threaded tracing, we record the number of simulated instructions and the run-time of the executing simulator and show the achieved simulation performance in Fig. 4.

Without dynamic register tracing, our RISC-V 32-bit emulator achieves 13% of the performance of Bochs (and Spike), which simulate at around 1.2 MHz. For the considerably simpler 8-bit AVR architecture, SailFAIL achieves 327 KHz. With dynamic register tracing, which is only required for golden run tracing and can be disabled for the actual FI, the simulation frequency is at 11 KHz (RISC-V) and 23 KHz (AVR).

The less-desirable performance results of Sail-generated simulators have two origins: (1) Quality of the model: As the authors admit, the RISC-V model has "many opportunities for optimisation" [17] as it only achieves around 300 KHz without instruction tracing. (2) Sail's C-emulator backend: Although our AVR model is a straight-forward implementation of a rather simple 8-bit ISA, its performance is still by a factor of three from Bochs and Spike. From this, we conclude that the translation from Sail to C is not yet fully optimized. Nevertheless, unlike hand-optimized per-ISA backends, all SailFAILFI platforms will automatically become faster with improvements to the Sail toolchain.

For checkpoint saving, Bochs requires 0.54 s, while the RISC-V emulator only requires 0.024 s. These long checkpointing times stem from the fact that Bochs is not only a CPU emulator, but emulates a whole execution platform including periphery. This is also reflected in Boch's startup time of 3.82 s, which makes checkpointing absolutely necessary for reasonable FI times. With SailFAIL, the 0.011 s setup time is even faster than saving the checkpoint. So, while the hand-optimized simulator will outperform Sail's generated one in the long run, SailFAIL can already be faster for short running programs.

4.2 Register Trace Coverage

To validate our register tracing approach, we compare the recorded register accesses to the result of FAIL*'s trace analysis, which statically extracts register access patterns from the disassembled binary. At the very least, SailFAIL must record all accesses that can be also be statically extractable. For RISC-V 32-bit, we traced the mentioned program for the first 500 Fibonacci numbers (30 510 instructions), loaded the golden run into the database, and executed (bit-wise) def-use pruning.

In total, the disassembler approach reported $2.58 \cdot 10^5$ register byte accesses[2], while SAILFAIL reported $6.27 \cdot 10^5$ accesses. SAILFAIL faithfully covered all statically inferred register accesses, but moreover found accesses to six additional architecture-specific registers (MISA, MSTATUS, MIP, MIE, MCYCLE, MTIME), which the CPU implicitly uses to decide on the instruction semantic and interruptions. While these registers are not listed in the disassembler information, SAILFAIL makes it possible to also cover them in a FI campaign.

4.3   Efficiency Improvements by Bit-Wise Pruning

Our bit-wise pruning method, combined with the fine-grained access information, allows SAILFAIL to cover partially read/written registers without planning a FI for each bit in each accessed register. As the disassembler-based approach would only report full-width accesses to those six registers, the byte-granular def-use pruning method would require $4.43 \cdot 10^6$ pilot injections into the registers. By taking the access masks into account, we are able to reduce this number to $3.58 \cdot 10^6$ (-19.28%).

For the CRC32-Fibonacci program on AVR ($N = 500$, 85 511 instructions), the situation looks similar: a disassembler-based approach would require $9.42 \cdot 10^5$ single-bit register injections, while SAILFAIL plans $7.9 \cdot 10^5$ injections (-16.16%). For AVR, this reduction stems from the 8-bit wide SREG register, which, in contrast to RISC-V's machine status word, is essential to the instruction semantic as it stores condition codes. From 21 000 SREG reads, our dynamic tracing recorded that 96.4% interpreted a single bit and 3.6% accessed two bits. Unlike a byte-wise def-user pruner, which would plan 8 injections per access, our bit-wise pruning only plans one resp. two injections.

4.4   Case Study: SDC Counts for Bubblesort

To demonstrate the flexibility of SAILFAIL, we execute a comparative FI campaign to quantify the resilience of different bubblesort implementations on different RISC-V derivatives. With bubblesort, we sort ten integers (register width) that are stored in a *static* array, a *single*-linked list, and a *double*-linked list; for the CHERI variants, the link pointers were capability-protected. Besides RISC-V and CHERI-enabled RISC-V, we also execute our benchmarks on a CHERI-RISC-V variant that we extended with parity-protected capabilities. We also compare the 32-bit and 64-bit ISA variants. We chose these benchmark (variants) as we expect that capabilities, which also provide hardware-enforced bounds checking, positively influence the SDC rate.

---

[2] FAIL* splits up an access to a 32-bit register in four 4-byte accesses.

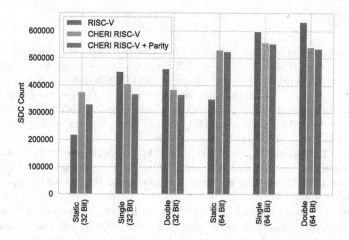

Fig. 5. SDCs for different bubblesort implementations

With our toolchain, we covered the full FS for memory and registers and show the weighted absolute failure counts [22] for the SDC class in Fig. 5. In total, this comparative campaign requires six different FI platforms; each with tooling for tracing, pruning, campaign coordination, and analysis. With SAIL-FAIL, we could provide these toolchains from two basic Sail models with a small modification to the CHERI RISC-V model.

From the results, we can deduce the following observations: (1) If using static arrays, the protection from capabilities does not outweigh the increased attack surface that is induced by managing those capabilities. (2) Our parity extension improves the SDC rate of CHERI RISC-V ISA always and up to 12%. (3) Although doubling the size of the sorted integers from 32 to 64 bit, the SDC does not increase linearly but between 33% (Single Linked List on RISC-V) and 60% (Static Array on RISC-V). (4) Using double-linked list instead of single-linked lists the SDC rate decreases for CHERI-protected ISAs, while it increases for the RISC-V without capabilities.

5 Conclusion

With SAILFAIL, we derived five new simulation-assisted FI platforms from three formal ISA models written in the Sail modeling language. With limited manual effort, we combined automatically generated C emulators with the FAIL* toolchain, whereby SAILFAIL supports all phases of systematic FI campaigns (tracing, injection planing, and injection). We also modified the Sail compiler and let the emulator dynamically record register accesses, down to the level of individual bits. In combination with our bit-wise def-use pruning, we were able to cover implicitly used architectural registers (e.g., machine status words) while reducing necessary injections by up to 19%. In a case study FI, we compared different (CHERI) RISC-V ISAs and showed that parity-checked capabilities improved the SDC rate by up to 12%.

References

1. Armstrong, A., et al.: ISA semantics for ARMv8-A, RISC-V, and CHERI-MIPS. In: Proceedings of 46th ACM SIGPLAN Symposium on Principles of Programming Languages, January 2019. https://doi.org/10.1145/3290384
2. Berrojo, L., et al.: New techniques for speeding-up fault-injection campaigns. In: Design, Automation and Test in Europe Conference and Exhibition 2002 (DATE 2002), pp. 847–852, Washington, DC, USA. IEEE Computer Society Press (2002). https://doi.org/10.1109/DATE.2002.998398
3. Carreira, J., Madeira, H., Silva, J.G., Silva, J.G.: Xception: software fault injection and monitoring in processor functional units. In: Proceedings of the Conference on Dependable Computing for Critical Applications (DCCA 1995), pp. 135–149, September 1995
4. Chisnall, D., et al.: Beyond the PDP-11: architectural support for a memory-safe C abstract machine. In: Proceedings of the Second International Conference on Architectual Support for Programming Languages and Operating Systems. ACM, New York (2015). https://doi.org/10.1145/2694344.2694367
5. Cho, H., Mirkhani, S., Cher, C.Y., Abraham, J.A., Mitra, S.: Quantitative evaluation of soft error injection techniques for robust system design. In: Proceedings of the 50th Annual Design Automation Conference, pp. 1–10 (2013). https://doi.org/10.1145/2463209.2488859
6. Civera, P., Macchiarulo, L., Rebaudengo, M., Reorda, M.S., Violante, M.: An FPGA-based approach for speeding-up fault injection campaigns on safety-critical circuits. J. Electron. Test. **18**(3), 261–271 (2002). https://doi.org/10.1023/A:1015079004512
7. Constantinescu, C.: Trends and challenges in VLSI circuit reliability. IEEE Micro **23**(4), 14–19 (2003). https://doi.org/10.1109/MM.2003.1225959. ISSN 0272-1732
8. Dietrich, C., Bargholz, M., Loeck, Y., Budoj, M., Nedaskowskij, L., Lohmann, D.: SailFail: Model-Derived Simulation-Assisted ISA- Level Fault-Injection Platforms (Software Artifact), May 2022. https://doi.org/10.5281/zenodo.6553206
9. Entrena, L., Garcia-Valderas, M., Fernandez-Cardenal, R., Lindoso, A., Portela, M., Lopez-Ongil, C.: Soft error sensitivity evaluation of microprocessors by multi-level emulation-based fault injection. IEEE Trans. Comput. **61**(3), 313–322 (2012). https://doi.org/10.1109/TC.2010.262. ISSN 0018-9340
10. Guan, Q., Debardeleben, N., Blanchard, S., Fu, S.: F-SEFI: a fine-grained soft error fault injection tool for profiling application vulnerability. In: 2014 IEEE 28th International Parallel and Distributed Processing Symposium, pp. 1245–1254, May 2014. https://doi.org/10.1109/IPDPS.2014.128
11. Guthoff, J., Sieh, V.: Combining software-implemented and simulation-based fault injection into a single fault injection method. In: Proceedings of the 25rd International Symposium on Fault-Tolerant Computing (FTCS-25), pp. 196–206. IEEE Computer Society Press, June 1995. https://doi.org/10.1109/FTCS.1995.466978
12. Hari, S.K.S., Adve, S.V., Naeimi, H., Ramachandran, P.: Relyzer: exploiting application-level fault equivalence to analyze application resiliency to transient faults. In: Proceedings of the 17th International Conference on Architectural Support for Programming Languages and Operating Systems (ASPLOS 2012). ACM Press, New York (2012). https://doi.org/10.1145/2150976.2150990. ISBN 978-1-4503-0759-8
13. Hochschild, P.H., et al.: Cores that don't count. In: Proceedings of the Workshop on Hot Topics in Operating Systems, pp. 9–16 (2021)

14. Hoffmann, M., Ulbrich, P., Dietrich, C., Schirmeier, H., Lohmann, D., Schröder-Preikschat, W.: A practitioner's guide to software-based soft-error mitigation using AN-codes. In: Proceedings of the 15th IEEE International Symposium on High-Assurance Systems Engineering (HASE 2014), pp. 33–40. IEEE Computer Society Press, January 2014. https://doi.org/10.1109/HASE.2014.14. ISBN 978-1-4799-3465-2

15. ISO 26262-9:2018: Road vehicles - Functional safety - Part 9: Automotive Safety Integrity Level (ASIL)-oriented and safety-oriented analyses. International Organization for Standardization, Geneva, Switzerland (2018)

16. Mukherjee, S.: Architecture Design for Soft Errors. Morgan Kaufmann Publishers Inc., San Francisco (2008). ISBN 978-0-12-369529-1

17. Mundkur, P., et al.: RISCV sail model. https://github.com/riscv/sail-riscv. Accessed 04 Feb 2022

18. Nassif, S.R., Mehta, N., Cao, Y.: A resilience roadmap. In: Design, Automation Test in Europe Conference Exhibition (DATE 2010), pp. 1011–1016 (2010). https://doi.org/10.1109/DATE.2010.5456958

19. Papadimitriou, G., Gizopoulos, D.: Demystifying the system vulnerability stack: transient fault effects across the layers. In: 48th ACM/IEEE Annual International Symposium on Computer Architecture, ISCA 2021, Valencia, Spain, 14–18 June 2021, pp. 902–915 (2021). https://doi.org/10.1109/ISCA52012.2021.00075

20. Pusz, O., Dietrich, C., Lohmann, D.: Data-flow-sensitive fault-space pruning for the injection of transient hardware faults. In: Proceedings of the 2021 ACM SIGPLAN/SIGBED Conference on Languages, Compilers and Tools for Embedded Systems (LCTES 2021), pp. 97–109. ACM Press, New York, June 2021. https://doi.org/10.1145/3461648.3463851

21. Schirmeier, H., Breddemann, M.: Quantitative cross-layer evaluation of transient-fault injection techniques for algorithm comparison. In: 15th European Dependable Computing Conference, EDCC 2019, Naples, Italy, 17–20 September 2019, pp. 15–22 (2019). https://doi.org/10.1109/EDCC.2019.00016

22. Schirmeier, H., Borchert, C., Spinczyk, O.: Avoiding pitfalls in fault-injection based comparison of program susceptibility to soft errors. In: Proceedings of the 45th International Conference on Dependable Systems and Networks (DSN 2015), Washington, DC, USA. IEEE Computer Society Press, June 2015. https://doi.org/10.1109/DSN.2015.44

23. Schirmeier, H., Hoffmann, M., Dietrich, C., Lenz, M., Lohmann, D., Spinczyk, O.: FAIL*: an open and versatile fault-injection framework for the assessment of software-implemented hardware fault tolerance. In: Sens, P. (ed.) Proceedings of the 11th European Dependable Computing Conference (EDCC 2015), pp. 245–255, September 2015. https://doi.org/10.1109/EDCC.2015.28

24. Skarin, D., Barbosa, R., Karlsson, J.: GOOFI-2: a tool for experimental dependability assessment. In: Proceedings of the 39th International Conference on Dependable Systems and Networks (DSN 2009), pp. 557–562. IEEE Computer Society Press, June 2010. https://doi.org/10.1109/DSN.2010.5544265

25. Smith, D.T., Johnson, B.W., Profeta, J.A., Bozzolo, D.G.: A method to determine equivalent fault classes for permanent and transient faults. In: Annual Reliability and Maintainability Symposium 1995 Proceedings, pp. 418–424. IEEE (1995). https://doi.org/10.1109/RAMS.1995.513278

26. Venkatagiri, R., et al.: gem5-approxilyzer: an open-source tool for application-level soft error analysis. In: 2019 49th Annual IEEE/IFIP International Conference on Dependable Systems and Networks (DSN), pp. 214–221 (2019). https://doi.org/10.1109/DSN.2019.00033

Quality of Fault Injection Strategies on Hardware Accelerator

Iban Guinebert[1]([✉]), Andres Barrilado[2], Kevin Delmas[1][ID], Franck Galtié[2], and Claire Pagetti[1][ID]

[1] ONERA, 2 Avenue Edouard Belin, 31000 Toulouse, France
`iban.guinebert@onera.fr`
[2] NXP Semiconductors, 134 Avenue du Général Eisenhower, 31100 Toulouse, France

Abstract. Safety-critical systems require understanding and mitigating the behavior of processors in case of failures. In order to analyze and verify hardware architectures, intensive fault injection campaigns are made. This work focuses on assessing the quality of fault injection strategies. The idea is to identify all failure scenarios associated to a hardware accelerator and estimate the coverage associated to a strategy. We have applied the approach on a LeNet5 streaming architecture accelerator.

Keywords: Formal modelling of hardware · Failure modes · Fault injection

1 Introduction

In the automotive domain, ISO 26262 [19] is the standard defining the *functional safety* process. Among the objectives, any semiconductor component (e.g. processor) must be able to detect and mitigate hardware failures that have an impact on the safety of the function running on it.

1.1 Context

The traditional approach [7] to develop ISO26262 compliant processors consists of (1) identifying the failure modes, (2) defining an adequate detection mechanism that permits to detect hardware failures at run-time and (3) realizing intensive fault injection campaigns to verify and validate the design. A classical detection mechanism consists of duplicating the computing units and of comparing each instruction in lock step manner [18]. If this solution has worked perfectly so far, the introduction of hardware accelerator to execute more demanding applications (such as machine learning applications) changes the situation. Indeed, duplicating all computing units would imply the use of a large amount of silicon space and require a lot of power as illustrated by the system-on-a-chip of Tesla [31]. Thus, in the future, new detection strategies will have to be defined.

In any case, verification and validation activities are of paramount importance to assess the *quality* of a detection mechanism, i.e. *does it lead indeed to*

M. Trapp et al. (Eds.): SAFECOMP 2022, LNCS 13414, pp. 222–236, 2022.
https://doi.org/10.1007/978-3-031-14835-4_15

the expected detection capacity? These V & V activities start by understanding in depth the *failure scenarios*, in particular by identifying the safety impact of failures combinations. Then, intensive and representative fault injection campaigns must be defined in order to stress the architecture when activating the *failure scenarios*. We focus on hardware-level fault injection because this encompasses real abnormal behaviors. Most of the works propose random fault injection [26], which is insufficient to provide a full coverage of all *failure scenarios*. On the other hand, realizing naive exhaustive fault injection campaigns is unrealistic as it could take too much time (e.g. one year). Thus, we propose to explore tractable exhaustive/systematic analyses.

1.2   Contributions

A fault injection campaign is composed of a *fault injection strategy* (specifying where to inject the faults and how to code them) and of an *activation strategy* (indicating how to identify and generate a set of representative covering inputs). The *activation strategy* is outside the scope of the present article, the interested reader can find numerous methods (like [15]) addressing the Automatic Test Pattern Generation problem (ATPG). The purpose of the present work is to help assess the quality of fault injection strategies. For this purpose, we first define a formalization of the hardware behavior (Sect. 2) under normal circumstances or under fault. Then, we proposed a methodology (Sect. 3) to identify and quantitatively evaluate the failure scenarios involving a SDC (silent data corruption) failure. We define a coverage metric for fault injection strategies with respect to the full set of failure scenarios. We applied the methodology (Sects. 2.3 and 4) on a LeNet5 streaming architecture accelerator and compared the quality of three injection strategies.

2   Abstract Semantics of Hardware Architecture

In the following we define an abstraction of hardware architectures that allows to describe the behavior of circuits at the Register Transfer Level (RTL).

2.1   Semantics of Atomic Components

The hardware is composed of several components where the smallest units are the *atomic components*. The design is hierarchical, meaning that a component contains several (atomic or non-atomic) components. The description consists of the combination of two parts: the topology details the components and their connections, whereas the dynamic details the data flow driving the communication between or within components. We consider typical atomic components building modern hardware.

Definition 1 (Atomic component). *An atomic component c is:*

– *either* combinational *(e.g. mult, add, max); in this case it applies an operation on several inputs and computes several outputs;*

– *or a* register *of size* b_{reg}; *in this case it can store some data of size* $\leq b_{reg}$
*bits. A register has one input and possibly more than one output if the data
is required by several components.*

The set of atomic components is denoted by $\mathcal{C}$.

We abstract from the complex logic of the hardware design in order to only represent the behavior by its *data-flow*. The logic is encoded by some inputs to be instantiated for each specific hardware. The formalization reuses the notion of flow, *à la.* LUSTRE [17] or *à la tagged signal model* [24]. We consider finite executions of a program that traverse some components and terminate. The next execution will start after the end of the previous execution.

Definition 2 (Flow). *A flow* $f = ((t_k, d_k))_{k<N}$ *is a finite sequence of pairs where* $t_k \in \mathbb{N}$ *is a time stamp and* $d_k \in \mathbb{R}$ *is the value of* f *at time* t_k. *The time stamps of* f *are accessed by the function* $T_f(k) = t_k$ *for* $k < N$. *The values* d_k *are all encoded with the same fixed number of bits denoted by* b_f. *The length of a flow* f *(i.e. the number of elements of* f*) is accessible by* length(f).

The set of flows is denoted by $\mathcal{F}$. *Two flows* f *and* f' *are synchronous, denoted by* $f \bowtie f'$, *if and only if* $T_f = T_{f'}$.

Definition 3 (Input/output flows associated to a component). *Let* c *be a component with* $n_{\text{in}}(c)$ *inputs (resp.* $n_{\text{out}}(c)$ *outputs); we denote by* $(c.in_i)_{i<n_{\text{in}}(c)}$ *(resp.* $(c.out_i)_{i<n_{\text{out}}(c)}$*) the flows associated to these inputs (resp. outputs).*

The input and output flows of combinational components are all synchronous. Indeed, the computation is considered to be instantaneous because the propagation delay within those components is less than a clock period.

Property 1 (Combinational components semantics). Let c be a combinational component, then $\forall i < n_{in}(c), j < n_{out}(c)$: $c.in_i \bowtie c.out_j$.

The registers store data and cannot be read instantaneously. Data within the register is pushed out by the input flow. So when data arrives, it is stored until a new one overwrites it. In that case, a reader can read any instance between two successive data writings.

Definition 4 (Shift function). *Let* $f = ((t_k, d_k))_{k<N} \in \mathcal{F}$, *let* $I \subseteq [0, N[$ *denote a finite subset of indices, let* $(e_k)_{k\in I}$ *denote a sequence of integers. The function* shft$_f$ *is defined by* shft$_f(I, (e_k)_{k\in I}) = ((T_f(k) + e_k, d_k))_{k\in I}$.

Definition 5 (Register semantics). *A register* $r = (O_k, (e_j)_{j\in O_k})_{k<n_{out}(r)}$ *is defined by* O_k *denoting the set of indices of data* d_j *that can be read from* $r.out_k$ *and* $(e_j)_{j\in O_k}$ *the delays before reading the data* d_j. *For an input flow* $f = r.in = ((t_k, d_k))_{k<N}$, *the semantics of* r *is: for all* $p < n_{out}(r)$, $r.out_p = $ shft$_f(O_p, (e_k)_{k\in O_p})$. *The following constraints must hold for the delays: for all* $k \in O_p$, $1 \leq e_k$ *and for all* $k \in O_p \setminus \{N-1\}$, $e_k \leq T_f(k+1) - T_f(k)$.

2.2   Semantics of Components

A design consists in assembling components by connecting them or grouping them in higher-level components.

Property 2 (Communicating components). Let c_1, c_2 be two components (atomic or not) such that $\exists i, j : c_1.out_i$ is connected to $c_2.in_j$. Then, $c_1.out_i = c_2.in_j$.

Property 3 (Hierarchical components). Let c be a hierarchical component. Let c_1 be a component inside c such that $\exists i, j : c.in_i$ (resp. $c.out_i$) is connected to $c_1.in_j$ (resp. $c_1.out_j$). Then $c.in_i = c_1.in_j$ (resp. $c.out_i = c_1.out_j$).

Example 1 (Example of non-atomic component). Let c_1 and c_2 two components within a component c as presented in Fig. 1. According to Properties 2 and 3, $\forall i \in [0, 3]: c.in_i = c_1.in_i$ and $c_2.in_i = c_1.out_i$; $\forall i \in [0, 1]: c.out_i = c_2.out_i$.

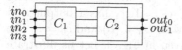

Fig. 1. Hierarchical component   **Fig. 2.** Example of an *extractor*

Extractors are very common components, they consist of a series of connected registers that allow to select from an input flow the sub-set of data needed by other components (see Fig. 2).

Definition 6 (Extractors). *An* extractor $e = (r_p)_{p < N_e}$ *is defined by a series of N_e connected registers r_p. We assume that the first output flow of each register is connected to the next register, i.e. for $p < N_e - 1$, $r_p.out_0$ is connected to $r_{p+1}.in$. Note that atomic registers are a particular case of extractors where $N_e = 1$.*

Property 4 (Sub-flow extracted by an extractor). For an *extractor* $e = (r_p)_{p < N_e}$, we can reconstruct the indices I^p of the data extracted from the input flow $r_0.in$ that are output by each register r_p. Let $r_p = (O_k^p, (e_j)_{j \in O_k^p})_{k < n_{out}(r_p)}$, let $O_k^p(i)$ (resp. $I_k^p(i)$) the function returning the i-th element of the sorted set O_k^p (resp. I_k^p). First we decompose I^p per output flow, thus $I^p = \cup_{k < n_{out}(r_p)} I_k^p$. Then, for all $p < N_e - 1$ and $k < n_{out}(r_p)$, we can compute I_k^p knowing the sets $(O_j^i)_{i,j}$ (or vice versa, compute O_k^p knowing the sets $(I_j^i)_{i,j}$) as follows:

- For r_0, by Definition 5, the indices I_k^0 extracted from $r_0.in$ are directly given by O_k^0. So $\forall k < n_{out}(r_0), I_k^0 = O_k^0$;
- The indices extracted for $r_p.out_0$ are those required for the outputs of r_{p+1}. So $\forall p < N_e - 1, I_0^p = \bigcup_{k < n_{out}(r_{p+1})} I_k^{p+1}$;

	1	4	7	8	9	10
$r_0.in$	d_0	d_1	d_2			
$r_0.out_0$			d_2			
$r_0.out_1$		d_1		d_2		
$r_1.out_0$				d_2		
$r_2.out_0$					d_2	

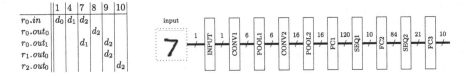

Fig. 3. Execution of Example 2

Fig. 4. LENET5 hardware implementation

- The indices extracted for $r_p.out_k$ are those extracted by r_{p-1} and required for O_k^p. So $\forall p < N_e, k < n_{out}(r_p)$, $I_k^p = \{I_0^{p-1}(i)|i \in O_k^p\}$;
- The indices extracted for $r_p.out_k$ are those extracted by r_{p-1} required for r_p. So $\forall p < N_e, k \leq n_{out}(r_p), O_k^p = \{i < |I_0^{p-1}| \mid I_0^{p-1}(i) \in I_k^p\}$.

Example 2 (Sub-flow extracted by an extractor). Let us compute the semantics of the extractor of Fig. 2 when $N_e = 3$ (the extractor is composed of 3 registers). r_0 has 2 output flows with for the first output $O_0^0 = \{2\}$ and $e_2 = 1$; the second $O_1^0 = \{1,2\}$ with $e_1 = T_{r_0.in}(2) - T_{r_0.in}(1)$ and $e_2 = 1$. r_1 has 1 output flow with $O_0^1 = \{0\}$ and $e_0 = 1$. r_2 has 1 output flow with $O_0^2 = \{0\}$ and $e_0 = 1$. The execution when $r_0.in = (1, d_0)(4, d_1)(7, d_2)$ is given in Fig. 3. Let us illustrate the Property 4 by computing first the sets I_k^p. For $p = 0$, $I_0^0 = O_0^0 = \{2\}$ and $I_1^0 = O_1^0 = \{1,2\}$. For $p = 1$, $I_0^1 = \{I_0^0(i)|i \in O_0^1\} = \{2\}$. For $p = 2$, $I_0^2 = \{I_0^1(i)|i \in O_0^2\} = \{2\}$

Let us illustrate the Property 4 by computing the sets O_k^p. We do not need all sets I_k^p because some can be reconstructed. For $p = 0$, we can compute $I_0^1 = I_0^2 = \{2\}$ and $I_0^0 = I_0^1 \cup I_0^2 = \{2\}$ thus $O_0^0 = I_0^0 = \{2\}$ and $O_1^0 = I_1^0 = \{1,2\}$. For $p = 1$, $O_0^1 = \{i < 1|I_0^0(i) \in I_0^1\} = \{0\}$. For $p = 0$, $O_0^2 = \{i < 1|I_0^1(i) \in I_0^2\} = \{0\}$.

2.3   Application of the Semantics to a Streaming Architecture

A *streaming architecture* is a very simple hardware where the function to be implemented is directly mapped as a set of blocks. We have implemented the LENET5 [22] with HADDOC2 [2] as shown in Fig. 4. LENET5 is a convolutional neural network (CNN) trained to recognize handwritten digits between 0 and 9 from the MNIST [23] dataset. A CNN [1,22] is a deep neural network composed of successive convolution and pooling layers, sometimes followed by fully connected layers. Input and output of CNNs (resp. of each layer) are multidimensional vectors also called *tensors*.

Due to lack of space, we only present how convolutions have been coded in the LENET5 hardware and their semantics. Note that the hardware architectures and semantics of other layers are quite similar to the convolutions. Our convolution hardware is composed of several extractors (see Fig. 5), the role of which is to extract from the input tensor the values that will be used during the convolution. From the tensor stored in the *extractors*, the convolution for one feature map is computed by means of several *multipliers* and one *adder* adding all the multiplication results (see Fig. 6); this is often referred to as a *dot product*. On the output side, a *max* implements the ReLU function.

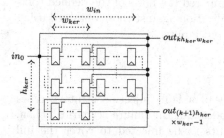

Fig. 5. Extractor for the kth channel

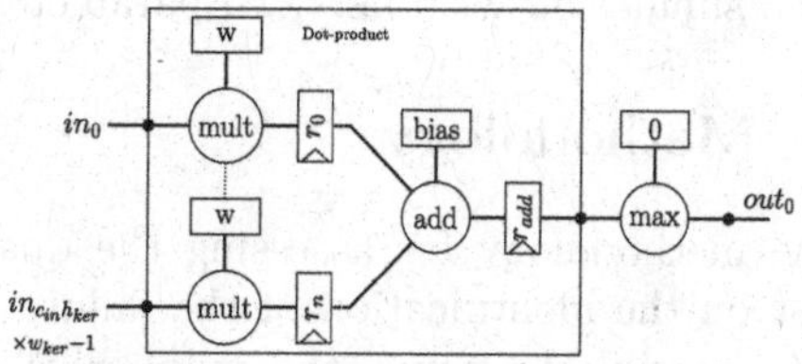

Fig. 6. A convolution for one feature map

Definition 7 (Convolution extractor). *The input tensor of the convolution is $T_{in} = (h_{in}, w_{in}, c_{in})$ where h_{in} is the height, w_{in} the width and c_{in} the number of channels (or feature maps). A convolution layer starts with c_{in} convolution extractors (cf. Definition 6) $e = (r_p)_{p<N_e}$. Let us denote by $h_s, w_s, h_p, w_p, w_{\text{ker}}, h_{\text{ker}} \in \mathbb{N}$ the hyperparameters of the convolution where (h_s, w_s) are the vertical and horizontal stride parameters, (h_p, w_p) are the vertical and horizontal padding parameters, $(h_{\text{ker}}, w_{\text{ker}})$ are the height and width of the kernel. Then*

- $N_e = (w_{in}(h_{\text{ker}} - 1) + w_{\text{ker}})$
- *for all $p \leq N_e$, if $p \in \{c + w_{in}l \mid c \leq w_{\text{ker}} - 1, l \leq h_{\text{ker}} - 1\}$ then $n_{\text{out}}(r_p) = 2$ else $n_{\text{out}}(r_p) = 1$.*
- *we denote $w_{out} = \frac{w_{in} + 2w_p - w_{\text{ker}}}{w_s} + 1$ and $h_{out} = \frac{h_{in} + 2h_p - h_{\text{ker}}}{h_s} + 1$. Note that the parameters $w_{in}, h_{in}, h_s, w_s, h_p, w_p, w_{\text{ker}}, h_{\text{ker}}$ are chosen such that $w_{out}, h_{out} \in \mathbb{N}$.*
  - O_k^p *can be computed (cf. Property 4) from $I_0^{N_e-1} = (w_s c + l h_s w_{in})_{c<w_{out}, l<h_{out}}$ and from all $p < N_e$ such that $n_{\text{out}}(r_p) = 2$, $I_1^p = (N_e - 1 - p + w_s c + l h_s w_{in})_{c<w_{out}, l<h_{out}}$.*
  - *The delays are defined as follows: for all $j \in O_k^p$ if $j < \text{length}(r_p.in)$ then $e_j = T_{r_p.in}(j+1) - T_{r_p.in}(j)$ otherwise $e_j = T_{r_p.in}(j) + 1$.*

Definition 8 (Dot product). *After the c_{in} extractors, there are c_{out} dot products as shown in Fig. 6. Each dot product d contains $N_d = c_{in} \times w_{\text{ker}} \times h_{\text{ker}}$ multipliers $(\text{mult}_p)_{p<N_d}$. Each multiplier is followed by a register $r_p = (O_0^p, (e_i)_{i \in O_0^p})$. The outputs of the $(r_p)_{p<N_d}$ are connected to an adder add followed by a register $r_{\text{add}} = (O_0, (e_i)_{i \in O_0})$. The dot product semantics is given by:*

1. $\forall p < N_d$, $\text{mult}_p.in = \text{extr}.out_p$, $r_p.in = \text{mult}_p.out$ *and* $\text{add}.in_p = r_p.out$;
2. $\forall p < N_d$, $O_0^p = O_0 = \{0, \ldots, \text{length}(\text{extr}.out_p) - 1\}$
3. *for all register r of d, if $i < \text{length}(r.in) - 1$ then $e_i = T_{r.in}(i+1) - T_{r.in}$ otherwise $e_i = T_{r.in}(i) + 1$*

Property 5 (Validation). An abstract model of a system or an architecture is necessary for analyses, but it is mandatory for the model to represent correctly and accurately the system *i.e.* the model must be a valid representation of the architecture. In order to ensure this, we compared the flows of the defined components and layers obtained with the formalization against those obtained using RTL simulation with LENET5 parameters and inputs.

3 Methodology

The methodology for assessing the quality of a fault injection strategy relies first on the identification of the failure modes and the failure scenarios. Then, it is possible to count the number of faults to be injected to cover the full spectrum of possible failure scenarios. This first enumeration can be seen as a *naive estimation*. Successively, the definition of equivalence rules may help reduce the number of fault injections while preserving the same level of *coverage* (see Definition 14).

3.1   Fault Model

A *fault model* addresses the way *a component is expected to fail* [21]. This can also be referred to as a *failure mode* [33].

Definition 9 (Failure mode). *A failure mode is defined by a* type, *a* location *(i.e. spatial location within a hardware), a* time of activation *(i.e. logical time when the failure mode is activated) and a* duration *(i.e. number of logical instants when the failure mode remains activated).*

There are several types of fault models for VLSI circuits [5]. In this work, we focus on *silent data corruptions* (SDC) because they can have a severe functional safety impact, they are the hardest to detect and are predominant compared to non-SDC failures. We consider the two main types of SDC failure modes [4,16].

Definition 10 (Stuck-at X). *A permanent stuck-at X (SX) models a defect where a flow is erroneously connected to logical level X where $X \in \{0, 1\}$. The location of a stuck-at is on a bit b of some input/output flow of an atomic component c. We assume stuck-at faults to be activated at $t = 0$ and because they are permanent, their duration is infinite.*

   Let $f = ((t_k, d_k))_{k<N}$ a flow, a stuck-at $SX_{f,b}$ on f at bit b, modifies f into $((t_k, d_k^*))_{k<N}$ where d_k^* is the modified value of d_k.

Definition 11 (Bit-flip). *A transient bit-flip (BF) is a bit inversion of a stored data. It is located on a bit b stored in a register $r = (O_k, (e_i)_{i \in O_k})_{k<n_{out}(r_p)}$. It is activated at time t and is assumed (without loss of generality) to last 1 time unit. A bit-flip on r, denoted $BF_{r,b,t}$, modifies the values stored from input flow r.in at t and has an effect on the output flows r.out$_k$ if t belongs to $[T_{r.in}(i), T_{r.in}(i) + e_i]$ and $i \in O_k$. We denote the modified value r.out$_k$ = $((t_0, d_0), \dots, (t_i, d_i^*), \dots, (t_n, d_n))$ where $n = |O_k| - 1$ and d_i^* is the modified value of d_i. Otherwise, there is no effect on r.out$_k$.*

3.2   Identification of Failures Scenarios

We have to identify the set of *failure scenarios*, where a failure scenario is a combination of failures. According to ISO26262, single-point failure scenarios (i.e. involving a unique failure mode) must be studied in priority in automotive systems. This is the reason why we focus on them only.

Property 6 (Failure scenarios). The set of single-point failure scenarios is $FM = \bigcup_{c \in C} FM(c)$. Since we consider two types of failure modes, this can be refined as for all $c \in C$ $FM(c) = S1(c) \cup S0(c) \cup BF(c)$ where $SX(c)$ is the set of stuck-at X and $BF(c)$ is the set of bit-flips that may occur on c.

Indeed, it is sufficient to enumerate the failure scenarios per atomic component and concatenate the resulting list.

Definition 12 (Stuck-at X identification). *Let $c \in C$ be an atomic component. Then $SX(c) = \bigcup_{io \in \{in, out\}, k < n_{io(c)}, b < bc.io_k} \{SX_{c.io_k, b}\}$.*

Combinational components are only subject to stuck-at because they take no (RTL logical) time to execute. To compute $BF(r)$, we need to know all the activation times where a data has been stored and will be read.

Property 7 (Bit-flip identification). Let $r = (O_k, (e_j^k)_{j \in O_k})_{k < n_{out}(r)}$ be a register and $r.in = ((t_i, d_i))_{k < N}$ its input flow. We define the set of time intervals V_r where a bit-flip may have an impact on data. Let $E_i = \{0\} \cup_{k < n_{out}(r_p), i \in O_k} \{e_i^k\}$ be the set of delays for the i-th data read, $E_i(j)$ the j-th element of the sorted set E_i then $V_r = \cup_{i < N, j < |E_i| - 1} \{[t_i + E_i(j), t_i + E_i(j+1)]\}$. Injecting a bit-flip at any t of a given interval will result in the same corruption. So the set of bit-flip is $BF(r) = \bigcup_{[t, t'] \in V_r, b < b_r} \{BF_{r, b, t}\}$.

Example 3 (Bit-flip identification). Let us consider the register r_0 of the Example 2, we have $E_0 = \{0\}$, $E_1 = \{0, 3\}$, $E_2 = \{0, 1, 2\}$ so $V_{r_0} = \{[4, 7], [7, 8], [8, 9]\}$. A bit-flip occurring during $[4, 7]$ corrupts d_1 on $r_0.out_0$. A bit-flip occurring during $[7, 8]$ corrupts d_2 on $r_0.out_0$ and $r_0.out_1$. Finally, a bit-flip occurring during $[4, 7]$ corrupts d_2 on $r_0.out_1$.

3.3   Coverage/Fault Collapsing

The purpose of the methodology is to assess the *quality* of a fault injection strategy. The quality consists in estimating how many single-point failure scenarios have been really triggered by the strategy among the exhaustive set identified by the Property 6. This problem shares some commonality with *fault collapsing* [9], a method used to reduce the number of faults to inject by merging those producing exactly the same safety impact. We were inspired by the collapsing rules of [8]. We define an equivalence relation, valid for any input, that characterizes the effect of failures on a component.

Definition 13 (Failure mode equivalence). *For a component c and two failure modes fm_1 and fm_2, fm_1 and fm_2 are equivalent for c, denoted $fm_1 \equiv_c fm_2$, iff for all possible values $c.in_0, \ldots, c.in_{n_{in}(c)}$, the flows output by c under a fm (denoted $fm(c, c.in_0, \ldots, c.in_{n_{in}(c)}).out_k$) are the same for fm_1 and fm_2, i.e. for all $k < n_{out}(c)$, $fm_1(c, c.in_0, \ldots, c.in_{n_{in}(c)}).out_k = fm_2(c, c.in_0, \ldots, c.in_{n_{in}(c)}).out_k$.*

Thanks to this relation, it will be possible to identify failure modes having (or never having) equivalent impacts. We define specific rules inducing failure mode equivalence; these rules, however, may not identify all equivalent failure modes (Figs. 7, 8 and 9).

Rule 1 (Connected flows). *Let c_1, c_2 be two connected components with $c_1.out_0$ connected to $c_2.in_0$ (fixing the port id to 0 and the number of connected ports does not change the genericity of the rule) and let c be the assembly component incorporating the connection c_1, c_2. Let fm_1 a failure mode the effect of which is impacting several output flows of c_1.*

1. *if $c_1.out_0$ is the only output corrupted by fm_1 that is if $n_{out}(c_1) = 1$ or $fm_1 \equiv_{c_1} SX_{c_1.out_0,b}$ (resp. $fm_1 \equiv_{c_1} BF_{c_1.out_0,b,t}$) then $fm_1 \equiv_c fm_2$ where $fm_2 \equiv_{c_2} SX_{c_2.in_0,b}$ (resp. $BF_{c_2.in_0,b,t}$);*
2. *otherwise, several outputs are corrupted and the connected component c_2 interacting with one output cannot emulate all the corruptions. Thus, for all $fm_2 \in \{SX_{c_2.in_0,b'}, BF_{c_2.in_0,b',t'}\}$, $fm_1 \not\equiv_c fm_2$*

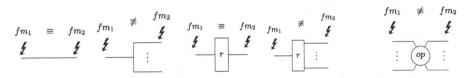

Fig. 7. Rule 1   **Fig. 8.** Rule 2   **Fig. 9.** Rule 3

Rule 2 (Registers). *Let r be a register, then the rules are almost the same as for Rule 1. A failure mode affecting r can affect none or a subset of the outputs of r.*

- *stuck-at always affects all the outputs. Thus, if $n_{out}(r) = 1$ we have $SX_{r.in_0,b} \equiv_r SX_{r.out_0,b}$. Otherwise, we have $SX_{r.in_0,b} \not\equiv_r SX_{r.out_j,b'}$*
- *bit-flip at time t only affects the outputs that can be read at t. Thus,*
  - *if exactly one output $r.out_k$ contains the corrupted data d_i of in that is $E_i = \{e_i^k\}$ then $\exists![t - a, t + b] \in V_r$ and $BF_{r.in,b,t} \equiv_r BF_{r.out_k,b,t_i+e_i^k}$;*
  - *otherwise several outputs are corrupted and there is no equivalence, that is $BF_{r.in,b,t} \not\equiv_r BF_{r.out_k,b',t'}$.*

Rule 3 (Failure modes equivalence on combinational components). *Let c be a combinational component. For all $i < n_{in}(c)$ and $j < n_{out}(c)$, for all $fm_1 \in \{SX_{c.in_i,b}, BF_{c.in_i,b,t}\}$ and $fm_2 \in \{SX_{c.out_j,b}, BF_{c.out_j,b,t}\}$, $fm_1 \not\equiv_c fm_2$.*

Thanks to the equivalence rules we can define the coverage of a fault injection campaign.

Definition 14 (Coverage). *Let* $FM_P \subseteq FM$ *be the subset of fault injections of a campaign* P *on a component* c, *and* $\equiv_c^*$ *the reflexive and transitive closure of* $\equiv_c$ *then the coverage of* P *(denoted* $Cov(P, FM)$*) is:*

$$Cov(P, FM) = \frac{|\{fm \in FM | \exists fm' \in FM_P, fm \equiv_c^* fm'\}|}{|FM|}$$

4 Experiments

The methodology has been applied on the LENET5 hardware defined in Sect. 2.3. As identified in the Sect. 5, many fault injection strategies have been proposed for DNN accelerators. We selected three of them:

- **Input Registers:** failure modes are injected at the interface of each layer. Such a strategy is inspired from the activation layer fault injection of [28];
- **First Registers:** failure modes are injected on the first register of each extractor. This strategy extends the previous one considering not only input registers. Note that a single register between two combinational components is an extractor.
- **Combinational Registers:** failure modes are injected in all registers providing at least one output to a combinational component. This strategy is a deterministic version of the fault injection strategy of [30].

The coverage rules, defined in Sect. 3.3, have been implemented in a SCALA code executed on an Intel-i7 CPU @2.9 GHz 8 GB RAM. This code can be easily adapted to assess the coverage on another streaming-based DNN accelerator.

Table 1 provides the fault coverage of each fault injection strategy per layer type (convolution, pooling, sequencer, and fully connected layers). Moreover, the estimated fault injection execution time provided by the Table 1 is extrapolated from a saboteur-based fault injection platform similar to [3] and implemented on a Xilinx Virtex Ultrascale (XCVU440). The average injection time for a $SX_{f,b}$ or

Table 1. Coverage and execution time estimations for one activation

FM	Strategy	Layers				Total	Estimated execution time (h:mm:ss)	Coverage assessment time (s)
		Conv	Pool	FC	Seq			
SX	Input Registers	1%	7%	0%	15%	<1%	0:00:01	$3.7.10^{-2}$
	First Registers	81%	14%	85%	15%	81%	0:02:50	$3.9.10^{-2}$
	Combinational Registers	83%	21%	87%	15%	83%	0:03:02	$2.2.10^{-2}$
BF	Input Registers	3%	94%	0%	100%	11%	0:02:35	23.1
	First Registers	76%	100%	100%	100%	81%	3:27:41	23.6
	Combinational Registers	100%	100%	100%	100%	100%	3:44:13	145.4

$BF_{f,b,t}$ has been estimated at 1.2ms for one full inference of the LeNet5 on an image of the MNIST test dataset. Finally, the coverage assessment time column provides the processing time of the Scala code.

The *input registers* strategy reaches a poor coverage (11%) for BF and almost no coverage (<1%) for SX. The coverage is especially poor on the convolution (1% for SX, 3% for BF) and fully connected (0% for SX, 0% for BF) layers. These results suggest that DNN model-level (and software) injection may not be sufficient to ensure a significant coverage of hardware accelerator's internal faults. Indeed, the effects of an internal fault may not be equivalent to a failure at a layer interface.

The two other strategies provide considerably better BF (resp. 81% and 100%) and SX (resp. 81% and 83%) coverage. Obviously, this high coverage comes with an explosion of the estimated execution time (from 2 minutes for BF with *input registers strategy* to almost 4 hours with the *combinational registers strategy*). This result highlights the classical quality/efficiency trade-off that must be considered during the definition of a fault injection strategy.

Since the rules defined in Sect. 3.3 do not capture all equivalent failure modes, the coverage obtained is an under-approximation of the actual coverage. Nonetheless, this under-approximation is still able to ensure that all failure modes are covered by the last injection strategy.

5 Related Work

Abstract Model of Hardware Platform. The formalization of VHDL/verilog hardware descriptions has been widely studied in the literature. Many of the proposed formal semantics for VHDL can be found in [20]. These semantics can abstract the hardware component either as a state/transition system – typically timed automata – enabling to perform formal verification with temporal logic like [6]; or as a data processing flow – typically flow graphs like [29]. We focused on the propagation and final effects of a failure of the system components. That is why, like [29], the formalization of Sect. 2 represents only the data flow processing, the control logic being captured by the parametric definition of the registers (see Definition 5) and of their assembly (e.g. see Definition 6).

Fault Injection Strategies. As identified by [14], due to the tremendous complexity of industrial circuits, the number of failure modes in modern digital circuits makes naive systematic fault injection intractable. To tackle this issue, fault injection strategies provide guidelines to inject a fraction of the possible failure modes, small enough to be performed in a reasonable amount of time. This selection method can be statistical like [10] or systematic like [11]. In both cases, the quality of these methods should be demonstrated.

Statistical Assessment of Fault Injection Strategies. A way to assess the quality is to derive statistical confidence bounds on the fault injection campaign, knowing the failure mode distribution density. The method [25] identifies the number of scenarios that should be sampled and tested to achieve a given error margin and level of confidence. This approach is totally agnostic of the actual system under test, and needs an a priori estimation of the proportion (called p) of failure modes leading to a failure of the system. Due to the lack of in-operation feedback on DNN accelerator, the method must be applied by using a default (pessimistic) value of p. As identified by [32], doing so deeply weakens the benefit of the approach (requiring to inject 18% of the total number of failure modes to obtain a 10^{-3} error margin). Other methods such as [27] use the architecture of the system to identify the component failures that may lead to a system failure. More precisely the method of [27] can be used to identify, knowing the activation of the system, the bits within the architecture that can affect the system outputs (ACE bits). The authors propose to derive from it a statistical indicator assuming that failures are uniformly distributed. The main limitations of this method are the exclusive consideration of *BF* failure modes and the quality assessment the injection strategy based on a given activation, *i.e.* an image for LeNet5.

Formal Assessment of Fault Injection Strategies. Another way to assess the quality of the approach is to formalize and analyze the notion of failure mode *equivalence classes*. To define these classes, the method proposed in [8] defines a list of equivalence rules for microprocessor's internal failure modes. It also relies on the notion of data life instants to identify which *BF* may have an impact. The authors of [12] propose a way to identify these life instants with VHDL behavioral simulation. This method only requests one simulation to identify all the life instants resulting in a system failure. Nevertheless, the activation must be known to assess these critical life instants. So, unlike our method, the quality is only assessed for a given activation. Eventually, methods like [13] use formal methods (like SAT solvers) to assess the equivalence between failure modes. More precisely, the authors of [13] focus their work on permanent failure modes of gate-level combinational circuits. The formal methods are used to decide whether the resulting circuit (whose semantics has been altered) is semantically equivalent to the initial one. A failure mode is said equivalent to another one if and only if their impacts will be semantically equivalent whatever the activation. The notion of equivalence presented in Sect. 3.3 is inspired from this work. Nevertheless, we have adapted the equivalence rules to our description level (operation-level components) and considered the transient and permanent failure modes of sequential components.

6   Conclusion

We defined a generic method to assess the quality of a fault injection strategy for a given hardware. This consists in assessing how many failure scenarios equivalence sets have been explored. The coverage of a fault injection strategy requests a deep knowledge of both the behavior of the hardware accelerator and the fault model (and the effects of these faults). That is why this kind of framework may help the designer to assess efficiently (the coverage assessment execution time requires at most few minutes) the trade-off between the coverage and the efficiency of the strategy adopted. It shall be pointed out that depending on the actual implementation, some single point failures at physical-level may result in multiple failures at our abstraction level. Indeed, several atomic components may use a common cell (e.g. LUT cell) and this may lead to common cause problems. Nonetheless, these kinds of problems are known and are handled afterwards with a common cause analysis. In the future, we plan to generalize our approach by integrating more complex failure modes and lowering the level of abstraction. We will evaluate the scalability of our approach on industrial accelerators. We also plan to combine the identification of optimal fault injection strategies with ATPG and to use our formalization to generate optimal strategies, that are covering and efficient.

Acknowledgement. The research has benefited from the AI Interdisciplinary Institute ANITI. ANITI is funded by the French program "Investing for the Future – PIA3" under the Grant agreement No ANR-19-PI3A-0004.

References

1. Abdelouahab, K., Pelcat, M., Serot, J., Berry, F.: Accelerating CNN inference on FPGAs: a survey. arXiv:1806.01683 (2018)
2. Abdelouahab, K., Pelcat, M., Serot, J., Bourrasset, C., Berry, F.: Tactics to directly map CNN graphs on embedded FPGAs. IEEE Embed. Syst. Lett. **9**, 1–4 (2017)
3. Abideen, Z.U., Rashid, M.: EFIC-ME: a fast emulation based fault injection control and monitoring enhancement. IEEE Access **8**, 207705–207716 (2020)
4. Abraham, J.A., Fuchs, W.K.: Fault and error models for VLSI. Proc. IEEE **74**(5), 639–654 (1986)
5. Avizienis, A., Laprie, J., Randell, B., Landwehr, C.: Basic concepts and taxonomy of dependable and secure computing. IEEE Trans. Depend. Secur. Comput. **1**(1), 11–33 (2004)
6. Bara, A., Bazargan-Sabet, P., Chevallier, R., Encrenaz, E., Ledu, D., Renault, P.: Formal verification of timed VHDL programs. In: 2010 Forum on Specification & Design Languages (FDL 2010), pp. 1–6. IET (2010)
7. Benso, A., Bosio, A., Di Carlo, S., Mariani, R.: A Functional verification based fault injection environment. In: 22nd IEEE International Symposium on Defect and Fault-Tolerance in VLSI Systems (DFT 2007), pp. 114–122 (Sep 2007)
8. Benso, A., Rebaudengo, M., Impagliazzo, L., Marmo, P.: Fault-list collapsing for fault-injection experiments. In: Annual Reliability and Maintainability Symposium. 1998 Proceedings. International Symposium on Product Quality and Integrity, pp. 383–388, January 1998
9. Berrojo, L., et al.: New techniques for speeding-up fault-injection campaigns. In: Automation and Test in Europe Conference and Exhibition Proceedings 2002 Design, pp. 847–852, March 2002
10. Berrojo, L., et al.: New techniques for speeding-up fault-injection campaigns. In: Automation and Test in Europe Conference and Exhibition Proceedings 2002 Design, pp. 847–852, March 2002
11. Chen, J., Lee, C., Shen, W.: Single-fault fault-collapsing analysis in sequential logic circuits. IEEE Trans. Comput. Aid. Des. Integr. Circ. Syst. **10**(12), 1559–1568 (1991)

12. Chibani, K., Portolan, M., Leveugle, R.: Evaluating application-aware soft error effects in digital circuits without fault injections or probabilistic computations. In: 2016 IEEE 22nd International Symposium on On-Line Testing and Robust System Design (IOLTS), pp. 54–59, July 2016

13. Dao, A.Q., Lin, M.P.H., Mishchenko, A.: SAT-based fault equivalence checking in functional safety verification. IEEE Trans. Comput.-Aid. Des. Integr. Circ. Syst. **37**(12), 3198–3205 (2018)

14. Ebrahimi, M., Sayed, N., Rashvand, M., Tahoori, M.B.: Fault injection acceleration by architectural importance sampling. In: 2015 International Conference on Hardware/Software Codesign and System Synthesis (CODES+ISSS), pp. 212–219, October 2015

15. Eggersglüß, S., Schmitz, K., Krenz-Bååth, R., Drechsler, R.: On optimization-based ATPG and its application for highly compacted test sets. IEEE Trans. Comput.-Aid. Des. Integr. Circ. Syst. **35**(12), 2104–2117 (2016)

16. Eghbal, A., Yaghini, P.M., Bagherzadeh, N., Khayambashi, M.: Analytical fault tolerance assessment and metrics for TSV-Based 3D network-on-chip. IEEE Trans. Comput. **64**(12), 3591–3604 (2015)

17. Halbwachs, N., Caspi, P., Raymond, P., Pilaud, D.: The synchronous data flow programming language LUSTRE. Proc. IEEE **79**(9), 1305–1320 (1991)

18. Iturbe, X., Venu, B., Ozer, E., Das, S.: A triple core lock-step (TCLS) ARM® cortex®-R5 processor for safety-critical and ultra-reliable applications. In: 2016 46th Annual IEEE/IFIP International Conference on Dependable Systems and Networks Workshop (DSN-W), pp. 246–249 (2016)

19. Jeon, S.H., Cho, J.H., Jung, Y., Park, S., Han, T.M.: Automotive hardware development according to ISO 26262. In: 13th International Conference on Advanced Communication Technology (ICACT2011), pp. 588–592, February 2011

20. Kloos, C.D., Breuer, P.: Formal semantics for VHDL, vol. 307. Springer, New York (2012). https://doi.org/10.1007/978-1-4615-2237-9

21. Koopman, P.J.: Lost message and system failures. Embed. Syst. Program. **9**, 38–52 (1996)

22. LeCun, Y., et al.: Backpropagation applied to handwritten zip code recognition. Neural Comput. **1**(4), 541–551 (1989)

23. Lecun, Y., Bottou, L., Bengio, Y., Haffner, P.: Gradient-based learning applied to document recognition. Proc. IEEE **86**(11), 2278–2324 (1998)

24. Lee, E.A., Sangiovanni-Vincentelli, A.: A framework for comparing models of computation. IEEE Trans. Comput.-Aid. Des. Integr. Circ. Syst. **17**(12), 1217–1229 (1998)

25. Leveugle, R., Calvez, A., Maistri, P., Vanhauwaert, P.: Statistical fault injection: quantified error and confidence. In: Automation Test in Europe Conference Exhibition 2009 Design, pp. 502–506, April 2009

26. Mittal, S.: A survey on modeling and improving reliability of DNN algorithms and accelerators. J. Syst. Architect. **104**, 101689 (2020)

27. Mukherjee, S., Weaver, C., Emer, J., Reinhardt, S., Austin, T.: A systematic methodology to compute the architectural vulnerability factors for a high-performance microprocessor. In: Proceedings. 36th Annual IEEE/ACM International Symposium on Microarchitecture, 2003. MICRO-36, pp. 29–40, December 2003

28. Neggaz, M.A., Alouani, I., Lorenzo, P.R., Niar, S.: A reliability study on CNNs for critical embedded systems. In: 2018 IEEE 36th International Conference on Computer Design (ICCD), pp. 476–479, October 2018

29. Reetz, R., Schneider, K., Kropf, T.: Formal specification in VHDL for hardware verification. In: Proceedings Design, Automation and Test in Europe, pp. 257–263. IEEE (1998)

30. Salami, B., Unsal, O.S., Kestelman, A.C.: On the resilience of RTL NN accelerators: fault characterization and Mitigation. In: 2018 30th International Symposium on Computer Architecture and High Performance Computing (SBAC-PAD), pp. 322–329, September 2018

31. Talpes, E., et al.: Compute solution for tesla's full self-driving computer. IEEE Micro **40**(2), 25–35 (2020)

32. Tuzov, I., de Andrés, D., Ruiz, J.C.: Accurate robustness assessment of HDL models through iterative statistical fault injection. In: 2018 14th European Dependable Computing Conference (EDCC), pp. 1–8, September 2018

33. Villemeur, A.: Reliability, Availability, Maintainability and Safety Assessment, vol. 1. Wiley, Methods and Techniques (1991)

Assessment of the Impact of U-space Faulty Conditions on Drones Conflict Rate

Anamta Khan[1]([✉]), Carlos A. Chuquitarco Jiménez[2], Morcillo-Pallarés Pablo[2], Naghmeh Ivaki[1], Juan Vicente Balbastre Tejedor[2], and Henrique Madeira[1]

[1] CISUC, Department of Informatics Engineering, University of Coimbra, Coimbra, Portugal
{anamta,naghmeh,henrique}@dei.uc.pt
[2] Universitat Politècnica de València, València, Spain
{carchuji,pabmorpa,jbalbast}@upv.edu.es

Abstract. Unmanned Aerial Vehicles (UAVs) have gained notable importance in civil airspace. To ensure their safe operation, U-space services are being defined. We argue that the target level of safety of UAS can be threatened by faults, abnormal conditions, and security attacks. In this paper, we propose a fault-injection-based approach to build a framework to allow the safety assessment of UAS under these conditions. We created a simulation-based setup to mimic a realistic scenario to study the impact of these conditions on UAS conflict metrics and surveillance performance metrics. Results show a correlation between the faults (impairments) introduced and the degradation of some performance metrics indicating the quality of the measured trajectory by the U-space. These metrics can be used by the UAV conflict management service to ensure UAS safe operation.

Keywords: UAS · U-space · Target level of safety · Fault injection

1 Introduction

Although Unmanned Aircraft Systems (UAS) [7] were significantly used in some military operations in the 1990s (Gulf War I), it was not until the beginning of the 21st century when the interest in this technology showed up in the civil world. Nowadays, there is a huge expectation of a variety of potential professional uses in many fields (e.g., urban mobility, delivery, public safety and security).

One of the main hazards to the operation of UAS is nearby UAS and manned aircraft with which they may collide, especially in urban scenarios where a high density of UASs is likely. To mitigate the risk of mid-air collisions, the UAS traffic management (UTM) concept was conceived in the early 2010s "to support the real-time or near-real-time organization, coordination, and management of UA operations" [15]. The UTM concept is currently being developed and implemented in many countries around the World.

M. Trapp et al. (Eds.): SAFECOMP 2022, LNCS 13414, pp. 237–251, 2022.
https://doi.org/10.1007/978-3-031-14835-4_16

The European implementation of the UTM concept is the U-space, a set of services relying on a high level of digitalization and automation of functions, whether they are onboard, or are part of the ground-based environment [23], allowing the safe and efficient operation of a large number of UASs (especially, but not only, in urban VLL (very low level)). The maturity achieved by several U-space services [24] led the European Commission to lay down a regulatory framework for the U-space [1–3], hereinafter referred to as "the U-space regulation". The U-space regulation introduces the "U-space airspace" concept as a designated portion of the airspace where U-space services are provided by U-space service providers (USSP) and used by UASs operators when planning and conducting flights therein.

1.1   Conflict Management by the U-space

Conflict management is one of the safety pillars in aviation, *aiming at limiting the risk of collision between aircraft and hazards to an agreed level deemed as acceptable* [17]. When the hazard is another aircraft, a conflict is defined as *a predicted converging of aircraft in space and time which constitutes a violation of a given set of separation minima*, which are the *minimum distance between aircrafts that maintain the risk of collision at an acceptable level of safety* [16].

The U-space tackles conflicts between aircraft at two levels **(1) strategic** and **(2) tactical** . At the strategic level, UASs operators have to submit their flight plans, including the 4D trajectory of the UAS during the entire mission, to the *Flight Authorisation Service*, which checks whether it intersects both in space and time with trajectories in already approved flight plans.

At the tactical level, UASs have to submit their position, speed, and orientation to the *Network Identification Service* in real-time. The *Traffic Information Service* receives UAS information from the *Network Identification Service* and makes this information available to UASs operators, which have to *take the relevant action to avoid any collision hazard*. Although not required by the U-space regulation, a conflict detection capability can be added to the *Traffic Information Service* to serve as a safety net alerting pilots when a predefined separation threshold is infringed. In future U-space implementations, it is expected that tactical conflicts will be tackled by a *Tactical Conflict Resolution service* [7] that will apply a stepped process for conflict resolution.

1.2   Safety Assessment in the U-space

Safety is the cornerstone of aviation. The usual way to express the safety goal is the **Target Level of Safety (TLS)**, which represents the level of risk as the number of risk events divided by an exposure unit. In manned aviation, the risk event used to express TLS is *accidents*, whereas the exposure units can be either *flight-hours* for en-route aircraft or *movements* for taking-off, landing, and taxiing aircraft. Defining TLS for UASs is still controversial, and there is no common agreement either on the risk event or the exposure time. We will use

mid-air conflicts per flight hour as the primary safety measure. Although other risks (e.g., direct ground impacts) could also affect safety, mid-air conflicts per flight hour is the common TLS measure often used by U-space projects.

The ultimate purpose of the U-space is to guarantee safe and efficient access of UASs to the airspace. From the safety perspective, the U-space raises mitigation barriers between UASs and hazards both at strategic and tactical levels, as described in Sect. 1.1. When designating a part of the national airspace as U-space airspace, competent authorities are required by the U-space regulation to assess the effectiveness of these barriers in that local scenario by means of a risk assessment meant. This assessment is a twofold process encompassing both **(1) a success approach** and **(2) a failure approach**. The success approach aims at demonstrating that U-space services can mitigate risks posed by *pre-existing hazards*, i.e., those arising during usual aviation operations under *normal* or *abnormal* conditions (rare *external* events that can negatively affect safety). The failure approach is conducted to assess how *system-generated failures* affect safety. Due to the complexity of the aviation system, most of this risk assessment is qualitative and based on experts' judgment. However, whenever a quantitative approach is possible, it should be applied.

This paper presents a fault-injection-based approach to quantitatively assess the effect of abnormal and faulty conditions (some of them caused by security issues) to the effectiveness of the tactical barrier provided by the U-space to mitigate the collision risk. The research is focused on the detection of the conflict, which is the first and most critical step in the tactical conflict resolution process as described in Sect. 1.1 (non-detected conflicts will never be solved). Hence, the number of conflicts will be used instead of the number of collisions as a measure of the risk. The results show the importance of considering abnormal, faulty, and security conditions in the safety assessment of UASs and U-space services. Moreover, the results prove the effectiveness of our approach.

2   Related Work

This section reviews the related work on the safety assessment of UAVs and, in particular, fault-injection-based assessment of UAVs.

2.1   Safety Assessment of UAVs

For assessment of UAVs operations management systems like the U-space services, the Joint Authorities on Rulemaking for Unmanned Systems (JARUS) [18] developed a risk-based methodology as Specific Operations Risk Assessment (SORA), which determines the safety level required for these operations considering both drone and ground stakeholders [21]. Then, U-space safety assessment (MEDUSA) is developed, which identifies and mitigates the relevant risks of drone operations supported by U-Space services by integrating the SESAR safety principles for the overall airspace system with the SORA approach that is focused on risk assessment of individual missions [4].

In addition to the above analytical approaches, we can find efforts in the literature that experimentally assess the safety (or security) of UAVs operations. A UAVs safety assessment approach is presented in [8], where a series of attacks (e.g., DoS) were injected into a real commercial drone to show how easily one can remotely control or bring the UAV down. In a similar study [13], a De-Authentication attack is emulated to demonstrate that anyone with access to a computer could potentially take down a drone. Similar studies are performed in [26] and [14] aiming to assess the security of commercially available drones. They present several security vulnerabilities found in drones and exploit them through a series of attacks (e.g., De-Authentication attack and buffer overflow).

2.2 Fault Injection for Safety Assessment

In a study [19] to create fault tolerance for UAVs, the authors created a Hardware in Loop Simulation (HILS) environment and studied three subsystems (Navigation, GPS, and transmission) injecting two types of faults (failure and signal strength), thus in a total of 6 faults to identify mitigation and define recovery mechanism for them. A similar study [12] using Simulink identified two common difficulties: a) in general, there are not enough fault samples in historical data to make it possible to cover most fault modes in UAVs; b) test flights does not offer a realistic way to identify and study these faults. The approach in this paper helps to solve both of the identified challenges in this study by using simulations to inject faults and study the impacts without using real vehicles. In a similar approach as previous works [20], the authors analyze the effects of GPS spoofing on drones through a series of tests in a HILS environment.

An attempt to study the impact of faults and also verify HILS environments is presented in [25]. The authors created their own simulator for fault injection purposes and also verified its accuracy, showing that the results of fault injection in simulation models (such as done in our paper) can be considered very close to real-world scenarios. Another recent fault injection platform [5], is using a very similar simulation model as in our approach, with PX4, Dronekit, and ArduPilot instead of Gazebo. It considers nine fault types including GPS faults (5 faults types) and Actuator Faults (4 faults types).

3   Approach and Experimental Setup

To verify and validate the behaviour of UAVs in faulty conditions, this work aims at creating a software-based fault injection framework providing all necessary tools for running experiments in faulty conditions. To achieve that, the following steps are required: i) definition and characterization of the system under assessment (SUA) and its environment (this is required for the definition of the missions); ii) identification and characterization of failure scenarios, helping to create a representative and fault model which is as complete as possible; iii) definition of safety assessment metrics for analysis of the obtained results, and finally iv) design and implementation of fault injection framework that can be served in diverse types of UAV systems within diverse missions.

To realize the first step, it is important to identify diverse representative drone models in terms of hardware and software suitable for different application scenarios. It is also necessary to analyze, compare and identify the critical components of autonomous drones. Then, for each application scenario, it is needed to identify the most important environmental parameters. These help to define a set of realistic and representative missions, which are used as the workload for the experiments.

In the second step, a field data analysis is performed to identify and characterize the failure scenarios for the SUA, resulting in the definition of a fault model.

The third step is to identify the metrics allowing us to qualify and quantify the impact of each fault/failure/threat. This step is done by adapting the concept of surveillance performance monitoring from manned aviation to the U-space framework. As a result, we defined a set of metrics that evaluate the surveillance system performance quality. In parallel, a computation of the number of conflicts is done to assess and set safety thresholds for these metrics.

Finally, the last step is focused on the definition, design, and implementation and required techniques and tools for i) defining fault injection campaigns (e.g., software faults, security attacks, and network issues), ii) running the missions, iii) injecting the faults, iv) obtaining an analyzing the results.

When these essential requirements are met, experiments can be run. To assess the impact of faulty conditions, two sets of experiments need to be executed: **fault free runs (Gold runs)** and **Faulty runs**. The results obtained from gold runs are used as an oracle to assess the impact level of the injected faults.

3.1   Scenarios and Missions

In order to define a representative scenario with representative missions, we need to define the characteristics of the scenario, including i) dimensions of the area, ii) number of UASs per hour, and iii) type of trajectory to be followed.

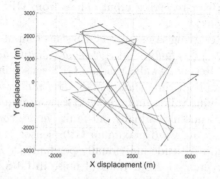

Fig. 1. General view of the scenario generated for the assessment

These features are introduced in a trajectory generation software, namely BB-Planner, which generates a trajectory for each selected UASs. A file with all the necessary parameters and way-points (WPs) is generated for each trajectory.

In this work, we generated one scenario for running the experiments. This scenario is defined in an area of high-density controlled air traffic in the urban center of Valencia, Spain. It was designed to represent one of the most representative scenarios defined in [6] and also to meet with a TLS of 10E–6 fatalities/hour. The simulated zone covers an area of 25 km^2 with a height limit of 120 m (VLL) and a density of 28 UAS/h (i.e., 28 missions). Multirotor UAS of several categories with different power and velocity were used. Figure 1 shows a general view of the scenario generated for this study, where each line represents a UAS mission. The whole scenario takes about 1 h to be completed.

3.2   Fault/Failure Model

Nowadays, GPS is the only surveillance system regulated for drones. Also, it has been shown that GPS is a highly vulnerable component [22] whose failures can lead to many conflicts, crashes, and even casualties. In the U-space framework, GPS information encapsulated in a surveillance data packet transmitted through the Network Identification Service is the only source of surveillance available for UTM. For these reasons, we selected GPS as the most critical component of UAV systems to be used as the target for our fault injection campaigns.

In this experiment, 14 **fault/failure types** were identified, taking into consideration 3 different condition types, i) *Faulty Conditions* (i.e., internal GPS failure or reception of incorrect data); ii) *Abnormal Conditions* caused by external factors (e.g., unavailability of GPS signals), and iii) Security conditions (e.g., hijacking), which are the most common conditions that a drone's GPS may face. The list of 14 fault/failure types is presented below:

1. **Fixed Valid Values:** Fixed valid value as GPS sensor input for Latitude, Longitude and Altitude (*faulty* and *security conditions*)
2. **Fixed Invalid Values:** Fixed invalid value as GPS sensor input for Latitude, Longitude and Altitude (*faulty* and *security conditions*)
3. **Missing Values:** Not receiving input values from GPS sensor (*faulty* and *Abnormal conditions*)
4. **Freeze Values:** Receiving same frozen GPS sensor input values for Latitude, Longitude and Altitude (*faulty* and *Abnormal conditions*)
5. **Random Value:** Receiving valid random GPS sensor input values for Latitude, Longitude and Altitude (*faulty* and *Abnormal conditions*)
6. **Min Value:** Receiving valid minimum GPS sensor input values for Latitude, Longitude and Altitude individually per fault (*faulty conditions*)
7. **Max Value:** Receiving valid maximum GPS sensor input values for Latitude, Longitude and Altitude individually per fault (*faulty conditions*)
8. **Fixed Noise:** Receiving a fixed value of noise in GPS sensor input values for Latitude, Longitude and Altitude (*faulty* and *Abnormal conditions*)

9. **Random Noise:** Receiving a random value (in range) of noise in GPS sensor input values for Latitude and Longitude (*faulty* and *Abnormal conditions*)
10. **Random Latitude:** Receiving a random value in GPS sensor input values for Latitude (*faulty* and *security conditions*)
11. **Random Longitude:** Receiving a random value in GPS sensor input values for Longitude (*faulty* and *security conditions*)
12. **Random Position:** Receiving a random value in GPS sensor input values for Latitude, Longitude and Altitude (*faulty* and *security conditions*)
13. **Slow Force Landing:** Forcing a drone to land by slowly increasing it's GPS sensor input values for Altitude (*security conditions*)
14. **Hijack:** Forcing the drone to move/land by tampering with its GPS sensor input values for Latitude, Longitude and Altitude (*security conditions*)

For each fault/failure type, the fault injection experiment is conducted for 4 different durations (namely, 2, 5, 10, and 30 s). Each fault instance was injected in the tactical phase at a random time between 30 s to 60 s after the completion of take-off. More than one test case was tested for some fault types (e.g., Random Noise). The result is a total of 74 cases to be studied.

3.3 Safety Assessment Metrics

As described in Sect. 1.2, evaluating the TLS is fundamental in civil aviation safety. Since it is not possible to obtain this variable directly (as one metric), this study focuses on metrics related to conflict detection. In this study, two sets of safety assessment metrics are defined: i) conflict metrics and ii) surveillance performance metrics. The **conflicts metrics** are defined to assess and set safety thresholds (e.g., separation minima) and the surveillance performance metrics are considered to assess and evaluate the effect of the impairment on the aeronautical surveillance service. The conflict metrics defined are as follows:

- **Number of conflicts:** Is calculated as the number of times the separation volume of each UAS is intersected by the separation volume of a different UAS. This calculation is performed pairwise, and the number of conflicts is independent of the duration of the conflicts, 5 s being the minimum duration to consider a positive conflict.
- **Frequency of conflicts (conflicts/h):** Is calculated as the ratio of the total number of conflicts of the selected scenario divided by the sum of the total flight time of all UAS. These values indicate, together with the traffic density and the selected area, how effective the selected separation is.

To calculate the **surveillance performance metrics**, a Surveillance Performance Monitoring Tool is used, which works based on some generic specifications and requirements for Air Traffic Control (ATC) surveillance systems [11].The performance-based surveillance approach aims to evaluate surveillance systems in a technology-agnostic way.

The tool compares the data provided by the surveillance systems (in this case, it is just the system that provides the U-space Network Identification surveillance service) with the high-quality trajectories computed from the received telemetry. To statistically obtain relevant performance metrics, a minimum of 50,000 position data cases are needed.

The telemetry received from the UAVs must be suitable in various aspects for the UTM system that want to use it. The data must be delivered with certain minimum conditions of completeness, codification, precision, update rate, latency, and integrity. These requirements can be reduced to a set of performance metrics [9,10] that are defined as follows:

- **Probability of Update (PU):** This metric refers to the probability that a True Target Report (TR) is associated with a reference trajectory within an Update Interval (UI) defined by the user (one second in this case). A True Target Report is a target report whose positioning distance between the position measurement in a time and the position in the reference trajectory at the same time is below a threshold. The UI is a requirement of the application in which this data is used, in this case, 1 s.
- **Probability of Long Gap (PLG):** This metric refers to the probability of not receiving a True TR during a number of UIs greater than or equal to n.
- **Probability of False Track (PFT):** This metric refers to the probability of having a false track in a trajectory. A false track is defined as a consecutive number of false target reports (3 TRs in this study) correlated in the 3D space. A False Target Report is a target report in which the distance between the position of a UAV in a faulty trajectory and its position in the reference trajectory is higher than a certain threshold.

3.4   Experimental Framework

Figure 2 presents a general view of the process followed to run the whole experiment from the definition of flight plans to analysis of the results.

The BBPlanner generates flight plans/missions for a given scenario. The generated missions are executed within the fault injection environment. The generated telemetry in this environment is then transmitted to the Conflict Computation module (running on BBPlanner) and the Surveillance Performance Monitoring Tool for calculation of the safety assessment metrics. This setup intends to emulate a non-real-time U-space [6] architecture with the minimum modules and interfaces needed to make a safety assessment. This justifies the existence of Tracker between the telemetry source and the conflict detection module.

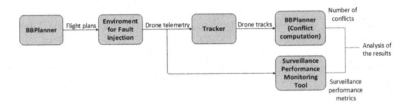

Fig. 2. General experimentation setup

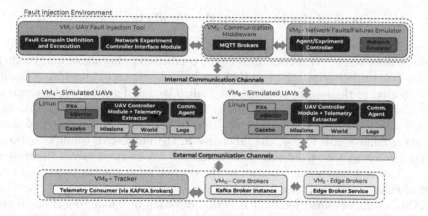

Fig. 3. Detailed view of the fault injection environment.

Fault Injection Environment, whose overall view is presented in Fig. 3, contains all required components for the definition of a fault injection campaign, the injection of faults, the execution of the missions on several UAVs, the extraction of flight logs, and the analysis of the trajectories. All these components are completely developed, deployed, and running within a VMware ESXi virtualized environment.

The fault injection campaigns are defined on the fault inject tool (VM_1). The defined faults will either be injected into the UAVs flight controller (currently only PX4 is supported by our fault injection environment) or into communication network (not done in this study) through the network emulator (VM_3) which is triggered after receiving the fault injection command through a communication middleware (VM_2). The UAVs are all running on a simulation environment created using Gazebo and PX4. Currently five machines $(VM_4$ to $VM_8)$, each one with the capacity of running multiple UAVs, are dedicated to the UAVs. The tracking system (including a tracker, core brokers, edge brokers are running on VM_9 to VM_{11}) consumes the generated telemetry of UAVs for the calculation of the safety assessment metrics.

4   Results and Analysis of the Results

The effect of the impairments injection can be directly seen comparing the faulty trajectories against the gold trajectories. Although a straightforward and quantitative analysis of the impact of faults could be done, this may not represent the real effects of impairments from a UTM point of view. A more thorough study in two perspectives in line with the U-space concept of operations [7] was carried out. Thus, this approach intends, on one hand, to assess and analyse the impairment effects on a UAS conflict detection tool and on a surveillance performance evaluation tool and, on the other hand, to relate the assessment done for each tool to find a preliminary set of metrics values in the surveillance performance metrics that may lead to a safety action concerning UAS separation management/conflict management.

4.1 Assessment of the Impact on the Conflicts

In order to make the trajectories as realistic as possible, they are processed by a Kalman filter before being consumed by the conflict-counting algorithm. We do it to simulate the behaviour of a real UAS tracker. The effects of impairment/faults are reflected in the results in which the fault injection duration is of 2 s, where the difference between the faulty and gold run are practically negligible and do not affect the system (because the Kalman filter absorbs the effect of short duration failures). In Fig. 4, the difference in the number of conflicts between the faulty run and the Gold run, does not exceed 2 conflicts in any of the studied cases. This maximum value occurs in the case of minimum altitude error, the rest of values varies between 1 or 0.

The results obtained for fault injection duration of 5 and 10 s (Figs. 5 and 6) shows that the number of conflicts increases significantly when *Minimum Lat/Lon* and *Maximum Lat/Lon* fault types are injected. This is because, at the same instant of time, all the drones move in the same direction, resulting in drones' trajectories approaching each other and thus increasing the number of conflicts. In the cases in which the position of the drones is modified, such as *random lat/lon* and *random position* fault types, a similar effect is observed, but the number of conflicts is not as high as in the previous cases. Since the values selected for these cases are random, the directions the drones will take are highly dependent on these points.

The results for the fault injection duration of 30 s (Fig. 7) show that the impact of previously mentioned fault types (*Minimum Lat/Lon* and *Maximum Lat/Lon*) becomes even more significant when the fault is injected for a longer period of time. For instance, in the case of *Random Lat/Lon*, the number of conflicts increases from 21 to 45 with a fault duration of 30 s.

From the results presented in Fig. 7, we also observed that the fault type of *Missing Values* causes a significant decrease in the number of conflicts when compared to the gold run results. This happens due to the fact that the PX4 position estimate falls below acceptable levels, which is caused by GPS loss (injected fault). This triggers the Position Loss Failsafe, causing UAVs to descend to the ground, aborting the mission.

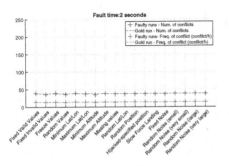

Fig. 4. Impact on conflict metrics (fault injection duration: 2 s)

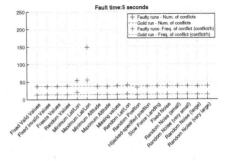

Fig. 5. Impact on conflict metrics (fault injection duration: 5 s)

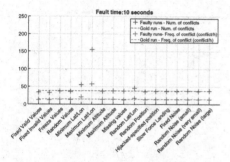

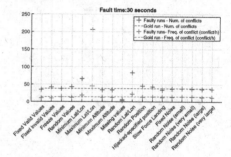

Fig. 6. Impact on conflict metrics (fault injection duration: 10 s)

Fig. 7. Impact on conflict metrics (fault injection duration: 30 s)

The rest of the fault types shown in the figures are not affecting the conflict metrics to the same extent as those analyzed in this section. This is due, on the one hand, to smoothing of the trajectories by the Kalman filtering that Tracker uses internally and, on the other hand, to the conflict algorithm, in which a conflict must last for at least 5 s to be considered as a positive conflict.

4.2   Assessment of the Impact on the Surveillance Performance

Figure 8 shows the impact of injected fault types on the Probability of Update for various fault injection durations. The probability of update depends on several factors: lost/incomplete/damaged reports/packages, latency, jitter, and, to a less important extent, positioning error. Here, this metric is mainly affected by GPS errors caused either by faulty, abnormal, or security conditions.

The results show that most of the fault types (Valid/Invalid Fixed Values; Random values, position, latitude, and longitude; Min/Max latitude, longitude and altitude; Random noise (large), and the Hijack), even when injected for a short period of time, had an impact on this metric, and the impact increased by increasing the fault injection duration.

The degradation of the performance metrics happens due to the fact that these impairments increase the positioning error greatly. The impact on this metric is even more significant when the fault injection duration goes above 30 s. In these cases the PU falls below 90%. In contrast, *Freeze Values, Minimum Altitude, Slow Force Landing, Small Fixed Noise,* and *Small Random Noise* faults do not affect this metric critically.

Figure 9 presents the impact of impairments on Probability of Long Gap (PLG). When the "gap" between true TRs becomes beyond 3UI or 4UI, we consider it a sensitive situation as the UI is equal to 1 s, and the maximum speed considered for each drone in this study is up to 20 m/s. The results show a similar impact on PLG when compared to PU. The reference values (based on gold runs) for this metric are around 0.03%. Therefore, when faults are injected for more than 2 s, this metric hardly meets the requirement for TLS.

Figure 10 presents the impact of the injected faults on the Probability of False Track (PFT). This metric is only affected by the positioning error and,

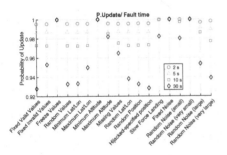
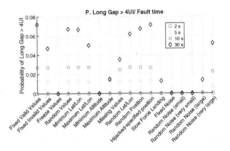

Fig. 8. Probability of update   **Fig. 9.** Probability of long gap

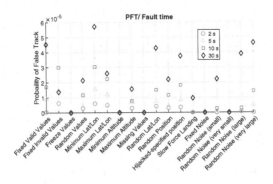

Fig. 10. Impact on probability of false tracks

by definition, indicates how likely it is that there is a given time-correlated spatial error bias on a given sensor. Thus, small random values injected into latitude, longitude, and altitude do not affect PFT significantly. The impact becomes severe when large random values are injected. No negative effect is observed in the case of *Freeze Values*, *Minimum Altitude*, and *Fixed Noise* faults. This happened because no positioning error is injected with the freeze and missing values. In the other cases, the injected values are not high enough to observe any false telemetry report in the faulty runs.

4.3 Discussion

Considering that the faults analyzed in this study are worst-case scenarios, it is interesting to relate the results obtained in Sects. 4.1 and 4.2 to suggest threshold values or at least a range for the surveillance performance metrics. Values selected are the following: PU = [0.995–0.987], PLG = [0.001–0.0128], PFT = [4.956E-6–1.197E-5]. These ranges were selected, taking into account the worst case in the conflict assessment. The conflict metrics are defined for a defined level of safety (TLS). An increase of 5% in the frequency of conflict is considered unacceptable. This increase, for the worst cases, happens between the faults of duration between 2 and 5 s. Since the PU is the most sensitive metric (as being affected by various impairments), it is more likely that this metric is the factor that triggers an alert on the degradation of the surveillance service and its possible effect on the overall safety of the airspace volume analyzed. This alert would lead to a conflict management action taken by the USSP and the pilots/operators in charge of the corresponding UAS. As is proposed in [6] the USSP would receive the surveillance degradation alert and consequently would update the separation minima between drones. Updating the minimum separation between drones would instantly increase conflicts between drones in operation and then reduce them by mechanism targeting the appropriate level of security. This is because when a drone has a conflict, the pilot/operator receives an alert from the USSP that must resolve by a deconflict decision through their own judgment or by an indication provided by the USSP.

5 Threats to Validity

Although the results of this study are very representative for realistic scenarios, there are some limitations that could be taken into consideration for future studies. To verify the results and compare them among each other, the study uses a single scenario. Despite the scenario being pragmatic, in future studies, more scenarios can be experimented with and can be compared with each other. This study also considers the same drone model in each experiment and uses a single flight mode; in future studies, diverse types of UAVs can be observed with multiple flight modes. This study only considers GPS faults, but it would be really insightful to include different communication cases (e.g., latency).

6 Conclusion

Aiming to assess conflict and surveillance performance of the U-space services through qualitative analysis, a fault-injection-based framework was developed to simulate drone flights and emulate 14 types of faulty/abnormal/security issues concerning the UAV GPS module in realistic scenarios. The results suggest that these conditions significantly impact both the conflict and surveillance performance metrics. Internal GPS failures such as maximum values and missing values (which forced the drone to land) tend to have a greater impact on conflict metrics. On the other hand, it has also been observed that a short duration of such faults/failures does not affect the metrics. However, a longer duration, such as 30 s or more, has a significant impact, especially on surveillance performance metrics. The framework developed and results give us indications on how the U-space services can collaborate to continuously monitor the communications and surveillance systems in order to manage conflicts to supports safe UAV operations.

Acknowledgment. This work was partially funded by the European Union in the scope of the BUBBLES Project (SESAR JU, 2020), funded in the scope of the SESAR Joint Undertaking (SESAR JU), under the Horizon 2020 Research and Innovation Program (agreement number 893206).

References

1. Commission Delegated Regulation (EU) 2021/664 of 22 April 2021 on a regulatory framework for the U-space. OJ 64. 23 April 2019
2. Commission Delegated Regulation (EU) 2021/665 of 22 April 2021 amending Implementing Regulation (EU) 2017/373. OJ 64, 23 April 2019
3. Commission Delegated Regulation (EU) 2021/665 of 22 April 2021 amending Regulation (EU) No 923/2012 as regards requirements for manned aviation operating in U-space. OJ 64, 23 April 2019
4. Barrado, C., et al.: U-space concept of operations: a key enabler for opening airspace to emerging low-altitude operations. Aerospace **7**(3), 24 (2020)
5. Bo, C., Benkuan, W., Yuntong, M., Yu, P.: A fault injection platform for multirotor UAV PHM. In: IEEE International Conference on Electronic Measurement Instruments (ICEMI) (2019)
6. Bubbles: Bubbles project. https://bubbles-project.eu/
7. CORUS project: U-space Concept of Operations. SESAR JU (2019)
8. Deligne, E.: ARDrone corruption. J. Comput. Virol. **8**, 5–27 (2012)
9. EUROCAE: ED-129B: Technical specification for a 1090 MHz extended squitter ADS-B ground system (2016)
10. EUROCAE: ED-142A: Technical specification for a wide area multilateration GroundSystem with composite surveillance functionality (2019)
11. EUROCAE: ED-261-1: Safety and performance requirements standard for a generic surveillance system (GEN-SUR SPR). www.eurocae.net/news/posts/2020/january/eurocae-open-consultation-ed-261-1/
12. Gong, S., et al.: Hardware-in-the-loop simulation of UAV for fault injection. In: 2019 Prognostics and System Health Management Conference (PHM-Qingdao) (2019)
13. Gordon, J., Kraj, V., Hwang, J.H., Raja, A.: A security assessment for consumer WIFI drones. In: IEEE International Conference on Industrial Internet (ICII) (2019)
14. Hooper, M., et al.: Securing commercial WIFI-based UAVs from common security attacks. In: MILCOM 2016–2016 IEEE Military Communications Conference. IEEE (2016)
15. International Civil Aviation Organisation: Unmanned Aircraft Systems Traffic Management (UTM) - A Common Framework with Core Principles for Global Harmonization, 3rd edn. International Civil Aviation Organisation (2020)
16. International Civil Aviation Organisation: ICAO Doc. 9426 Air Traffic Services Planning Manual (1992)
17. International Civil Aviation Organisation: ICAO Doc. 9854 Global Air Traffic Management Operational Concept. International Civil Aviation Organisation (2005)
18. JARUS: JAR doc 06 SORA. http://jarus-rpas.org/content/jar-doc-06-sora-package
19. Kumar Chandhrasekaran, V., Choi, E.: Fault tolerance system for UAV using hardware in the loop simulation. In: 4th International Conference on New Trends in Information Science and Service Science (2010)
20. Mendes, D., Ivaki, N., Madeira, H.: Effects of GPS spoofing on unmanned aerial vehicles. In: 2018 IEEE 23rd Pacific Rim International Symposium on Dependable Computing (PRDC). IEEE (2018)
21. Miles, T., Suarez, B., Kunzi, F., Jackson, R.: SORA application to large RPAS flight plans. In: IEEE/AIAA 38th Digital Avionics Systems Conference (DASC) (2019)

22. Nighswander, T., Ledvina, B., Diamond, J., Brumley, R., Brumley, D.: GPS software attacks. In: Proceedings of the 2012 ACM Conference on Computer and Communications Security. Association for Computing Machinery (2012)
23. SESAR JU: U-space blueprint. SESAR JU (2017)
24. SESAR JU: Consolidated report on SESAR U-space research and innovation results. SESAR JU (2020)
25. Wen, J., Wang, H., Zhang, M., Li, D., Wu, J.: Design of a real-time UAV fault injection simulation system. In: IEEE International Conference Unmanned Systems (ICUS) (2019)
26. Lakew Yihunie, F., Singh, A.K., Bhatia, S.: Assessing and exploiting security vulnerabilities of unmanned aerial vehicles. In: Somani, A.K., Shekhawat, R.S., Mundra, A., Srivastava, S., Verma, V.K. (eds.) Smart Systems and IoT: Innovations in Computing. SIST, vol. 141, pp. 701–710. Springer, Singapore (2020). https://doi.org/10.1007/978-981-13-8406-6_66

ACTOR: Accelerating Fault Injection Campaigns Using Timeout Detection Based on Autocorrelation

Tim-Marek Thomas[1(✉)], Christian Dietrich[2(✉)], Oskar Pusz[1],
and Daniel Lohmann[1]

[1] Leibniz Universität Hannover, Hanover, Germany
{thomas,pusz,lohmann}@sra.uni-hannover.de
[2] Technische Universität Hamburg, Hamburg, Germany
christian.dietrich@tuhh.de

Abstract. Fault-injection (FI) campaigns provide an in-depth resilience analysis of safety-critical systems in the presence of transient hardware faults. However, FI campaigns require many independent injection experiments and, combined, long run times, especially if we aim for a high coverage of the fault space. Besides reducing the number of pilot injections (e.g., with def-use pruning) in the first place, we can also speed up the overall campaign by speeding up individual experiments. From our experiments, we see that the timeout failure class is especially important here: Although timeouts account only for 8% (QSort) of the injections, they require 32% of the campaign run time.

In this paper, we analyze and discuss the nature of timeouts as a failure class, and reason about the general design of dynamic timeout detectors. Based on those insights, we propose ACTOR, a method to identify and abort stuck experiments early by performing autocorrelation on the branch-target history. Applied to seven MiBench benchmarks, we can reduce the number of executed post-injection instructions by up to 30%, which translates into an end-to-end saving of 27%. Thereby, the absolute classification error of experiments as timeouts was always less than 0.5%.

1 Introduction

Functional safety standards, such as ISO 26262 or IEC 61508 [14,15], demand that we assess (and, if necessary, mitigate) the effects of transient hardware faults (soft errors) on our systems. As soft errors are rare in reality [21,28], we often use *fault injection (FI)* [1,29] to quantify the resilience of a program. Unlike radiation or heat experiments [9], which are probabilistic by nature, FI also gives us the chance to gain systematic insights as we can inject different *faults* into repeated re-executions of the same program. By observing the resulting erroneous misbehavior(s), we can classify the *failure* of the *system-under-test (SUT)* and provide a summarized overview. Figure 1a shows the (unweighted) failure classification for seven MiBench [10] benchmarks if injected on the ISA level.

© The Author(s), under exclusive license to Springer Nature Switzerland AG 2022
M. Trapp et al. (Eds.): SAFECOMP 2022, LNCS 13414, pp. 252–266, 2022.
https://doi.org/10.1007/978-3-031-14835-4_17

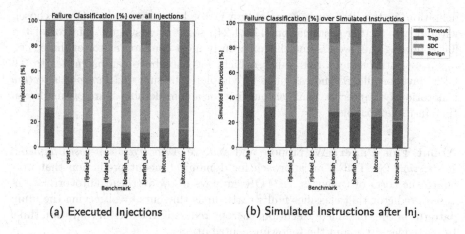

(a) Executed Injections   (b) Simulated Instructions after Inj.

Fig. 1. Injection count vs. simulated executions

If the campaign designer wants to cover the entire *fault space (FS)*, which gives the most comprehensive picture of the potential misbehavior, we have to execute millions of injections. Even after applying standard fault-pruning methods [11,27], our benchmarks require $2.8 \cdot 10^7$ injections. For these, our simulation-assisted FI platform [25] executed $1.3 \cdot 10^{12}$ instructions after the injection, which took us around 13 CPU days (at 1.16 MHz simulation rate). And although FI sampling [8] can reduce the number of injections, long-running programs with a large state will still require many independent injections.

Whenever the injected program execution deviates from the *golden run* (i.e., the fault is not *benign*), this typically also impacts its execution time, that is, the time it takes until the error is detected and the simulation terminates with a failure classification. However, the different failure classes can differ significantly in their share of the simulation time (see Fig. 1b): For example, although 15.6% of all QSort injections yield a trap (e.g., division by zero), they only account for 0.4% of the simulated instructions, so apparently, trap errors are detected early. On the other hand, *timeout* faults are detected late: 8.1% of faults in QSort account for 32.3% of the simulated instructions.

Timeout is meant to catch fault-induced endless loops and is a special failure class: It does not convey a ground truth, as deriving the ground truth would imply a solution for the halting problem. Instead, we need to heuristically classify an experiment as a timeout (and abort the simulation) by invoking the timeout-handler after some time $t_{inv} \in [t_1, \infty)$, with t_1 being the fault-free execution time. The selection of t_{inv} is a tradeoff between accidentally misclassifying longer-running experiments as timeout (false positives) and prolonging simulation time (as each true positive runs until t_{inv}).[1] The common approach is to select t_{inv} by stretching the execution time t_1 by a *timeout factor*. This factor is arbitrary by

---

[1] In hard real-time settings, the situation is somewhat different: Here, the respective task's deadline would actually define a ground truth for timeout errors and, thus, also the upper bound for t_{inv}. However, depending on the tightness of the deadline, this might still prolong the simulation time too much.

definition; in the literature, commonly a factor between two and five is chosen without any further justification [17,23,24], some even suggest a factor of ten [6]! Following this, we assume the apparently most common factor of three (i.e., $t_{inv} = 3t_1$) throughout this paper, which, for our above campaign, let to 3.6 CPU days for alleged endless loops to complete. To sum up: *Timeout detection* is notoriously imprecise, while accounting for a considerable share of simulation time in FI campaigns.

About This Paper. We propose and analyze *Autocorrelation-based Timeout Restriction* (ACTOR), an approach for dynamic timeout prediction that mitigates the costs of timeouts. ACTOR employs a low-overhead autocorrelation-based predictor that classifies faults early on as timeouts by observing the jump patterns of the continued execution, thereby reducing the overall campaign time. In particular, we claim the following contributions:

- We analyze the nature of the timeout failure class, reason about the maximal achievable savings of any timeout detector, and give guidelines for their design.
- We propose and implement autocorrelation to heuristically detect faulty executions that will lead to a timeout.
- We evaluate our ACTOR prototype on seven MiBench benchmarks and quantify the achieved end-to-end savings (up to 27.6%) and the classification error.

The rest of the paper is structured as follows: In Sect. 2, we describe our fault-injection model and discuss the problem of timeout detection. Sourced by those insights, we design ACTOR in Sect. 3 and evaluate it in Sect. 4. After the discussion of our results (Sect. 5) and the related work (Sect. 6), we conclude this paper in Sect. 7.

2   Problem Analysis

In a nutshell, we aim to reduce FI-campaign run times by detecting experiments that are most likely to result in a timeout early and abort their continuation. For this, we will first describe our targeted models of FI campaigns and reason afterwards in general about *timeout detectors*.

2.1   Fault-Injection Model

ACTOR targets systematic FI campaigns, were a single deterministic program run on a specific system is examined for its resiliency. For this, we record a fault-free *golden run* of the SUT and plan a number of faults that cover the (partial or complete) FS. The start of the golden run is t_0, its end is t_1. Each fault is identified by its fault location (e.g., register r0 bit 3) and its relative fault time t_f (i.e., $t_f = t_0 + a$, $t_0 \le t_f \le t_1$).

For injecting a specific fault, the *FI platform* (e.g., a modified ×86 emulator) *forwards* the program to the fault time and injects the fault (e.g., toggling one or multiple fault-location bits). Depending on the FI platform, forwarding is made more efficient using checkpointing [3,18] or (hardware-assisted) break points [26]. In contrast, we cannot speedup the *post-injection execution* as the faulty control flow can deviate from the golden run. Therefore, this paper looks only on the time-budget spent *after* injecting the fault.

After injection, the platform continues the SUT, observes its behavior, and comes to a failure classification. While such classification is always application-specific, the classes *benign*, *silent-data corruption (SDC)*, *trap*, and *timeout* are commonly used.

For our approach, we furthermore assume that the FI platform can report the last m jumps. This can either be done via actively recording jumps (in a simulator) or by a hardware-implemented branch-history buffer. Without loss of generality, we explore the ACTOR approach on an ISA-level fault injection.

2.2   Timeout Detectors

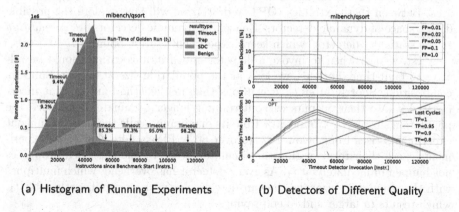

(a) Histogram of Running Experiments   (b) Detectors of Different Quality

Fig. 2. Running experiments for QSort and the influence of the timeout-detector quality

As already mentioned, timeout is a special failure class as the FI platform cannot surely classify stuck programs into one of the other classes. Therefore, the campaign designer must define a *timeout detector* that classifies the currently injection as a timeout.

These detectors can either be *static* and ignore the current system state or they are *dynamic* and make a heuristic decision. Furthermore, the detector-invocation time t_{inv} can either be *relative* to the FI time t_{f} (e.g., 50 cycles after injection, $t_{\text{inv}} = t_{\text{f}} + 50$), *absolute* with regard to the golden run (e.g., 300% of the normal run time, $t_{\text{inv}} = 3t_1$), or *continuously* applied after injection.

Also, any real-world detector induces an overhead and will produce incorrect results (as they can only be a heuristic).

Usually, campaign designers define that executions that take N-times longer (usually $N = 2 \ldots 10$ [6,17,23,24]) than the golden-run length are considered as a timeout. In our taxonomy, this is a static detector with an absolute invocation point at $N \cdot t_1$, whose *true positive (TP)* and *false positive (FP)* rate is 1.

To give you a better intuition, Fig. 2a shows a stacked histogram of the FI-experiment "population" (for QSort). Thereby, the population is the number of parallel running experiments that execute at a given point if we would start them all in parallel. For example, at $t_0 + 20000$, we execute one million experiments and from those 9.4% will still execute at $3t_1$. Please note that this graph ramps up until t_1 as we only consider the post-injection time. Furthermore, the integral over Fig. 2a is the total number of executed post-injection instructions (i.e., the minimal campaign time) that, if broken down by resulting failure class, has been shown in Fig. 1b.

For QSort and the static $3t_1$ detector, we spend 32% of the campaign time for executing stuck programs. With the (hypothetical) timeout detector called OPT (relative, $TP = 1$, $FP = 0$), which surely stops all timeouts at fault time $t_{inv} = t_f$, we reach the theoretical optimum. In Fig. 2a, OPT removes the complete blue area. Between these extremes (OPT and $3t_1$), we will now explore the possible design space of dynamic detectors. Hence, the dynamic detectors are an *addition* to the static $3t_1$ detector, which keeps experiments surely bounded.

First, we ask when to invoke a detector and if its invocation should be relative to fault-time. For this, we look at the population size at a given t and its composition. Shortly after t_1, executions that masked the fault or that incorporated it into their outputs without running longer terminate. For QSort, the population shrinks by around 80% from its maximum, while the share of timeout experiments rises from below 10% to over 80%. Please note that these experiments check their result within the simulator, whereby the described drop does not happen immediately at t_1. As every detector has overhead, which multiplies with the population size, the timeout-detection cost drops significantly after t_1, which results in larger end-to-end savings.

Furthermore, real-world detectors will have a FP rate > 0 that, if applied to a population with many non-stuck experiments, will lead to a large number of *false positives (FPs)*. As FPs skew the failure classification, we consider them to be more important than *false negatives (FNs)*, which only prolong the campaign. To illustrate this, Fig. 2b (upper half) shows the influence of the FP rate for an absolute detector on the percentage of false decisions. Before t_1, a detector that is 90% correct makes wrong decisions in about 9% of the cases, while after t_1, even a detector that labels all experiments as timeout ($FP = 1$) quickly becomes usable. Even better for detectors that have a lower FP rate. Therefore, we argue that detectors should be invoked after t_1, which also rules out relative detectors as they would often become active before t_1.

On the other hand, we should invoke the detector as early as possible to maximize its effect and avoid executing stuck programs. For this, Fig. 2b (lower half) shows the campaign-time reduction that absolute detectors with different

TP rates can achieve over the $3t_1$ detector. Before t_1, which we already ruled out, an absolute detector cannot help much as many timeout experiments have not started yet. However, with progressing time, we lose saving potential (Lost Cycles) as the $3t_1$ limit comes closer and closer. Nevertheless, we also see that right after t_1 even detectors that achieve only a TP rate of 80% save 20% of our overall campaign run time. Please also note that absolute detectors invoked at or after t_1 have a benchmark-specific maximum that they can reach. For QSort, this upper limit is at 80% of OPT's savings.

To conclude our considerations: We should use absolute timeout detectors that we invoke shortly after t_1, where they cannot do much harm, even if they have a high FP rate. At this point, even if they are bad at detecting stuck programs (low TP rate), their saving potential is still high.

3   Timeout Detection Using Autocorrelation

The core idea of ACTOR is that stuck programs will probably execute in a (rather tight) loop, whereby their instruction stream becomes periodic. If the observed periodicity exceeds a certain threshold, which we have to choose above the periodicities of the fault-free execution, we abort the FI experiment and classify it as a timeout although we have not waited until $3t_1$. We base our detector on Ibing et al. [16], who use autocorrelation on the branch-target history to detect stuck executions on the fly. We adapt this technique for the FI context to achieve actual end-to-end savings and chose parameters for the specific benchmark.

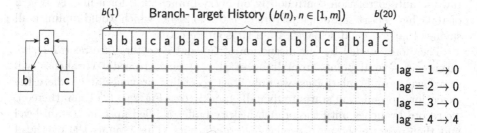

Fig. 3. Autocorrelation for branch-target history. $b(m)$ is the latest branch, while $b(1)$ is the oldest recorded branch. For lag 1–3, we cannot fit a periodic pattern, while with lag 4, the pattern continues throughout the branch-target history.

First, we want to give you a brief overview of the autocorrelation, which is often used in signal processing and statistical analysis, in the context of detecting periodic infinite loops [16]. The authors of this article apply discrete autocorrelation on the branch-target history instead of the full program trace, since the sequence of jump targets is sufficient to reconstruct the full path through a program. At a certain point in time, we look at the last m branches and compare the recorded branch-target sequence with a time-lagged version of itself.

The discrete autocorrelation can be simplified to a recursion $R_{bb}(l, m)$, where l is the currently examined *lag*:

$$R_{bb}(l, m) = \begin{cases} R_{bb}(l, m - l) + 1, \text{if } b(m) = b(m - l) \\ 0, \text{else} \end{cases} \tag{1}$$

In a nutshell, we count, beginning from the last taken branch $(b(m))$, how often we can jump l branches backwards in time before we hit a branch target unequal to $b(m)$. If we repeat this with different lags (e.g., $l \in [1, 64]$) on a fixed branch history, we end up with a vector of autocorrelation values $\vec{R}_{bb}(m)$. For example, in Fig. 3, the program is stuck within an endless loop that takes alternating conditional branches with each iteration. As the last branch target c is taken every 4 jumps, we end up with $\vec{R}_{bb} = \langle 0, 0, 0, 4 \rangle$. If the autocorrelation value exceeds a given threshold T, it can be classified as a timeout.

3.1   Adaption as Timeout Detector

To use autocorrelation as an absolute, dynamic timeout detector, we have to make adaptions and choose parameters. A static $3t_1$ detector is used as a fallback for potential false negatives. The main problem with the integration is the overhead of the detector and detection latency, as both are crucial to achieve actual end-to-end savings.

First, we have to decide on the history length and when to execute the *autocorrelation (AC)*. Ibing et al. [16], which looked at natively run programs, used the binary-instrumentation package Pin [22] to hook all branches. They ran the autocorrelation continuously on every branch and, for a history length of 100, they report slowdown *factors* of 100× to 225×, which would diminish all savings that we could achieve with a timeout detector.

Therefore, guided by our discussion of timeout detectors (see Sect. 2.2), we diverge in several points from Ibing et al.: (1) Since recording branches will slowdown most FI platforms, we only start recording branches at t_1 where the execution's population starts to dwindle quickly (see Fig. 2a). (2) From thereon, we record branches until the branch-history buffer is filled up to a certain level and then execute the autocorrelation *exactly once*. This bounds the overhead per experiment but comes at the cost of detecting less timeouts. If ACTOR does not detect a timeout, no further overheads are induced afterwards. Now, we only have to choose three parameters: the history length, the maximal lag l_{max}, and the threshold T at which we classify an experiment as a timeout.

For the history length m, we look at the development of the population size (Fig. 2a). As we have argued that time detector should run shortly after t_1, we choose to run the detector-invocation point at around $1.2t_1$. To achieve this, we derive the size of the history buffer from the average-branch density and the length of the golden run. For example, for a benchmark where every tenth instruction is a branch and $t_1 = 1000$ instrs., we set the history length to $0.2 \cdot \frac{1000}{10} = 20$ branches. Please note that, since the faulty programs can deviate from the original program, the branch buffer can be filled before or after $1.2t_1$.

The second parameter that we have to choose is the maximal lag l_{max}. With a large l_{max}, our detector becomes sensitive to patterns with a larger periodicity, which we expect to result in more brittle decisions (higher FP rate). For example, with a lag of 128, ACTOR could detect periodic sequences that repeat only every 128 branches. Therefore, we choose our maximum lag to be 16, which also is in concordance with our goal of detecting tight loops.

At the threshold T, we classify an experiment as a timeout, which challenges us to choose T such that ACTOR does not trigger on regular program behavior but is still able to detect timeouts. Since Ibing et al. [16] did not restrict the history length, they could use a rather large threshold (i.e., $T = 500$) that was applied regardless of the lag. However, with our fixed-sized history length, $R_{bb}(l, m)$ is always less than $\lfloor m/l \rfloor$, whereby the need for a lag-specific threshold vector $\vec{T} = (T_1, \ldots, T_{l_{max}})$, which we will compare against $\vec{R}_{bb}(m)$, arises. If any observed value surpasses its threshold, we report a timeout.

$$T_l = 1 + \max_{s \in [0, (|H| - m)]} R_{bb}(l, H[s, s + m]) \tag{2}$$

To calculate T_l for lag l, we find the maximum R_{bb} value that we observe if we perform autocorrelation on the golden run and increase it by 1. For this, we shift an m-sized window over the branch-target history H of the golden run and calculate the autocorrelation. With the resulting $\vec{T}$, ACTOR cannot trigger if confronted with a regular program run even if the injected fault shifts the execution beyond t_1.

3.2 FAIL* Integration

We integrated the ACTOR approach in the simulation-assisted open-source FI framework FAIL* [25], which provides infrastructure for golden-run tracing, fault planning, distributed and parallelized campaign execution, and result analysis. FAIL* utilizes the independence of injections using a client-server-architecture to highly parallelize FI campaigns. We integrated ACTOR into the IA-32 injector client, which is based on the Bochs simulator [19]. With a deterministic timer breakpoint, we start recording the branch-target history at t_1, whereby we use the FAIL* infrastructure to record branches directly from Bochs' simulator loop which keeps the overheads as low as possible. The source code is publicly available.[2]

4 Evaluation

With our evaluation, we demonstrate that ACTOR is able to reduce the end-to-end campaign run-times without skewing the result statistic towards the timeout class. We use the classification results and the campaign run time of the static $3t_1$ detector as the ground truth and the baseline. We also show the theoretical optimum that OPT would achieve (see Sect. 2) if invoked at injection time t_f (OPT_{t_f}) and compare ACTOR to a static detector invoked at $1.2t_1$.

---

[2] https://doi.org/10.5281/zenodo.6534708.

Table 1. Quality of the failure classification. For each failure class, we report the relative classification error compared to a static $3t_1$ timeout detector. For ACTOR, we report the TP and FP rates, the percentage of experiments involving a detector invocation (Inv.). For comparison, we also show the classification error in percentage points that a $1.2t_1$ detector would exhibit.

Benchmark	Classification error [Δ%]				$1.2t_1$ detector	ACTOR detector		
	Ben.	SDC	Trap	TO	TO [Δ%]	Inv.	TPR	FPR
BitCount	+0.00	−0.02	+0.00	+0.02	+0.04	4.69%	98.51%	93.40%
BitCount-TMR	−0.21	−0.01	+0.00	+0.22	+38.14	43.86%	86.12%	0.59%
QSort	−0.05	−0.35	−0.03	+0.43	+1.41	9.01%	88.55%	37.72%
SHA	+0.00	−0.16	−0.11	+0.27	+13.75	27.50%	99.75%	42.29%
Blowfish (enc)	−0.06	−0.12	−0.01	+0.19	+0.31	8.37%	98.27%	82.40%
Blowfish (dec)	−0.07	−0.13	+0.00	+0.20	+0.28	8.21%	96.76%	84.12%
AES (enc)	−0.03	−0.26	−0.11	+0.40	+0.46	5.63%	99.92%	56.39%
AES (dec)	−0.07	−0.08	−0.03	+0.19	+1.49	8.51%	85.65%	5.27%

We ran seven benchmarks from the automotive and security branch of the MiBench [10] benchmark suite on FAIL*'s IA-32 backend (Bochs). Additionally, ACTOR was also applied to a modified BitCount benchmark using *triple modular redundancy (TMR)*. As a fault model for this evaluation, we use uniformly-distributed single-bit flips in registers and memory, and classify the failure into benign, SDC, trap, and timeout (TO). For the evaluation, we also record whether a timeout was detected by ACTOR or by the static fall-back 3_{t_1} detector. We performed the FIs on a 17-node Intel X5650 @ 2.67 GHz (12 cores) cluster, leading to 204 simultaneously run simulations. Timestamps were both taken in simulated instructions and in wall-clock time.

First, we look at the influence of ACTOR on the failure-classification statistic (see Table 1, Δ%). In total, we see that ACTOR has only a small impact on the failure classification over all benchmarks and that it shifts less than 0.5% of all FIs from another failure class into the timeout class. We also see that our invocation strategy (at around $1.2t_1$) successfully restricts the usage of the ACTOR detector to less than 10% of all experiments. Only for SHA, which exhibits a high number of long-running timeouts (see Fig. 1a), and BitCount-TMR, which naturally has a longer runtime when one of the results is corrupted, our detector is invoked more often. Furthermore, the ACTOR detector is very good (TPR > 85%) at aborting experiments that would still execute at $3t_1$. In all cases, the static $1.2t_1$ detector, which is invoked at around the same time as ACTOR, shifts more experiments into the TO class.

However, the FP rate of our ACTOR detector varies widely between 1 to 94%, which means that ACTOR marks experiments as timeouts although they would eventually result in a different classification before $3t_1$. We still achieve good results for the classification error for two reasons: (1) we invoke the detector only on a small share of experiments (see Table 1, Inv.), and (2) from these experiments, only a small share will yield a non-timeout (e.g. Fig. 2a). Therefore, even a large FP rate yields small changes in the result. We will discuss the FP-rate issue in more detail in Sect. 5.

Table 2. Campaign run-time reductions. Besides the achieved end-to-end savings (w/ overheads), we show the reduction of simulator time for ACTOR, the OPT_{t_f}-detector, and a $1.2t_1$ detector. We also quantify the autocorrelation with the history length (H-Ln.), the average abort lag l_{avg}, and the run-time cost.

Benchmark	Autocorrelation			Sim. post-inj. instr. [%]			E2E saving
	H-Ln.	l_{avg}	Cost	ACTOR	$1.2t_1$	OPT_{t_f}	
BitCount	2 705	4.0	64 µs	−13.1	−17.3	−25.2	−12.66%
BitCount-TMR	5 296	4.6	62 µs	−9.9	−14.6	−21.1	−7.39%
QSort	1 385	1.6	53 µs	−19.5	−23.3	−32.3	−16.07%
SHA	1 766	1.0	68 µs	−30.6	−44.4	−61.7	−27.64%
Blowfish (enc)	1 019	9.6	67 µs	−16.1	−20.7	−28.7	−15.91%
Blowfish (dec)	981	9.5	65 µs	−15.8	−20.4	−28.4	−15.72%
AES (enc)	851	1.0	47 µs	−17.2	−16.0	−22.2	−17.59%
AES (dec)	794	1.0	38 µs	−13.1	−14.5	−20.1	−12.24%

In Table 2, we show the run-time savings that ACTOR achieves by aborting experiments early. For the number of simulated post-injection instructions, we reduce the campaign run time by at least 9.9% and by up to 30%. In comparison to the theoretical optimum (OPT), ACTOR achieves a respectable reduction, although it is invoked on average $0.7t_1$ time units later. In direct competition with a $1.2t_1$ detector, which acts around the same time as ACTOR, we stay within 5% points (except for SHA). Please note, that ACTOR sometimes reaches bigger savings than the static detector since executions that are stuck in a tight loop often fill the history buffer before $1.2t_1$.

We are able to translate these simulation-time reduction into actual end-to-end savings for the campaign run time by at least 9.9% and up to 30%. This success is rooted in two design decisions: (1) The AC itself is fast (<70 µs) since we bound the lag and the branch-target history and we invoke the AC exactly once. (2) Recording the branch-target history within the simulator loop reduces the simulation frequency by 28%. However, as we only activate this in the interval $[1.0, 1.2] \cdot t_1$, the simulation-time reductions translate well into end-to-end savings.

5   Discussion

Clearly, the decision between aborting an experiment as a timeout and continuing its execution (also beyond $3t_1$) is a trade-off between campaign run-time and result quality. In essence, for programs without a hard deadline, no timeout detector can distinguish between stuck programs that will never halt and faulty-programs that execute for a (very) long but bounded time. So, in general, there is no ground truth for timeout detection but only similarity between different timeout detectors. Therefore, the absolute share of timeouts is a source of uncertainty in the resilience assessment of a program and the campaign designer has to decide whether the observed uncertainty is acceptable in the current design stage.

Without ACTOR, the only way to reduce the number of timeouts and to classify more experiments as non-timeouts is to prolong the observation time. With ACTOR, we are able to achieve campaign run-times similar to an aggressive $1.2t_1$ detector (see Table 2), but at timeout rates close to the $3t_1$ detector (see Table 1). For example, in the best case (SHA), we produce 13% points less timeouts than $1.2t_1$ while the end-to-end campaign run time reduces by 27%. Therefore, a viable route for a campaign designer is to use ACTOR in combination with a $3t_1$ fall-back detector. If the timeout rate exceeds his safety margins, e.g. those required by a certain standard, he can re-run aborted experiments with an ACTOR-variant that gets activated later (e.g., $1.4t_1$).

The other important aspect to discuss is the widely varying FP rate of our AC-based detector, which sometimes results in high (>80%) FP rates. These FPs stem from the detection principle of ACTOR to abort highly periodic executions. For our *non-TMR* benchmarks, which perform no error mitigation, timeouts occur if the injected fault hits a loop counter that prolongs the execution by a certain time depending on the flipped bit: *least-significant bit (LSB)* flips prolong the execution only slightly, while a *most-significant bit (MSB)* hit results in a large number of additional iterations. While both injections result in a highly-periodic branch pattern, which triggers ACTOR, some experiments still terminate before $3t_1$. In our eyes, the categorization of those injections as timeouts at $3t_1$ is quite arbitrary as they could still terminate with an SDC or a benign after this static time mark. We basically chose $3t_1$ as our "ground truth", because it best reflects the numbers commonly reported in the literature [6,17,23,24].

To put these results in more context, we build the TMR-protected variant of BitCount, which actively schedules a third execution on a detected error, whereby 86% of the executions at $1.2t_1$ will terminate before $3t_1$. While this is a similar execution-prolongation pattern as a loop-counter injection, ACTOR is able to differentiate with a very low FPR of 0.59% between the third execution and a behavior that leads to a timeout. Therefore, we conclude that ACTOR is well suited to work on benchmarks with enabled mitigation techniques – which are of special interest for the campaign designers.

ACTOR is furthermore limited to FI scenarios where a fault-free execution trace is available, which we use to derive the detector parameters (H and $\vec{T}$). If those parameters can be chosen otherwise, ACTOR can also be used without a trace. Furthermore, we found the third parameter $l_{\max} = 16$ worked quite well for our benchmarks. However, for SUTs with many convoluted loops and conditional branches a higher limit could be chosen to detect more timeouts.

A threat to the external validity is our limited selection of benchmarks, which we chose from the automotive and security branch of the MiBench suite [10] and which is generally considered to be representative for applications in safety-critical environments. We also evaluated ACTOR only on the ISA level. However, ACTOR can be generalized to other levels (e.g., RTL, gates) as long as a mechanism to collect branch targets (i.e., branch-target buffer) is available.

6   Related Work

ACTOR is a fault-outcome prediction, which makes heuristic decisions about the outcome of a running experiment. To our knowledge, ACTOR is the first attempt at *dynamic* timeout detection for the FI of transient hardware faults into running programs; usually timeout detectors with a static execution budget [24] are used. Nevertheless, others have proposed outcome-prediction strategies for other failure classes. For example, SmartInjector [20] chooses predictor instructions and trigger values for which the predictor instruction will produce a benign or SDC result. During the FI experiment, when the faulty control-flow reaches a predictor instruction, they compare the actual value to trigger value and abort the experiment in case. On the gate level, we [7] have proposed fault-masking terms to detect benign faults within the first cycle after injection. GangES [13] runs several FI experiments in parallel and looks for equal execution states in different experiments. If two experiments have the same state, only one experiment is completed and its outcome is transferred to the other. However, they only perform matching for a limited time after injection, whereby their measures become ineffective for experiments that become stuck late.

In a broader sense, infinite loops can, as discussed throughout the paper, be detected by autocorrelation [16], although the original 100× to 225× overhead makes the unmodified approach unsuitable for FI. Another approach is Looper [4], which use an SMT theorem solver to generate non-termination formulas, which are checked at run-time. However, they also report prohibitive run-time overheads of up to 10 000×. The third route is to detect recurring program states, which was done by Carbin et al. [5]. They record the *whole* program state and report an infinite loop if that state did not change in between two loop iterations. However, for our FI benchmarks, we have observed that timeouts often continue to change their program state (e.g., decrementing a faulty loop counter).

Fault pruning, which reduces the number of planned faults by choosing pilot injections that represent a group of faults, are a different way to speed up FI campaigns. These techniques are complementary to ACTOR. Bartsch et al. [2] have proposed a static program analysis based on unrolled data-flow graphs ("program netlists") that finds faults that will surely become benign. Relyzer by Hari et al. [12] applies heuristic known-outcome pruning to reduce the amount of experiments but is only able to find benign, SDC and trap experiments.

7   Conclusion

With this paper, we investigate on the nature of the failure classification *timeout* in the context of FI campaigns for transient hardware faults. We observe that timeouts require an over-proportional large amount of execution time, which makes them a prime target for experiment-speedup techniques. From our analysis, we derive that *timeout detectors* should execute shortly after the fault-free program run-time to achieve the highest end-to-end savings while limiting their negative effect of the failure classification.

Based on this, we present ACTOR, an autocorrelation-based dynamic timeout detector that detects highly-periodic branch patterns and aborts the FI experiment early if it exceeds thresholds we derive from the golden run. Applied to seven benchmarks from the MiBench benchmark suite, ACTOR achieves end-to-end savings that range from 7.4% up to 27.6% in comparison to a static timeout detector. Thereby, ACTOR maintains a low classification error of less than 0.5% points and a high (>85%) true-positive rate for experiments that can be stopped early.

References

1. Arlat, J., et al.: Fault injection for dependability validation: a methodology and some applications. IEEE Trans. Softw. Eng. **16**(2), 166–182 (1990). https://doi. org/10.1109/32.44380. ISSN: 0098-5589
2. Bartsch, C., Villarraga, C., Stoffel, D., Kunz, W.: A HW/SW cross-layer approach for determining application-redundant hardware faults in embedded systems. J. Electron. Test. **33**(1), 77–92 (2017). https://doi.org/10.1007/s10836-017-5643-3
3. Berrojo, L., et al.: New techniques for speeding-up fault-injection campaigns. In: Design, Automation and Test in Europe Conference and Exhibition, pp. 847–852. IEEE (2002)
4. Burnim, J., Jalbert, N., Stergiou, C., Sen, K.: Looper: lightweight detection of infinite loops at runtime. In: Automated Software Engineering (ASE 2009), pp. 161–169. IEEE Computer Society (2009). https://doi.org/10.1109/ASE.2009.87
5. Carbin, M., Misailovic, S., Kling, M., Rinard, M.C.: Detecting and escaping infinite loops with jolt. In: Mezini, M. (ed.) ECOOP 2011. LNCS, vol. 6813, pp. 609–633. Springer, Heidelberg (2011). https://doi.org/10.1007/978-3-642-22655-7_28
6. Di Leo, D., Ayatolahi, F., Sangchoolie, B., Karlsson, J., Johansson, R.: On the impact of hardware faults – an investigation of the relationship between workload inputs and failure mode distributions. In: Ortmeier, F., Daniel, P. (eds.) SAFE-COMP 2012. LNCS, vol. 7612, pp. 198–209. Springer, Heidelberg (2012). https:// doi.org/10.1007/978-3-642-33678-2_17 ISBN: 978-3-642-33678-2
7. Dietrich, C., Schmider, A., Pusz, O., Payá-Vayá, G., Lohmann, D.: Cross-layer fault-space pruning for hardware-assisted fault injection. In: 55th Annual Design Automation Conference (DAC 2018). ACM Press (2018). https://doi.org/10.1145/ 3195970.3196019. ISBN: 978-1-4503-5700-5/18/06
8. Ebrahimi, M., Sayed, N., Rashvand, M., Tahoori, M.B.: Fault injection acceleration by architectural importance sampling. In: Hardware/Software Codesign and System Synthesis (CODES+ISSS), pp. 212–219. IEEE (2015). https://doi.org/10. 1109/CODESISSS.2015.7331384

9. Gunneflo, U., Karlsson, J., Torin, J.: Evaluation of error detection schemes using fault injection by heavy-ion radiation. In: 19th International Symposium on Fault-Tolerant Computing (FTCS-2019), pp. 340–347. IEEE Computer Society Press, June 1989. https://doi.org/10.1109/FTCS.1989.105590

10. Guthaus, M.R., Ringenberg, J.S., Ernst, D., Austin, T.M., Mudge, T., Brown, R.B.: MiBench: a free, commercially representative embedded benchmark suite. In: Fourth Annual IEEE International Workshop on Workload Characterization, WWC-4, pp. 3–14, December 2001. https://doi.org/10.1109/WWC.2001.990739

11. Guthoff, J., Sieh, V.: Combining software-implemented and simulation-based fault injection into a single fault injection method. In: 25nd International Symposium on Fault-Tolerant Computing (FTCS-25), pp. 196–206. IEEE Computer Society Press, June 1995. https://doi.org/10.1109/FTCS.1995.466978

12. Hari, S.K.S., Adve, S.V., Naeimi, H., Ramachandran, P.: Relyzer: exploiting application-level fault equivalence to analyze application resiliency to transient faults. ACM SIGPLAN Not. **47**, 123–134 (2012). https://doi.org/10.1145/2189750.2150990

13. Hari, S.K.S., Venkatagiri, R., Adve, S.V., Naeimi, H.: GangES: Gang error simulation for hardware resiliency evaluation. In: ACM/IEEE 41st International Symposium on Computer Architecture, ISCA 2014, Minneapolis, MN, USA, 14–18 June 2014, pp. 61–72. IEEE Computer Society (2014). https://doi.org/10.1109/ISCA.2014.6853212

14. IEC. IEC 61508 - Functional safety of electrical/electronic/programmable electronic safety-related systems. International Electrotechnical Commission, December 1998

15. ISO 26262-9: ISO 26262-9:2011: Road vehicles - functional safety - part 9: automotive safety integrity level (ASIL)-oriented and safety-oriented analyses. International Organization for Standardization, Geneva, Switzerland (2011)

16. Ibing, A., Kirsch, J., Panny, L.: Autocorrelation-based detection of infinite loops at runtime. In: IEEE International Conference on Dependable, Autonomic and Secure Computing, pp. 368–375. IEEE Computer Society (2016). https://doi.org/10.1109/DASC-PICom-DataCom-CyberSciTec.2016.78

17. Kaliorakis, M., Tselonis, S., Chatzidimitriou, A., Foutris, N., Gizopoulos, D.: Differential fault injection on microarchitectural simulators. In: 2015 IEEE International Symposium on Workload Characterization, IISWC 2015, Atlanta, GA, USA, 4–6 October 2015, pp. 172–182. IEEE Computer Society (2015). https://doi.org/10.1109/IISWC.2015.28

18. King, S.T., Dunlap, G.W., Chen, P.M.: Debugging operating systems with time-traveling virtual machines (awarded general track best paper award!). In: 2005 USENIX Annual Technical Conference, pp. 1–15 (2005). http://www.usenix.org/events/usenix05/tech/general/king.html

19. Lawton, K.P.: Bochs: a portable PC emulator for Unix/X. Linux J. (29), 7 (1996)

20. Li, J., Tan, Q.: SmartInjector: exploiting intelligent fault injection for SDC rate analysis. In: Defect and Fault Tolerance in VLSI and Nanotechnology Systems (DFT 2013), pp. 236–242. IEEE Computer Society Press, October 2013. https://doi.org/10.1109/DFT.2013.6653612

21. Li, X., Huang, M.C., Shen, K., Chu, L.: A realistic evaluation of memory hardware errors and software system susceptibility. In: 2010 USENIX Annual Technical Conference (2010). https://www.usenix.org/conference/usenix-atc-10/realistic-evaluation-memory-hardware-errors-and-software-system

22. Luk, C.-K., et al.: Pin: building customized program analysis tools with dynamic instrumentation. ACM SIGPLAN Not. **40**(6), 190–200 (2005)

23. Mansour, W., Velazco, R.: SEU fault-injection in VHDL-based processors: a case study. In: 13th Latin American Test Workshop (LATW 2012), pp. 1–5. IEEE Computer Society (2012). https://doi.org/10.1109/LATW.2012.6261258

24. Schirmeier, H., Breddemann, M.: Quantitative cross-layer evaluation of transient-fault injection techniques for algorithm comparison. In: 15th European Dependable Computing Conference, EDCC, pp. 15–22 (2019). https://doi.org/10.1109/EDCC.2019.00016

25. Schirmeier, H., Hoffmann, M., Dietrich, C., Lenz, M., Lohmann, D., Spinczyk, O.: FAIL*: an open and versatile fault-injection framework for the assessment of software-implemented hardware fault tolerance. In: Sens, P. (ed.) 11th European Dependable Computing Conference (EDCC 2015), pp. 245–255, September 2015. https://doi.org/10.1109/EDCC.2015.28

26. Schirmeier, H., Rademacher, L., Spinczyk, O.: Smart-hopping: highly efficient ISA-level fault injection on real hardware. In: 19th IEEE European Test Symposium (ETS 2014). IEEE Computer Society Press, May 2014

27. Smith, D.T., Johnson, B.W., Profeta, J.A., Bozzolo, D.G.: A method to determine equivalent fault classes for permanent and transient faults. In: Reliability and Maintainability Symposium, pp. 418–424. IEEE (1995). https://doi.org/10.1109/RAMS.1995.513278

28. Sridharan, V., Stearley, J., DeBardeleben, N., Blanchard, S., Gurumurthi, S.: Feng shui of supercomputer memory: positional effects in DRAM and SRAM faults. In: High Performance Computing, Networking, Storage and Analysis, SC 2013, pp. 22:1–22:11. ACM Press, New York (2013). ISBN: 978-1-4503-2378-9. https://doi.org/10.1145/2503210.2503257

29. Ziade, H., Ayoubi, R.A., Velazco, R.: A survey on fault injection techniques. Intl. Arab J. Inf. Technol. 1(2), 171–186 (2004)

Object Detection and Perception

Formally Compensating Performance Limitations for Imprecise 2D Object Detection

Tobias Schuster, Emmanouil Seferis, Simon Burton, and Chih-Hong Cheng[⊠]

Fraunhofer Institute for Cognitive Systems, Hansastr. 32, 80686 Munich, Germany
{tobias.schuster,emmanouil.seferis,simon.burton,
chih-hong.cheng}@iks.fraunhofer.de

Abstract. In this paper, we consider the imperfection within machine learning-based 2D object detection and its impact on safety. We address a special sub-type of performance limitations related to the misalignment of bounding-box predictions to the ground truth: the prediction bounding box cannot be perfectly aligned with the ground truth. We formally prove the minimum required bounding box enlargement factor to cover the ground truth. We then demonstrate that this factor can be mathematically adjusted to a smaller value, provided that the motion planner uses a fixed-length buffer in making its decisions. Finally, observing the difference between an empirically measured enlargement factor and our formally derived worst-case enlargement factor offers an interesting connection between quantitative evidence (demonstrated by statistics) and qualitative evidence (demonstrated by worst-case analysis) when arguing safety-relevant properties of machine learning functions.

Keywords: Safety · Object detection · Deep learning · Post-processing

1 Introduction

Safety has become a crucial factor in the deployment of automated driving (AD) functions. Deep neural networks (DNNs) are widely used to implement key modules of AD functions such as object detection. It is thus essential to systematically analyze the impact of performance limitations of DNNs on the safety of the system. The objective must be to understand residual performance limitations of the DNN-based models such that these can be minimised during design or compensated for in the system architecture such that they do not lead to an unreasonable risk of hazardous system failures.

In this paper, we consider a specific class of performance limitations, namely *bounding box non-alignment* in 2D object detection. Bounding box

---

T. Schuster and E. Seferis—Equal contribution.

This work is funded by the Bavarian Ministry for Economic Affairs, Regional Development and Energy as part of a project to support the thematic development of the Fraunhofer Institute for Cognitive Systems.

M. Trapp et al. (Eds.): SAFECOMP 2022, LNCS 13414, pp. 269–283, 2022.
https://doi.org/10.1007/978-3-031-14835-4_18

non-alignment refers to the property where the prediction does not suitably cover the object. This may result in safety risks, as any object not surrounded by the prediction bounding box can be viewed as empty space, thereby inducing the risk of collision. This property is typically measured during training of the model by computing the Intersection-over-Union (IoU) ratio between the ground-truth (GT) label bounding box and the predicted bounding box. Provided that the degree of non-alignment is bounded, which can be characterized by the computed IoU ratio always being larger than a constant α, the key contribution of this paper is to formally derive the *minimum required enlargement factor* to be imposed on the prediction bounding box to fully cover the GT label. As a consequence, by adding a conservative post-processor after the DNN to enlarge the prediction bounding box using the derived enlargement factor, the imprecision (to the degree governed by α) may be assumed not to have a safety impact. The value α may be observed from the collected data and acts as a Safety Performance Indicator (as specified in UL4600 [10]) due to the connection with the bounding box enlargement[1]. The observed value α can also be further categorized depending on the operational design domain (e.g., subject to weather conditions) and the distance to the object, thereby creating a fine-grained and dynamically adjusted enlargement factor.

Subsequently, we consider the problem of choosing an optimal factor for bounding-box enlargement. Following the practical observation that the motion planner always reserves a fixed width as a safety buffer, one can utilize the buffer and employ a smaller enlargement, provided that the combined effect of the bounding box enlargement (from the safety post-processor) and the buffer from the motion planner is larger than the computed bound. We show that such a sound estimation that ensures sufficient bounding-box coverage is conditional on an assumption over the maximum width of the detected object type (e.g., car).

Finally, we compare the formally derived enlargement factor with an enlargement factor directly *measured from the training data*, following the methodology in [4]. There can be many interpretations of the difference between the two. The measured enlargement factor to cover the GT label bounding box is smaller, as the formal derivation considers *the worst case scenario* while the worst case scenario may not be present in the training dataset. However, considering the distance between the measured mean enlargement factor to the worst-case computed factor also offers an interesting link between the quantitative evidence (as supported by statistics) and the qualitative evidence (as supported by the worst-case analysis), as the gap can be further rewritten by the multiple of the standard deviation σ measured from data.

The rest of the paper is structured as follows. After reviewing related work in Sect. 2, in Sect. 3 we summarize the basic principles of the conservative post-processing algorithm. In Sect. 4 we derive the connection between IoU and safety

---

[1] Precisely, when the DNN has not-so-good performance where within the collected dataset the observed intersection-over-union α is small, one needs to enlarge the bounding box more conservatively to ensure box coverage.

and subsequently in Sect. 5, we consider the situation where motion planners also reserve some buffer to compensate the imprecision. Finally, we evaluate the result by comparing the formal result with the data-driven approach using a case study in Sect. 6, and conclude in Sect. 7 by outlining further research opportunities.

2   Related Work

The safety of DNN-based systems is currently being addressed from a number of different perspectives; we recommend readers to a current survey [5] conducted by the German national project KI-Absicherung for an overview. On the methodology side, many results on safety argumentation use semi-formal/structural notations with variations on argumentation strategies (to list a few [2,8,15,19]). The value of these results is the development of generic safety argumentation structures, where the purpose of this paper is to demonstrate implementation aspects for a specific type of performance insufficiencies. For DNN testing, apart from proposing concrete testing techniques [14], another key direction is to introduce novel coverage criteria where the goal is to include diversified test cases such that the computed coverage is sufficiently high. For white box coverage criteria, neuron coverage [13] and extensions (e.g., SS-coverage [17]) motivated by MC/DC coverage in classical software have been proposed. For black box coverage criteria, various approaches apply combinatorial testing [1,3] to argue about the relative completeness of the test data. Readers are referred to Section 5.1 of a recent survey paper [6] for an overview of existing results in coverage-driven testing. However, the key issue for these coverage criteria is that they do not have a direct connection to safety, which is in many cases task-specific. Very recently, Lyssenko et al. [12] proposed to include a task-oriented relevance factor in the evaluation of DNNs. They used the distance from the sensor to the object to derive a relevance metric based on the IoU with a focus on semantic segmentation. Additionally, Volk et al. [18] defined a comprehensive safety score by considering various factors such as quality, relevance, and reaction time. The safety score is based on extending the basic IoU value. Again, to be used in safety argumentation, these metrics need to be connected to concrete performance limitations and to concrete applications, as suggested in safety standards such as ISO 21448 [7]. Our result overcomes the above mentioned limitation: even for the commonly used IoU metric, we can establish a precise and mathematically sound connection with the safety goal by properly restricting ourselves to a particular performance limitation of non-aligning bounding boxes.

Finally, the recent work from Cheng et al. [4] initiated the concept of safety post-processing attached to the standard post-processor to address the insufficiency of imprecise prediction. In [4], the enlargement threshold is estimated based on the data. This is in contrast to the concept stated in this paper where the enlargement factor is computed using worst-case analysis. The safety guarantee of the data-driven approach is conditional to an assumption on the generalizability between in-sample and out-of-sample data; this is not the case for

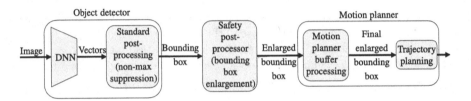

Fig. 1. The safety post-processor is inserted between the object detector and the motion planner. Here sensor fusion is omitted for simplicity purposes; the basic principle still applies when sensor fusion modules are introduced.

our worst-case derivation. The data-driven and the logical approach complement each other; in our experiments we also consider their connection.

3   Data-Driven Safe Post-processing in Addressing 2D Object Detection Imprecision

We first review the commonly used definition of the IoU between two rectangles.

Definition 1. *Given two 2D rectangles R_A and R_B, the intersection-over-union is defined to be the ratio between the overlapping area of R_A and R_B (nominator) and the union area of R_A and R_B (denominator), where* **area**(R) *denotes the area of some region R on the 2D plane.*

$$\mathsf{IoU}(R_A, R_B) = \frac{\mathsf{area}(R_A \cap R_B)}{\mathsf{area}(R_A \cup R_B)} \tag{1}$$

Within 2D object detection, the two rectangles used for calculating the IoU are the prediction bounding box R_{PR} and the associated GT bounding box R_{GT}. We also assume that all considered bounding boxes are horizontally laid out rectangles, i.e., all rectangles are *axis-aligned*.

We now summarize the principle of safe post-processors (SPP) as defined in [4] using Fig. 1, where introducing the post-processor between object detector and motion planner is meant to *compensate the performance insufficiency caused by non-alignment between prediction bounding box and the GT label bounding box*. While the general principle is applicable also for 3D detection, in this paper we restrict ourselves to the discussion on 2D front-view detection.

1. For each image collected in the training dataset, and for each predicted bounding box (R_{PR_i}) that only partially covers the associated GT bounding box R_{GT_i} but has $\mathsf{IoU}(\mathsf{R}_{PR_i}, \mathsf{R}_{GT_i}) \geq \alpha$, the minimum enlargement factor required to enclose the GT bounding box is measured. An illustration is shown in Fig. 3, where R_{PR} does not enclose R_{GT}: R_{PR} can be properly enlarged to $\mathsf{R}_{PR'}$, and the enlargement factor from R_{PR} to $\mathsf{R}_{PR'}$ is the ratio of the two widths (or two heights) between the two rectangles.

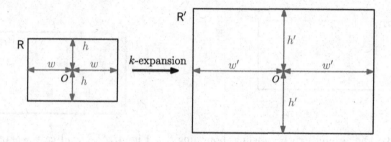

Fig. 2. A rectangle R (left), and it's k-expansion R' (right)

2. Aggregate the enlargement factor for all images in the training dataset and for all bounding boxes analyzed in the previous step. This can be done by taking the maximum value, in the following denoted as $k_{max,data}$, or by taking the mean value $k_{\mu,data}$ plus some additional buffer if desired.
3. Finally, add an SPP unit after the standard bounding box detector, as illustrated in Fig. 1. During operation, for each image captured by the camera sensor, the SPP always enlarges each predicted bounding box by the factor computed in the previous step.

This method for determining the enlargement factor is *learned/measured from the training data*, while in the following section we will describe a method that computes the required enlargement factor by conservatively considering, under the condition where $\mathsf{IoU}(\mathsf{R}_{PR}, \mathsf{R}_{GT}) \geq \alpha$, all possible overlapping scenarios.

4   Mathematically Associating the IoU Metric and Safety

In this section, we present the key result of the paper, namely the formal derivation of the *minimum enlargement factor required* to fully cover the ground truth bounding box (a situation we refer to as "safe" w.r.t. the coverage of the GT bounding boxes) under the condition $\mathsf{IoU} \geq \alpha$, by considering *the theoretical worst case scenario*.

4.1   The Mathematical Connection Between IoU and Safety

We first formally define the enlargement factor with the help of Fig. 2. Consider a rectangle R with center O, half-width w and half-height h, as depicted on the left of Fig. 2. Then the definition of an enlargement factor can be stated using Definition 2. The enlarged rectangle R' is shown on the right of Fig. 2. Note that this is equivalent to multiplying the length and width of R by k, while keeping the center fixed.

Definition 2. *The k-expansion ($k \geq 1$) transforms a rectangle R to a new rectangle R' by keeping the center O fixed while multiplying w, h by k, i.e., $w' = k \cdot w$, $h' = k \cdot h$. The value k is called the enlargement factor.*

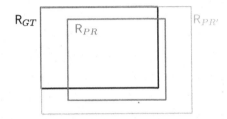

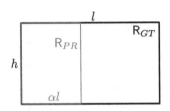

Fig. 3. The ground-truth labeling bounding box R_{GT}, prediction R_{PR}, and the k-expanded prediction $R_{PR'}$ that covers R_{GT}.

Fig. 4. A special case where R_{GT} and R_{PR} have the same height.

Assuming that no safety-aware post-processing exists, a complete enclosure of an object (in training or testing, an object is represented by the GT label) by the predicted bounding box is necessary to achieve safe detection. However, when considering a safety-aware post-processing step that enlarges the predicted bounding box by a certain margin, the risk due to a small amount of imprecision in detection can be compensated by the enlargement strategy. As a consequence, the IoU metric could still be used to determine a safe detection and leads to the following research question:

Question 1. Within 2D object detection, assume that a ground-truth label R_{GT} is intersecting with the prediction R_{PR}, both as horizontally laid out rectangles as shown in Fig. 3, with an $IoU(R_{GT}, R_{PR}) \geq \alpha$, where $\alpha \in (0, 1]$. What is the minimum k-expansion to be applied on R_{PR} such that it can fully cover R_{GT}?

We introduce the following example as a special case, which is later used in answering Question 1.

Example 1. Consider the ground-truth label R_{GT}, and the prediction R_{PR} that is fully covered by R_{GT} and only deviates from R_{GT} in one direction as depicted in Fig. 4. Let the width of R_{GT} to be l and the height to be h and let the prediction width be αl with $\alpha \leq 1$. What is the minimum k-expansion so that the k-expanded R_{PR} covers R_{GT}?

Solution to Example 1. Note that the height dimension is already covered, therefore, we focus on the width. Currently, the half-width of R_{PR} is $w = \frac{\alpha l}{2}$. In order to cover R_{GT}, the half-width w of R_{PR} has to increase by the distance $l - \alpha l$, to reach the bottom-right corner of R_{GT} to cover it. Thus, the new half-width will be $w' = w + (l - \alpha l)$, and the minimum k value is:

$$k = \frac{w'}{w} = \frac{\frac{\alpha l}{2} + l - \alpha l}{\frac{\alpha l}{2}} = \frac{2 - \alpha}{\alpha}$$

Moreover, noticing that the IoU in this case is exactly α, we can also express k in terms of the IoU:

$$k = \frac{2 - IoU(R_{PR}, R_{GT})}{IoU(R_{PR}, R_{GT})} \tag{2}$$

$\square$

Before extending the previous example to the general case of Question 1, we introduce the following Lemma 1, which states that an axis-aligned rectangle contained in a larger axis-aligned rectangle will still be contained when enlarging both rectangles by the same factor $k \geq 1$. This is based on the fact that the expansion does not change the center for R' and R. Therefore, when both rectangles enlarge themselves by an identical constant factor, the original area containment relation remains. The complete proof can be found in the extended version [16].

Lemma 1. *Consider an axis-aligned rectangle R, and a second axis-aligned rectangle R' that contains R. The region containment relation holds subject to the k-expansion, i.e., the k-expanded R will still be contained in the k-expanded R', for any $k \geq 1$.*

We now state the main theorem and its proof answering Question 1, where it turns out that the situation stated in Example 1 actually characterizes *the theoretical worst case scenario* concerning the prediction bounding box and the GT label.

Theorem 1. *Let $\alpha \in (0, 1]$ be a constant, and let R_{PR} and R_{GT} be the axis-aligned prediction and ground-truth bounding boxes that satisfy the following constraint:*

$$IoU(R_{PR}, R_{GT}) \geq \alpha$$

Then the minimum required k-expansion for R_{PR} to cover R_{GT} is characterized by $k = \frac{2-\alpha}{\alpha}$.

Proof. There are many different cases for the intersection and union between the prediction and the GT rectangles (e.g., prediction overlapping with GT, prediction completely inside GT, etc.). Therefore, we start the proof by considering the relation between the GT label and the *intersection*, not the prediction. This leads to a simplified sub-problem which we can easily solve to find the required k value. Subsequently, by using Lemma 1, we extrapolate from the intersection to the prediction bounding box and finally we show the tightness of the result.

We denote the intersection of R_{GT} and R_{PR} as R_I, and their union by R_U. Moreover, we denote the areas of R_{GT}, R_I and R_U as area(R_{GT}), area(R_I) and area(R_U). From Definition 1 of the IoU, we derive:

$$IoU(R_{GT}, R_{PR}) = \frac{area(R_I)}{area(R_U)} \geq \alpha \tag{3}$$

Since area(R_U) is always larger or equal to area(R_{GT}), we derive:

$$\alpha \leq IoU(R_{GT}, R_{PR}) = \frac{area(R_I)}{area(R_U)} \leq \frac{area(R_I)}{area(R_{GT})} \Leftrightarrow area(R_{GT}) \leq \frac{area(R_I)}{\alpha} \tag{4}$$

Consider now the intersection and the GT label as shown in Fig. 5. Note that Fig. 5 represents only one case; in fact, the only prerequisite for the proof

Fig. 5. Example ground-truth (black) and intersection (blue) rectangle. (Color figure online)

Fig. 6. The two line segments x_{GT}, x_I and the distance d between their (right) endpoints.

is that the intersection is contained in R_{GT}-its exact location does not change the proof. Let x_{GT} and y_{GT} be the width and height of R_{GT}, and let x_I and y_I be the width and height of the intersection R_I respectively (s. Fig. 5). Let $r_x = x_{GT}/x_I$ be the ratio of the widths of R_{GT} and R_I, and $r_y = y_{GT}/y_I$ the ratio of the heights of R_{GT} and R_I. Then, the area of R_{GT} in terms of r_x, r_y is given by Eq. 5.

$$\text{area}(R_{GT}) = x_{GT} \cdot y_{GT} = r_x x_I \cdot r_y y_I = r_x r_y (x_I \cdot y_I) = r_x r_y \text{area}(R_I) \quad (5)$$

From Eq. 4 it is known that $\text{area}(R_{GT}) \leq \text{area}(R_I)/\alpha$, thus, combining it with Eq. 5, we get Formula 6.

$$\text{area}(R_{GT}) = r_x r_y \text{area}(R_I) \leq \frac{\text{area}(R_I)}{\alpha} \Leftrightarrow r_x r_y \leq \frac{1}{\alpha} \quad (6)$$

That is, the product of r_x, r_y is bounded by $\frac{1}{\alpha}$. Since $r_x \geq 1, r_y \geq 1$ (the intersection is contained in GT and cannot be larger than GT), the maximum value one can take for one of these ratios is $\frac{1}{\alpha}$. Without loss of generality, we consider the width (the proof can be derived for the height in the same way). That is, x_{GT} is at most $\frac{x_I}{\alpha}$ due to the following inequality:

$$x_{GT} = r_x x_I \leq \frac{1}{\alpha} \cdot x_I = \frac{x_I}{\alpha} \quad (7)$$

Given the above result, how much do we need to k-expand x_I in order to cover x_{GT}? Now, we can focus solely on the line segments x_{GT} and x_I, as shown in Fig. 6. For x_I to cover x_{GT}, we must add the distance d from the endpoint of x_I up to the endpoint of x_{GT}. This distance is at most $d \leq d_{max} = x_{GT} - x_I$, since x_I is contained within x_{GT}, and the maximum possible distance occurs when x_I and x_{GT} align on one side. Therefore, the original half-width $w_I = \frac{x_I}{2}$ of the intersection must increase at most by a distance $d_{max} = x_{GT} - x_I$, leading in the worst case (i.e. in the case requiring maximal enlargement) to the following enlarged half-width obtained by Formula 7:

$$w_I' \leq w_I + d_{max} = w_I + x_{GT} - x_I \leq w_I + x_I(\frac{1}{\alpha} - 1) \Rightarrow$$
$$w_{I,max}' = w_I + x_I(\frac{1}{\alpha} - 1) \quad (8)$$

With this, the worst-case expansion factor k for R_I to cover R_{GT} will be

$$k = \frac{w'_{I,max}}{w_I} = \frac{w_I + x_I(\frac{1}{\alpha} - 1)}{w_I} \Rightarrow$$

$$k = \frac{\frac{x_I}{2} + x_I(\frac{1}{\alpha} - 1)}{\frac{x_I}{2}} \Leftrightarrow$$

$$k = \frac{x_I + 2x_I(\frac{1}{\alpha} - 1)}{x_I} \Leftrightarrow \tag{9}$$

$$k = 1 + 2(\frac{1}{\alpha} - 1) = \frac{2}{\alpha} - 1 \Leftrightarrow$$

$$k = \frac{2 - \alpha}{\alpha}$$

Now, the rectangle that should be expanded is the prediction R_{PR}, not the intersection R_I. However, due to Lemma 1, since R_{PR} contains the intersection R_I, the k-expanded R_{PR} will contain the k-expanded intersection, which in turn contains R_{GT}. Thus, expanding R_{PR} by k can also cover R_{GT} in all cases.

Finally, the bound k obtained in Eq. 9 for expanding R_{PR} is tight, since there are cases such as Example 1 where $k = \frac{2-\alpha}{\alpha}$ is necessary. □

The consequence of Theorem 1 is that by inverting Question 1, one can compute a safe IoU threshold based on a fixed k value[2]. From now on, the *theoretically derived* k value using Theorem 1 will be denoted as k_{math}.

Note that Theorem 1 considers the expansion for a single object. The validity of the argument does not change when one has multiple objects that overlap: If every object is fully covered by its bounding box, then object coverage is again ensured.

5 Connecting Motion Planners with Safety Post-processing

In this section, we present the mathematical relation between motion planning and safety-aware post-processing. As can be seen in Fig. 1, after the prediction bounding boxes are enlarged by the SPP, the enlarged predictions are then passed to the motion planner that can also add a physical buffer before planning the trajectory. However, the formally derived k value in Sect. 4.1 assumes no extra motion planner buffer to be applied to the enlarged bounding box. If the motion planner always adds a physical buffer to the enlarged bounding box, it is not required to apply the SPP with a k value following Theorem 1. More precisely, as long as the effect of the SPP and the motion planner is larger than the k value from Theorem 1, the prediction can be considered safe.

Precisely, let $k_{res,W}$ be the (residual) enlargement factor for the width (similar methodology is equally applicable to height) when considering the physical

---

[2] Due to space limits, we refer readers to the extended version [16] for further details.

buffer X_W to be added by the motion planner to each bounding box on both sides, as seen in Fig. 7. Furthermore, we consider that a prediction bounding box R_{PR} of an object has an initial physical width of W. After applying $k_{res,W}$, the new width is $W \cdot k_{res,W}$. Finally, considering the motion planner buffer, the final width is $2X_W + Wk_{res,W}$. Then, the effect of SPP and motion planner can be characterized by Eq. 10, which requires that the total enlargement factor due to the SPP and the motion planner exceeds the given enlargement threshold k_{math} derived from Theorem 1. For simplicity, in this paper we further assume that all objects as well as the point-of-view are placed on a flat surface environment.

$$\frac{\frac{2X_W + Wk_{res,W}}{2}}{\frac{W}{2}} \geq k_{math} \Leftrightarrow$$

$$\frac{2X_W}{W} + k_{res,W} \geq k_{math} \tag{10}$$

Further, by transforming Eq. 10 we derive the $k_{res,W}$ value to be used by the SPP in Eq. 11. As one can see, the smallest $k_{res,W}$ enabling object coverage is determined by the lower bound of combined enlargement k as well as the physical motion planner buffer X_W, and is conditional on an assumption over the **maximum observed width** W_{max} of the detected object type, e.g., "car". Furthermore, note that the SPP does not decrease the bounding box size, leading to the constraint in Eq. 12. Combining Eqs. 11 and 12 leads to the minimum $k_{res,W}$ ensuring object coverage and denoted as $k_{res,W,min}$, which is determined in Eq. 13.

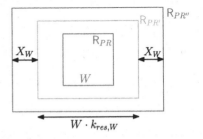

Fig. 7. Motion planner buffer enlargement on top of safety post-processing. R_{PR} denotes the predicted bounding box, $R_{PR'}$ the k-expanded R_{PR} and $R_{PR''}$ the $R_{PR'}$ with additional motion planner buffer X_W.

$$k_{res,W} \geq k_{math} - \frac{2X_W}{W} \tag{11}$$

$$k_{res,W} \geq 1 \tag{12}$$

$$k_{res,W,min} = max\left(k_{math} - \frac{2X_W}{W_{max}}, 1\right) \tag{13}$$

Situations when W_{max} appears can be computed analytically. Consider the identified object to be of class "car". One can derive that the largest observed width occurs when a "car" object satisfies the following two conditions:

- The car's diagonal has maximum length.
- The car's diagonal is oriented 90 degree towards the ego vehicle's front-facing axis.

As an example, let the physical buffer be $X_W = 50\,\text{cm}$ and $k_{math}(\alpha = 0.5) = 3$. According to German traffic law, the largest "car" has a width of $250\,\text{cm}$ and a length of $700\,\text{cm}$. Therefore, the largest observed object width will be the diagonal, i.e., $W_{max,car} = \sqrt{700^2 + 250^2} = 743\,\text{cm}$.[3] These considerations result in the enlargement factor $k_{res,W,min,car} = 2.87$ for the object with type "car". For any other "car" object with an observed width $W'_{car} \le W_{max,car}$, the combined enlargement is larger or equal to k_{math}.

$$\frac{2X_W}{W'_{car}} + k_{res,W,min,car} \ge \frac{2X_W}{W_{max,car}} + k_{res,W,min,car} = k_{math} \qquad (14)$$

Here we omit further details, but a similar analysis technique can be applied for the height of the detected objects. Finally, the similar analysis technique is also applicable for data-driven SPP as stated in Sect. 3: instead of taking the formally derived k_{math} in Theorem 1, one simply replaces k_{math} by a measured value such as $k_{max,data}$.

6 Evaluation

We perform an empirical study to understand the difference between an empirically measured enlargement factor (s. Sect. 3) and our formally derived worst-case enlargement factor (using Theorem 1). On the whole, this offers an interesting connection between the quantitative evidence (demonstrated by statistics) and qualitative evidence (demonstrated by worst-case analysis).

For the case study, we choose YOLO V5s [9], a single-stage object detector pretrained on the COCO dataset [11]. Moreover, we use a small automotive image dataset[4] generated with the CARLA[5] simulator, containing 820 training images and 208 test images with objects of the classes bike, motorbike, traffic light, traffic sign and vehicle which was split into car and truck. The dataset is generated via driving in autopilot, taking images from the ego vehicle's perspective and the bounding box labels were generated from the semantic segmentation information, successively manually adjusted and corrected. All other hyperparameters maintain their default values (and are not tuned as we are not interested in finding the best model but rather want to show the connection between IoU and safety). For training and validation, we apply a 90–10 split, resulting in 738 and 82 images for the respective datasets. For generating the predictions on the training dataset, we set the standard post-processing parameters confidence threshold and non-maximum suppression threshold to be 0.5. Based on

---

[3] Based on the analysis, for low IoU values, the required expansion factors can be very large. For example, for $\alpha = 0.4$, Eq. 9 would give an enlargement factor of $k_{math} = 4$, thus a vehicle with a bounding box of length $w = 5\,\text{m}$ would be enlarged to $w' = 20\,\text{m}$, which is forbiddingly large in practice. Hence, for meaningful practical applications, the implication of our result is the need of high IoUs within the collected dataset.

[4] https://github.com/DanielHfnr/Carla-Object-Detection-Dataset.

[5] https://carla.org/.

Table 1. The formally derived and measured k values for the object class "car".

IoU	0.1	0.2	0.3	0.4	0.5	**0.6**	0.7	0.8	0.9
k_{math}	19.000	9.000	5.667	4.000	3.000	2.333	1.857	1.500	1.222
$k_{max,W,data}$	4.400	2.360	2.360	2.360	2.261	2.000	1.588	1.444	1.128
$k_{\mu,W,data}$	1.083	1.078	1.078	1.078	1.075	1.070	1.057	1.044	1.023
$\sigma_{W,data}$	0.176	0.130	0.130	0.129	0.118	0.105	0.078	0.058	0.030
$k_{\mu,W,data} + 3\sigma_{W,data}$	1.612	1.468	1.468	1.464	1.428	1.383	1.291	1.216	1.112
$k_{\mu,W,data} + 6\sigma_{W,data}$	2.141	1.857	1.857	1.850	1.780	1.697	1.524	1.389	1.202

the above configuration, for a given IoU threshold value α from 0.1 to 0.9, we have conducted the following experiments for the width of the object class "car":

1. **Mathematical worst-case enlargement factor.** First, we derive the mathematical worst-case k value k_{math} following Theorem 1 where no physical buffer is assigned. The results are reflected in the first row of Table 1.
2. **Data-enabled worst-case enlargement factor.** We further use the method in Sect. 3 to derive the measured worst-case k value where no physical buffer is assigned. $k_{max,W,data}$ records the maximum observed enlargement factor for width in the second row of Table 1.
3. **Data-enabled average enlargement factor.** We again use the method in Sect. 3 to derive the measured average k value $k_{\mu,W,data}$ and the standard deviation $\sigma_{W,data}$ for width where no physical buffer is assigned. They are recorded in Table 1, row three and four. Additionally, we record the measured average k value plus three times the standard deviation ($k_{\mu,W,data}+3\sigma_{W,data}$) and plus six times the standard deviation ($k_{\mu,W,data}+6\sigma_{W,data}$), with values stored in Table 1, row five and six.
4. **Combined effect of SPP and motion planner.** Lastly, we investigate the combination of SPP and motion planner buffer by analyzing the influence of the physical buffer for width X_W on the $k_{res,W,min}$ values.

Mathematical and Measured Enlargement Factors. We first compare the *measured* and *formally derived* k values by comparing the first and the second rows of Table 1.

Without surprise, we can observe that $k_{math} > k_{max,W,data}$, i.e., all k values observed on the data are lower than the theoretical ones. This is expected since the mathematically derived k-expansion factor provably considers all possible cases, but these worst cases rarely appear in reality. Moreover, one can observe that for an increasing IoU threshold, the measured values $k_{max,W,data}$ and $k_{\mu,W,data}$ decrease, similarly to the mathematical value k_{math}, as the predicted bounding boxes deviate less from the GT bounding box with increasing IoU. Additionally, we observe the following points:

1. For high IoU thresholds such as 0.8 or 0.9, the measured worst case value $k_{max,W,data}$ and $k_{\mu,W,data} + 6\sigma_{W,data}$ are only slightly lower than the

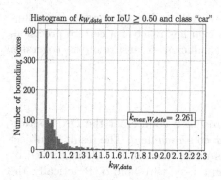

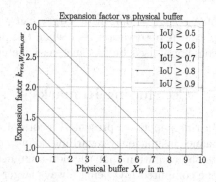

Fig. 8. Histogram of $k_{W,data}$ values for class "car" at IoU ≥ 0.5.

Fig. 9. The relation between $k_{res,W,min}$ and X_W for class "car" with respect to varying IoU values.

theoretical worst case value k_{math}. Considering low IoU values such as 0.1 or 0.2, we observe the opposite; the measured worst case value $k_{max,W,data}$ and $k_{\mu,W,data} + 6\sigma_{W,data}$ are significantly lower than the theoretical worst case k_{math}.[6]

2. From the distribution of measured k values $k_{W,data}$, e.g. for IoU ≥ 0.5 in Fig. 8, we can observe that it is a one-sided distribution with the majority of values close to one. Still, the probability of requiring a large k value is low.

3. We see that for any IoU threshold, the distance between k_{math} and $k_{max,W,data}$ is always larger than three standard deviations $\sigma_{W,data}$, except for IoU ≥ 0.8.

Connecting SPP and Motion Planner. We present the results of experiment 4 on the connection between the SPP and the motion planner buffer. For different IoU thresholds and k_{math} values, assuming a maximum observed "car" width of $W_{max,car} = 7.43$ m, we can derive $k_{res,W,min,car}$ as a function of the physical buffer X_W using Eq. 13. The result is visualized by Fig. 9, where we plot $k_{res,W,min,car}$ with respect to X_W for various IoU thresholds.

From Fig. 9, we can observe that $k_{res,W,min,car} = 1$ when the physical buffer exceeds a certain value. Indeed, as we can also see from Eq. 13, when the physical buffer becomes large enough and surpasses a threshold $X_{W,thres}$, the motion planner is by itself sufficient to ensure object coverage, and no further enlargement by the SPP module is required. Otherwise, without a physical buffer, the enlargement is purely based on the SPP module. Moreover, we can see that this threshold value $X_{W,thres}$ is larger for lower IoU values. This is also reasonable, since for a small IoU, a larger physical buffer is necessary to ensure object coverage. Finally, for large IoU values such as IoU ≥ 0.9, a physical buffer

---

[6] If we assume that the occurrence of bounding box non-alignment is a random variable, and the measured mean and variance match the real ones, then from Chebyshev's inequality we know that the probability of exceeding $6\sigma_{W,data}$ is below 2.78%.

of $X_{W,thres} = 0.82\,\text{m}$ or larger can already ensure object coverage. This supports the observation that when the prediction has reached a certain precision, commonly used buffers such as 1 meter are sufficient to ensure object coverage.

7   Concluding Remarks

In this paper, we presented a formal approach to counteract the DNN performance insufficiency regarding *bounding box non-alignment*. The result is subject to the condition that the non-alignment is under control, i.e., characterized by the computed IoU being always larger than a fixed threshold α. Practically, the decision of the threshold is measured from the collected data at a given confidence level. Based on the threshold, the main result of this paper (Theorem 1) provides a criterion to conservatively enlarge the prediction bounding box via an additional post-processing step after DNN-based object detection, in order to safely cover the object. We further studied the case when the motion planner also reserves some buffer, where the introduced post-processing and the buffer should altogether achieve the expansion governed by Theorem 1. Altogether, the merit of Theorem 1 is to connect the performance of the DNN (characterized by the value α) with safety (by appropriately enlarging the bounding box or the motion planner buffer). Having such a unified analysis ensures that the resulting system is not acting overly conservatively without considering the capabilities of other components. Finally, our empirical evaluation on a simulation-based dataset showed that the mathematically derived expansion factor was mostly larger than the one empirically measured by one standard deviation.

This work continues our vision of offering a rigorous methodology to systematically analyze performance limitations for DNNs and subsequently provide counter-measures that are rooted in scientific rigor. We conclude by outlining some research directions currently under investigation: (a) Consider the impact of the IoU threshold and the post-processor with other types of DNN insufficiencies such as false negatives (disappearing objects) or false positives (ghost objects). (b) Extend the formalism by considering the interplay among multiple perception pipelines and the resulting sensor fusion. (c) Extend the theoretical framework to also cover DNN insufficiencies in 3D object detection. (d) Consider a fine-grained IoU metric and the corresponding worst-case expansion that is less conservative.

References

1. Abrecht, S., Gauerhof, L., Gladisch, C., Groh, K., Heinzemann, C., Woehrle, M.: Testing deep learning-based visual perception for automated driving. ACM Trans. Cyber-Phys. Syst. **5**(4), 1–28 (2021)
2. Burton, S., Gauerhof, L., Heinzemann, C.: Making the case for safety of machine learning in highly automated driving. In: Tonetta, S., Schoitsch, E., Bitsch, F. (eds.) SAFECOMP 2017. LNCS, vol. 10489, pp. 5–16. Springer, Cham (2017). https://doi.org/10.1007/978-3-319-66284-8_1

3. Cheng, C.-H., Huang, C.-H., Yasuoka, H.: Quantitative Projection Coverage for Testing ML-enabled Autonomous Systems. In: Lahiri, S.K., Wang, C. (eds.) ATVA 2018. LNCS, vol. 11138, pp. 126–142. Springer, Cham (2018). https://doi.org/10.1007/978-3-030-01090-4_8

4. Cheng, C.H., Schuster, T., Burton, S.: Logically sound arguments for the effectiveness of ML safety measures. arXiv preprint arXiv:2111.02649 (2021)

5. Houben, S., et al.: Inspect, understand, overcome: a survey of practical methods for AI safety. arXiv preprint arXiv:2104.14235 (2021)

6. Huang, X., et al.: A survey of safety and trustworthiness of deep neural networks: Verification, testing, adversarial attack and defence, and interpretability. Comput. Sci. Rev. **37**, 100270 (2020)

7. Safety of the intended functionality - SOTIF (ISO/DIS 21448). Standard, International Organization for Standardization (2021)

8. Jia, Y., Lawton, T., McDermid, J., Rojas, E., Habli, I.: A framework for assurance of medication safety using machine learning. arXiv preprint arXiv:2101.05620 (2021)

9. Jocher, G., et al.: ultralytics/yolov5: v4.0 - nn.SiLU() activations, weights & biases logging, PyTorch hub integration, https://zenodo.org/record/4418161

10. Koopman, P., Ferrell, U., Fratrik, F., Wagner, M.: A safety standard approach for fully autonomous vehicles. In: Romanovsky, A., Troubitsyna, E., Gashi, I., Schoitsch, E., Bitsch, F. (eds.) SAFECOMP 2019. LNCS, vol. 11699, pp. 326–332. Springer, Cham (2019). https://doi.org/10.1007/978-3-030-26250-1_26

11. Lin, T., et al.: Microsoft COCO: common objects in context. In: Fleet, D., Pajdla, T., Schiele, B., Tuytelaars, T. (eds.) ECCV 2014. LNCS, vol. 8693, pp. 740–755. Springer, Cham (2014). https://doi.org/10.1007/978-3-319-10602-1_48

12. Lyssenko, M., Gladisch, C., Heinzemann, C., Woehrle, M., Triebel, R.: From evaluation to verification: towards task-oriented relevance metrics for pedestrian detection in safety-critical domains. In: CVPR Workshop, pp. 38–45. IEEE (2021)

13. Pei, K., Cao, Y., Yang, J., Jana, S.: DeepXplore: automated whitebox testing of deep learning systems. In: SOSP, pp. 1–18. ACM (2017)

14. Pezzementi, Z., et al.: Putting image manipulations in context: robustness testing for safe perception. In: SSRR. pp. 1–8. IEEE (2018)

15. Salay, R., Czarnecki, K., Kuwajima, H., Yasuoka, H., Nakae, T., Abdelzad, V., Huang, C., Kahn, M., Nguyen, V.D.: The missing link: Developing a safety case for perception components in automated driving. arXiv preprint arXiv:2108.13294 (2021)

16. Schuster, T., Seferis, E., Burton, S., Cheng, C.H.: Unaligned but safe-formally compensating performance limitations for imprecise 2D object detection. arXiv preprint arXiv:2202.05123 (2022)

17. Sun, Y., Huang, X., Kroening, D., Sharp, J., Hill, M., Ashmore, R.: Structural test coverage criteria for deep neural networks. In: ACM TECS, vol. 18, pp. 1–23 (2019)

18. Volk, G., Gamerdinger, J., Bernuth, A.v., Bringmann, O.: A comprehensive safety metric to evaluate perception in autonomous systems. In: ITSC, pp. 1–8. IEEE (2020)

19. Zhao, X., et al.: A Safety Framework for Critical Systems Utilising Deep Neural Networks. In: Casimiro, A., Ortmeier, F., Bitsch, F., Ferreira, P. (eds.) SAFECOMP 2020. LNCS, vol. 12234, pp. 244–259. Springer, Cham (2020). https://doi.org/10.1007/978-3-030-54549-9_16

Architectural Patterns for Handling Runtime Uncertainty of Data-Driven Models in Safety-Critical Perception

Janek Groß[1]([⊠]), Rasmus Adler[1] [ID], Michael Kläs[1], Jan Reich[1] [ID], Lisa Jöckel[1], and Roman Gansch[2]

[1] Fraunhofer IESE, Kaiserslautern, Germany
{janek.gross,rasmus.adler,michael.klaes,jan.reich,
lisa.joeckel}@iese.fraunhofer.de
[2] Corporate Research, Robert Bosch GmbH, Renningen, Germany
roman.gansch@de.bosch.com

Abstract. Data-driven models (DDM) based on machine learning and other AI techniques play an important role in the perception of increasingly autonomous systems. Due to the merely implicit definition of their behavior mainly based on the data used for training, DDM outputs are subject to uncertainty. This poses a challenge with respect to the realization of safety-critical perception tasks by means of DDMs. A promising approach to tackling this challenge is to estimate the uncertainty in the current situation during operation and adapt the system behavior accordingly. In previous work, we focused on runtime estimation of uncertainty and discussed approaches for handling uncertainty estimations. In this paper, we present additional architectural patterns for handling uncertainty. Furthermore, we evaluate the four patterns qualitatively and quantitatively with respect to safety and performance gains. For the quantitative evaluation, we consider a distance controller for vehicle platooning where performance gains are measured by considering how much the distance can be reduced in different operational situations. We conclude that the consideration of context information concerning the driving situation makes it possible to accept more or less uncertainty depending on the inherent risk of the situation, which results in performance gains.

Keywords: Uncertainty quantification · Architectural patterns · Machine learning · Safety · Autonomous systems

1 Introduction

Data-driven models (DDM) based on machine learning are an enabler for many innovations. A huge field of application concerns the perception of the environment in increasingly autonomous systems. Considering self-driving road vehicles, DDMs can be used, for instance, to detect and classify traffic participants or road signs. The main issue that limits the usage of DDMs for such perception tasks is the assurance of safety. A solution

M. Trapp et al. (Eds.): SAFECOMP 2022, LNCS 13414, pp. 284–297, 2022.
https://doi.org/10.1007/978-3-031-14835-4_19

that would make it possible to use DDMs for realizing safety-critical functionalities would be extremely valuable for all industries dealing with safety.

A major safety concern is that DDM outputs are subject to uncertainty due to implicit behavioral definitions based on available training data. One promising approach to address this safety concern is to estimate the uncertainty for a particular output during operation and to handle it by adapting the system behavior. This approach leads to two related challenges. The first one is how to determine uncertainty during operation in a dependable way. The second one is how to handle estimated uncertainties by means of behavior adaptations. Most existing work focuses on the first challenge. In previous work, we also already proposed and evaluated a solution for estimating uncertainties during operation [1–4]. Therefore, this paper focuses on the second challenge, i.e., uncertainty handling and the interface to uncertainty estimation. In a previous paper, we elaborated one possible solution for handling uncertainties [5]. In this paper, we systematically derive alternative patterns and evaluate them by means of a simple application example.

As for the application, we will consider a distance controller for keeping a safety distance between two vehicles. Traditionally, such a distance controller is realized without any DDM. Thus, we use this traditional approach as a reference baseline and evaluate how much we could reduce the distance if we use a DDM to consider additional information; namely, the friction coefficient of the leading vehicle. Traditionally, a fixed worst-case value would be defined for this friction coefficient. We hypothesize that using a dynamically estimated value instead of the worst-case value bears utility potential. However, using a DDM comes with uncertainties in the predicted friction value. Therefore, the achievable utility gain varies depending on the level of uncertainty that is realistically expectable and acceptable, but also on the architectural pattern we apply to handle uncertainty at runtime. This raises the research questions we address in this work: *RQ1* – What are general patterns for dealing with DDM-related runtime uncertainty on an architectural level? *RQ2* – Which advantages and disadvantages does each pattern have compared to (a) using worst-case approximation and (b) situation-independent uncertainty estimates obtained at design time? *RQ3* – How do relevant parameters such as the prediction performance of the DDM and the accepted level of uncertainty affect the perceived utility gain?

This paper offers the following contributions to answer these questions: (1) systematically derived architectural patterns to deal with DDM-related uncertainty and (2) an initial evaluation of these patterns. The evaluation comprises (a) an implementation of the distance controller example; (b) an analysis of our implementation by means of an evaluation of the impact of parameters such as the degree of accepted uncertainty; and (c) a comparison and discussion of the different patterns.

The paper is structured as follows: First, we will discuss related work and provide a quantitative definition of uncertainty. Second, we will introduce the running example. Third, we will answer *RQ1* and describe the architectural patterns for handling uncertainty. Fourth, we will present our approach for evaluating the patterns by means of the example. Finally, we will present the evaluation results and use them to answer the *RQ2* and *RQ3* before concluding the paper.

2 Related Work

Our proposed patterns for handling uncertainty estimates at runtime are related to approaches that can provide these uncertainty estimates. They complement each other like error detection and error handling. Our work is more closely related to approaches that estimate uncertainties during operation for a concrete DDM output. However, there is also a link to approaches that estimate a situation-independent general uncertainty value at design time, e.g., by statistical testing, because the patterns are also applicable if the uncertainty is assumed constant. Uncertainty estimates during operation can be determined, e.g., by extending existing models like Bayesian neural networks or deep ensembles [6], or by using model-agnostic approaches like uncertainty wrappers [1]. The latter considers a required confidence level in the uncertainty estimates, which is preferable for safety-related contexts.

A basis for combining approaches for uncertainty estimation with approaches for uncertainty handling is a clear *interface* with an unambiguous definition of uncertainty. In previous work, we related uncertainty to the probability that DDM output or a statement about the outcome is not correct [1]. More formally, *uncertainty* is the complement of certainty, where certainty is a lower bound on the probability of correctness justifiable on a given level of confidence considering the current state of knowledge. In the following, we will use the term *data-driven component* (DDC) for a component that comprises a DDM but enhances the DDM output with uncertainty information.

In this paper, we relate uncertainty to a certain safety-critical failure mode like 'too high' or 'too low' for a given output of a DDM. Our estimated uncertainty is thus related to the probability of a failure mode. Hereby, 100% uncertainty means that we do not know at all whether the failure mode is present, whereas 100% failure probability means that the failure mode is definitely there.

Our patterns for handling uncertainty abstract from the causes that contribute to uncertainty. Their application is thus not limited to DDCs and also relates to the handling of random events in the environment or other kinds of random events considered in existing safety standards such as IEC 61508. However, following traditional safety standards, it is not common to estimate failure probabilities during operation. Safety analyses such as fault tree analyses are used at design time to identify the relationship between causes and top-level system failures and perform related probabilistic reasoning. For instance, the occurrence probability of every cause is estimated and the occurrence probability of the top-level failure is derived. However, in practice, all this is done at design time. The concept of component fault trees [7] supports automation of such analyses by modularizing fault trees and making them composable so that compositional fault trees can be generated and analyzed when components are composed into systems at design time. In the context of the DEIS project [8], related runtime analyses concepts were developed, but this work did not consider DDCs. Accordingly, runtime estimation of uncertainty was not considered and all probabilities of causal events were statically defined at design time.

As mentioned above, uncertainty estimation and uncertainty handling complement each other like error detection and error handling. In this sense, the patterns for handling uncertainty are related to error handling. The latter can be seen as a special case of uncertainty handling that considers only the uncertainty values 0 and 1. Reactions concerning values in between are not considered. We address this gap with our approach.

Salay et al. propose to work with an imprecise world model comprising a set of precise world models to handle uncertainties in perception, yet they do not further elaborate their idea by proposing an architectural pattern that could serve as a reference to implement their approach, neither do they investigate validity of assumptions or implications on performance [9]. Henne et al. proposed an architectural pattern for handling uncertainties at different stages of the perception chain [10]. These uncertainties are fed into a dynamic dependability management component that merges outputs from the perception chain and from a verified low-performance safety path. Compared to our patterns, this pattern is at a much higher level of abstraction. For instance, it does not describe which uncertainty information is delivered and how it is processed.

The Situation-Aware Dynamic Risk Assessment (SINADRA) approach uses Bayesian networks to determine the likelihood that a possible system behavior in the current operational situation will lead to an accident [11]. This approach is related to some patterns that allow dynamic adaptation of a threshold for acceptable uncertainty and can be used as an alternative solution to our patterns. The estimated uncertainties could be fed into Bayesian networks, so the accident likelihood would consider not only uncertainties due to the behavior of other traffic participants and other environmental aspects but also the uncertainty that environmental aspects might not be perceived correctly.

As our patterns are not limited to the handling of uncertainties of DDCs, many approaches for estimating perception uncertainties could be compatible with our patterns. However, most approaches focus on design-time estimation of uncertainty. For instance, the work in [12] presents an approach for expressing perception uncertainties of LIDAR by means of Bayesian networks.

3 Example Use Case

As an example for explaining and evaluating our patterns, we will consider a vehicle function intended to ensure a safe distance to the vehicle in front. We will denote by d_{safe} the safety-related distance required to avoid collisions; it is determined by the following rule from [13]:

$$d_{safe} = \left[v_F \rho + \frac{1}{2} a_{max,acc,F} \rho^2 + \frac{\left(v_F + \rho a_{max,acc,F}\right)^2}{2 a_{min,brake,F}} - \frac{v_L^2}{2 a_{max,brake,L}} \right]_+ \quad (1)$$

where $[x]_+ := \max\{x, 0\}$.

The first three terms together represent the stopping distance of the follower vehicle considering (i) the reaction distance based on follower speed v_F and reaction time ρ that is required until the follower can initiate the braking maneuver after the leader has started to brake, (ii) the acceleration distance (assuming the follower constantly accelerates with $a_{max,acc,F}$ during reaction time), and (iii) the follower braking distance when the follower constantly brakes with deceleration $a_{min,brake,F}$. The last term represents the leader's braking distance. To estimate the safe distance d_{safe}, we subtract the leader's braking distance from the follower's stopping distance. Using this formula, we can formalize the safety constraint 'keep a safe distance' with $d_{current} \geq d_{safe}$ where $d_{current}$ refers to the current distance. To discuss the handling of uncertainties, we focus on the road friction coefficient of the leading vehicle μ_L, which affects the lead vehicle's traction during braking. We assume that the leader's road friction is estimated by means of a DDC, e.g., one of those used in the context of [14] or [15]. The following two equations concretize the physical relationship between $a_{max,brake,L}$ from the safe distance formula and the friction coefficient μ_L.

$$a_{max,brake,L} = min\left(\frac{F_{b,traction,limit,L}}{m_L}, \frac{F_{b,brakesystem,limit,L}}{m_L} \right) \tag{2}$$

$$F_{b,traction,limit} = m_L \cdot g \cdot \mu_L \tag{3}$$

In general, the effective maximum leader deceleration limit $a_{max,brake,L}$ is influenced by all driving resistance forces acting in the longitudinal direction (brake system, brake force, air resistance, rolling resistance, road inclination resistance). For the sake of exemplification, Eq. (2) only considers the effective deceleration to be bound by the maximum brake force $F_{b,brakesystem,limit,L}$ the brake system is capable of generating at the wheels, and the traction limit $F_{b,traction,limit,L}$ determining how much of the generated force can be transferred effectively to the road. Since the stronger of the two forces overcomes the weaker one, the slippage either of the brakes or of the tires on the road is zero at any moment in time. Thus, only the weaker of the two forces limits the overall brakeforce and the maximal deceleration is calculated using the minimum of the two force values. While the brake system's limit is mainly influenced by construction, brake pad wear, and the pedal force a driver is likely to apply, the traction limit depends on the vehicle's mass m_L, the gravitational constant g, and the friction coefficient μ_L. We assume that the friction coefficient μ_L of the leading vehicle is estimated by a DDM and thus subject to uncertainty. In previous work [5], we argued that it is reasonable to use a DDM, apart from the safety challenge that we address with our approach.

In order to apply our architectural patterns, we consider the architecture depicted in Fig. 1, which shall ensure the safety constraint $d_{current} \geq \hat{d}_{safe}$ as a starting point; hereby, $\hat{d}_{safe}$ denotes the "determined safety distance", i.e. the value obtained when determining d_{safe} on the basis of uncertainty-affected parameters.

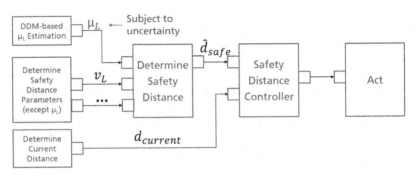

Fig. 1. Architectural perspective on the function ensuring the safety distance constraint

A 'safety distance controller' receives the current distance and determined safety distance as input. It checks whether the current distance approaches the safety distance and sends, if required, brake commands so that the current distance does not go below the safety distance. For this purpose, the RSS framework [13] defines the concept of 'proper response' to ensure that the safety distance constraint is met.

The current distance is measured directly, whereas the safety distance is derived according to the formulas mentioned above. High-integrity distance measurements are possible with radar sensors and are already used in series, e.g., in adaptive cruise control systems. Accordingly, one component determines the required parameters like μ_L and another component calculates the safety distance from these values.

The critical failure mode of the estimated friction coefficient μ_L of the leading vehicle is 'too low' because the braking capability of the leading vehicle would be underestimated, causing the safety distance to be underestimated as well. Accordingly, we focus on the uncertainty with respect to this critical failure mode.

4   Architectural Patterns for Dealing with Uncertainty

In this section, we address *RQ1* 'What are general patterns for dealing with DDM-related runtime uncertainty at an architectural level?' by proposing and discussing patterns for handling uncertainty. We consider the robotic paradigm *sense-plan-act* and focus on the uncertainty that a safety-critical failure mode in the sensing or perception of the environment is present. In our example case, the uncertainty that the determined friction coefficient μ_L of the leading vehicle has the failure mode 'too low' causes an uncertainty regarding the fulfillment of the safety constraint. The objective of all patterns is to limit this uncertainty to an acceptable level. For the remainder of this work we will focus on μ_L as the uncertainty-affected variable and assume that other variables are either measured with perfect accuracy or are worst-case estimates. We only consider established platoons and disregard situations where a platoon is formed or dissolved.

Next, we will first systematically derive the patterns and then briefly discuss implications if we need to deal with multiple uncertain variables.

We see two elementary *design decisions* for the patterns. The first one addresses the interface, i.e., whether we provide a single value x and related uncertainty u or an uncertainty distribution regarding possible values $u(x)$. The second decision addresses whether we assume a fixed target for the degree of acceptable uncertainty $u_{acceptable}$ or consider the option that $u_{acceptable}$ depends on further situational information y.

In our further discussion, we will focus on the resulting alternative *uncertainty handlers*, which are illustrated in Fig. 2, and which would be placed between the sensing component providing the required information and the decision component using it. In our example architecture given in Fig. 1, it would be placed between the DDC providing μ_L and the component determining the safety distance.

The **uncertainty supervisor** shown in the top-left part of Fig. 2 receives an input x that is estimated by a DDC. Furthermore, it receives an uncertainty u representing the uncertainty that x has a certain failure mode. It compares this uncertainty u with a fixed threshold $u_{acceptable}$ defining what is acceptable from a safety perspective. If the uncertainty is not acceptable, it overwrites the input variable x by a default value, e.g., the worst-case value. In our example, the variable x would be the friction coefficient μ_L and the uncertainty u would refer to the failure mode 'too low'. As default value, we would choose a value we can assure to be the highest value (μ_{max}) that the leading vehicle could encounter in the intended usage context.

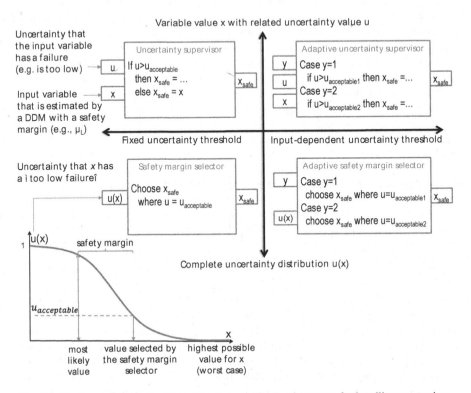

Fig. 2. Checker options to implement the four architectural patterns for handling uncertainty

The ***adaptive uncertainty supervisor*** in the top-right part of Fig. 2 has an additional input y that is used to adapt the acceptable uncertainty threshold. This can make sense because the safety criticality of the DDC output may depend on the current operational situation. In our example of assuring a safe distance, a rear-end collision would be less severe if the vehicle speed is very low. Accordingly, one could think of two safety goals addressing different situations with different integrity levels and values for $u_{acceptable}$. If we apply this approach, we need to consider that situations must not be too fine-grained as described in clause 6.4.2.7, part 3 of ISO 26262: 'It shall be ensured that the chosen level of detail of the list of operational situations does not lead to an inappropriate lowering of the ASIL [of the corresponding safety goals].'

The ***safety margin selector*** in the lower-left part of Fig. 2 receives an uncertainty distribution, which is also illustrated in the figure. The x-axis refers to value x, e.g., the friction coefficient μ_L. The y-axis assigns to each x-value the associated uncertainty $u(x)$. In our example, $u(x)$ would be the uncertainty concerning the failure mode 'too low'.

This implies that higher x values have lower uncertainties and the highest practically possible x value μ_{max} has uncertainty zero. Based on this distribution, the safety margin selectors choose the x such that $u(x) \leq u_{acceptable}$.

The ***adaptive safety margin selector*** in the lower-right part finally combines an uncertainty distribution with an adaptable uncertainty threshold.

So far, we have assumed that only the friction coefficient of the leading vehicle is estimated by a DDM. Yet, we can apply the patterns in the same way for further uncertain variables when assigning uncertainty to them.

Considering uncertainties from many variables, (static) budgeting of the uncertainty threshold would lead to behavior that is not optimal in all situations. If we consider uncertainty supervisors, in some situations some variables might not need the uncertainty budget that has been assigned to them, while other variables would be overwritten as they are just above the uncertainty threshold. If we consider safety margin selectors, we may have a similar effect, as the safety margins are not selected optimally. An approach to overcoming this issue is to propagate the uncertainties and then apply an uncertainty handler after all uncertainties are combined. In our example, an uncertainty handler for $\hat{d}_{safe}$ would replace an uncertainty handler for μ_L and further input variables.

However, this requires that the 'determine safe distance' component appropriately integrates the different variables and their uncertainties in the calculation of d_{safe}.

5 Simulation-Based Evaluation Approach

In this section we describe how we simulated the application of the previously derived patterns to answer *RQ 2* and *RQ 3* in Sect. 6. To answer our RQs in the example use-case, we need to evaluate the impact that each pattern has on the safety distance $\hat{d}_{safe}$ when we estimate the leader's friction coefficient μ_L by means of a DDC and use the patterns to deal with related uncertainties. For this purpose, we need to generate the parameter values from which we can calculate d_{safe}. In the following, we will thus first provide an overview of our approach to generating this information. Then we will describe the assumptions we made, i.e., the values of the constants and the anticipated distributions. Finally, we will report on technical aspects of our implementation.

Overview – Figure 3 illustrates the data flow of the implemented simulation approach. As shown in the left part, we use two random variables called *Weather Conditions* and *Behavioral Conditions* as input to allow for a variation of the considered situations. The *Weather Conditions* are used to generate situational friction information and related uncertainty information as we assume that the friction depends on the situational weather conditions. We vary the estimated friction value $E[\mu]$ as well as the related dispersion σ to get a situational probability distribution. We define a situational uncertainty threshold $u_{acceptable}$ in case a human is actively supervising the vehicle because we assume that supervision allows for less strict uncertainty thresholds. The generated information is used to apply the different patterns and calculate their output, namely the friction coefficient $\hat{\mu}_{safe}$. As illustrated in Fig. 3, we also use the *Behavioral Conditions* to generate velocity values for both vehicles. These velocity values are used together with μ_{safe} and the predefined *Safety Distance Parameters* to compute the minimum required safety distance $\hat{d}_{safe}$.

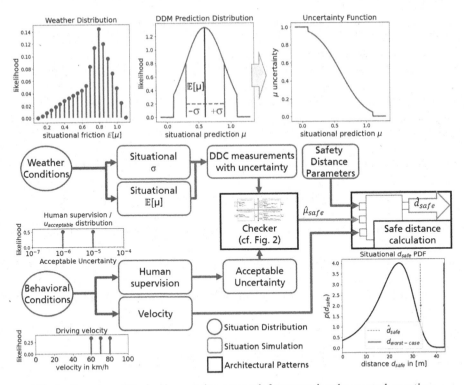

Fig. 3. Overview of the implementation approach for answering the research questions

Assumptions – Discussing the underlying simulation assumptions, we start from the bottom left in Fig. 3 where we defined several distributions that characterize the simulated situations. To generate the vehicle velocities from the *Behavioral Conditions,* we assumed a discrete distribution of velocities between 60 and 80 km/h in order to comply with speed limits for commercial vehicles on German highways. We considered only situations with established platoons where both vehicles drive at the same speed. For specifying the acceptable uncertainty, we assumed a distribution where the driver supervises the distance controller 50% of the operating time and $u_{acceptable} = 10^{-5}$ in case of supervision and 10^{-6} in case of no supervision.

The *Weather Conditions* are defined by a discrete unidimensional distribution. This distribution describes multiple degrees of one of the four conditions: (i) dry weather, (ii) light rain, (iii) snow, and (iv) heavy rain/freezing rain with a respective frequency of 300, 100, 60, and 5 days per year. For the distribution of *Situational Friction* coefficients, we considered empirical friction measurements [16] and assumed the road conditions dry asphalt, wet asphalt, snow/wet leaves, glaze/aquaplaning with the respective friction coefficients 0.8, 0.64, 0.41, and 0.14. To achieve a more fine-grained distribution, we used friction values in steps of 0.05 and derived the corresponding likelihoods from the *Weather Conditions* distribution through linear interpolation.

To model the inaccuracy of the DDM-based friction predictions, we assumed unobservable random variables including events like sensor noise or road surface irregularities leading to disparities. For simplicity, we assumed independent unobservable random variables that influence the DDM friction prediction uncertainty. According to the central limit theorem, the distribution of the mean of n independent and integrable random variables converges to the normal distribution with increasing n. Thus, we assumed that the friction coefficients are normally distributed with expected situational friction $E[\mu]$ as mean and situational dispersion σ as standard deviation. However, both the maximal and minimal friction on the road are limited by physical constraints. We therefore assumed $\mu = 0.1$ as the lower limit and $\mu = 1.1$ as the upper limit and cut off the normal distribution at these limits. The dispersion σ is assumed to decrease linearly with better weather conditions and higher friction values with a maximum dispersion of $\sigma = 0.075$ for glaze and a minimum of $\sigma = 0.02$ under perfect road conditions.

Further assumptions relate to the simulated DDC and the architectural patterns themselves. For the two uncertainty supervisors, the DDC returns a pair (μ_L, u) consisting of the prediction and a corresponding uncertainty value. The uncertainty is computed using the cumulative distribution function F of the situation-dependent friction distribution where $u = P(\mu > \mu_L) = 1 - F(\mu_L)$. We considered a safety margin $\Delta\mu$ with $\mu_L = \mu_{predicted} + \Delta\mu$ which is determined by a grid search optimization on the safety distance. Thereby, we chose the $\Delta\mu$ value that minimizes the expected safety distance over all situations. For the safety margin selector patterns, the DDC returns the inverse of the complete uncertainty function $(1 - F)^{-1}$.

For the *Safety Distance Parameters* that we considered as constants, we assumed a maximum acceleration of the following vehicle of $acc_f = 2\frac{m}{s^2}$ and the gravity acceleration of $g = 9.81 \frac{m}{s^2}$. To simulate both a highly efficient and a human-like reaction time, we ran our simulation with either $\rho = 0.1$ s for use case A or $\rho = 0.8$ s for use case B.

Implementation – We used the programming language Python3 [17] and Jupyter Notebooks [18] in a web-based development environment supported by interactive widgets using the ipywidgets library. Using these widgets, interactive plots were created in combination with the matplotlib [19] library for rapid prototyping. The implemented probability distributions are specified using NumPy [20] and SciPy [21], two libraries for linear algebra, statistics, and scientific computing in Python.

6   Study Results and Discussion

In this section, we will present and discuss the results of our simulation study based on the study design and implementation presented in the previous section.

RQ2 – Comparison of patterns with static approaches – To estimate the expected utility gain from dynamic handling of uncertainty and to compare the patterns for two anticipated use cases A and B, the expected utility, measured as the expected reduction in the required safety distance $\hat{d}_{safe}$, was determined using the assumed distributions over the situational and behavioral distributions as introduced above. The observed expected friction $E(\hat{\mu}_L)$ and distances $E(\hat{d}_{safe})$ are summarized in Table 1.

Table 1. Comparison between different patterns for uncertainty handling of estimated friction values. The columns contain safety distance calculations for use case A - platooning with a low latency distance controller and use case B - platooning with human reaction time. Distances are compared between scenarios that use (a) the worst-case assumption, (b) static design time uncertainty estimates and (c) the four proposed patterns for dynamic uncertainty handling at runtime. Each cell contains the expected minimum required safety distance and the corresponding expected minimum safety friction that is assumed for the leading vehicle (lower is better).

	Expected safety distance (expected safety friction)			
	Use Case A – Platooning reaction time $\rho = 100$ ms		Use Case B – Default reaction time $\rho = 800$ ms	
(a) Worst-case μ_{max}	14.670 m (1.100)		33.350 m (1.100)	
(b) DDC with static uncertainty estimate	13.727 m (1.060)		32.407 m (1.060)	
(c) DDC with dynamic uncertainty estimates	Single value (μ_L, u)	Distribution $u(\mu_L)$	Single value (μ_L, u)	Distribution $u(\mu_L)$
Constant threshold $u_{acceptable}$	12.649 m (1.011)	10.638 m (0.922)	31.329 m (1.011)	29.318 m (0.922)
Input-dependent $u_{acceptable}(y)$	12.305 m (1.000)	10.364 m (0.913)	30.985 m (1.000)	29.044 m (0.913)

Interpretation: As expected, the worst-case baseline performed worse than all other patterns in terms of utility in both use cases. Considering uncertainty at design time with a situation-independent uncertainty estimate provides some benefits compared to this baseline but is outperformed by any of the dynamic situation-aware uncertainty patterns. For the dynamic patterns, the use of an input-dependent acceptable uncertainty threshold $u_{acceptable}$ led to utility improvements as well as to propagating uncertainty as a distribution $u(\mu_L)$ instead of a single value.

The magnitude of improvement differs depending on the use case. For use case A, which focuses on platooning with a highly efficient solution with short reaction times, the best solution reduced the average requirement on d_{safe} by ~29%. For use case B, which focuses on default driver assistance with a more relaxed requirement on the reaction time, the reduction was only ~13%, which could increase the capacity on the road under optimal conditions by approximately the same amount.

RQ3 – Sensitivity analysis of the results – To understand the impact on key parameters of the perceived simulation outcomes, we conducted a sensitivity analysis. Sensitivity analysis hereby refers to an analysis that is applied to determine how an output variable is affected by changes in one or more input variables. We investigated the effects of choosing different thresholds for the accepted uncertainty $u_{acceptable}$ and varied the dispersion σ of the predicted friction values μ_L provided by the DDC. This corresponds to using a DDM in the DDC that is either more or less accurate in its predictions. Figure 4 provides the results of the sensitivity analysis with respect to the acceptable uncertainty $u_{acceptable}$ considering situations that differ regarding the friction μ_L.

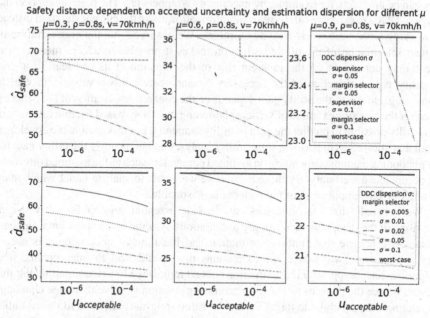

Fig. 4. Sensitivity of the safety distance to the accepted uncertainty threshold for multiple levels of dispersion σ. In the first row the proposed margin selector and uncertainty supervisor patterns are compared. In the second row, the safety distance is computed only using the margin selector.

Interpretation: The results in the first row of Fig. 4 illustrate that margin selectors are more flexible compared to supervisors in dealing with different thresholds on the accepted uncertainty. In the case of $\mu = 0.9$ and $\sigma = 0.1$, the patterns do not yield any benefit over the worst-case assumption. The results in the second row of Fig. 4 indicate that the safety distance requirement is less sensitive to DDCs that have a low accuracy, i.e., a high dispersion σ. For stricter, i.e., lower, acceptable uncertainty thresholds, such DDCs do not outperform the worst-case baseline, yet they are more sensitive to changes in the threshold on the accepted uncertainty. On the other hand, for very accurate DDCs, the safety distance requirement is significantly reduced and the reduction is hardly affected by the acceptable uncertainty threshold.

In conclusion, the use of an input-dependent acceptable uncertainty threshold is most beneficial for DDCs with higher dispersion. On the other hand, DDC-based predictions can become useless in some situations, e.g., if there are strict thresholds for the acceptable uncertainty and at the same time their predictions have high dispersion.

7 Summary and Conclusion

We proposed novel safety patterns for handling runtime estimations of uncertainty, as they can be provided, for example, by uncertainty wrappers [1]. The patterns support the usage of DDCs to estimate safety-relevant information about the current situation instead of working with static worst-case assumptions. We observed that the consideration of context information of the driving situation makes it possible to accept more or less uncertainty depending on the inherent risk of the situation. This can lead to a gain in utility, e.g., a reduction of the necessary distance between two vehicles in vehicle platooning. However, the utility gain depends on the concrete application of the patterns. Even for the concrete example of vehicle platooning and DDC-based friction estimation, it is hardly possible to predict the gain in utility manually. For this reason, we developed a tool that allowed us to perform some utility analyses and to quantify the utility gain for the platooning example depending on assumed parameters such as the assumed threshold for acceptable uncertainty. By these means, we were able to analyze under which main assumptions the application of the patterns is reasonable.

We conclude that such analyses can provide essential support for early design decisions in the design of increasingly autonomous systems in complex environments because we believe that runtime estimation and handling of uncertainties is necessary to overcome worst-case approximations that would lead to unacceptable utility/performance, especially if the situation context indicates a low risk situation. For this reason, we see the patterns as part of a promising solution to solve this huge challenge by relating the probabilistic target values for safety-relevant functions to uncertainties of DDCs and the confidence that uncertainties are not underestimated.

An open issue in this regard is the consideration of stochastic dependencies between uncertainties estimated in different time steps. Further open issues concern the stochastic dependencies between uncertainties of different DDCs.

References

1. Kläs, M., Sembach, L.: Uncertainty wrappers for data-driven models – increase the transparency of AI/ML-based models through enrichment with dependable situation-aware uncertainty estimates. In: 2nd International Workshop on Artificial Intelligence Safety Engineering (WAISE 2019). Turku, Finland (2019)
2. Kläs, M., Jöckel, L.: A framework for building uncertainty wrappers for AI/ML-based data-driven components. In: 3rd International Workshop on Artificial Intelligence Safety Engineering (WAISE) (2020)
3. Jöckel, L., Kläs, M.: Could we relieve AI/ML models of the responsibility of providing dependable uncertainty estimates? A study on outside-model uncertainty estimates. In: 40th Int. Conference on Computer Safety, Reliability and Security, SafeComp 2021. York, United Kingdom (2021)
4. Gerber, P., Jöckel, L., Kläs, M.: A study on mitigating hard boundaries of decision-tree-based uncertainty estimates for AI models. In: Safe AI @ AAAI2022, Virtual (2022)
5. Kläs, M., Adler, R., Sorokos, I., Jöckel, L., Reich, J.: Handling uncertainties of data-driven models in compliance with safety constraints for autonomous behaviour. In: European Dependable Computing Conference (EDDC) (2021)

6. Arnez, F., Espinoza, H., Radermacher, A., Terrier, F.: A comparison of uncertainty estimation approaches in deep learning components for autonomous vehicle applications. In: Workshop in Artificial Intelligence Safety (AISafety) (2020)
7. Kaiser, B., et al.: Advances in component fault trees. In: ESREL (2018)
8. Kabir, S., et al.: A runtime safety analysis concept for open adaptive systems. In: 6th International Symposium on Model-Based Safety and Assessment. Thessaloniki, Greece (2019)
9. Salay, R., Czarnecki, K., Elli, M., Alvarez, I., Sedwards, S., Weast, J.: PURSS: towards perceptual uncertainty aware responsibility sensitive safety with ML. In: SafeAI @ AAAI2020. New York (2020)
10. Henne, M., Schwaiger, A., Roscher, K., Weiß, G.: Benchmarking uncertainty estimation methods for deep learning with safety-related metrics. In: Proceedings of the Workshop on Artificial Intelligence Safety, co-located with 34th AAAI Conference on Artificial Intelligence, SafeAI@AAAI 2020. New York, USA (2020)
11. Reich, J., Trapp, M.: SINADRA: towards a framework for assurable situation-aware dynamic risk assessment of autonomous vehicles. In: 16th European Dependable Computing Conference (EDCC). Munich, Germany (2020)
12. Adee, A., Gansch, R., Liggesmeyer, P.: Systematic modeling approach for environmental perception limitations in automated driving. In: 17th European Dependable Computing Conference (EDCC). Munich, Germany (2021)
13. Shalev-Shwartz, S., Shammah, S., Shashua, A.: On a formal model of safe and scalable self-driving cars. arXiv preprint (2017)
14. Hartmann, B., Eckert, A.: Road condition observer as a new part of active driving safety. ATZelektronik worldwide 12(5), 34–37 (2017)
15. Predictive road condition services, Robert Bosch GmbH, 2022. https://www.bosch-mobility-solutions.com/en/solutions/automated-driving/predictive-road-condition-services/. Accessed 22 02 2022
16. Wassertheurer, B.: Reifenmodellierung für die Fahrdynamiksimulation auf Schnee, Eis und nasser Fahrbahn, Karlsruhe. KIT Scientific Publishing, Germany (2020)
17. Van Rossum, G., Drake, F.: Python 3 Reference Manual. CreateSpace, Scotts Valley, CA (2009)
18. Kluyver, T., et al.: Jupyter Notebooks-a publishing format for reproducible computational workflows. In: 20th International Conference on Electronic Publishing. Göttingen, Germany (2016)
19. Hunter, J.D.: Matplotlib: a 2D graphics environment. Comput. Sci. Eng. 9(03), 90–95 (2007)
20. Harris, C.R., et al.: Array programming with NumPy. Nature 585(7825), 357–362 (2020)
21. Virtanen, P., et al.: SciPy 1.0: fundamental algorithms for scientific computing in Python. Nat. Meth. 17(3), 261–272 (2020)

Hardware Faults that Matter: Understanding and Estimating the Safety Impact of Hardware Faults on Object Detection DNNs

Syed Qutub[1](✉) ⓘ, Florian Geissler[1] ⓘ, Yang Peng[1] ⓘ, Ralf Gräfe[1],
Michael Paulitsch[1] ⓘ, Gereon Hinz[2], and Alois Knoll[2]

[1] Dependability Research Lab, Intel Labs, Munich, Germany
`syed.qutub@intel.com`
[2] Technical University of Munich, Munich, Germany

Abstract. Object detection neural network models need to perform reliably in highly dynamic and safety-critical environments like automated driving or robotics. Therefore, it is paramount to verify the robustness of the detection under unexpected hardware faults like soft errors that can impact a system's perception module. Standard metrics based on average precision produce model vulnerability estimates at the object level rather than at an image level. As we show in this paper, this does not provide an intuitive or representative indicator of the safety-related impact of silent data corruption caused by bit flips in the underlying memory but can lead to an over- or underestimation of typical fault-induced hazards. With an eye towards safety-related real-time applications, we propose a new metric **IVMOD** (Image-wise Vulnerability Metric for Object Detection) to quantify vulnerability based on an incorrect image-wise object detection due to false positive (FPs) or false negative (FNs) objects, combined with a severity analysis. The evaluation of several representative object detection models shows that even a single bit flip can lead to a severe silent data corruption event with potentially critical safety implications, with e.g., up to $\gg100$ FPs generated, or up to $\sim90\%$ of true positives (TPs) lost in an image. Furthermore, with a single stuck-at-1 fault, an entire sequence of images can be affected, causing temporally persistent ghost detections that can be mistaken for actual objects (covering up to $\sim83\%$ of the image). Furthermore, actual objects in the scene are continuously missed (up to $\sim64\%$ of TPs are lost). Our work establishes a detailed understanding of the safety-related vulnerability of such critical workloads against hardware faults.

1 Introduction

Research communities seek to make the deployment of general artificial intelligence (AI) and deep neural networks (DNNs) used in everyday life as dependable as possible. Significant emphasis is placed on handling corrupted input (e.g. due

© The Author(s), under exclusive license to Springer Nature Switzerland AG 2022
M. Trapp et al. (Eds.): SAFECOMP 2022, LNCS 13414, pp. 298–318, 2022.
https://doi.org/10.1007/978-3-031-14835-4_20

to visual artifacts or to attacks) provided to the model. However, less effort has been dedicated to studying corruptions of the internal state of the model itself, most importantly caused by faults in the underlying hardware. Such faults can occur naturally, such as memory corruption induced by external (e.g., cosmic neutron) radiation or electric leaking in the circuitry itself, typically manifested as bit flips or stuck-at-0/1s in the memory elements [1,16], which may alter the DNN model parameters (*weight faults*) or the intermediate states (*neuron faults*). Platform faults can also impact the input while it is held in memory, yet this work focuses on the computational part of the DNN as our goal is to estimate the vulnerability of the model. The impact of these faults is often unpredictable in systems with large complexity. Alterations can be of transient or permanent nature: Transient faults have a short life span of the order of a few clock cycles and are therefore harder to detect by the system. On the contrary, permanent faults may silently corrupt the system output for a longer period. Memory protection techniques like error correcting code (ECC) can mitigate the risk of hardware faults [20]; however, they are typically applied only to selected elements to avoid significant cost overheads. Given the rise in technology scaling with smaller node sizes and larger memory areas, future platforms are expected to become even more vulnerable to hardware faults [20].

Object detection DNNs are among the most common examples of highly safety-critical DNN applications as they are in autonomous vehicles or in medical image analysis. Typically, autonomous systems process events based on perception techniques. Hence, it is critically important that any potential hazards does not impact the system-level evaluation of events. While the chances for a hardware fault to occur (for example, the chance of a neutron radiation event hitting a memory element) can be estimated statistically, it remains unclear how to quantify the safety-related impact of the failure of a DNN applied for the purpose of object detection. In contrast to simpler classification problems, the model output here typically consists of a multitude of bounding boxes and classes per image, of which a subset can be altered in the presence of a fault while others remain intact, see Fig. 1. We find that commonly used average precision (AP) [19] metrics inappropriately rely on the count of false objects irrespective of their interrelations (grouping in the same image or distributed across multiple frames). In real-time applications of DNNs, it further matters if the corrupted output is volatile or temporally stable across multiple input frames. The user is typically behind a tracking module that can regularize instantaneous alterations. We, therefore, see the need to establish a safety-related assessment of the vulnerability of object detection workloads under soft errors. Depending on the specifications from safety assessment, we adopt a generalized notion of a safety hazard as a perturbation that causes a potentially unsafe decision by the end-user of the object detection module.

Therefore, we introduce two variants of the metric IVMOD (Image-wise Vulnerability Metric for Object Detection), namely $IVMOD_{SDC}$ in case of an image-wise silent data corruption (SDC), and $IVMOD_{DUE}$ in case of detectable uncorrectable errors (DUE)s.

(a) Inference from Yolov3 model and Kitti dataset

(b) Inference from Faster-RCNN model and Kitti dataset

Fig. 1. Examples of the impact of a single neuron bit flip (at bit position b and layer index l, see image insets). TPs are marked by green, FPs by red and FNs by blue rectangles, comparing the fault-free (top) and the faulty (bottom) predictions. In example (a) multiple FPs are generated right in front of the ego vehicle, while in (b) all previous detections are erased due to the fault. (Color figure online)

In this paper, we discuss the characteristics of the AP-based metrics in detail when used to quantify a model's vulnerability. For example, AP50 is found to be hypersensitive to rare single corruption events compared to an evaluation at the image level. Our work supports maintaining the relationship of the system-level hazard evaluation to the impact of any hardware faults. We find that a hardware fault - if it hits the crucial bits of either neuron or weight - can silently lead to excessive amounts of additional false positives (FPs) and increase the rate of false negatives (FNs) misses. We further study the impact of permanent faults in a real-time situation by considering continuous video sequences and observing a significant frequency that the error manifestation persists for a critical time interval.

In summary, this paper makes the following contributions:

- We demonstrate that AP-based metrics lead to misleading vulnerability estimates for object detection DNN models (Sect. 4.1).
- We propose an SCD-based/DUE-based metric IVMOD to quantify the vulnerability of object detection DNN models under hardware faults (Sect. 4.2).
- We evaluate the vulnerability of various representative object detection DNN models using the proposed IVMOD, illustrating the probability of a single bit flip resulting in a potentially safety-critical event (Sect. 5.1).
- For each such event, we propose various quantitative metrics to estimate the impact severity for typical safety-critical applications (Sect. 5.2).
- We extend our image-based evaluation to a video-based safety-critical system and measure the vulnerability of temporal persistency ($A_{FP_{blob}}$ and $A_{FN_{blob}}$) due to a permanent fault, by tracking the FPs and FNs across multiple video frames (Sect. 6).

2   Related Work

The effort to estimate the vulnerability or resilience of the DNNs against hardware faults affecting the model has been explored recently to study the safety criticality of a model when used in real-time operation.

To this extent, faults are injected in DNNs during inference either at the application layer on weights/neurons [6,16], or by neutron beam experiments ([4,9], black-box techniques). Authors of Ref. [2,16] considered transient faults, which are multiple event upsets occurring in data or buffers of DNN accelerators. Many prior works claimed DNNs to have inherent tolerance towards faults. Li et al. [2] studied the vulnerability of DNNs by injecting faults in data paths and buffers with different data type levels and quantified it in the form of SDC probabilities and FIT (failure in time) rates. It is seen that errors in buffers propagate to multiple locations compared to errors in data-path. These works estimated the resiliency of the model by injecting multiple fault injections during the feedforward inference. This analysis is limited to image classification models like AlexNet [14], VGG [24], and ResNets [7]. Our analysis does not characterize the faults in buffer and faults in the data-path. We assume the faults will propagate to the application layer, which may impact either the weights or the neurons. Hence we analyze them independently, assuming equal probabilities. The Ares framework [21] demonstrated that activations (neurons) in image classification networks are $50\times$ more resilient than weights. These works focus mainly on fault models involving multiple bit flips captured by bit error rate (BER). There is limited research done on understanding the vulnerability of object detection DNNs. The work in Ref. [4] quantified the architectural vulnerability factor (AVF) of Yolov3 using metrics like SDC AVF, DUE AVF, and FIT rates. This work studies fault propagation by injecting a random value in the selected register file and not flipping a bit. The authors argue that not all SDCs are critical, given that change in objects' confidence scores after injecting faults is tolerable. The definition of SDC used in this work is not straightforward. They use the precision and recall values computed at the object level by combining all the images, obscuring the actual vulnerability. The vulnerability of object detection DNNs is studied by injecting faults using neutron beam [18]. The authors analyzed both transient and permanent faults but not on continuous video sequences. Also, the dataset considered in these experiments was primarily limited to only one object per image. Also, they injected faults into the input image. We limit our fault injections to neurons and weights and only to convolution layers of the DNNs as the fully connected layers did not change much of the observed data. We believe fault-injected images do not fall into the category of the model vulnerability. They rather find their place in adversarial input space within various adverse fault/noise models. The results obtained from many of these works are not easy to compare as the failure and SDC definitions differ and do not follow standard baseline. To our best knowledge, our paper is the first to demonstrate vulnerabilities of the object detection models in detail using the proposed (**IVMOD**) metrics to measure the severities at the image level. Also, we introduce a new metrics $A_{\mathrm{FP_{blob}}}$ and $A_{\mathrm{FN_{blob}}}$ quantifying the area occupancy of FP/FN blobs, which is essential to establish the safety criticality of the object detection models concerning specific real-time applications.

3   Preliminaries

3.1   Hardware Faults Vocabulary

Our fault injection technique includes transient and permanent faults. Transient faults refer to random bit flips ($0{\to}1$ or $1{\to}0$) of a randomly chosen bit, which occur during a single image inference and are removed afterward. Permanent faults are modeled as stuck-at-0 and stuck-at-1 errors, meaning that a bit remains consistently in state '0' or '1' without reacting on intended updates. Those faults are assumed to persist across many image inferences. We inject faults either into intermediate computational states of the network (neurons) or into the parameters (weights) of the DNN model, focusing only on convolutional layers, which constitutes a significant part of all operations in the studied DNNs. Both types of faults represent bit flip in the respective memory elements, holding either temporary states such as intermediate network layer outputs or learned and statically stored network parameters. A fault can potentially induce critical alterations of the model predictions, measured by $IVMOD_{SDC}$ or $IVMOD_{DUE}$ as shown in Eq. 1.

3.2 Experimental Setup: Models, Datasets and System

We use standard object detection models - Yolov3 [22], RetinaNet [17], Faster-RCNN (F-RCNN [23]) - together with the test datasets CoCo2017 [19], Kitti [5] and Lyft [12]. We retrained Yolov3 on the Kitti and Lyft dataset, and the Faster-RCNN model on Kitti for comparative experiments. We used open-source trained weights for the rest of the models and datasets. The base performances of these models in terms of AP50 and mAP can be found in Fig. 3. The parameter configurations used for these models (NMS threshold, confidence score, etc.) are taken from the original publications. Since fault injection is compute-intensive, we select a subset of 1000 images for each dataset to perform the transient fault analysis and use a single Lyft sequence of 126 images for the permanent fault analysis. All experiments adopt a single-precision floating-point format (FP32) according to the IEEE754 standard [10]. Our conclusions also apply to other floating-point formats with the same number of exponent bits, such as BF16 [11], since no relevant effect was observed from fault injections in mantissa bits.

4 Methodology of Vulnerability Estimation

4.1 Issues with Average Precision

In object detection, evaluation and benchmarking methods are most commonly selected from the family of average precision (AP)-based metrics (in combination with specific IoU thresholds such as AP50 or mAP). Libraries such as CoCo API [19] perform the following relevant steps to obtain AP values from a set of object predictions: i) ground truth and the predicted objects are collected in groups of the same class label, ii) within a group, the predicted objects are sorted w.r.t their confidence scores, iii) the sorted predictions are consecutively assigned to the ground truth objects within the same class group, using an appropriate IoU threshold, iv) precision and recall (PR) curves are evaluated sequentially through the confidence-ranked TP, FP, and FN objects, v) the class-wise AP is calculated as the area under the interpolated PR curve of a class, and vi) the overall AP is determined as the average of the class-wise AP values.

It has been pointed out that such AP metrics can lead to non-intuitive results in the detection performance of a model on a specific data set [22]. In the following, we illustrate that an AP-based evaluation can be misleading when estimating the vulnerability of a model against corruption events such as soft errors in a safety-critical real-time context concerning the probability and severity of corruption. Corruption events lead to additional FP and FN objects merged into or eliminated from the healthy list of detected objects. We identified the following issues when trying to quantify model vulnerability based on AP metrics:

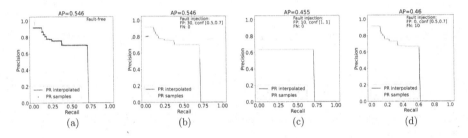

Fig. 2. Simulation of the effect of fault injection on the AP metric. Here, an artificial data set of 100 objects was generated, where each object was classified as TP with a chance of 0.7 or as a FN otherwise. In addition, FPs were created with a rate of 0.3 per true detection. Both TPs and FPs are assigned random confidence values between 0.7 and 1. To this setup (a), additional FPs simulating the effect of fault injection were augmented or existing TPs were randomly eliminated to model fault-induced FNs ((b)–(d)). The diagrams show the PR curves and the effect of fault injection on them. Number and confidence range of the faulty objects are given in the insets.

- **Object-level evaluation:** The AP is calculated on an object level, i.e., the amount of TP, FP, FN objects accumulated across all images is used for evaluation. This does not consider how corrupted boxes are distributed across images, i.e., one image with a large number of fault-induced FP detections can have the same effect as many corrupted images with few FP detections each. From a real-time safety perspective, however, the amount of corrupted image frames is typically relevant, as this may determine, for example, the robustness of a video stream used for environment perception.
- **Dependency of PR on confidence:** Due to the sequential and integration-based characteristic of the average precision, the fault-induced FP object's impact depends highly on those sample's confidence. This does not reflect the potential safety relevance a low-confidence FP object may have, see more below.
- **Dependency of box assignment on confidence:** The strict confidence ranking can, in some cases, lead to a non-optimal global assignment of bounding boxes. For example, a better matching box might have slightly lower confidence than a global optimization would demand.
- **Class-wise average:** Common and rare classes have the same weight in the overall AP metric. However, their detection performance and vulnerability can be quite different as they typically relate to the samples the model encountered during training.

In particular, the second point above is non-intuitive; we therefore illustrate this in more detail in Fig. 2 with the help of a generic example from a randomly generated data set of 100 objects. Additional FPs with low confidence compared to the reference set of objects have a negligible impact on the metric as they get appended to the tail of the PR curve, even when numerous and potentially safety-critical. On the contrary, few high-confidence FP objects can lead to significant drops in the AP as those samples get sorted in at the head of the PR curve to lower it. Fault-induced FNs reduce the area under the PR curve by pushing the samples towards smaller recalls.

4.2 Proposed Metrics: IVMOD

We introduce IVMOD metrics to measure the image-wise vulnerability of the object detection DNNs. Our evaluation strategy described in the following seeks to counter the issues with AP-based metrics described in the last section in order to reflect vulnerability estimation better addressing safety targets. In particular, our approach is characterized by:

- **Image-level evaluation:** We evaluate vulnerability on an image level instead of an object level. This approach reflects that those faults jeopardize safety applications that silently alter the free and occupied space by inducing false detections in an image, particularly sequences thereof, even if such an alteration involves only few false objects per frame. We register image-wise SDC and DUE events, see Sect. 4.2, to determine the probability of a relevant fault impact. The severity of the latter is evaluated separately in terms of the amount of induced FPs and FNs. Due to their image-based character, $IVMOD_{SDC}$ and $IVMOD_{DUE}$ metrics are naturally independent of the object confidences.
- **Confidence-independent box assignment:** False-positive objects can be critical whether they have high or low confidence, which is masked in the AP metric. We apply a different assignment scheme for FPs and FNs that omits confidence ranking and hence makes the model vulnerability metric independent of the confidence of FPs, see Sect. 4.2. The assignment strategy can also be varied to relax class correspondence requirements, which are often overemphasized from a safety perspective. The system can perform at degraded level if its sure of object location and not much about the class.
- **Class-independent average:** We evaluate the overall sample mean instead of the mean of individual class categories to reflect typical imbalances in the data set concerning object classes.

Assignment Policy. In contrast to the sequential and class-wise matching described in Sect. 4.1, we calculate the cost matrix from a set of predictions and ground truth objects for a single image. The cost for matching objects is the IoU between the bounding boxes. If the IoU is below the specified threshold $IoU_{eval} = 0.5$, or if the classes of the two objects are not the same, we assign a maximum cost. To analyze the relevance of exact class predictions for an application, we can harden or soften the class matching from a one-to-one correspondence to compatible class clusters or neglect class matching altogether. A Hungarian association algorithm [15] is then deployed to obtain the global optimal cost assignment. As usual, the number of accepted matches per image represents the true positive (TP) cases. False detections are registered in the following cases: i) a FP and a simultaneous FN detection occurs if the IoU with

the assigned ground truth object is below the threshold, independent of the predicted class, or if the IoU is sufficiently large, but the classes are not compatible,
ii) a single FP occurs if there is a predicted object that cannot be assigned to
any ground truth object with acceptable costs, iii) a single FN occurs if there
is a non-assigned ground truth object. Figure 1 shows an illustrative example
of assigned TP, FP, FN boxes. In our setup, we clip predicted bounding boxes
reaching out of the image dimensions – e.g., due to faults – to the actual image
boundaries.

IVMOD (IVMOD$_{SDC}$ and IVMOD$_{DUE}$). We define the IVMOD$_{SDC}$ rate
as the ratio of events where a fault during inference causes a silent corruption
of an image and the total number of image inferences. IVMOD$_{SDC}$ is an SDC
defined as a change in either of the TP, FP, or FN count of the respective image,
compared to the original fault-free prediction, given that no irregular *NaN* (not
a number) or *Inf* (infinite) values occur during the inference as shown in Eq. 1.
Since TPs and FNs are complementary to each other, we can eliminate either
TP or FN in IVMOD$_{SDC}$ in Eq. 1. On the other hand, the IVMOD$_{DUE}$ rate
is the ratio of events where irregular *NaN* or *Inf* values are generated during
inference and detected inside the layers or in the predicted output due to the
injected fault in the respective image during inference and are computed using
the Eq. 1. As DUE events are naturally detectable, they typically are less critical
than SDC events. Explicitly,

$$\text{IVMOD}_{\text{SDC}} = \frac{1}{N} \sum_{i=1}^{N} \Big\{ \big[(FP_{\text{orig}})_i \neq (FP_{\text{corr}})_i \vee (FN_{\text{orig}})_i \neq (FN_{\text{corr}})_i \big] \wedge \neg \text{Inf}_i \wedge \neg \text{NaN} \Big\},$$

$$\text{IVMOD}_{\text{DUE}} = \frac{1}{N} \sum_{i=1}^{N} [\text{Inf}_i \vee \text{NaN}_i].$$

$$(1)$$

5 Transient Faults

Our evaluation concept is guided by the assumption that in safety-critical applications, both the miss of any existing object as well as the creation of any false
positive object can be potentially hazardous. Therefore, we consider the probability that such an SDC event occurs and our primary metrics IVMOD$_{SDC}$
and IVMOD$_{DUE}$ (Eq. 1) captures the vulnerability of a model. For transient
faults, this evaluation is performed in Sect. 5.1. Accordingly, we independently
inject 50,000 random single-bit flips in neurons and weights at each inference of
the chosen test datasets. Subsequently, Sect. 5.2 discusses the severity of each
of those SDC events in terms of the average impact of additional FP and FN
objects, their size, and confidence. If a specific use case is given, the factors of
probability and severity can be used to derive the risk of an error [13].

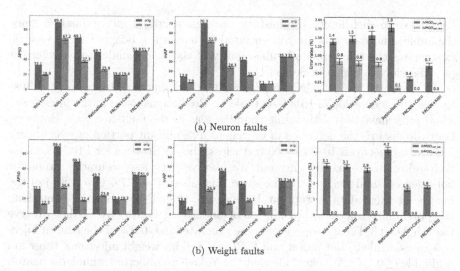

(a) Neuron faults

(b) Weight faults

Fig. 3. Key metrics to interpret the vulnerability of object detection DNNs in the presence of transient hardware faults: (left) AP50, (center) mAP, (right) error rate, distinguishing IVMOD$_{SDC}$ and IVMOD$_{DUE}$. We study both neuron faults (a) and weight faults (b).

5.1 Corruption Probability

In Fig. 3, we present the fault injection campaigns of all studied networks, comparing the typical benchmark metrics AP-50 and mAP to the IVMOD$_{SDC}$ and IVMOD$_{DUE}$ rate as defined in Sect. 4.2. Both Yolov3 and RetinaNet show a significant change in the AP-50 and mAP metrics under the injected neuron and weight faults: The accuracy can drop as much as from 89.4% to 34.4% (AP-50) due to a single weight fault in the scenario of Yolov3 and Kitti. On the other hand, F-RCNN does not showcase much sensitivity to the injected faults ($\lesssim$0.8% change in AP-50). At the same time, the IVMOD$_{SDC}$ rates vary between 0.4% and 1.8% (neu-

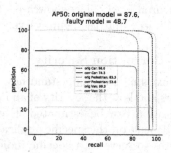

Fig. 4. Example of the AP50 PR curves of few classes from Yolov3 and Kitti in the fault free and faulty cases.

ron faults), and from 1.5% to 4.2% (weight faults). This discrepancy illustrates the need for a more realistic vulnerability estimate. As shown below, in Table 1, fault injections in Yolov3 and RetinaNet tend to produce many FPs with statistically increased confidence. This leads to a drastic shift of the PR curves, as shown in the example in Fig. 4, where only 3.2% out of 1000 samples have corrupted prediction (demonstrated the similar effect in Fig. 2(c)). Rare classes are susceptible to such faults, diminishing the class-averaged metric further. Since the induced false objects are concentrated on only a few images, the AP metric exaggerates the safety-related vulnerability of the model under software errors (see also the discussion in Sect. 4.1).

In contrast, the F-RCNN model architecture appears to be very robust against the generation of FPs (see Table 1). Predictions made in the presence of a soft error have nearly the same confidence as in the fault-free case. However, faults do disturb the detection of objects as a significant portion of FNs appear (on average between 10–33%). Nevertheless, the AP metrics for FRCNN under fault injection are hardly affected: We observe very few accuracies drops for both neurons and weights. At the same time about 0.4–0.7% (1.5–1.8%) of the images see silent data corruption. In this case, the AP-based metric is masking the potentially safety-critical impact of underlying faults. We further observe that for Yolov3, $IVMOD_{DUE}$ events are generated in $\sim$0.9% of the neuron injection cases, while in RetinaNet and F-RCNN and for weight injections, those are negligible ($\lesssim$0.1%). We conclude that the Yolov3 architecture stimulates neuron values that have a higher chance if being flipped to a configuration encoded as *NaN* or *Inf* (in FP32, all exponential bits have to be in state '1'), compared to RetinaNet and F-RCNN. The weight values of all networks, on the other hand, are closely centered around zero, which makes it very unlikely to reach a *NaN* or *Inf* bit configuration [6] (typically MSB and at least another exponential bit are in state '0' at the same time). We observe that the faults injected in weights at any bit of FP32 cause higher $IVMOD_{SDC}$ rates than the faults injected at the neuron level. They showcase $\sim$2× more adverse effects on predictions than faults injected at the neuron level.

5.2   Corruption Severity

We next aimed to understand how faults leading to $IVMOD_{SDC}$ events corrupt images and how the severity of an $IVMOD_{SDC}$ event on a potential safety-critical application can be estimated. Even though the relevance of a safety feature may depend on the specific application, we identified the following fundamental features to serve as a specific indicative measure of an SDC fault severity, see Table 1:

- The average number of FP objects induced by a given $IVMOD_{SDC}$ fault and the proportion of boxes lost due to a fault, referred to as ΔFP and ΔFN_n, respectively as described in Eq. 2 (subscript 'n' represents normalization as the upper limit of FNs is known, in contrast to FPs).
- The average size of objects in the presence and absence of SDC (avg(size)) since a significant change of the object size can be safety-critical,
- The average area of the image that is erroneously occupied due to $IVMOD_{SDC}$ induced FP objects ($A_{FP_{blob}}$) and the average portion of the vacant area created by not detecting the objects due to $IVMOD_{SDC}$ faults ($A_{FN_{blob}}$).
- The average confidence of objects in the presence and absence of $IVMOD_{SDC}$, avg(conf).

We motivate this choice more in the following subsections.

Table 1. Severity features averaged over all IVMOD$_{SDC}$ events.

	Yolo+Coco	Yolo+Kitti	Yolo+Lyft	Retina+Coco	F-RCNN+Coco	F-RCNN+Kitti
Neurons:						
avg(ΔFP)	**333**	36	174	33	0	0
avg(ΔFN_n)(%)	42.2	41.3	**46.6**	16.1	25.3	33.3
avg(conf) (corr, orig)	0.99, 0.52	0.99, 0.51	0.99, 0.65	**0.79, 0.11**	0.73, 0.73	0.90, 0.89
avg(size)/$1e^3$px (corr, orig)	4.3, 11.2	**34.5, 2.3**	17.8, 7.3	5.6, 20.3	17.0, 18.6	6.3, 6.8
$A_{fp\text{-}occ}$(%)	36.8	**62.5**	59.8	0.7	1.7	0.0
$A_{fn\text{-}vac}$(%)	4.0	5.1	4.8	**53.1**	41.1	39.8
Weights:						
avg(ΔFP)	**198**	59	145	7	0	0
avg(ΔFN_n)(%)	23.3	21.7	21.3	4.0	9.6	**29.6**
avg(conf) (corr, orig)	1.00, 0.53	1.00, 0.52	1.00, 0.65	**0.62, 0.11**	0.72, 0.73	0.89, 0.88
avg(size)/$1e^3$px (corr, orig)	5.5, 12.1	21.4, 2.5	**30.8, 6.9**	7.9, 19.8	10.0, 15.0	4.9, 5.0
$A_{fp\text{-}occ}$(%)	40.1	**81.0**	79.1	1.5	0.3	0.0
$A_{fn\text{-}vac}$(%)	15.1	2.5	6.8	42.3	77.8	**85.8**

Fault-Induced Object Generation and Loss. Object detection is commonly used in scenarios where the number of objects, combined with their location and class, is input to safety-critical decision making. Examples include face detection or vehicle counting in traffic surveillance, automated driving, or medical object detection. Therefore, to assess IVMOD$_{SDC}$ severity, we quantify the impact of a fault injection by the differences (a loss in TPs equals the gain in FNs)

$$\Delta FP = (FP_{corr} - FP_{orig}),$$
$$\Delta FN_n = (TP_{orig} - TP_{corr})/TP_{orig}, \tag{2}$$

In Table 1, we observe that all Yolov3 and RetinaNet scenarios exhibit large numbers of fault-induced FPs ($\gg$100 in Yolov3 and Coco experiments). For neuron faults, the generation of FPs is, on average, more pronounced. Furthermore, the normalized FN rates show that already a single fault can cause a significant loss of accurate positive detections. Average FN rates are higher for neuron faults than weight faults and reach averages up to 47% (Yolov3 and Lyft). F-RCNN models are robust against the generation of FP objects but not immune against fault-induced misses (e.g. Fig. 1b). The number of generated FPs and FNs varies in a broad sample range, up to the maximum limit of allowed detections (here 1000), due to the inhomogeneous impact of flips in different bit positions (see Sect. 5.3). In some situations, additional objects created by faults will match actual ground truth objects, leading to a negative FP or FN difference. This effect originates from the imperfect performance of the original fault-free model and is tolerated here due to the minor impact. By relaxing the class matching constraints from one-to-one correspondence to no class matching, we can further segment the type of FPs that the IVMOD$_{SDC}$ events cause. It appears that situations where an FP is due to a change in the class label only or due to a shift of the bounding box only (on average $\lesssim 3$ for Yolo models, 0 for others). In most cases, *both* the bounding box gets shifted, and the class labels is mixed up, or predicted objects cannot be matched with any ground truth object at all.

Object Size and Confidence. Box sizes and confidence values are other severity indicators since large erroneous objects take up a more significant portion of the image space, and high-confidence objects might be handled with priority in some use cases. Table 1 shows the change of the average box size and confidence of all model detections across the identified $IVMOD_{SDC}$ events. In most models, the typical box size is reduced in the presence of faults, which is partially due to the creation of boxes with zero width or height. However, there are also scenarios where faults tend to induce overly large objects (Yolov3 and Kitti, Lyft, see Table 1) that can even fill the entire picture. An object's average confidence score after fault injection significantly increases in the scenario of Yolov3 and RetinaNet, while there is hardly any impact on F-RCNN predictions. This explains why confidence-sensitive metrics based on AP react differently to fault injections in the respective architectures; see the discussion in Sect. 4.1.

Area Occupancy. safety-related decision-making.in a dynamic environment is most importantly based on the detected free and occupied space. For example, an automated vehicle will determine a driving path depending on the detected drivable space. A large number of false-positive objects, even when small in size, can, in combination, cover a significant portion of the image, which will leave only little free space. On the opposite, in some situations, they may overlay each other and occupy only a little space. To reflect a realistic severity of free space, we first cluster all FP and FN objects to *blobs* by projecting them to a binary space of occupancy and vacancy (see Fig. 6). As we are only interested in fault-induced false objects, our blobs for a given frame at time t are defined as follows:

$$FP_{blob} = \mathcal{I}(det_{corr} - det_{orig}),$$
$$FN_{blob} = \mathcal{I}(det_{orig} - det_{corr}). \tag{3}$$

$$A_{FP_{blob}} = |FP_{blob}|/A_{image},$$
$$A_{FN_{blob}} = |FN_{blob}|/|\mathcal{I}(det_{orig})|. \tag{4}$$

In Eq. 3, det denotes the set of all detected bounding boxes (TP and FP), and $\mathcal{I}(x)$ represents the pixel-wise projection to binary occupancy space, i.e., for any pixel u in a blob x it is $\mathcal{I}(u < 0) = 0$, $\mathcal{I}(u \geq 0) = 1$ (see Fig. 6). We define the occupancy coefficients in Eq. 4, where A_{image} is the size of the image in pixels and $|\ldots|$ denotes the sum of all nonzero pixels in a blob. In Table 1, we see Yolo+Kitti creates significantly less ΔFP than Yolo+CoCo, but the average $A_{FP_{blob}}$, in this case, is $\sim 2x$ greater than $A_{FP_{blob}}$ of Yolo+CoCo. This can even be observed using the feature $avg(size)/1e^3$ (average size of bounding boxes of all the detections combined - TPs+FPs). In the case of Yolo+Kitti, the $avg(size)/1e^3$ is $15x$

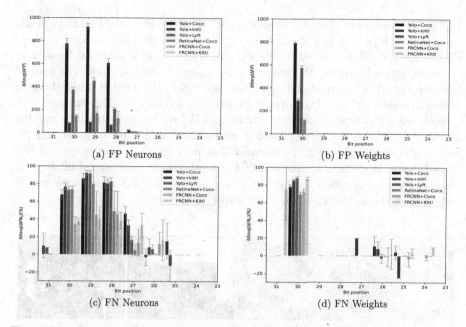

Fig. 5. Bit-wise analysis of the severity of IVMOD$_{SDC}$ events. Diagrams show the FP difference (a), (b) and FN rates (c), (d) for neurons and weights, respectively. Bit 31st is the sign bit, 30th bit being the most significant bit and 23rd bit is the lowest bit of exponent part.

and $\sim 8x$ larger than its original detections when a fault is injected in neurons and weights. This implies that ΔFP alone cannot determine the safety impact during an IVMOD$_{SDC}$ event. Similarly, F-RCNN creates no ΔFP, but large free space ΔFN_n by missing the TPs. F-RCNN+Kitti, when induced with weight faults, is more safety-critical as the $A_{FN_{blob}}$ is highest compared to other studied models. Furthermore, in case of neuron faults, the RetinaNet and F-RCNN have higher $A_{FN_{blob}}$.

5.3   Bit-Wise Analysis of False Object Count

The severity of an IVMOD$_{SDC}$ event typically depends on the magnitude of the altered values, where values with a considerable absolute value are more likely to propagate and disrupt the network predictions [6,8,16]. Therefore, the severity features are expected to form a non-uniform distribution depending on the flipped bit position. To gain a better intuition, we here choose to present a bit-wise analysis of the ΔFP and ΔFN_n samples during the IVMOD$_{SDC}$ events. To quantify the impact of bits, we define the bit-averaged false-positive difference, bitavg(ΔFP), which intuitively tells us how many FPs an SDC event with a particular bit position induces, on average. Similarly, for FNs, the normalized bit-averaged difference, bitavg(ΔFN_n), represents what portion of the originally detected objects disappears due to an SDC event with a specific bit position.

In Fig. 5, we observe that, for neuron faults, those additional FPs are typically caused by bitflips in either of the three highest exponential bits, as long as those do not lead to DUE instead. For weight faults, we find a situation similar to classifier networks where the specific value range of weights centered around zero is encoded in bit constellations where the MSB is in state '0' while the next higher exponential non-MSB bits are in state '1', see Ref. [6]. This explains why almost only MSB flips induce large values and IVMOD$_{SDC}$ (with a high number of FPs). Given the respective relevant neuron and weight bit flips, the ΔFN_n ratio is increased up to ~90% (meaning that portion of all true positive detections is lost), in particular, due to MSB and other high exponential bit flips, in some of the models (see Fig. 5(c),(d)). We observe that FN alterations can, to some extent, be induced also by lower exponential bits.

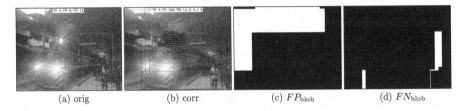

(a) orig   (b) corr   (c) FP_{blob} (d) FN_{blob}

Fig. 6. Illustration of the clustering of bounding boxes to binary occupancy blobs. In this example we find from (c) and (d) that $A_{FP_{\text{blob}}} = 33.3\%$, $A_{FN_{\text{blob}}} = 7.5\%$ (white pixels indicate space occupied by fault FPs).

6 Permanent Faults

Our analysis in this section aims to understand whether permanent stuck-at faults (see Sect. 3.1) leads to temporally consistent errors on an object level leading to continuous failure. The object detection model typically receives sequential images from a continuous video stream in real time applications. We assume a permanent hardware fault hitting the inference module which in turn causes persistent miss detections on consecutive images. In this case, they will appear either as ghost objects in the output (as FPs) or lead to a consecutive miss of an object (as FNs) - both situations can be highly safety-critical. A perception pipeline typically also includes a tracking module for detected objects, which can then be used to predict an object's trajectory and make an informed decision concerning the next maneuver of the vehicle. Therefore, we simulate a simple tracking of instantaneous fault-induced FPs and FNs clusters to determine whether they would be persistent in a realistic scenario. For the analysis in this section, we use Yolov3 and the Lyft data set. This is the only dataset used in our analysis that provides consecutive images from video sequences (Lyft sequence of the *CAM_FRONT* channel featuring 126 frames is considered). From our experiments with transient faults injections in Sect. 5, we understand that no effect is observed by altering mantissa bits or by flips in the direction $'1' \rightarrow '0'$ since

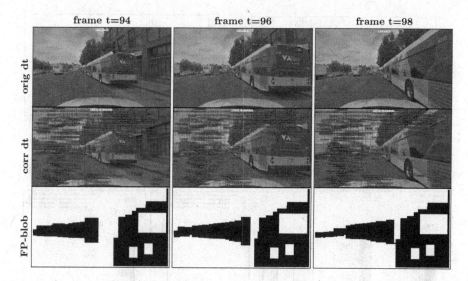

Fig. 7. Pixel wise tracking of FP blobs. First row: orig dt are fault free detections. Second row: corr dt are faulty detections. Third row are tracked FP-blobs (white pixels are occupied by FP blobs).

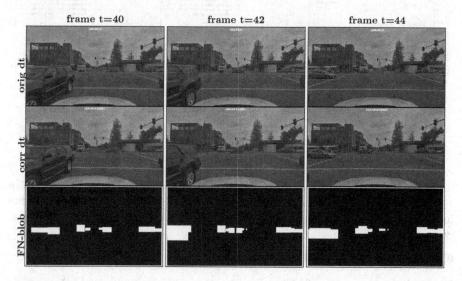

Fig. 8. Pixel wise tracking of FN blobs. First row: orig dt are fault free detections. Second row: corr dt are faulty detections. Third row are tracked FN-blobs (white pixels is the free space created by FNs).

this does not generate large values. Therefore, the experiments of this section are accelerated by using only stuck-at-1 faults in the exponential bits of FP32. However, results have been rescaled to account for the probability of injections

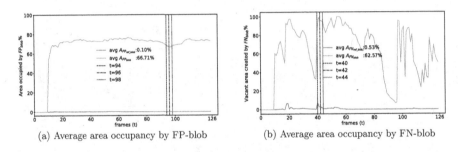

(a) Average area occupancy by FP-blob   (b) Average area occupancy by FN-blob

Fig. 9. Tracking of FP- and FN-blob area

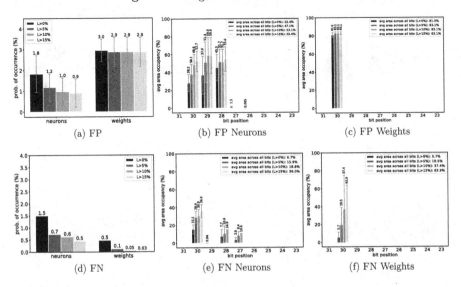

(a) FP   (b) FP Neurons   (c) FP Weights

(d) FN   (e) FN Neurons   (f) FN Weights

Fig. 10. Vulnerability of Yolov3 and Lyft for permanent faults.

in all 32 bits. In this section, we designed an experiment where we inject each of 1000 single random permanent faults (exponential bits) at neurons and weights independently for the above considered sequence to understand its safety impact.

6.1   Evaluating Fault Persistence

We track the movement of blobs (Eq. 3) using a simple pixel-wise M/N tracking scheme [3]. The proposed tracker incorporates the following criteria to establish that a given pixel of FP or FN blob is persistent, at a given frame t: i) The pixel occupied in at least M/N consecutive frames. (if it is also occupied in the current frame, this corresponds to t track update; otherwise it is a coasting track), ii) If the occupancy of that pixel in the last N frames is below M, we check the vicinity around that pixel for past occupancy. Deploying a simplified unidirectional motion model, we register a persistent dynamic pixel for the current frame if occupancies above M are found in the past N frames in a close enough (here 50 pixel, abbr. px) vicinity.

For FN blobs, we omit coasting due to the nature of detection misses. After registering the persistent pixels computed by the pixel-wise tracker, the occupied $(A_{FP_{blob}})$ or free-space $(A_{FN_{blob}})$ area is calculated using Eq. 4. The tracking parameters are chosen as $(10/15)$: The upper frame number is hereby estimated from a critical time of reaction to a persistent false target (≈ 0.5 s) and the frame rate of the Lyft sequence (30 Hz), leading to $N = 0.5\,\text{s}\cdot 30\,\text{s}^{-1} = 15$ key sequential frames. This estimated upper number can be application specific relevant to its safety specifications.

6.2   Corruption Probability and Severity

In Fig. 7 and Fig. 8, we show examples of persistent FP and FN blobs in selected frames. The occupied $(A_{FP_{blob}})$ and free $(A_{FN_{blob}})$ space of an entire video sequence is presented in Fig. 9a and Fig. 9b. For orientation, we also give the area difference between original and ground truth predictions (Fig. 9), $A_{FP_{ref\_blob}} = |\mathcal{I}(\det_{orig} - gt)|/A_{image}$ and $A_{FN_{ref\_blob}} = |\mathcal{I}(gt - \det_{orig})|/|\mathcal{I}(\det_{orig})|$ (where gt is ground truth). We neglect these contributions originating from the model imperfection as it is a function of training and is found to be small (in the above examples <1%) compared to the fault-induced occupancy ($\sim$66% and $\sim$62%, respectively). The example demonstrates that tracked FP blobs may persist across the entire image sequence and occupy a significant amount of free space. Similarly, a significant portion of the image can be lost persistently across the sequence (it reaches as high as $\sim$96%). Our statistical evaluation from 1000 permanent fault injections on the selected image sequence is given in Fig. 10 for FP and FN. The Fig. 10(a) and (d) shows both the SDC probability (in the form of persistant occurance) and the severity ((b)–(c), (e)–(f)) in detail. We register an SDC for a given fault if any persistent FP or FN is found during the sequence with a severity of at least level L. The severity L is quantified as the average area occupied by the blob (for FP normalized by the image size, for FN by the TP blob size, see above). The severity levels are varied from 0% to 15% in Fig. 10 to illustrate the effect of softening or hardening of the safety requirements. As the severity of a fault is again expected to depend on the bit position of the injected fault, we present both bit-selected and bit-averaged numbers in Fig. 10(b,c,e,f).

In this figure, the permanent faults in neurons and weights have a probability of 1.8% and 3% to create persistent ghost FP objects with a minimal area of $L > 0$, respectively. With $L > 15\%$ of an image area, this reduces to 0.9% and 2.9%, respectively. On average, faults hitting MSB bit in weights on this model have 96% probability to manifest into a persistent FP blob of area >81%. On the other hand, persistent FN blobs incorrectly indicating vacant spaces occur with a much lower chance. Bitflips cause persistent objects only in the highest exponential bits in case of neurons or in the MSB bits in the case of weights. This observation is consistent with the findings from transient faults in Sect. 5. Using the given area occupancy metrics, permanent weight faults have a higher severity than neuron faults; in particular, weight faults on average induce massive ghost FP blobs of >83% of the image area.

7   Conclusion

This work points out the challenges in estimating the vulnerability of object detection models under bit flip faults. Average precision-based metrics are either very sensitive or not sensitive to the corruption events, which can be misleading in a safety context. For example, for F-RCNN+Kitti, neuron injections experiments showed almost no impact (<0.1%) in the AP50 and mAP metrics. Using the image-based evaluation metric IVMOD proposed here, however, we see that 0.7% of all images lose substantial amounts (>30%) of the total TP detections due to a single bit flip. The evaluation method presented in this work allows us to come to a vulnerability estimate better addressing safety targets. Given the $IVMOD_{SDC}$ probabilities and severities (see Fig. 3 and Table 1), we conclude that the chances of safety-related corruptions due to soft errors are minor to moderate (0.4%–4.2%) in the studied setups. $IVMOD_{SDC}$ events due to weight faults are about two times as likely as neuron faults. However, if SDC occurs, the severity can be grave. The IVMOD metric should always be considered in combination with severity features for safety purposes. This is because IVMOD does not quantify the severity, but only considers the existence of false and missed bounding boxes. Our metric is defined relative to the original performance. This means that even if a fault also acts in a beneficial way, i.e. fixing some FP or FN occurrences, it will be categorized as a SDC here. We estimated this severity with the help of different safety-related features. We observed that high bits of the exponent of floating point numbers, when hit by either neuron or weight faults, can lead to a significant increase in ΔFP and ΔFN_n. This effect is also translated into an average occupancy value that reflects the area portion of the image that is critically altered by a fault. We find that large average occupancies (up to $A_{FP_{blob}} \sim 81\%$ for FP and $A_{FN_{blob}} \sim 86\%$ for FN) are common, reflecting significant safety hazards. Finally, we studied the use case of a sequential real-time image sequence from Lyft to show that permanent *stuck-at* faults on neurons or at weights can induce FP objects covering as much as $\sim$83% of the image area, creating dangerous ghost objects. Similarly, up to $\sim$63% of the TP area in the scene can be missed. Overall, the weight faults are more likely impactful than neuron faults and have a higher severity in area occupancy (except for permanent FNs).

Acknowledgment. This project has received funding from the European Union's Horizon 2020 research and innovation programme under grant agreement No 956123. Our research was partially funded by the Federal Ministry of Transport and Digital Infrastructure of Germany in the project Providentia++ (01MM19008).

References

1. Athavale, J., Baldovin, A., Graefe, R., Paulitsch, M., Rosales, R.: AI and reliability trends in safety-critical autonomous systems on ground and air. In: Proceedings - 50th Annual IEEE/IFIP International Conference on Dependable Systems and Networks, DSN-W 2020 (2020)
2. Beyer, M., et al.: Fault Injectors for TensorFlow: evaluation of the impact of random hardware faults on deep CNNs. In: 30th European Safety and Reliability Conference, ESREL 2020 and 15th Probabilistic Safety Assessment and Management Conference, PSAM 2020 (2020)
3. Blackman, S., Popoli, R.: Design and Analysis of Modern Tracking Systems (Artech House Radar Library). Artech House (1999)
4. Dos Santos, F.F., Navaux, P., Carro, L., Rech, P.: Impact of reduced precision in the reliability of deep neural networks for object detection. In: Proceedings of the European Test Workshop (2019)
5. Geiger, A., Lenz, P., Stiller, C., Urtasun, R.: Vision meets robotics: the KITTI dataset. Int. J. Robot. Res. **32**, 1231–1237 (2013)
6. Geissler, F., et al.: Towards a safety case for hardware fault tolerance in convolutional neural networks using activation range supervision. In: Proceedings of the Workshop on Artificial Intelligence Safety 2021 co-located with the Thirtieth International Joint Conference on Artificial Intelligence (IJCAI 2021), Virtual, August 2021 (2021)
7. He, K., Zhang, X., Ren, S., Sun, J.: Deep residual learning for image recognition. In: Proceedings of the IEEE Conference on Computer Vision and Pattern Recognition (2016)
8. Hong, S., Frigo, P., Kaya, Y., Giuffrida, C., Dumitras, T.: Terminal brain damage: exposing the graceless degradation in deep neural networks under hardware fault attacks. In: Proceedings of the 28th USENIX Security Symposium (2019)
9. Hou, X., Breier, J., Jap, D., Ma, L., Bhasin, S., Liu, Y.: Security evaluation of deep neural network resistance against laser fault injection. In: Proceedings of the International Symposium on the Physical and Failure Analysis of Integrated Circuits, IPFA (2020)
10. IEEE: 754-2019 - IEEE Standard for Floating-Point Arithmetic. Tech. rep. (2019)
11. Intel Corporation: bfloat16 - Hardware Numerics Definition. Tech. rep. (2018)
12. Kesten, R., et al.: Level 5 perception dataset 2020 (2019)
13. Koopman, P., Osyk, B.: Safety argument considerations for public road testing of autonomous vehicles. SAE Technical Papers, April 2019
14. Krizhevsky, A., Sutskever, I., Hinton, G.E.: ImageNet classification with deep convolutional neural networks. Advances in Neural Information Processing Systems (2012)
15. Kuhn, H.W.: The Hungarian method for the assignment problem. Naval Res. Logist. Q. **2**, 83–97 (1955)
16. Li, G., et al.: Understanding error propagation in Deep learning Neural Network (DNN) accelerators and applications. In: Proceedings of the International Conference for High Performance Computing, Networking, Storage and Analysis, SC 2017. Association for Computing Machinery, Inc. (2017)
17. Lin, T.Y., Goyal, P., Girshick, R., He, K., Dollar, P.: Focal loss for dense object detection. IEEE Trans. Pattern Anal. Mach. Intell. **42**, 318–327 (2020)
18. Lotfi, A., et al.: Resiliency of automotive object detection networks on GPU architectures. In: Proceedings - International Test Conference (2019)

19. Microsoft: Coco 2017 dataset (2017)
20. Neale, A., Sachdev, M.: Neutron radiation induced soft error rates for an adjacent-ECC protected SRAM in 28 nm CMOS. IEEE Trans. Nucl. Sci. **66**, 1912–1917(2016)
21. Reagen, B., et al.: Ares: a framework for quantifying the resilience of deep neural networks. In: Proceedings - Design Automation Conference (2018)
22. Redmon, J., Farhadi, A.: YOLOv3: An Incremental Improvement (2018)
23. Ren, S., He, K., Girshick, R., Sun, J.: Faster R-CNN: towards real-time object detection with region proposal networks. IEEE Trans. Pattern Anal. Mach. Intell. **36** (2017)
24. Simonyan, K., Zisserman, A.: Very deep convolutional networks for large-scale image recognition. In: 3rd International Conference on Learning Representations, ICLR 2015 - Conference Track Proceedings (2015)

Application of STPA for the Elicitation of Safety Requirements for a Machine Learning-Based Perception Component in Automotive

Esra Acar Celik[1]([✉]), Carmen Cârlan[2], Asim Abdulkhaleq[3], Fridolin Bauer[4], Martin Schels[5], and Henrik J. Putzer[1]

[1] fortiss Research Institute of the Free State of Bavaria, Munich, Germany
{acarcelik,putzer}@fortiss.org
[2] Edge Case Research GmbH, Munich, Germany
ccarlan@ecr.ai
[3] Robert Bosch GmbH, Stuttgart, Germany
Asim.Abdulkhaleq@de.bosch.com
[4] BMW AG, Munich, Germany
Fridolin.Bauer@bmwgroup.com
[5] Continental AG, Regensburg, Germany
martin.schels@continental-corporation.com

Abstract. Approaches based on Machine Learning (ML) provide novel and promising solutions to implement safety-critical functions in the field of autonomous driving. Establishing assurance in these ML components through safety requirements is critical, as the failure of these components may lead to hazardous events such as pedestrians being hit by the ego vehicle due to an erroneous output of an ML component (e.g., a pedestrian not being detected in a safety-critical region). In this paper, we present our experience with applying the System-Theoretic Process Analysis (STPA) approach for an ML-based perception component within a pedestrian collision avoidance system. STPA is integrated into the safety life cycle of functional safety (regulated by ISO 26262) complemented with safety of the intended functionality (regulated by ISO/FDIS 21448) in order to elicit safety requirements. These requirements are derived from STPA unsafe control actions and loss scenarios, thus enabling the traceability from hazards to ML safety requirements. For specifying loss scenarios, we propose to refer to erroneous outputs of the ML component due to the ML functional insufficiencies, while adhering to the guidelines of the STPA handbook.

Keywords: Safety requirements · Machine Learning · Functional insufficiencies · STPA · ISO 26262 · ISO/FDIS 21448

1 Introduction

The safety life cycle of ISO 26262 [6] encompasses the main safety activities to design the system so that the consequences of internal malfunctions that may

M. Trapp et al. (Eds.): SAFECOMP 2022, LNCS 13414, pp. 319–332, 2022.
https://doi.org/10.1007/978-3-031-14835-4_21

occur in the system components are mitigated. However, for Autonomous Driving (AD) systems addressing hazards caused by component faults is not enough, as such systems heavily rely on sensors (leading to high-dimensional inputs) and on dynamically evolving data sets (e.g., for training neural networks) in an open world context [9]. Consequently, the activities recommended by ISO/FDIS 21448 [7] shall also be executed to address the risk associated with functional insufficiencies. According to ISO/FDIS 21448, *functional insufficiencies* refer to the insufficiencies of the specification of the intended functionality at vehicle level, or the insufficiencies of the specification or performance limitations of system elements [7]. *Performance limitation* is a limitation of the technical capability and *insufficiency of specification* is a possibly incomplete specification leading to a hazardous behavior in combination with one or more triggering conditions [7]. Here, *triggering conditions* refer to specific conditions of a scenario that serve as an initiator for a subsequent system reaction contributing to either a hazardous behavior or an inability to prevent or detect and mitigate a reasonably foreseeable indirect misuse [7]. However, providing a complete specification of a Deep Neural Network (DNN) is hard to achieve, mainly due to the black box nature of these algorithms.

For the elicitation of safety requirements in a systematic manner, one can execute one or more state-of-the-art safety analyses. Traditional safety analysis methods are based on the reliability theory, and are not adequate to address hazards related to Safety Of The Intended Functionality (SOTIF) and caused by human errors, dysfunctional component interactions or ML functional insufficiencies [1]. STPA is a more recent hazard analysis technique based on the system and control theory, and is more than a mere fault analysis as it also addresses types of hazardous causes in the absence of failure [11,12]. In the case of ML components, classical fault definitions do not apply, but the output of an ML component can be safety critical when used as input to a controller (e.g., "Pedestrian Avoidance Controller" in Fig. 3). Consequently, as also stated in ISO/FDIS 21448, STPA is an appropriate candidate for the analysis of functional insufficiencies that may be root causes for hazardous events. A more comprehensive comparison between STPA and other safety analyses can be found in [16]. The main contributions of the paper can be summarized as follows:

– *Integration of STPA into the safety life cycle of ISO 26262 and ISO/FDIS 21448:* In order to address both functional safety and SOTIF, we follow the reference safety life cycle from ISO 26262 and complement each phase in this life cycle with ISO/FDIS 21448 specific activities (similarly to Becker et al. [3] and Kirovskii et al. [9]). The STPA technique is then integrated into this life cycle for the elicitation of safety requirements in a systematic manner. The STPA integration is necessary due to the following reasons: (1) ISO 26262 does not explicitly mention how to deal with deep learning algorithms; (2) The complementary ISO/FDIS 21448 provides no guidance on how to derive safety measures from system level to algorithm level. The presented approach that integrates STPA into the safety life cycle addresses this gap and enables the provision of traceability from hazards to safety requirements assigned to DNN components.

- *Elicitation of safety requirements based on ML safety concerns:* We provide guidance for identifying SOTIF-specific loss scenarios via STPA based on DNN safety concerns that are defined as the root causes of DNN functional insufficiencies in [18].
- *Guideline for defining safety-relevant metrics for ML safety requirements:* We discuss how to define safety-relevant metrics for exemplary ML safety requirements that are derived from DNN safety concerns using STPA.

The paper is organized as follows. Section 2 explores recent developments that have been proposed for the safety assurance of ML components in the field of AD. In Sect. 3, we introduce our approach for the elicitation of ML safety requirements while using STPA and how it is applied for a pedestrian detection Learning Enabled Component (LEC). Finally, we present concluding remarks and future directions to expand our approach in Sect. 4.

2   Related Work

On the one hand, Abdulkhaleq et al. [1] discuss the usability of STPA for the execution of certain activities within the ISO 26262 life cycle and present a concept to extend the safety scope of ISO 26262 and to support the Hazard Analysis and Risk Assessment (HARA) process. On the other hand, Zhang et al. [19] propose an approach for identifying and evaluating SOTIF-relevant hazardous factors via STPA. In contrast to these works, we focus on SOTIF-related triggering conditions associated to DNN functional limitations. Kramer et al. [10] provide an integrated method for the safety assessment of AD functions, which covers both aspects of functional safety and SOTIF. They also provide a functional insufficiency and causal chain analysis technique to identify and model SOTIF-related hazards. Still, their approach addresses system level, whereas our focus is on the level of ML.

In addition, there is ongoing research on deriving safety requirements for ML and/or providing a traceable link between system level and component level safety requirements. For example, Gauerhof et al. [5] provide a traceable link between system level safety requirements and ML safety requirements that address data management, and model learning stages of the ML life cycle for pedestrian detection at crossings. The paper focuses mainly on the derivation and the sufficiency of data management requirements that target different concerns of the data used in the generation of ML models. Similarly, Salay et al. [13] address the missing link between system level safety requirements and component level performance requirements using a so-called "linkage argument" that connects component related claim at system level to component level argument. Further, Schwalbe et al. [15] present an assurance case to argue about confidence for ML components and propose a pattern to structure the part of a safety argument specific to DNNs with a case study based on pedestrian detection. They suggest to derive DNN-related safety requirements from types of DNN-specific functional insufficiencies along with a structure for evidences related to these insufficiencies. The main difference from our work is that they focus on the completeness of safety requirements on DNN level and provide no traceable link between system level and component level safety requirements.

Complementary to existing works, we present a systematic approach that integrates STPA into the safety life cycle of ISO 26262 and ISO/FDIS 21448 to elicit safety requirements for an ML-based perception function. Our approach uses STPA for the identification of SOTIF-related triggering conditions based on ML functional insufficiencies and safety concerns. To the best of our knowledge, no systematic guidance exists on how to derive safety requirements based on ML functional insufficiencies and ML safety concerns for ML-based perception components from system level safety requirements.

3   Safety Requirement Elicitation for Pedestrian Detection Component

In this section, we present our approach for integrating STPA into the combined safety life cycle of ISO 26262 and ISO/FDIS 21448, and show how we used the presented approach to derive safety requirements for an ML-based perception function of a pedestrian collision avoidance system. More specifically, this function is a DNN-based component that is assumed to be embedded in an SAE Level 4 autonomous vehicle. In Subsect. 3.1, the integration of STPA into the combined safety life cycle is presented. The elicitation of safety requirements based on the proposed approach is presented in Subsect. 3.2 and guidance on safety-relevant metrics for derived ML safety requirements is provided in Subsect. 3.3. Finally, in Subsect. 3.4, based on the experiences gained in the KI Absicherung project[1], we discuss open points that should be addressed in the future for the safety assurance of systems with LECs.

3.1   Integrating STPA into the Safety Life Cycle of ISO 26262 and ISO/FDIS 21448

We integrate the safety assurance activities recommended by ISO 26262 and ISO/FDIS 21448 by complementing each phase in the ISO 26262 safety life cycle with ISO/FDIS 21448 specific activities, similarly to Becker et al. [3] and Kirovskii et al. [9]. In Fig. 1, we present how we also integrate STPA activities into this combined safety life cycle.

As shown in Fig. 1, the first two phases of STPA, namely *define the purpose of the analysis* and *model the control structure*, have overlapping activities with clause 5 and clause 6 in ISO/FDIS 21448, and part 3–5 and part 3–6 in the ISO 26262 safety life cycle. The aim of the phase of *defining the purpose of the analysis* is to identify hazards and safety constraints, whereas the *modeling the control structure* can be seen as a part of *specification and design* (ISO/FDIS 21448), or *item definition* (ISO 26262).

---

[1] https://www.ki-absicherung-projekt.de/.

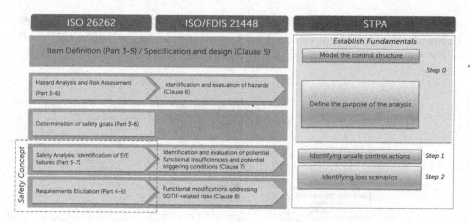

Fig. 1. Pillars of the proposed integrated assurance approach

The next phase of STPA, namely *identify unsafe control actions* - Step 1 in Fig. 1, overlaps with the execution of safety analysis (part 3–7) as recommended by ISO 26262 and with the identification and evaluation of triggering conditions recommended by ISO/FDIS 21448 (clause 7). The aim of STPA, part 3–7 of ISO 26262 and clause 7 of ISO/FDIS 21448 is similar, namely to identify the causal factors of hazardous events. While in the scope of ISO/FDIS 21448, causal factors related to algorithms, sensors and actuators are identified, in the scope of ISO 26262, hazardous events caused by the occurrence/presence of hardware, software, communication, or integration faults are identified.

The final phase of STPA, namely *identify loss scenarios* - Step 2 in Fig. 1, aims at identifying the causal factors that can lead to unsafe control actions (UCAs), i.e., loss scenarios [12]. In order to prevent the occurrence of loss scenarios, we define safety requirements. In this activity of definition of safety requirements, clause 8 of ISO/FDIS 21448 overlaps with part 4–6 of ISO 26262. The remaining activities from ISO 26262 and ISO/FDIS 21448 are not discussed as they are out of the scope of this paper. However, ISO/FDIS 21448 explains how SOTIF activities including verification and validation are aligned with ISO 26262.

3.2 Case Study: Deriving Safety Requirements of a Perception Component with STPA

In this subsection, we explore the application of the proposed method, where STPA is used as the safety analysis method for an ML-based perception component. Safety requirements for the considered component are derived from identified UCAs and loss scenarios. The identification of STPA loss scenarios helps identifying SOTIF-related unsafe scenarios, thus reducing the number of unknown unsafe scenarios. Known unsafe scenarios can be then eliminated by the implementation of a safety concept in the scope of ISO 26262 (part 3–7 and

4–6), or of functional modifications in the scope of ISO/FDIS 21448 (clause 8). In Fig. 2, we show how a top-level safety goal of the system boils down to ML safety requirements.

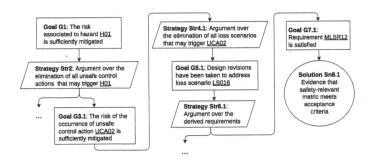

Fig. 2. Goal Structuring Notation (GSN) showing the derivation of ML safety requirements using STPA

Inspired by the work of Abdulkhaleq et al. [1], in Fig. 1 we present how STPA can support the systematic refinement of hazards to safety requirements. However, since the scope of this paper is to provide the safety assurance of a DNN component, in contrast to [1] we mainly focus on SOTIF-related triggering conditions associated to DNN functional limitations. In addition, we propose our own approach for specifying loss scenarios, while basing our usage of STPA on the guidelines from the STPA Handbook [12].

In the initial phase of STPA, losses, system level hazards and constraints are identified. For our use case (i.e., pedestrian detection), we define the following losses/harms: (1) $L01$: Loss of life or serious injury to people, and (2) $L02$: Damage to the vehicle or objects outside the vehicle. Then, based on the addressed losses along with the item definition and the possible operational situations, we determine relevant hazardous events and their consequences (severity, exposure, controllability as described by ISO 26262): (1) $H01$: Collision with pedestrians when driving with velocity greater than 10 km/h in urban area (S1–S3 - depending on velocity, E4, C3), and (2) $H02$: Collision with trailing vehicle due to unnecessary braking (S1–S2 - depending on velocity, E4, C2/C3). In the second phase of STPA, a highly abstract system architecture (from a functional point of view), having a control structure and used for the safety analysis, is modelled. Figure 3 shows the control structure modelled for our use case.

Based on the modelled control structure and the identified hazards, UCAs are defined in the third phase of the STPA by using guiding words provided in the STPA handbook (i.e., *provided, not provided, too soon/too late/out of sequence, stopped too soon/applied too long*). A UCA is a control action that will lead to a hazard in a particular context and worst-case environment [12]. We define the following exemplifying UCAs for our use case: (1) $UCA02$: The "Pedestrian Avoidance Controller" does not provide brake when pedestrian present in the

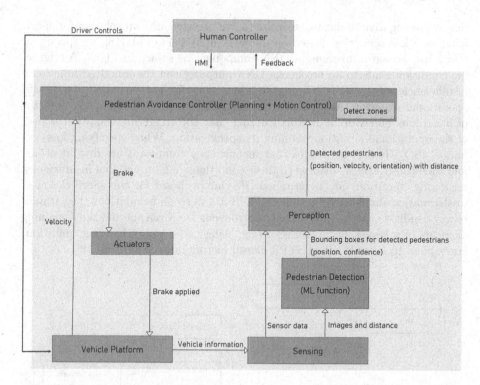

Fig. 3. STPA control structure presenting the system architecture of the pedestrian collision avoidance system. "Detect zones" information consists of velocity-dependent reachability zones of the ego vehicle in which the system should accurately detect all pedestrians.

must-detect area corresponding to current velocity - traced back to *H01*; and (2) *UCA03:* The "Pedestrian Avoidance Controller" provides brake when not needed - traced back to *H02*. Here, *must-detect area* is a safety-critical region defined according to the field of view of the camera and a braking distance according to the effective braking deacceleration defining the radius of the must-detect area. This area is then used to determine safety-relevant pedestrians (i.e., pedestrians that shall be detected by the DNN component). From each UCA, a functional safety requirement (FSR) is derived by inverting the UCA. Each FSR is then refined to technical safety requirements based on the system architecture, control structure and its effect chain.

In the last phase of the STPA analysis, the possible causes of the UCAs are identified as loss scenarios. The STPA handbook provides guidelines on how to identify such loss scenarios and an inadequate process model is stated as a possible cause of UCAs in the handbook [12]. In this work, LECs implementing perception functionality are treated as part of the process model of a decision making controller. As such, we are interested in identifying when the controller receives incorrect feedback from an inadequate process model, namely the LEC (e.g., false negative in must-detect area). We present our own solution for specifying such loss scenarios. Based on the work of Willers et al. [18], we specify an STPA loss scenario involving a DNN component as shown in Fig. 4. A triggering condition leads to an erroneous DNN output given the inherited functional insufficiencies of the DNN component, when occurring in the context of a certain operational situation. As a result, this erroneous output becomes a causal factor of hazardous behavior. It is worth noting that the triggering condition is part of the operational situation, refining its specification. When specifying loss scenarios, ISO/FDIS 21448 states that insufficiency conditions are first identified and then causal factors leading to these conditions (e.g., functional insufficiency, triggering condition) are determined [7]. Our proposal for the specification of loss scenarios aligns with these ISO/FDIS 21448 recommendations (i.e., insufficiency condition can be interpreted as erroneous DNN output and the remaining elements of a loss scenario in Fig. 4 (e.g., safety concerns, triggering condition) correspond to what is called STPA causal factors in ISO/FDIS 21448).

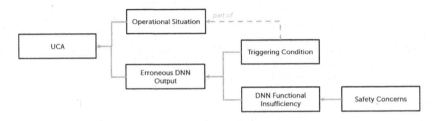

Fig. 4. The relation between safety concerns, functional insufficiencies, triggering condition, and unsafe control actions

To reason about different types of erroneous output of DNNs, we use domain knowledge about DNNs and adapt the service failure taxonomy proposed by Avizienis et al. [2] to DNNs. Consequently, we realize a taxonomy for erroneous DNN outputs, which can be seen in Fig. 5. According to this taxonomy, the following types of erroneous outputs of DNNs are claimed to cause the occurrence of a UCA: (1) The controller receives incorrect feedback from the DNN component, (2) the controller does not receive feedback from the DNN component when needed (i.e., receives a delayed feedback).

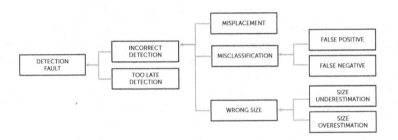

Fig. 5. Taxonomy of erroneous DNN outputs

There are different possible triggering conditions for incorrect feedback (output) from the DNN, namely the occurrence of:

- **SOTIF Factors:** The occurrence of triggering conditions, in the context in which the DNN component has certain functional insufficiencies caused by safety concerns.
- **ISO 26262 Functional Safety Factors:** Software faults in the software implementation of the DNN model. UCAs based on these factors are considered as violating functional safety (FuSa).

Exemplifying ISO/FDIS 21448 and ISO 26262 related loss scenarios for our use case are the following: (1) ISO/FDIS 21448: Performance limiting factors such as strong occlusion of pedestrians and low contrast of people in camera image due to environmental conditions; (2) ISO 26262: Hardware or software fault occurring in the camera sensor or lack of efficiency. As shown in Fig. 4, erroneous DNN outputs are triggered due to DNN functional insufficiencies. In this paper, we consider *insufficient generalization capability* [14] as the functional insufficiency of DNN and use the DNN safety concerns that are defined by [8] as the root causes of this functional insufficiency.

Table 1. ISO/FDIS 21448 and ISO 26262 relevant exemplary loss scenarios: LS016, LS017 and LS024 are ISO/FDIS 21448 relevant, whereas LS030 is an ISO 26262 relevant one (OS: Operational Situation, OS1: Pedestrians in must-detect area; Pedestrian Collision Avoidance system is enabled, FN: DNN provides a false negative output, TL: DNN provides bounding boxes too late.)

ID	Safety concerns	Triggering condition	OS	Erroneous output
LS016	Brittleness of DNNs	Presence of natural noise	OS1	FN
LS017	Brittleness of DNNs	Presence of natural adversarial attacks	OS1	FN
LS024	Unreliable confidence information Unknown behavior in rare critical situations Brittleness of DNNs Missing label details or meta-labels	Strong occlusion of pedestrians	OS1	FN
LS030	N/A	Lack of efficiency	OS1	TL

In the light of the discussion above, we provide exemplifying loss scenarios both for ISO/FDIS 21448 and ISO 26262 for our use case in Table 1. To prevent the occurrence of the identified loss scenarios, which would imply the occurrence of UCAs causing harm, a safety requirement shall be derived from each identified loss scenario and the derived requirement can be allocated to system components, where one safety requirement may address several loss scenarios. In Table 2, we provide exemplifying ML safety requirements (MLSRs) derived for our use case.

Table 2. Exemplary safety requirements derived by the proposed approach

ID	Requirement Text	Related Loss Scenario
MLSR12	The 2D bounding box detector shall detect pedestrians if a foreseeable type of perturbation is present (e.g., strong rain, dirt on sensor, noise due to electromagnetic interference below high voltage lines, ...).	LS016
MLSR13	The 2D bounding box detector shall detect pedestrians if known adversarial attacks are present.	LS017
MLSR08	The 2D bounding box detector shall detect pedestrians if they are partially occluded.	LS024
MLSR05	The 2D bounding box detector shall detect pedestrians with a processing time per frame of at most 40 ms (due to camera frame rate of 25 Hz)	LS030

3.3 Defining Safety-Relevant Metrics

According to ISO/FDIS 21448, the definition of acceptance criteria (e.g., a validation target) is required in the development process of AD systems. Such acceptance criteria could be the minimum length of the required endurance run combined with a maximum number of observed failures for each type (e.g., false positives, false negatives) [7]. Therefore, for each DNN safety requirement, a safety-relevant metric should be defined. Safety-relevant metrics are basically performance metrics that enable to evaluate safety requirements (i.e., that are used for safety assurance). For example, our derived safety requirements such as MLSR12 address ML safety concerns but they provide no explicit reference to any specific metric (Table 2 and Table 3). In this work, we determine the safety-relevant metrics based on the addressed safety concerns along with triggering conditions. This enables the linkage between the derived SOTIF ML requirements to the properties of ML components such as performance and, as a result, to have a holistic view that combines top-down and bottom-up assurance approaches for ML-based systems. A top-down approach refers to a safety argument that begins with system level hazards and continues with the derivation and the refinement of safety requirements from system level to component level. A bottom-up approach, on the other hand, refers to the incorporation of the properties of ML components into the system safety case. We perform the connection of top-down and bottom-up approaches by the use of safety concerns as being a part of STPA loss scenarios (Fig. 4). Therefore, in order to determine which evidences can be used to meet a safety requirement assigned to an ML component, we focus on evidences that can be generated to mitigate related safety concerns. More specifically, metrics are defined based on mechanisms and methods that address the safety concerns along with related triggering conditions. These metrics can then be used as safety measures for fault removal, tolerance, prevention and forecasting. In Table 3, we provide exemplary MLSRs with related safety concerns and safety-relevant metrics.

Table 3. Exemplary MLSRs with related safety concerns and safety-relevant metrics.

Requirements	Safety concerns	Safety-relevant metrics
MLSR12 (foreseeable type of perturbation is present) **MLSR13** (known adversarial attacks are present)	Brittleness of DNNs	– Robustness metric = correlation between performance metric and image metric measuring the degree of perturbation (specifics depend on perturbation type) – Robustness under domain shift – ...
MLSR08 (pedestrian is partially occluded)	– Unreliable confidence information – Unknown behavior in rare critical situations – Brittleness of DNNs – Missing label details or meta-labels	Occlusion sensitivity ...

The safety-relevant metrics outlined in Table 3 are defined in the context of the KI Absicherung project and providing details about each metric is beyond the scope of this paper. However, as shown in Table 3, these metrics are determined mainly based on the safety concern being addressed by the MLSR and related triggering condition. *MLSR12* and *MLSR13* are related to the safety concern of brittleness of DNNs and the related triggering condition is the presence of perturbation (noise or adversarial attacks). Therefore, robustness related metrics are suggested to support these MLSRs in the safety argument. Similarly, *MLSR08* is related to the following safety concerns: Unreliable confidence information, unknown behavior in rare critical situations, brittleness of DNNs and missing label details or meta-labels. The triggering condition for *MLSR08* is the strong occlusion of pedestrians. As a result, metrics that address the sensitivity to occluded objects of a DNN model are used to support this safety requirement.

3.4 Discussion

Failure Modes and Effects Analysis (FMEA) and Fault Tree Analysis (FTA) are both recommended by ISO 26262 as safety analysis methods and they mainly focus on the analysis of safety-critical Electrical/Electronic (E/E) failures based on the available design of the system. STPA, on the other hand, is a method which is used to design a system while regarding the safety concerns at an early stage of the development process (*safety by design*) and it does not only focus on the E/E failures of the system, but also on hazardous behaviors in the absence of the E/E failures and the interaction between the system and its environment. Therefore, in line with what ISO/FDIS 21448 recommends, in this paper we proposed an approach using STPA during the execution of a safety life cycle which entails both ISO 26262 and SOTIF activities, and our approach mainly focuses on hazardous behaviors which are not related to the E/E failures. Still, in a real world context, all these approaches are applicable at different steps within the safety life cycle. For example, STPA is applicable at the concept phase part 3 of ISO 26262 to derive the hazardous events including SOTIF (ML algorithms) hazardous events, whereas FTA and FMEA can be applied at the part 9 of ISO 26262 to identify the failure and faults of system components.

Within the context of elicitation of safety requirements for ML components, the definition of acceptance criteria was one of the major topics discussed during the KI Absicherung project. More specifically, the discussion point was how to map the system target level of safety (acceptable risk) to safety metrics at the level of ML component as discussed in the previous subsection. Arguing whether an autonomous vehicle with LECs meets quantitative safety targets (acceptable risk) is still a largely open research question addressed in some studies [4] [17]. Vaicenavicius et al. [17] decompose the validation target defined for the perception function into two, namely: (1) the performance of the perception function of the system, and (2) properties of the environment. The properties of the environment can be seen as the environmental factors to be considered such as the average number of pedestrians expected for the pedestrian detection function. Berk et al. [4] provide a much clearer system-component linking compared to [17]. They state that an overall approval criterion for the system is that the sum of the failure rates of the perception (λ_{per}), planning (λ_{func}), and actuation subsystems (λ_{actu}) is smaller than a given threshold rate (determined by the target safety level of the system) [4]. The rate of failures of the perception (λ_{per}) is decomposed into *overall rate of perception errors (i.e., false positives and false negatives)* and *safety-criticality* of a perception error that is defined as high, medium and low depending on the location of the error in the field of view [4]. For instance, perception errors directly in front of the ego vehicle can heuristically be estimated to be more safety critical than perception errors occurring further away [4]. A comprehensive approach that would both target different phases of ML life cycle (as in [5]) and that enables definition of a target safety at system level (via an acceptable risk) using component level performance requirements (as in [4]) seems to be a promising way to proceed and to extend our current approach.

4   Conclusion

In this paper, we presented an approach that applies STPA for the elicitation of safety requirements for an ML component implementing an AD function. The approach integrates STPA activities into the functional safety and SOTIF activities, and enables the traceability from hazards to safety requirements assigned to

DNN components. While adhering to the guidelines from the STPA handbook, loss scenarios are specified in a novel way by referring to erroneous DNN outputs due to DNN functional insufficiencies. In addition, we briefly discuss the usage of safety-relevant metrics that target the DNN safety concerns as performance evidence. In order to facilitate the understanding of the approach, we discuss its usage within the KI Absicherung project. However, the approach is agnostic to a specific project and is applicable to a diverse set of scenarios in which ML components are integrated into a safety-critical system.

One interesting and important line of future work would be providing a link between the SOTIF-related risk at vehicle level and the performance requirements at component level in order to define acceptance criteria for ML safety requirements. Another significant future work would be to investigate how process-related requirements such as adhering to data labeling guidelines can be incorporated into the safety argumentation of the system as indirect evidences.

Acknowledgement. The research leading to these results is funded by the German Federal Ministry for Economic Affairs and Energy within the project "KI Absicherung - Safe AI for Automated Driving". The authors would like to thank the consortium for the successful cooperation. C. Cârlan worked on this paper during her time as a researcher at fortiss Research Institute of the Free State of Bavaria.

References

1. Abdulkhaleq, A., Wagner, S., Lammering, D., Boehmert, H., Blueher, P.: Using STPA in compliance with ISO 26262 for developing a safe architecture for fully automated vehicles. In: Automotive - Safety & Security. LNI, vol. P-269, pp. 149–162. Gesellschaft für Informatik, Bonn (2017)
2. Avizienis, A., Laprie, J.C., Randell, B., Landwehr, C.: Basic concepts and taxonomy of dependable and secure computing. IEEE Trans. Depend. Secur. Comput. **1**(1), 11–33 (2004)
3. Becker, C., Brewer, J.C., Yount, L., et al.: Safety of the intended functionality of lane-centering and lane-changing maneuvers of a generic level 3 highway chauffeur system. Tech. rep, US National Highway Traffic Safety Administration (2020)
4. Berk, M., Schubert, O., Kroll, H.M., Buschardt, B., Straub, D.: Assessing the safety of environment perception in automated driving vehicles. SAE Int. J. Transp. Saf. **8**(1), 49–74 (2020)
5. Gauerhof, L., Hawkins, R., Picardi, C., Paterson, C., Hagiwara, Y., Habli, I.: Assuring the safety of machine learning for pedestrian detection at crossings. In: Casimiro, A., Ortmeier, F., Bitsch, F., Ferreira, P. (eds.) SAFECOMP 2020. LNCS, vol. 12234, pp. 197–212. Springer, Cham (2020). https://doi.org/10.1007/978-3-030-54549-9_13
6. ISO: ISO 26262 - Road vehicles - Functional safety (2011)
7. ISO: ISO/FDIS 21448 - Road vehicles - Safety of the intended functionality (2022)
8. KI-Familie Newsletter, https://ki-familie.vdali.de/ki-newsletter-nr-2/ki-absicherung-dnn-specific-safety-concerns
9. Kirovskii, O.M., Gorelov, V.A.: Driver assistance systems: analysis, tests and the safety case. ISO 26262 and ISO PAS 21448. IOP Conf. Ser. Mater. Sci. Eng. **534**, 012019 (2019)

10. Kramer, B., Neurohr, C., Büker, M., Böde, E., Fränzle, M., Damm, W.: Identification and quantification of hazardous scenarios for automated driving. In: Zeller, M., Höfig, K. (eds.) IMBSA 2020. LNCS, vol. 12297, pp. 163–178. Springer, Cham (2020). https://doi.org/10.1007/978-3-030-58920-2_11

11. Leveson, N.G.: Engineering a Safer World: Systems Thinking Applied to Safety. The MIT Press, Cambridge (2016)

12. Leveson, N.G., Thomas, J.P.: STPA Handbook. MIT Partnership for Systems Approaches to Safety and Security (PSASS) (2018)

13. Salay, R., et al.: The missing link: Developing a safety case for perception components in automated driving. arXiv:2108.13294 (2021)

14. Sämann, T., Schlicht, P., Hüger, F.: Strategy to increase the safety of a DNN-based perception for had systems. arXiv:2002.08935 (2020)

15. Schwalbe, G., et al.: Structuring the safety argumentation for deep neural network based perception in automotive applications. In: Casimiro, A., Ortmeier, F., Schoitsch, E., Bitsch, F., Ferreira, P. (eds.) SAFECOMP 2020. LNCS, vol. 12235, pp. 383–394. Springer, Cham (2020). https://doi.org/10.1007/978-3-030-55583-2_29

16. Sulaman, S.M., Beer, A., Felderer, M., Höst, M.: Comparison of the FMEA and STPA safety analysis methods-a case study. Softw. Qual. J. **27**(1), 349–387 (2019)

17. Vaicenavicius, J., Wiklund, T., Grigaitė, A., Kalkauskas, A., Vysniauskas, I., Keen, S.: Self-driving car safety quantification via component-level analysis. arXiv:2009.01119 (2020)

18. Willers, O., Sudholt, S., Raafatnia, S., Abrecht, S.: Safety concerns and mitigation approaches regarding the use of deep learning in safety-critical perception tasks. arXiv:2001.08001 (2020)

19. Zhang, S., Tang, T., Liu, J.: A hazard analysis approach for the SOTIF in intelligent railway driving assistance systems using stpa and complex network. Appl. Sci. **11**(16), 7714 (2021)

Testing

Exploring a Maximal Number of Relevant Obstacles for Testing UAVs

Tabea Schmidt[✉], Florian Hauer, and Alexander Pretschner

Department of Informatics, Technical University of Munich, Munich, Germany
{tabea.schmidt,florian.hauer,alexander.pretschner}@tum.de

Abstract. Autonomously operating Unmanned Aerial Vehicles (UAVs) must behave safely while performing their missions. For assessing the safe behavior of a UAV, scenario-based testing provides valuable insights into the UAV's behavior in various situations. However, we can always create new challenging situations to test by adding new obstacles to the UAV's environment. For reasons of practicality and cost, we need to focus on those that represent relevant situations for the system under test. In this work, we present an automated approach for exploring a maximal number of relevant obstacles for testing the safe behavior of UAVs. We evaluate our approach using different optimization algorithms to validate our results and understand which technique is more suited. Since we can base our understanding of challenging situations for the UAV on various fault hypotheses, we further display the effect of collecting different parameter values of the UAV. Our experiments show the applicability of the proposed methodology and imply that the MOEA/D optimization algorithm performs better than NSGAII for the proposed approach. Further, the results indicate that a maximum of $M = 5$ or $M = 8$ obstacles are relevant for the system under test, depending on the applied fault hypothesis. Based on these results, we can effectively limit the number of situations for testing the system under test by excluding those with more than M obstacles.

Keywords: Scenario-based testing · Unmanned Aerial Vehicles · Safety

1 Introduction

Companies such as Amazon [22] or Zipline [20] are actively working on autonomously operating Unmanned Aerial Vehicles (UAVs). Since these systems will operate more often in populated areas in the near future, we need to ensure that they behave safely during operation. Recent work has shown that scenario-based testing [6] provides valuable insights into the safe behavior of autonomous cars [7,13] and UAVs [21]. In scenario-based testing, the System Under Test (SUT) is tested in typical situations that it might encounter. For autonomous cars, we have a good intuition and understanding of the nature of these typical traffic situations. Further, available traffic rules and road elements provide a

M. Trapp et al. (Eds.): SAFECOMP 2022, LNCS 13414, pp. 335–349, 2022.
https://doi.org/10.1007/978-3-031-14835-4_22

rigid structure for these situations. In contrast, UAVs operate in the open field and have a wide range of possible missions and environments that we need to consider in these typical situations. A quadcopter with the mission to transport a package to a destination point while encountering three obstacles and medium wind conditions is an example of such a typical situation for a UAV. By adding further obstacles to the environment of the UAV in these typical situations, we can create a new situation that might be challenging for the UAV. Thus, we need to test the UAV's behavior in each of these novel situations. As it is infeasible to test a UAV in infinitely many typical situations, we have to derive a complete list of relevant situations. As a first step towards acquiring such a comprehensive list, we propose investigating the maximal number of relevant obstacles that we need to consider when testing the safe behavior of UAVs. In related work, the authors of [3,4,9,15,23] derive typical situations for autonomous cars or UAVs based on ontologies that describe the various aspects of these situations. They focus on the structure of these situations or specific use cases and do not concentrate on the completeness of the derived situations. As an alternative, the authors of [8,14,24] propose statistical approaches to explore the completeness and diversity of collected data. Since we still lack high amounts of data for testing UAVs to apply these approaches, we aim to focus instead on the relevant typical situations themselves. In addition, we are not aware of a test ending criterion for scenario-based testing of UAVs that would inherently provide insight into a maximal number of relevant obstacles. In this work, we aim to investigate the upper bound of the number of obstacles that we need to consider when testing UAVs. In this way, we provide a first step for deriving a comprehensive list of relevant typical situations for testing the safe behavior of UAVs.

The **contribution of this paper** is an automated approach for exploring a maximal number of relevant obstacles for UAVs. With our proposed approach, we can effectively limit the number of typical situations in which we need to test the safe behavior of UAVs. Our work, thus, *provides the basis* for a complete collection of relevant situations for testing UAVs. We further present experimental results to show the applicability of the proposed approach for two different optimization algorithms and various collected parameter values.

We present an overview of the process for testing UAVs with scenario-based testing in Sect. 2. Section 3 provides an automated approach for exploring the maximal number of relevant obstacles, whereas Sect. 4 presents experimental results. Section 5 discusses related work before Sect. 6 concludes.

2   Scenario-Based Testing of UAVs

Following the terminology in [18], we differentiate between logical and concrete scenarios for scenario-based testing. Logical scenarios represent typical situations the UAV will encounter in the real world and incorporate n parameters $P = \{p_1, p_2, \ldots, p_n\}$, such as characteristics of the obstacles or the wind conditions in the logical scenarios. By assigning specific values to these parameters P, we can create various concrete scenarios that resemble possible real-world situations for the given logical scenario and constitute test cases for the SUT.

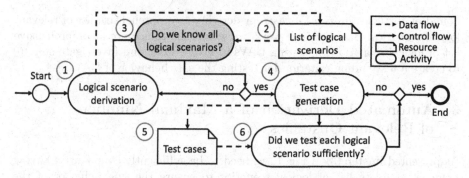

Fig. 1. Overview of the process for testing the safe behavior of UAVs with scenario-based testing. This work provides a basis for the highlighted activity.

In Fig. 1, we present an outline for testing the safe behavior of UAVs with scenario-based testing. First, we need to derive logical scenarios ① in which we aim to test the UAV's behavior. We can acquire these logical scenarios by (a) clustering real-flight data [12] we collected beforehand or by (b) deriving them from mental models of challenging situations presented by experts, literature, or specifications. As a result of this first step, we gain a list of logical scenarios ②. However, we can only ensure a safe behavior of a UAV when we test its behavior in all relevant situations that it might encounter. Thus, in the next step, we need to investigate whether we know all logical scenarios ③ and, therefore, all relevant situations to test the UAV's behavior. If we have enough confidence in knowing all relevant logical scenarios for our aspired safety argumentation, we can generate test cases for these scenarios in the next step. Note that this is an active research area and that we might only be able to give such confidence to a certain degree. Otherwise, we have to go back to step ① and derive more logical scenarios until we are sufficiently confident that we have gathered a suitable list of logical scenarios for the SUT. Since it is infeasible to test all concrete scenarios of each logical scenario, we need to select "good" test cases that represent challenging situations for the UAV for each logical scenario in the test case generation step ④. [19] argues that "good" test cases are those test cases that are able to reveal *potential* faults in the SUT. In these "good" test cases, a correct UAV behaves safely, whereas a faulty one behaves unsafely. As a result of step ④, we gain "good" test cases ⑤ that represent challenging situations for our SUT with the help of optimization algorithms, as presented in [21]. Finally, we need to ensure that we tested the SUT for each logical scenario sufficiently ⑥ to expect a safe behavior of the UAV in the concrete scenarios of each logical scenario. Evaluating the quality of the generated test cases by different optimization algorithms will be an essential part of this step. If we are not sufficiently sure that we tested each logical scenario adequately, we need to create additional test cases ④ before stopping the testing process.

In this work, we focus on step ③ by investigating the maximal number of relevant obstacles to incorporate in logical scenarios for UAVs. Finding this upper bound of obstacles *provides a basis* for deriving a comprehensive list of relevant logical scenarios. Based on this work, we would like to acquire a comprehensive list of logical scenarios for testing UAVs in future work and investigate step ⑥ to create a test ending criterion for testing the safe behavior of UAVs.

3   Automated Derivation of a Maximal Number of Relevant Obstacles

As presented in step ③ in Fig. 1, we need to be sufficiently confident in having found a complete list of logical scenarios to ensure the safe behavior of the tested UAV in all relevant situations. Thus, we need to provide lower and upper bounds for the parameters that characterize logical scenarios for UAVs, such as the number of included obstacles, the minimum and maximum wind force, or the number of wind directions to consider. If we lack expert knowledge about these bounds, we need to investigate the influence of different bounds on the UAV's behavior experimentally. In this work, we present an automated approach for finding such bounds with the example of investigating an upper bound for the number of obstacles to consider in logical scenarios for UAVs. As we limit the number of logical scenarios to test, this approach provides a first step toward acquiring a comprehensive and finite list of logical scenarios.

3.1   Relevant Obstacles for the UAV

When limiting the number of obstacles in a logical scenario, we can discard those obstacles that do not impact the behavior and trajectory planning of the UAV, e.g., ones located 100 m away. Relevant obstacles can influence the UAV's behavior and reside in its surrounding area. During the UAV's flight, the relevance of obstacles changes dynamically and depends, among others, on the UAV's type, size, and velocity. While the relevance of specific obstacles changes over time, we can derive a maximal number of relevant ones at each timestamp. In this work, we aim to obtain, for a given SUT, an upper bound for this number of relevant obstacles. In our proposed approach, we investigate the impact of a number of relevant obstacles N on the UAV's behavior *independent of a given logical scenario*. This independence is possible since we aim to explore how many obstacles have an effect on the UAV's behavior and do not aim to test the safe behavior of the UAV directly. After deriving a maximal number M of relevant obstacles that generally affect the UAV's behavior, we can create various logical scenarios for the tested system in the next step. In these logical scenarios, we incorporate 0 to M obstacles, various missions, and different environmental effects, such as weather effects or terrains, to thoroughly investigate the UAV's safe behavior. As an advantage of our proposed approach, we limit the number of relevant logical scenarios by excluding those with more than M obstacles.

3.2   Parameter Values Describing the UAV's Behavior

For investigating the UAV's behavior in a black-box manner, we focus on externally observable system states. The number of obstacles in the surrounding area of the UAV influences the range of these observable values. Additional obstacles are relevant for the UAV if they introduce new challenging situations. The pitch, roll, and yaw values of the UAV, which represent its orientation, are an example of a precise external description of the UAV's state. The rationale for using these values for our proposed approach is the fault hypothesis that we can represent challenging situations for the UAV by extreme orientation values. As an example, the following two ideas contribute to such a fault hypothesis: (a) extreme orientation values lead to temporarily unstable positions of the UAV, which might lead to control loss and a crash of the UAV; (b) when avoiding obstacles, more extreme orientations of the UAV are needed. Following this fault hypothesis, we investigate whether additional obstacles force the UAV into a new extreme orientation that it does not encounter for fewer obstacles. In case the UAV should perform maneuvers with extreme orientations as part of its mission, the orientation values of the UAV might not represent a suitable indicator for challenging situations. In this case, other parameter values such as the linear or angular velocity of the UAV might be more convenient. However, the proposed methodology is independent of the used parameter values. We show this in our experiments in Sect. 4 by investigating the performance of our proposed approach for orientation and linear velocity values of the UAV. In the following, we explain our proposed approach by using orientation values as exemplary parameter values.

3.3   Process Overview of the Automated Derivation of a Maximal Number of Relevant Obstacles

In general, our proposed methodology works as follows: We investigate the effect of different UAV starting positions and obstacle positions on the UAV's behavior by collecting the UAV's orientation values for each number of obstacles N. We further use an optimization algorithm to find challenging situations in which we can observe new extreme orientations of the UAV. A more detailed overview of this approach is provided in Fig. 2 and described subsequently. Note that this approach depicts one step towards deriving a complete list of logical scenarios, which presents step ③ in Fig. 1, and does *not* represent an approach for generating "good" test cases for testing the safe behavior of UAVs directly which depicts step ④ in Fig. 1.

As the first step in our approach, the optimization algorithm generates a population of candidates Ⓐ. These candidates Ⓑ represent concrete scenarios with specific parameter values from the search space, which contains all possible parameter values of a logical scenario. An example for a concrete scenario is the following: the UAV has the mission to fly to a target point starting at position $(x = -3.0, y = 1.3, z = 0.0)$ and avoiding obstacles at positions $(x = 5.0, y = -3.4, z = 1.0)$ and $(x = 7.1, y = 2.5, z = 1.2)$. We describe an exemplary

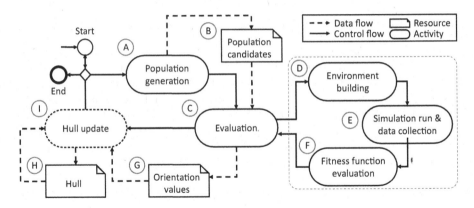

Fig. 2. Overview of the automated approach for exploring a maximal number of relevant obstacles for the system under test.

search space for our approach in the subsequent subsection. Next, the optimization algorithm evaluates the generated candidates. In this evaluation step Ⓒ, we build the simulation world Ⓓ according to the parameter values of each candidate and place the UAV and the obstacles at their corresponding positions. Then, the UAV receives and starts its mission, e.g., to fly to the destination point. Throughout the simulation, we collect the UAV's orientation representing its pitch, roll, and yaw angles Ⓔ. As mentioned earlier, we can also record other parameter values such as the UAV's velocity in this step. After the simulation has finished, the optimization algorithm needs to evaluate the quality of each candidate Ⓕ. This quality depends on the goal of the optimization and is described by the fitness function. We present potential fitness functions for our approach in the subsequent subsection. As a result of the evaluation step Ⓒ, we gain the detected orientation values Ⓖ of all candidates of this population. We store the discovered pitch, roll, and yaw values of all populations in a convex hull Ⓗ. After evaluating a population Ⓒ, we update this hull with the orientation values found in the current population Ⓘ. Finally, the algorithm checks whether the termination criterion is met after the current population. If this is the case, the process stops for the currently regarded number of obstacles N. Otherwise, the algorithm generates a new population Ⓐ and proceeds further.

We execute the complete process depicted in Fig. 2 for each number of obstacles N to detect a convergence of the results. When investigating the UAV's behavior for an additional obstacle $N + 1$, we should observe new extreme orientation values compared with those collected for N obstacles. However, we will detect fewer and fewer new orientations for an increasing number of obstacles N. If we discover no new orientations for $N+1$ obstacles, the additional obstacle does not influence the UAV's behavior.

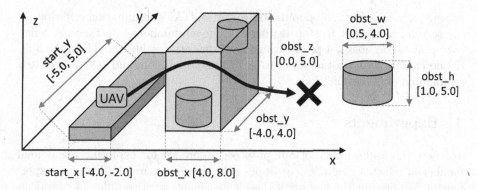

Fig. 3. Visualization of an exemplary search space for our approach. The UAV starts in the left orange area, flies through the middle blue area that includes the obstacles, and lands at the target point marked with an X. (Color figure online)

3.4 Search Space and Fitness Function

When we explore the search space of all possible candidates for our proposed approach, we need to consider the UAV and the obstacles. Figure 3 outlines an exemplary search space for our approach. In the depicted scenario, the UAV has the mission to fly to the destination point marked with an X. For each candidate, the optimization algorithm can choose a starting position of the UAV in the orange area on the left. Additionally, we enable the algorithm to adapt the x-, y-, and z-position of the static obstacles as well as their width and height for each candidate. Note that this search space describes only static obstacles of a specific form for simplicity of presentation. We can easily extend the search space for dynamic obstacles by including their velocity and trajectory points. To enable the optimization algorithm to produce adequate candidates, we need to set the fitness function f accordingly. In this work, we aim to discover whether additional obstacles introduce new challenging situations to the tested UAV. Thus, we search for concrete scenarios that provide new extreme parameter values that represent challenging situations for the SUT. These new extreme parameter values increase the volume of the convex hull storing all parameter values. Thus, we search for concrete scenarios that produce new extreme parameter values and compare the volume v of the existing hull h with the volume v of the hull extended with these new parameter values h_{new}:

$$f = v(h_{new}) - v(h)$$

In our search, we aim to maximize the fitness values of the produced candidates to find new extreme orientation values. We can apply this fitness function for all kinds of collected parameter values, e.g., finding extreme orientation values or extreme velocity values. Note that this is not the only possible fitness function. Other alternatives might be to maximize the average distance of the detected new parameter values to the hull or to maximize the distance of the discovered parameter values from one population to the hull. As a termination criterion for the search, we suggest to stop testing for a given number of obstacles N when (a) a population does not produce any new orientation values outside of the hull, (b) no crashes with obstacles occurred in this population, and (c) we executed a minimum of 500 evaluations.

4 Experiments

To show the applicability of our proposed approach for exploring a maximal number of relevant obstacles, we apply it to an open-source UAV in our experiments. We present the results of these experiments for two different optimization algorithms and when considering orientation or linear velocity values. As optimization algorithms, we compare the Multiobjective Evolutionary Algorithm Based on Decomposition (MOEA/D) [25] and the Non-dominated Sorting Genetic Algorithm II (NSGAII) [10]. We chose NSGAII since it generally provides decent results, as presented in [1,2], and effectively generates test cases for testing the safe behavior of UAVs in the current literature [21,26]. Since our optimization problem is dynamic, we evaluate MOEA/D as an alternative since it achieves the best optimization results when considering constraint dynamic problems according to the benchmark of [11].

4.1 Experimental Setup and Implementation

Since we aim to investigate the effect of two different optimization algorithms, we use the jMetalPy framework [5], which provides implementations for both algorithms. For MOEA/D, we use Tschebycheff as the aggregation function, while we apply SBX Crossover and Binary Tournament Selection for NSGAII. We set the population size for these two algorithms to 100 as this number showed the best performance in pre-experiments, where we investigated population sizes of 25, 50, and 100. In our experiments, we use the simulation environment Gazebo [16] for simulating the behavior of the obstacle avoidance extension of the PX4 drone [17]. In the simulations, this UAV flies autonomously to the specified target point while avoiding the obstacles on its path. We generate concrete scenarios for the logical scenario and search space depicted in Fig. 3 in our experiments. Note that we use only static obstacles for simplicity of presentation. Nonetheless, we can also apply our approach to dynamic obstacles by extending the search space with their velocity and trajectory points. Further, we use the termination criterion specified in Sect. 3.4, which states that we stop when we (a) detect no new parameter values outside the hull in the current population, (b) we discover no crashes in this population, and (c) we performed a minimum of 500 evaluations.

In our experiments, we collect the UAV's orientation or linear velocity values from concrete scenarios in which the UAV is in control and does not crash into any obstacle. As the open-source UAV produces a random set of parameter values that do not state anything about the challenge of the provided situation when it is out of control, we discard these situations to enable a clean collection of extreme parameter values. For the same reason, we exclude those concrete scenarios in which the UAV crashes without the present obstacles influencing the crash and loses control of its movements after the collision. Thus, if we can exclude that any of the obstacles had an influence on the crash, we exclude this concrete scenario. If we were testing the safe behavior of UAVs directly, such collisions would be particularly interesting. However, since we instead investigate the relevance of obstacles, we are dependent on not collecting a random set of parameter values caused without environmental impact. Thus, we exclude these cases to ensure a clean acquisition of parameter values. Note that we still catch the impact of the additional obstacle, if existing, as we collect the UAV's orientation in other concrete scenarios with the same amount of obstacles and include the crash information into our termination criterion. In the future, we would like to expand our experiments by investigating the performance of other optimization algorithms, including dynamic obstacles in the UAV's environment, and performing multiple runs per optimization algorithm to gain more robust results.

4.2   Experimental Results

Table 1 depicts the results of our experiments for the two optimization algorithms MOEA/D and NSGAII and when collecting orientation or linear velocity values. For each number of obstacles $N \in \{1, 2, ..., 15\}$, the table depicts the percentage volume increase vi to the previous hull:

$$vi = (v(h_{new}) - v(h))/v(h)$$

Since we build the first hull for $N = 0$ obstacles, we do not provide a volume increase for this N. When investigating the UAV's orientation values, MOEA/D converges after $N = 8$ obstacles with our proposed methodology, whereas NSGAII still produces a small number of new extreme orientation values for higher amounts of obstacles. When considering the linear velocity of the UAV, both algorithms converge for $N = 5$ relevant obstacles.

4.3   Discussion

For deriving a maximal number of relevant obstacles for testing the safe behavior of UAVs, we investigate the performance of the heuristic optimization algorithms MOEA/D and NSGAII in our experiments. While investigating the UAV's *orientation*, NSGAII does not converge to a maximal number of relevant obstacles. On the other hand, our experimental results for MOEA/D provide a maximal number of $M = 8$ relevant obstacles for the SUT. We derive this resulting number of relevant obstacles based on the fault hypothesis that extreme orientations of the UAV represent challenging situations. Note that the correctness of this fault hypothesis is dependent on the SUT. Figure 4 presents the plots of the convex hull that MOEA/D creates and updates when inspecting orientation values for

Table 1. The percentage volume increase vi [%] for different amounts of obstacles N when applying MOEA/D and NSGAII. Further, the table depicts the effect of collecting orientation or linear velocity values for the system under test.

MOEA/D			NSGAII		
N	Orientation vi	Lin. Velocity vi	N	Orientation vi	Lin. Velocity vi
1	15.78	8.32	1	147.11	0.08
2	110.49	0.48	2	0.00	0.00
3	0.00	0.00	3	9.37	0.00
4	0.00	0.00	4	14.96	12.07
5	7.95	0.06	5	1.38	28.15
6	0.01	0.00	6	0.00	0.00
7	4.01	0.00	7	5.00	0.00
8	0.01	0.00	8	0.00	0.00
9	0.00	0.00	9	1.39	0.00
10	0.00	0.00	10	0.00	0.00
11	0.00	0.00	11	0.00	0.00
12	0.00	0.00	12	0.31	0.00
13	0.00	0.00	13	0.00	0.00
14	0.00	0.00	14	0.22	0.00
15	0.00	0.00	15	1.26	0.00

$N \in \{1, 2, ..., 8\}$ obstacles. Note that the obstacles are only implicitly depicted in these plots as they influence the range of the orientation values. The newly discovered extreme orientation values for each N are depicted in pale blue and show the increase in the hull's volume. Further, the plots show in black the hull that our approach created for $N - 1$ obstacles.

When collecting *linear velocity values*, no new extreme orientation values—and thus challenging situations—are discovered for more than $M = 5$ obstacles with both algorithms. These results indicate that only $M = 5$ obstacles are relevant for the tested UAV when assuming that challenging situations are presented by extreme linear velocity values of the UAV. Further, we can discover a difference between the two optimization algorithms. MOEA/D collects most of the new extreme linear velocity values for $N = 1$ obstacles, while NSGAII acquires them mainly for $N \in \{4, 5\}$ obstacles.

In our experiments, both algorithms find challenging situations for the UAV and converge after a small number of obstacles, with the exception of NSGAII for orientation values. These experimental results show the applicability of our proposed approach for deriving a maximal number of obstacles. The results further indicate that MOEA/D is more suited for our approach than NSGAII since it detects new extreme parameter values for fewer obstacles more effectively. This early detection of new extreme parameter values enables MOEA/D to converge

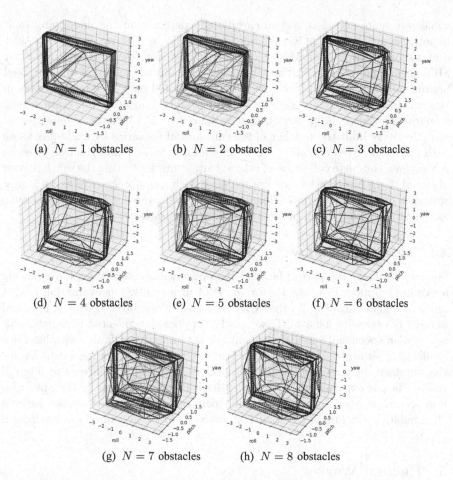

(a) $N = 1$ obstacles   (b) $N = 2$ obstacles   (c) $N = 3$ obstacles

(d) $N = 4$ obstacles   (e) $N = 5$ obstacles   (f) $N = 6$ obstacles

(g) $N = 7$ obstacles   (h) $N = 8$ obstacles

Fig. 4. The convex hulls created by MOEA/D for $N \in \{1, 2, ..., 8\}$ obstacles depicting the detected orientation values. We display the newly discovered extreme orientation values for N obstacles in pale blue and the existing ones for $N - 1$ obstacles in black. (Color figure online)

faster and consistently provide a maximal number of relevant obstacles. These characteristics fit very well for our approach as a fast convergence rate reduces the additional cost that we need to investigate to find an upper bound for the number of relevant obstacles and to limit the number of logical scenarios to test. Further, MOEA/D's reliability to detect an upper bound for the number of relevant obstacles is essential as without such an upper bound we cannot limit the number of logical scenarios. A reason for the better performance of MOEA/D might be that it inherently can handle dynamic optimization problems better than NSGAII.

In addition, we provide experimental results for different parameter values to guide the search for challenging situations. Whether orientation or linear velocity values are more suited is system-specific and depends on the underlying fault hypothesis for the SUT. Overall, the results indicate that we need to consider a maximum of $M = 5$ or $M = 8$ relevant obstacles in logical scenarios for our SUT depending on the used fault hypothesis. As an advantage of our proposed approach, the described process needs to be executed only once for each system version. In the next step, we can use the resulting insights to create logical scenarios for this system version that include 0 to M obstacles. Therefore, we can effectively limit the number of relevant logical scenarios by excluding those with more than $M = 5$ or $M = 8$ obstacles for our SUT. This reduction *provides a basis* for a complete collection of relevant situations for testing the safe behavior of our SUT. In future work, we aim to derive such a comprehensive list of logical scenarios by investigating additional relevant parameters for testing UAVs, such as the terrain, wind force, or fogginess of the environment.

4.4 Threats to Validity

Since we evaluate the performance of the optimization algorithms for exploring a maximal number of obstacles for the PX4 drone only, our evaluation results might not generalize to all other UAV systems. When investigating a maximal number of obstacles for a SUT, we need to choose the collected parameter values system-specifically and dependent on the underlying fault hypothesis for challenging situations for this SUT. Further, we focus on static obstacles for the simplicity of presentation in this work. We decrease the threats to internal validity in our experiments by using existing implementations of the optimization algorithms and by evaluating an open-source UAV. Further, we execute all simulations in isolated Docker containers to lower unwanted environmental effects.

5   Related Work

Several papers investigate the research area of deriving a (complete) list of logical scenarios in the context of autonomous driving. The authors of [15,23] further introduce ontologies for particular use cases for UAVs. To the best of our knowledge, no work about a complete list of logical scenarios for testing the safe behavior of UAVs exists yet. The authors of [3,4,9,15,23] derive logical scenarios based on existing ontologies. [3] concentrates on the positional and temporal descriptions of the elements of logical scenarios, whereas [4] focuses on describing the various layers of a logical scenario for autonomous cars. The authors of [9] specify that logical scenarios should include the environment, activities, events, and triggers. All mentioned ontologies concentrate on the structure of existing knowledge about logical scenarios for autonomous cars but do not provide completeness measures for their ontologies. Thus, the problem of deriving a complete list of logical scenarios remains an open issue for these approaches. In the context of UAVs, [15] specifies an ontology for UAV flight control and management systems, and [23] provides an ontology for modeling accessible aircraft resources for reconnaissance missions. Since both ontologies depict logical scenarios for specific use cases for UAVs, we can use them as a basis for deriving a complete list of UAVs. However, due to their limitation to one use case, they cannot provide such a list by themselves. As an alternative, the authors of [8,14,24] propose statistical approaches to explore the completeness and diversity of collected data. In [8], the authors investigate the completeness of the collected data by analyzing the density of several parameters. The authors of [14] use an instance of the Coupon Collector's Problem to indicate whether more real-world data needs to be collected, whereas [24] provides a statistical assessment of the diversity of gathered data. These statistical approaches focus on the data from which we can derive logical scenarios. Even though such data exists in large amounts for autonomous cars, it lacks for UAVs. Thus, we focus on the logical scenarios themselves instead of the data from which we can derive them. As a first step towards providing a complete list of logical scenarios for testing the safe behavior of UAVs, we explore a maximal number of relevant obstacles in this work. To the best of our knowledge, no related work about investigating such a maximal number for testing UAVs exists yet.

6 Conclusion

We outlined the challenge of deriving a complete list of logical scenarios for testing the safe behavior of UAVs. This work presents a solution to one part of this challenge by exploring the maximal number of obstacles that we need to consider in these logical scenarios for a given SUT. With our proposed approach, we investigate the effect of increasing numbers of obstacles on the UAV's behavior and search for challenging situations for the UAV. In our experiments, we compare the performance of the optimization algorithms MOEA/D and NSGAII and the effect of considering orientation or linear velocity values of the UAV. The experimental results show the applicability of the proposed approach and indicate that MOEA/D is more suited. Whether we should consider orientation or linear velocity values is system-specific and depends on the underlying fault hypothesis for challenging situations for the SUT. Finally, the experiments show that a maximal number of $M = 5$ or $M = 8$ obstacles is relevant for the SUT, depending on the applied fault hypothesis. Next, we can create logical scenarios for our SUT that include 0 to M obstacles. Thus, we effectively limit the number of logical scenarios to test by excluding those with more than M obstacles. Note that we focus on static obstacles in our experiments for simplicity of presentation. However, we can also apply our approach to dynamic obstacles by including their velocities and trajectory points in the search space. As an advantage, our proposed methodology needs to be executed only once for each system version. In the future, we aim to expand our experiments to include dynamic obstacles and investigate the performance of other optimization algorithms such as Particle Swarm Optimization or Bayesian Optimization. Further, we plan to derive a complete list of logical scenarios based on the results of this work by exploring additional relevant parameters for testing UAVs, such as the terrain, wind force, or fogginess of the UAV's environment.

References

1. Ali, S., Briand, L.C., Hemmati, H., Panesar-Walawege, R.K.: A systematic review of the application and empirical investigation of search-based test case generation. IEEE Trans. Software Eng. **36**(6), 742–762 (2009)
2. Arrieta, A., et al.: Search-based test case generation for cyber-physical systems. In: 2017 IEEE Congress on Evolutionary Computation, pp. 688–697. IEEE (2017)
3. Bach, J., Otten, S., Sax, E.: Model based scenario specification for development and test of automated driving functions. In: 2016 IEEE Intelligent Vehicles Symposium, pp. 1149–1155. IEEE (2016)
4. Bagschik, G., Menzel, T., Maurer, M.: Ontology based scene creation for the development of automated vehicles. In: 2018 IEEE Intelligent Vehicles Symposium, pp. 1813–1820. IEEE (2018)
5. Benitez-Hidalgo, A., et al.: jMetalPy: a python framework for multi-objective optimization with metaheuristics. Swarm Evol. Comput. **51**, 100598 (2019)
6. Cem Kaner, J.: An introduction to scenario testing. Florida Institute of Technology, Melbourne, pp. 1–13 (2013)
7. De Gelder, E., Paardekooper, J.P.: Assessment of automated driving systems using real-life scenarios. In: 2017 IEEE Intelligent Vehicles Symposium, pp. 589–594. IEEE (2017)
8. De Gelder, E., Paardekooper, J.P., Op den Camp, O., De Schutter, B.: Safety assessment of automated vehicles: how to determine whether we have collected enough field data? Traffic Inj. Prev. **20**, S162–S170 (2019)
9. De Gelder, E., et al.: Ontology for scenarios for the assessment of automated vehicles. arXiv preprint arXiv:2001.11507 (2020)
10. Deb, K., Pratap, A., Agarwal, S., Meyarivan, T.: A fast and elitist multiobjective genetic algorithm: NSGA-II. IEEE Trans. Evol. Comput. **6**(2), 182–197 (2002)
11. Grudniewski, P., Sobey, A.: Benchmarking the performance of genetic algorithms on constrained dynamic problems. Nat. Comput. 1–17 (2020). https://doi.org/10.1007/s11047-020-09799-y
12. Hauer, F., Gerostathopoulos, I., Schmidt, T., Pretschner, A.: Clustering traffic scenarios using mental models as little as possible. In: 2020 IEEE Intelligent Vehicles Symposium, pp. 1007–1012. IEEE (2020)
13. Hauer, F., Pretschner, A., Holzmüller, B.: Fitness functions for testing automated and autonomous driving systems. In: Romanovsky, A., Troubitsyna, E., Bitsch, F. (eds.) SAFECOMP 2019. LNCS, vol. 11698, pp. 69–84. Springer, Cham (2019). https://doi.org/10.1007/978-3-030-26601-1_5
14. Hauer, F., Schmidt, T., Holzmüller, B., Pretschner, A.: Did we test all scenarios for automated and autonomous driving systems? In: 2019 IEEE Intelligent Transportation Systems Conference, pp. 2950–2955. IEEE (2019)
15. Hu, X., Liu, J.: Ontology construction and evaluation of UAV FCMS software requirement elicitation considering geographic environment factors. IEEE Access **8**, 106165–106182 (2020)
16. Koenig, N., Howard, A.: Design and use paradigms for gazebo, an open-source multi-robot simulator. In: International Conference on Intelligent Robots and Systems, vol. 3, pp. 2149–2154. IEEE (2004)
17. Meier, L., Honegger, D., Pollefeys, M.: PX4: a node-based multithreaded open source robotics framework for deeply embedded platforms. In: 2015 IEEE International Conference on Robotics and Automation, pp. 6235–6240. IEEE (2015)

18. Menzel, T., Bagschik, G., Maurer, M.: Scenarios for development, test and validation of automated vehicles. In: 2018 IEEE Intelligent Vehicles Symposium, pp. 1821–1827. IEEE (2018)

19. Pretschner, A.: Defect-based testing. Dependable Softw. Syst. Eng. **84** (2015)

20. Rosen, J.W.: Zipline's ambitious medical drone delivery in Africa. MIT Technology Review, 8 June 2017 (2017)

21. Schmidt, T., Hauer, F., Pretschner, A.: Understanding safety for unmanned aerial vehicles in urban environments. In: 2021 IEEE Intelligent Vehicles Symposium, pp. 638–643. IEEE (2021)

22. Singireddy, S.R.R., Daim, T.U.: Technology roadmap: drone delivery – amazon prime air. In: Daim, T.U., Chan, L., Estep, J. (eds.) Infrastructure and Technology Management. ITKM, pp. 387–412. Springer, Cham (2018). https://doi.org/10.1007/978-3-319-68987-6_13

23. Smirnov, D., Stutz, P.: Use case driven approach for ontology-based modeling of reconnaissance resources on-board UAVs using OWL. In: 2017 IEEE Aerospace Conference, pp. 1–17. IEEE (2017)

24. Wang, W., Liu, C., Zhao, D.: How much data are enough? A statistical approach with case study on longitudinal driving behavior. IEEE Trans. Intell. Veh. **2**(2), 85–98 (2017)

25. Zhang, Q., Li, H.: MOEA/D: a multiobjective evolutionary algorithm based on decomposition. IEEE Trans. Evol. Comput. **11**(6), 712–731 (2007)

26. Zou, X., Alexander, R., McDermid, J.: Testing method for multi-UAV conflict resolution using agent-based simulation and multi-objective search. J. Aerosp. Inf. Syst. **13**(5), 191–203 (2016)

Data-Driven Assessment of Parameterized Scenarios for Autonomous Vehicles

Nicola Kolb[1]([✉]), Florian Hauer[1], Mojdeh Golagha[2], and Alexander Pretschner[1]

[1] Technical University of Munich, Arcisstraße 21, 80333 Munich, Germany
{nicola.kolb,florian.hauer,alexander.pretschner}@tum.de
[2] fortiss, Guerickestraße 25, 80805 Munich, Germany
golagha@fortiss.org

Abstract. Highly automated and autonomous driving systems are usually tested for their safe behavior using a so-called scenario-based testing approach. A common practice is to let experts create parameterized scenarios by selecting and varying parameters of a given scenario type, e.g., the initial speed of the participating vehicles. By assigning concrete values to the selected parameters, scenario instances are generated, which may be used as test scenarios for the driving system under test (SUT). For the generation of test cases, parameterized scenarios typically serve as input. Most works assume parameterized scenarios to be given without evaluating their quality. However, a parameterized scenario may be insufficient, leading to inadequately and incomplete generated test cases, unreliable test results, and even incorrect conclusions about the safety of the SUT. As contribution of this work, we present a quality criterion and a novel data-driven assurance approach to assess parameterized scenarios. We consider the quality of a parameterized scenario to be *acceptable* if it contains at least all scenario instances collected in real traffic for the studied scenario type. For this containment check, search-based techniques are used. We show experiments for a parameterized lane change scenario using 6736 lane change recordings from real traffic for the assessment. The experiment results show that in addition to shortcomings of a parameterized scenario, those of the simulation setup can be revealed.

Keywords: Parameterized scenario validation · Autonomous driving · Multi-objective search

1 Introduction

Since testing safety-critical highly automated and autonomous driving systems solely by real test drives is not feasible [18,32], they are usually tested in simulation using *scenario-based testing*. Experts make use of so-called *scenario types* [25], which textually describe recurring traffic situations, e.g.: *A vehicle (SUT) follows another vehicle on the right lane of a two-lane highway until it performs a lane change onto the left lane into the gap between two more vehicles.* There are many different instances of such scenario types such as lane changes at various

© The Author(s), under exclusive license to Springer Nature Switzerland AG 2022
M. Trapp et al. (Eds.): SAFECOMP 2022, LNCS 13414, pp. 350–364, 2022.
https://doi.org/10.1007/978-3-031-14835-4_23

velocities and gap sizes. This is why it is common practice in industry and existing works (see [28] for a survey) to operationalize scenario types to *parameterized scenarios* [25]. The idea is to describe parts of the scenario (e.g. starting positions) by parameters. Assigning concrete values to each such parameter yields a *scenario instance*. The goal of scenario-based testing is to identify instances that stress the SUT (e.g. by causing it to nearly crash) and to evaluate for these instances the behavior of the SUT w.r.t. safety. Besides others, one common approach is to apply search-based test case generation. The parameterized scenario with its parameter domains serves as *search space* for search-based test case generation, where each element in the search space is a potential test scenario, i.e. a test case. By search, "good" test scenarios can be found, where a "good" scenario is one in which a faulty system violates safety [15,21]. Demonstrating that the system works as expected in challenging scenario instances increases confidence in the system [20].

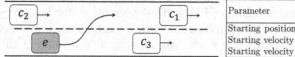

Parameter	Lower Bound	Upper Bound
Starting positions: $s_{c_i}(t_0)$ [m]	0	500
Starting velocity of c_i: $v_i(t_0)$ [km/h]	60	180
Starting velocity of e: $v_e(t_0)$ [km/h]	60	180

Fig. 1. Parameterized scenario with parameters incl. domains (prev. shown in [16])

An exemplifying parameterized scenario for the scenario type described above can be seen in Fig. 1. Several aspects of this scenario are parameterized, namely the starting positions and starting velocities of the vehicles $c_1 - c_3$ as well as the starting velocity of the ego vehicle e (SUT).

Creating such parameterized scenarios is currently a mostly manual process, conducted by experts based on their experience and mental models. Some works even suggest trial and error [13]. The **problem** is that usually such parameterized scenarios are not adequately evaluated. The parameters, the parameter domains, or the design of the non-parameterized part of the parameterized scenario may be inadequate. For instance, the parameter domains may be too narrow, such that during test case generation no good test cases are found for a particular scenario type. This may lead to the dangerous misconception that the SUT is safe, since no test cases could be found where safety is violated. However, with wider parameter domains, there would have been such test cases with a safety violation. As the parameterized scenario is a crucial input for test case generation techniques, its quality assessment is a necessary basis to allow valid interpretations on the SUT's safe behavior. Most works in the domain of testing automated and autonomous driving systems consider parameterized scenarios as given without investigating their quality. To the best of our knowledge, there is no quality criterion nor approach to measure if a given parameterized scenario is "acceptable" or not.

The **contribution** of this paper is twofold: (1) we define a quality criterion for parameterized scenarios in the domain of autonomous driving. To do so, we make use of recorded scenario instances that have been collected in real traffic: *A parameterized scenario is acceptable if it contains all recorded scenario instances for the respective scenario type.* (2) We also propose an automated, data-driven approach for validating such parameterized scenarios. Our approach receives as input the parameterized scenario as well as real traffic data of the respective scenario type. The goal is to check whether the parameterized scenario contains the recorded scenario instances of real traffic. Using search-based techniques, the approach aims to find a suitable scenario instance in the huge search space spanned by the parameterized scenario that reflects a recorded scenario instance respectively. If the parameterized scenario does not contain all recorded scenario instances, it either needs to be revised or an argumentation is necessary for each non-contained recorded scenario instance addressing why it may be ignored. If it contains all instances from real traffic, the parameterized scenario is deemed "acceptable". Note that this assessment is relative to data: if the data is bad (e.g. not comprehensive or diverse enough), the assessment will not yield meaningful results as usual with all data-driven approaches. We evaluate our approach using the parameterized lane change scenario of Fig. 1, 6736 recorded traffic instances of a lane change, and around 10^6 simulation runs during search. Also note that test case generation is **not** part of this work. We use search to identify if the parameterized scenario contains scenario instances recorded in real traffic, not to generate test cases.

2   Scenario-Based Testing

Scenario-based testing aims at increasing the confidence that the SUT is working safely in different traffic situations. Figure 2 provides an overview of the related steps of scenario-based testing. Initially, experts derive ① scenario types ② [25]. These are structured descriptions of recurring traffic scenarios. The idea is to partition [10,19] the operational design domain of an automated or autonomous driving system into such scenario types. For this derivation, experts use both potentially available specifications and requirements ③ as well as their mental model ④ of the traffic and the SUT. Literature suggests several ways to support experts with the derivation of scenario types, e.g. by using ontologies [4,12] as well as data-driven approaches, e.g. [14,31,34].

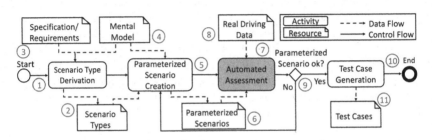

Fig. 2. Abstract depiction of the scenario-based testing process (prev. shown in [16])

Once the scenario type derivation is complete [16], experts create ⑤ parameterized scenarios ⑥ for the scenario types [24], again using their mental model and experience. Similar to existing works [2,15,25,26], we define a parameterized scenario as (F, P, D). We call F the non-parameterized part of the scenario. P describes the scenario elements that are parameterized by the parameters $p_i \in P, i = 1...n = |P|$ with corresponding domains $d_i \in D$. The domains span a huge space $A = d_1 \times d_2 \times ... \times d_{n-1} \times d_n \subseteq \mathbb{R}^n$ of scenario instances $a \in A$ [25].

This work aims at the automated assessment ⑦ of the quality of the derived parameterized scenarios (see Sect. 3) using real traffic data ⑧. Based on the assessment result ⑨, the test case generation follows ⑩ or insufficient parameterized scenarios get reworked similarly to the creation before. Literature provides a vast number of approaches that use parameterized scenarios for test case generation yielding "good" test cases ⑪ (see [28]).

3 Parameterized Scenario Assessment

3.1 Extracting Relevant Information from Traffic Data

Recorded traffic data usually contains vehicle trajectories (incl. positions, velocities, and accelerations) in form of timeseries. The goal is to filter these timeseries for scenario instances of the scenario type for which the parameterized scenario has been created and is being assessed for "acceptability". For filtering, we follow a rule-based approach, i.e. for each vehicle that appears in the data, its trajectory is analyzed for the respective scenario type, for instance "if the position of the vehicle indicates that the vehicle crosses the lane markings, a lane change is detected". Similar rules can be applied to ensure other aspects of the scenario type. Once the respective instances of the scenario type are identified within the data, characteristic values are extracted from the timeseries of these instances as commonly done by existing works (see e.g. [11]). Note that the kind of characteristic values heavily depends on the scenario type. We follow this strategy in the presented approach, i.e. for our example scenario type, the size of the gap as well as the velocities of the ego vehicle and of the front vehicle of the gap are extracted as characteristic values. Assuming that m characteristic values are chosen, the result of the data filtering process will be an m-dimensional point cloud B. Each point $b \in B$ represents one recorded scenario instance. Let b_i with i from 1 to m denote the characteristic values for the selected scenario instance b. Evidently, this resulting point cloud B is only meaningful if there is sufficient and representative data. In [11], it is discussed how much traffic data is needed to achieve a good representation for a scenario type.

3.2 Containment of a Single Recorded Scenario Instance

The aim is to assess if a selected concrete scenario instance $a \in A$, characterized by its concrete parameter values, reflects a recorded scenario instance b. The concrete parameter values of a selected a generally encode information about the structure of the scenario, but not about the actual behavior of the scenario participants. The latter only becomes apparent during the simulation of a and is encoded by the selected characteristic values, allowing a comparison of scenario instances in this regard. Simulating a yields a $\tilde{b}$. Simulation is done by putting the driving system in the scenario instance and recording the trajectory of all scenario participants during the simulation. Given these trajectories, the same characteristic values can be extracted as done for the traffic-recorded scenario instances. A parameterized scenario instance a *recreates* a recorded scenario instance b, if $\left| b_i - \tilde{b}_i \right| < \epsilon$ for some small predefined ϵ (depending on the use case considered), meaning that the data produced by simulating a produced characteristic values in $\tilde{b}$ very similar to b. If there is such a scenario instance a in the parameterized scenario search space A, we say that the parameterized scenario contains b. Further, if there is such an $a \in A$ for every recorded scenario instance $b \in B$, we deem the parameterized scenario to be "acceptable". This raises the question: *how do we find in the parameter space of the parameterized scenario a scenario instance* $\boldsymbol{a}$ *that recreates the recorded scenario instance* $\boldsymbol{b}$ *given there exists one?*

We suggest multi-objective search in the following way: Let the search-based technique select a somewhat arbitrary a, simulate it, and compute the difference $\left| b_i - \tilde{b}_i \right|$. If it is smaller than ϵ for all b_i, the search is done: a recreates b. Otherwise, the search-based technique will try another a'. Continue until a suitable a'' is found or the budget of available trials is spent. Search-based techniques require a fitness function, which we suggest to create as follows: For each of the m dimensions of b, one fitness value is computed by comparing the desired value b_i of a $b \in B$ with the observed value $\tilde{b}_i$ produced by an instance $a \in A$ during simulation. The final fitness function F looks as follows: $F = [f_1 \ \dots \ f_m]$ with

$$f_i = \begin{cases} \left| b_i - \tilde{b}_i \right|, & \left| b_i - \tilde{b}_i \right| > \epsilon \\ 0, & \text{otherwise} \end{cases}$$

Note: If some $\tilde{b}_i$ cannot be observed in a simulated scenario instance a, e.g. the velocity of the ego vehicle during a lane change cannot be observed if there is no lane change, the respective f_i evaluates to ∞ (f_i is to be minimized). Besides, we chose *difference per characteristic value* over an aggregated distance, e.g. euclidean distance, since it provides the search with more detailed information.

3.3   Containment of Many Recorded Scenario Instances

The intuitive approach to assess the containment of *all* recorded scenario instances consists in applying the presented method in Sect. 3.2 to all these instances. The result of the assessment will tell which recorded scenario instances are and which are not contained in the parameterized scenario. However, B may contain thousands of instances [11]. For every one, a search has to be executed, each needing many computationally expensive simulation executions. Overall, this is infeasible and not necessary, since many scenario instances b may be very similar to each other, e.g. lane changes at nearly the same velocities.

Thus, we aim at a reduction in the number of searches. This needs to be done with great care in order not to lose interpretability and reliability of the overall assessment of the parameterized scenario. Simply choosing an arbitrary low amount of random $b \in B$ and assessing their containment will not yield an interpretable nor a reliable result. Instead, we suggest a structured selection that considers recorded scenario instances at the extremes and representative recorded scenario instances in between the extremes.

The recorded scenario instances $b \in B$ describe a point cloud in a m-dimensional space. The points that lay on the outside of the point cloud are the extreme recorded scenario instances, e.g. very low or high velocities during a lane change. They can be identified by computing the multi-dimensional convex hull of the point cloud using *QuickHull* [5]. To provide reliable information about all the non-extreme points inside the convex hull, representatives need to be selected. For this, the inner points are clustered using classic *k-means* and a knee/elbow detector [30] to set the number of clusters. The characteristic values b_i are used as features for the clustering. From each cluster, the recorded scenario instance that is nearest to the cluster center is selected as representative. Thus, the overall number of searches is reduced to the number of recorded scenario instances on the convex hull plus the number of clusters.

4 Experiments

4.1 Parameterized Scenario

We apply the presented approach to the parameterized scenario described in Fig. 1: The driving system is tested in a scenario where the ego vehicle e drives on the right lane of a two lane highway. After approaching another vehicle c_3, e changes to the left lane in the gap between the vehicles c_1 and c_2. The **parameterized scenario** consists of three parts: (1) the non-parameterized part, (2) the seven parameters, (3) their domains (see Fig. 1), which span a seven-dimensional space of test cases. The vehicles start with a parameterized velocity at a parameterized longitudinal position. The ego vehicle's starting position is always 0. Note: the parameterized scenario to be assessed is assumed to have been defined by experts.

4.2 Traffic Data

To determine the point cloud B, the highD dataset [22] is used for our experiments. It contains German highway traffic data, which has been recorded from a bird's-eye perspective with a drone-mounted camera. The following characteristic values m are filtered from the recorded data (see Fig. 3), inspired by [11,29]: One might be interested in the velocities of the ego vehicle $v_e(t_{lc})$ and of the front vehicle of the gap $v_{c_1}(t_{lc})$ at the moment t_{lc} when e is changing lanes, i.e.

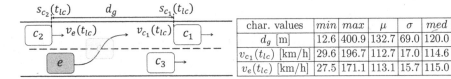

Fig. 3. Example scenario with three characteristic values (d_g, $v_e(t_{lc})$, $v_{c_1}(t_{lc})$) (left) and statistical information about extracted scenario instances (right) - μ denotes mean; σ denotes standard deviation, *med* denotes median

when e is at least half way on the target lane. Considered relevant is also the gap size $d_g = s_{c_1}(t_{lc}) - s_{c_2}(t_{lc})$. More complex models may be used as well, e.g. [33].

The extraction of the lane change scenario instances is done in a rule-based way, i.e. whenever the ego vehicle performs a lane change with the desired three vehicles around it, we extract the characteristic values. Within the highD dataset, we could find 6736 lane changes of the presented form (see aggregated information in Table in Fig. 3). To assess whether this is a sufficient amount of data to yield a meaningful representation of real traffic, literature provides statistical models [11], which is not focus of this work. We used all the data to which we had access.

Not unusual for German highways, the data (cf. Table in Fig. 3) contains lane changes at close to 200 km/h as well as lane changes at traffic jam velocities, i.e. velocities below 60 km/h. The mean velocities μ are around 113 km/h. Note that the considerably high gap sizes with a mean of 132 m are resulting from the fact that the highD data [22] has been recorded on a 420 m highway section allowing for such large gaps. To the best of our knowledge there exists no common understanding of how large such a gap may be to be still considered as a gap. To avoid inadequate assumptions, we allow for such large gaps.

4.3   Points to Be Reproduced

The 6736 identified lane change scenario instances (see points in Fig. 4) need to be reduced to a representative amount of relevant instances, for which the containment check can be performed via search (see Sect. 3.3).

For the computation of the **convex hull** we make use of Quickhull [5]. The result can be seen as black lines connecting the points on the hull in Fig. 4. There are 40 points on the hull which represent - with regard to the characteristic values - the extreme lane changes and thus are considerably far away from the majority of the other points. The remaining 6696 points are **clustered** using classic k-means based on the three characteristic values as features. To choose an adequate number of clusters without human influence, we let a knee/elbow detector [30] decide. Applied to the 6696 points, 14 clusters are yielded (see colored point groups in Fig. 4). For each cluster, the point closest to the cluster center is used as representative. This results in a total of 54 (40 + 14) points for the following containment check. This subset of 54 points is denoted as $B' \subseteq B$.

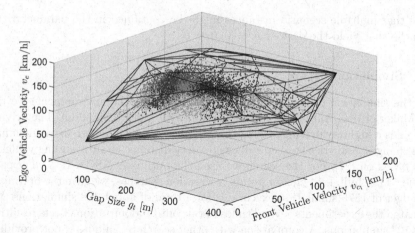

Fig. 4. 6736 lane changes: 40 points form the convex hull in black, the remaining 6696 points are grouped into 14 clusters within the convex hull

4.4   Fitness Function for Re-creation

The multi-objective fitness function that allows a search-based technique to search for a parameterized scenario instance a that recreates b consists of four objective functions. Since the subset of points $b \in B'$ have three dimensions, the template of Sect. 3.2 is used for three objective functions. The fourth objective function ensures that the identified lane changes in $\tilde{b}$ correspond to the situation as depicted in Fig. 3. For this we followed the method suggested in [15]: f_4 is set to a high value of 10000 if the ego vehicle does not perform a lane change within the scenario instance. If there is a lane change, but not into the gap, then the further away the lane change happened from the gap, the higher the fitness value. Otherwise, if the scenario instance is of the correct form, the fitness value is 0. The objective functions $f_{1/2/3}$ work as described in Sect. 3.2 and ensure that a suitable lane change is found. However, they got slightly modified: If there is no lane change in the gap ($f_4 > 0$), then one cannot measure the characteristic values and, thus, the fitness is set to a high value of 10000. The final fitness F function is $F = [f_1 \quad f_2 \quad f_3 \quad f_4]$ with $b \in B'$ and with

$$
\underset{i \in \{1,2,3\}}{f_i} = \begin{cases} 10000, & f_4 \neq 0 \\ \begin{cases} \left| \tilde{b}_i - b_i \right|, & f_4 = 0 \text{ and } \left| \tilde{b}_i - b_i \right| > \epsilon = 0.05 * b_i \\ 0, & f_4 = 0 \text{ and } \left| \tilde{b}_i - b_i \right| \leq \epsilon = 0.05 * b_i \end{cases} \end{cases}
$$

$$
f_4 = \begin{cases} 10000, & e \text{ does not change lanes} \\ \begin{cases} \left| \frac{s_{c_1}(t_{lc}) + s_{c_2}(t_{lc})}{2} - s_e(t_{lc}) \right|, & e \text{ changes lanes but not into the gap} \\ 0, & e \text{ changes lanes into the gap} \end{cases} \end{cases}
$$

The search-based technique will try to minimize the multi-objective function F. First, the value of f_4 will go to 0, before $f_{1/2/3}$ will get closer and closer to 0.

Note that multiple scenario instances might be contained in the parameterized scenario that yield the desired $F = [0 \ 0 \ 0 \ 0]$.

4.5   Simulation Setup

For the simulation of the driving scenario (including the environment) we use CarMaker of IPG Automotive in connection with Matlab Simulink. The driving system is a highway driving system that decides on which lane to drive including lane changes, and tries to keep sufficient safety distance to surrounding vehicles; it is based on [27]. For the search we used the optimizer NSGA-II [7]. For each of the 54 (40 hull + 14 cluster points) recreation searches, we gave the optimizer a budget of 1875 simulation executions for a total of about 10^5 simulations. We repeated the experiments several times to rule out randomization effects resulting in $\sim 10^6$ simulations. A comparison with other search techniques is not provided, as the focus is not on search performance, but on showing the soundness of this novel approach.

4.6   Experiment Results

Figure 5 shows which cluster and hull points could be recreated and which could not - the latter must be inspected manually in any case. In practice, an expert needs to either reject the parameterized scenario, because it does not contain all relevant lane changes from real data, or argue why it seems acceptable that some recorded scenario instance is not contained in the parameterized scenario. We showcase this analysis for some exemplifying points to demonstrate the types of insufficiencies the presented approach is able to detect.

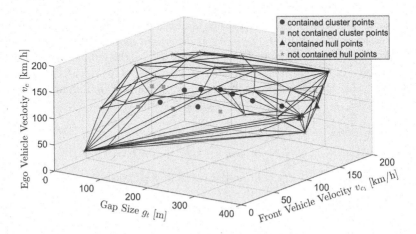

Fig. 5. Search results: blue points could be recreated, red not (Color figure online)

Parameter Domains Too Narrow: In Fig. 3 and Fig. 5, there is one extreme lane change scenario instance (a hull point) where the front vehicle c_1 is supposed to drive at 29.6 km/h when the ego vehicle's lane change happens. The parameter domains of the parameterized scenario only consider *starting velocities* for c_1 within 60 and 180 km/h (see Fig. 1). Since we configured the driver model of c_1 to keep, as far as safety permits, the starting velocity, the intuitive explanation seems to be that the parameter domains of the parameterized scenario are too narrow. Note that such a simple explanation is oftentimes not possible, when the characteristic values are less intuitive, as for example in [33].

Non-parameterized Scenario Part Not Adequate: Also the non-parameterized part may cause issues. For instance, in our case the parameterized scenario contains two vehicles on the left lane. Depending on their starting positions, the one is c_1 and the other c_2. Since their driver model is configured to keep safety distances, c_2 cannot drive faster than c_1 no matter which target velocities are selected as starting velocities. On the other hand, a faster c_2 will approach c_1 and eventually reduce its velocity to the velocity of c_1. For the presented experiment, this hinders recreation of some of the recorded scenario instances with small gap size, since c_2 will adjust its speed and distance depending on the speed of c_1. This shows that even with supposedly correct parameter domains, some instances may still not be contained in the parameterized scenario. This is hardly - if at all - detectable by an expert, but by the presented approach.

Simulation Models Not Suitable: In Fig. 5, there are multiple scenario instances where the front vehicle c_1 is supposed to drive at high velocities. However, the underlying driving model for traffic vehicles $c_{1/2/3}$ within CarMaker (version 8.1.1) is not designed to drive faster than 120 km/h in default mode. Even though the parameterized scenario may be adequate, unsuitable simulation models may still hinder containment of all scenario instances.

Scenario Design Not Suitable for Specific System: In Fig. 3 and Fig. 5, there are some lane change scenario instances where the driving system is supposed to perform a lane change into very narrow gaps. In reality, human drivers (as recorded in the dataset) perform high-velocity lane changes into such narrow gaps. However, the specific system used for the experiments is rather safety-conservative and cannot simply be triggered to perform lane changes into such a narrow gap. Thus, the parameterized scenario will not contain such lane changes. This does not necessarily mean that the parameterized scenario's quality is bad. The inspecting expert may accept that these lane changes are not contained.

4.7 Discussion

Search-based techniques are chosen as an approach to deal with the high-dimensional and complex search space. On the other hand, no simple relationship between parameter values and characteristic values of a scenario instance can be derived without simulation. The presented approach not only can detect problems concerning the description of the parameterized scenario itself, but also issues with the simulation models as well as suitability issues that relate to the specific SUT. However, even if all relevant scenario instances are contained, the parameterized scenario may still not be *complete*. The traffic data may simply not be representative and lack some rare special cases.

Yet, if not all relevant recorded scenario instances are contained, the parameterized scenario may still be valid, if the expert can argue why the non-contained recorded scenario instances do not necessarily have to be contained. In the presented example, the velocities lower bound is set to 60 km/h; any situation below this limit is considered as a *traffic jam*, which is tested using other parameterized scenarios. In such a case, non-contained lane change scenario instances below 60 km/h may be ignored. Without the presented approach it is usually unknown whether something is missing in the parameter space of the parameterized scenario. The presented approach enforces a structured validation and alerts the expert. Bad mistakes are ruled out, providing confidence and a basis for safety argumentation for the testing and release processes.

4.8 Limitations

Clearly, the presented experiments only consider a single source of data (highD dataset) that may or may not be representative, a single scenario type, selected characteristic values and a single driving system. Further evaluation is needed to understand how the approach works, e.g. for data from other highways or city centers, for other scenario types, and other driving systems. Similarly, search-based techniques might not be fully appropriate: While the approach involves considerable efforts, search-based techniques are based on heuristics which may or may not be suitable for specific parameterized scenarios' search spaces and fitness functions. Thus, the search as applied in this work may face the same issue as in other works: it may or may not find suitable scenario instances in the search spaces derived from parameterized scenarios. The search may mistakenly suggest that a recorded scenario instance is not contained in the parameterized scenario. While this may be inconvenient, the approach is still reliable in the following way: The presented approach can mistakenly reject a sound parameterized scenario, but it cannot not mistakenly accept it within the scope of realization (e.g. with regard to the selected characteristic values). In case of acceptance, we can base a safety argumentation on this result. If it is rejected, an expert may either argue that potentially non-contained recorded scenario instances do not matter, or re-run the search with a different configuration.

5   Related Work

Although a plethora of work on scenario-based testing exists, the number of papers addressing the derivation and quality of parameterized scenarios is scarce.

In [25], the different notions of scenarios have been introduced. The importance of parameterized scenarios is stated and fundamental concepts are presented. In their follow-up works, the authors make methodological suggestions on how to first derive scenario types [4] before refining them to parameterized scenarios [24]. Those are steps ① and ⑤ in Fig. 2, which are preliminary steps to the presented approach, but do not provide an assessment technique for parameterized scenarios.

In [33], characteristic values for lane changes are used to create a parameterized scenario and to determine parameter domains (step ⑤ in Fig. 2). The authors make use of traffic data to determine critical test cases for this parameterized scenario (step ⑩ in Fig. 2). This work is related, but does not provide an assessment approach for the parameterized scenarios.

Existing works address how to determine whether enough data has been collected to capture all scenario types [16] and all variations of a scenario type [11]. Such works are important as they can be used to supplement the presented approach: If the traffic data used for the presented assessment of parameterized scenario is *complete*, the presented assessment becomes more meaningful. The parameterized scenario assessment is not in the focus of their works.

Many existing works, e.g. [1–3, 6, 9, 13, 15, 23] (see [15, 28] for an overview), use search-based techniques for test case generation (step ⑩ in Fig. 2). In contrast, our approach does not use search-based techniques for test case generation, but for recreation of recorded scenario instances of real traffic to determine whether they are contained in the examined parameterized scenario. Another line of work [8, 17] aims at processing natural language police reports to reconstruct crashes. Their "reconstruction" is different from the "reconstruction" of our work in that they make use of path planners to find trajectories that lead to the target crashes. This is not possible for our setting, since we cannot pre-plan or influence the trajectory of the SUT. Additionally, their approach does not allow to assess the quality of parameterized scenarios.

All these works address important challenges in the scenario-based testing domain, leaving the quality assessment of parameterized scenarios unaddressed.

6   Conclusion

We argue that parameterized scenarios are the basis for scenario-based test case generation. Hence, their quality is fundamental, otherwise no "good" test cases can be generated which is, however, crucial for the safety argumentation of the SUT. So far, existing works do not provide a quality criterion nor the means to assess the quality of parameterized scenarios. This work contributes to such a novel data-driven criterion and assurance approach. It analyzes whether a parameterized scenario contains recorded scenario instances of the considered scenario type. Based on the analysis, a parameterized scenario can be deemed acceptable or not acceptable in terms of its quality.

The experiments show that the presented approach can detect issues resulting from (1) the parameterized and (2) non-parameterized part of the parameterized scenario as well as from (3) insufficient simulation models and (4) inadequate scenario design for the SUT. Even though the containment of real traffic instances is not a guarantee that a parameterized scenario is perfect, the presented quality assessment criterion and approach can increase confidence that no crucial mistakes were made during creation - representing an important step for safety argumentation of such systems.

References

1. Abdessalem, R.B., Nejati, S., Briand, L., Stifter, T.: Testing vision-based control systems using learnable evolutionary algorithms. In: Proceedings of the 40th International Conference on Software Engineering (ICSE), pp. 1016–1026. ACM (2018)
2. Abdessalem, R.B., Nejati, S., Briand, L.C., Stifter, T.: Testing advanced driver assistance systems using multi-objective search and neural networks. In: 31st IEEE/ACM International Conference on Automated Software Engineering, pp. 63–74 (2016)
3. Abdessalem, R.B., Panichella, A., Nejati, S., Briand, L.C., Stifter, T.: Testing autonomous cars for feature interaction failures using many-objective search. In: 33rd ACM/IEEE International Conference on Automated Software Engineering, pp. 143–154 (2018)
4. Bagschik, G., Menzel, T., Maurer, M.: Ontology based scene creation for the development of automated vehicles. In: IEEE Intelligent Vehicles Symposium (IV), pp. 1813–1820. IEEE (2018)
5. Barber, C.B., Dobkin, D.P., Huhdanpaa, H.: The quickhull algorithm for convex hulls. ACM Trans. Math. Softw. (TOMS) $22(4)$, 469–483 (1996)
6. Calò, A., Arcaini, P., Ali, S., Hauer, F., Ishikawa, F.: Generating avoidable collision scenarios for testing autonomous driving systems. In: 13th International Conference on Software Testing, Validation and Verification (ICST), pp. 375–386. IEEE (2020)
7. Deb, K., Pratap, A., Agarwal, S., Meyarivan, T.: A fast and elitist multiobjective genetic algorithm: NSGA-II. IEEE Trans. Evol. Comput. $6(2)$, 182–197 (2002)
8. Gambi, A., Huynh, T., Fraser, G.: Generating effective test cases for self-driving cars from police reports. In: Proceedings of the 2019 27th ACM Joint Meeting on European Software Engineering Conference and Symposium on the Foundations of Software Engineering, pp. 257–267 (2019)
9. Gambi, A., Mueller, M., Fraser, G.: Automatically testing self-driving cars with search-based procedural content generation. In: Proceedings of the 28th ACM SIGSOFT International Symposium on Software Testing and Analysis, pp. 318–328 (2019)
10. Gauerhof, L., Munk, P., Burton, S.: Structuring validation targets of a machine learning function applied to automated driving. In: Gallina, B., Skavhaug, A., Bitsch, F. (eds.) SAFECOMP 2018. LNCS, vol. 11093, pp. 45–58. Springer, Cham (2018). https://doi.org/10.1007/978-3-319-99130-6_4
11. de Gelder, E., Paardekooper, J., Op den Camp, O., De Schutter, B.: Safety assessment of automated vehicles: how to determine whether we have collected enough field data? Traffic Inj. Prev. 20(sup1), S162–S170 (2019)
12. de Gelder, E., et al.: Ontology for scenarios for the assessment of automated vehicles. arXiv preprint arXiv:2001.11507 (2020)
13. Gladisch, C., Heinz, T., Heinzemann, C., Oehlerking, J., von Vietinghoff, A., Pfitzer, T.: Experience paper: search-based testing in automated driving control applications. In: 34th IEEE/ACM International Conference on Automated Software Engineering (ASE), pp. 26–37. IEEE (2019)
14. Hauer, F., Gerostathopoulos, I., Schmidt, T., Pretschner, A.: Clustering traffic scenarios using mental models as little as possible. In: IEEE Intelligent Vehicles Symposium (IV), pp. 1007–1012. IEEE (2020)

15. Hauer, F., Pretschner, A., Holzmüller, B.: Fitness functions for testing automated and autonomous driving systems. In: Romanovsky, A., Troubitsyna, E., Bitsch, F. (eds.) SAFECOMP 2019. LNCS, vol. 11698, pp. 69–84. Springer, Cham (2019). https://doi.org/10.1007/978-3-030-26601-1_5

16. Hauer, F., Schmidt, T., Holzmüller, B., Pretschner, A.: Did we test all scenarios for automated and autonomous driving systems? In: IEEE Intelligent Transportation Systems Conference (ITSC), pp. 2950–2955. IEEE (2019)

17. Huynh, T., Gambi, A., Fraser, G.: AC3R: automatically reconstructing car crashes from police reports. In: 2019 IEEE/ACM 41st International Conference on Software Engineering: Companion Proceedings (ICSE-Companion), pp. 31–34. IEEE (2019)

18. Kalra, N., Paddock, S.M.: Driving to safety: how many miles of driving would it take to demonstrate autonomous vehicle reliability? Transp. Res. Part A Policy Pract. **94**, 182–193 (2016)

19. Koopman, P., Fratrik, F.: How many operational design domains, objects, and events? In: AAAI Workshop on Artificial Intelligence Safety (2019)

20. Koopman, P., Kane, A., Black, J.: Credible autonomy safety argumentation. In: 27th Safety-Critical Systems Symposium (2019)

21. Koopman, P., Wagner, M.: Challenges in autonomous vehicle testing and validation. SAE Int. J. Transp. Saf. **4**(1), 15–24 (2016)

22. Krajewski, R., Bock, J., Kloeker, L., Eckstein, L.: The highD dataset: a drone dataset of naturalistic vehicle trajectories on German highways for validation of highly automated driving systems. In: IEEE Intelligent Transportation Systems Conference (ITSC), pp. 2118–2125 (2018)

23. Li, G., et al.: AV-FUZZER: finding safety violations in autonomous driving systems. In: 31st International Symposium on Software Reliability Engineering (ISSRE), pp. 25–36. IEEE (2020)

24. Menzel, T., Bagschik, G., Isensee, L., Schomburg, A., Maurer, M.: From functional to logical scenarios: detailing a keyword-based scenario description for execution in a simulation environment. In: IEEE Intelligent Vehicles Symposium (IV), pp. 2383–2390 (2019)

25. Menzel, T., Bagschik, G., Maurer, M.: Scenarios for development, test and validation of automated vehicles. In: IEEE Intelligent Vehicles Symposium (IV), pp. 1821–1827 (2018)

26. Mullins, G.E., Stankiewicz, P.G., Gupta, S.K.: Automated generation of diverse and challenging scenarios for test and evaluation of autonomous vehicles. In: IEEE International Conference on Robotics and Automation (ICRA), pp. 1443–1450 (2017)

27. Nilsson, J., Silvlin, J., Brannstrom, M., Coelingh, E., Fredriksson, J.: If, when, and how to perform lane change maneuvers on highways. IEEE Intell. Transp. Syst. Mag. **8**(4), 68–78 (2016)

28. Riedmaier, S., Ponn, T., Ludwig, D., Schick, B., Diermeyer, F.: Survey on scenario-based safety assessment of automated vehicles. IEEE Access **8**, 87456–87477 (2020)

29. Roesener, C., et al.: A comprehensive evaluation approach for highly automated driving. In: 25th International Technical Conference on the Enhanced Safety of Vehicles (ESV) National Highway Traffic Safety Administration (2017)

30. Satopaa, V., Albrecht, J., Irwin, D., Raghavan, B.: Finding a "kneedle" in a haystack: detecting knee points in system behavior. In: IEEE International Conference on Distributed Computing Systems Workshops, pp. 166–171 (2011)

31. Tkachenko, P., Zhou, J., del Re, L.: Unsupervised clustering of highway motion patterns. In: IEEE Intelligent Transportation Systems Conference, pp. 2337–2342 (2019)

32. Wachenfeld, W., Winner, H.: The release of autonomous vehicles. In: Maurer, M., Gerdes, J.C., Lenz, B., Winner, H. (eds.) Autonomous Driving, pp. 425–449. Springer, Heidelberg (2016). https://doi.org/10.1007/978-3-662-48847-8_21

33. Zhou, J., del Re, L.: Identification of critical cases of ADAS safety by FOT based parameterization of a catalogue. In: IEEE Asian Control Conference, pp. 453–458 (2017)

34. Zhou, J., del Re, L.: Reduced complexity safety testing for ADAS & ADF. IFAC-PapersOnLine **50**(1), 5985–5990 (2017)

Optimising the Reliability that Can Be Claimed for a Software-Based System Based on Failure-Free Tests of Its Components

Peter Bishop[1,2(✉)] and Andrey Povyakalo[1]

[1] City, University of London, London, UK
{p.bishop,A.A.Povyakalo}@city.ac.uk
[2] Adelard, NCC Group, London, UK
pgb@adelard.com

Abstract. This paper describes a numerical method for optimising the conservative confidence bound on the reliability of a system based on statistical testing of its individual components. It provides an alternative to the sub-optimal test plan algorithms identified by the authors in an earlier research paper. For a given maximum number of component tests, this numerical method can derive an optimal test plan for any arbitrary system structure.

The optimisation method is based on linear programming which is more efficient than the alternative integer programming approach. In addition, the optimisation process need only be performed once for any given system structure as the solution can be re-used to compute an optimal integer test plan for a different maximum number of component tests. This approach might have broader application to other optimisation problems.

Keywords: Statistical testing · Confidence bounds · Software reliability · Fault tolerance · Linear programming

1 Introduction

Statistical testing [4,8,10] provides a direct estimate of the software probability of failure on demand (*pfd*) of a demand-based system to some confidence bound, and it is recommended in functional safety standards such as IEC 61508 [6]. The standard approach to deriving a confidence bound on the *pfd* of a software-based system is to perform statistical testing on the whole system as a "black-box". In practice, performing tests on the entire system may be infeasible for logistical reasons, such as lack of availability of all component subsystems at the same time during implementation. For example, the statistical tests performed on the Sizewell B computer-based Primary Protection System (PPS) were performed on a single hardware division of the PPS, while the complete fault tolerant system

M. Trapp et al. (Eds.): SAFECOMP 2022, LNCS 13414, pp. 365–378, 2022.
https://doi.org/10.1007/978-3-031-14835-4_24

consists of four divisions with 2-out-of-4 voting [5]. Similar constraints exist for the statistical testing of the Hinkley Point C protection system [9].

To address the constraint, testing can be restricted to a single component within the system architectures provided the fault tolerance mechanisms are pre-defined and static, i.e. there is no dependency between components (such as dynamic fail-over schemes). A general method was developed for deriving a conservative confidence bound based on independent statistical tests applied (with zero failures) to individual software-based components within the system [1]. The approach is completely general – it can be used to derive a conservative *pfd* bound for any system architecture (represented by a structure function) for a given component test plan.

The choice of component test plan affects the *pfd* bound that can be claimed under worst case failure dependency conditions. The paper showed that for symmetrical architectures (like r-out-of-m vote structures), an even split of N tests between components always produces the optimal *pfd* bound, where:

1. if all components have identical software, subjecting each component to N/m tests produces the same *pfd* bound as subjecting the full system to N tests;
2. if the software in each component is not identical, subjecting each component to N/m tests produces the same *pfd* bound as subjecting the full system to $N(m - r + 1)/m$ tests.

The first result is unsurprising. If all components have the same software, identical defects will be present in every component – so it does not matter which component is tested, the system *pfd* is determined by the total of number of tests in all m components.

The second result is counter-intuitive, as a complete system with diverse components would have the same *pfd* bound as a non-diverse system when tested as a "black-box". The difference arises because the components are tested separately. A worst case example of non-identical failure dependency is shown in Fig. 1 for a 2-out-of-3 vote structure. In this case, there is a common fault in just two of the components, so only the combined number of tests performed on components c_1 and c_2 determine the upper confidence bound on the system *pfd*.

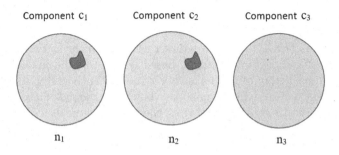

Fig. 1. Worst failure dependency example: non-identical software. *The dark patches represent defective regions in the input space of two components.*

There are other possible common failure mode states like $\{c_1, c_3\}$ or $\{c_2, c_3\}$, however in all cases, it was shown in [1] that the system *pfd* is determined by the two least tested components, and more generally for a r-out-of-m structure, the system *pfd* is determined by smallest total of tests in $(m - r + 1)$ components.

As a result, the optimal test plan is an even split of the available tests across the components, i.e. if N tests are available, N/m tests are allocated to each component.

Deriving optimal test plans for arbitrary, asymmetric structures was more challenging. Two sub-optimal test plan strategies were identified in [1] that are optimal for some asymmetric structures – but not in general.

This paper presents an alternative to the test plan algorithms described in [1] that derives an optimal test plan using linear programming. We first summarise the main elements of the theory presented in [1], and then present our alternative method for generating an optimal test plan using numerical methods.

2   Confidence Bounds from Component Tests

Failure-free testing over m individual components can be characterised by a test plan vector

$$\mathbf{n} = (n_1, n_2, \ldots, n_m)' \tag{1}$$

where m is a number of components, n_j is the number of (failure-free) tests for component j, and the total number of tests is

$$N = \sum_{j=1}^{m} n_j. \tag{2}$$

Failures of the overall system can be characterised by *minimal cutsets* where failure of all components in any minimal cutset will cause a system failure.

A general proof given in [1] shows that, for any structure characterised by a set X of minimal cutsets, the $(1 - \alpha)$ upper confidence bound q_s for the system *pfd* can be conservatively approximated as

$$q_s \leq \min\left(\frac{\ln(1/\alpha)}{N_{min}}, 1\right) \tag{3}$$

where N_{min} is the smallest total number of component tests in a minimal cutset, i.e.:

$$N_{min} = \min_{\forall \mathbf{x} \in \mathbf{X}} \sum_{i \in \mathbf{x}} n_i \tag{4}$$

where $i \in \mathbf{x}$ identifies the components in minimal cutset $\mathbf{x}$.

For example, a 2-out-of-3 vote structure with diverse components has three minimal cutsets $\{c_1, c_2\}$, $\{c_2, c_3\}$ and $\{c_1, c_3\}$ so

$$N_{min} = \min(n_1 + n_2, \quad n_2 + n_3, \quad n_1 + n_3).$$

For a 2-out-of-3 vote structure with identical components, the software failures in all components coincide, so there is only one minimal cutset: $\{c_1, c_2, c_3\}$ and

$$N_{min} = (n_1 + n_2 + n_3) = N.$$

The optimal test plans and confidence bounds derived in [1] for some common symmetrical structures are summarised in Table 1.

Table 1. Optimum test plan and confidence bounds for symmetrical structures

Structure	Software	n_j	N_{min}	Confidence bound
Series (m-out-of-m)	Diverse	$\frac{N}{m}$	$\frac{N}{m}$	$\frac{m}{N} \ln \frac{1}{\alpha}$
Vote (r-out-of-m)	Diverse	$\frac{N}{m}$	$\frac{(m-r+1)N}{m}$	$\frac{m}{(m-r+1)N} \ln \frac{1}{\alpha}$
Vote (r-out-of-m)	Identical	Any split	N	$\frac{1}{N} \ln \frac{1}{\alpha}$
Vote (1-out-of-m)	Either	Any split	N	$\frac{1}{N} \ln \frac{1}{\alpha}$

The "series" structure is a chain of m components where the failure of any component causes system failure, so all m components must be functional for the system to be functional.

The "vote" structure (assuming voter correctness) combines the outputs of m components so that only r components need to be functional for the overall system to be functional.

It can be seen that for symmetrical structures, it is always optimal to apportion the N tests equally across the m components.

3   Optimising Test Plans for Asymmetric Structures

An asymmetric structure has a variable number of components in its minimal cutsets, such as the reliability block diagram (RBD) shown in Fig. 2.

For such structures, explicit test plan optimisation is needed to ensure that the maximum value of N_{min} is obtained.

It was shown in [1] that it should always be possible to construct an allocation of component tests such that:

$$N_{min} \geq N/k_p. \tag{5}$$

where k_p is the length of the shortest possible success path.

For example, in Fig. 2, the dashed lines denote the shortest success paths where $k_p = 3$.

Two sub-optimal allocation plans where identified in [1] that always satisfy this constraint:

- *Single shortest path*, where N/k_p tests are allocated equally to all components on just one shortest success path.

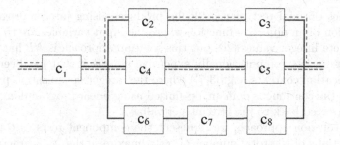

Fig. 2. Reliability block diagram. *The dashed lines are the shortest success paths*

– *Balanced shortest path*, where the number of tests per component is proportional to the number of shortest success paths that include the component.

Both allocation methods are optimal for cases where each component appears only once in the RBD. The balanced path test plan also produces the optimal result for symmetric r-out-of-m vote structures (where the same component is present in more than one RBD branch).

Figure 3 shows the result of applying the balanced path allocation procedure to the RBD shown in Fig. 2.

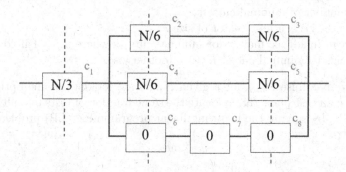

Fig. 3. Allocation of tests to components. The dashed lines are example minimal cutsets (there are further minimal cutsets).

Component c_1 has twice as many tests as the other shortest path components (because it is present in two shortest paths). It can be seen that the total number of tests in all minimal cutsets is the same ($N/3$).

Components c_6, c_7 and c_8 have no tests and could potentially fail on every demand, but this test plan is optimal because it maximises the number of tests in each cutset and hence the system reliability that can be claimed.

It proved to be more difficult to identify a general optimal test allocation strategy that was applicable to any arbitrary asymmetric structure. While further test plan allocation algorithms were examined, it was always possible to identify a counter-example structure where the allocation would be sub-optimal.

An exact optimal test plan could be produced using integer programming (optimisation of an objective function where the input variables are constrained to be discrete integer values [2]), but this solution approach is *NP* hard [12].

We chose a less computationally expensive approach that has been used in other application contexts (e.g. [3,7]) where the integer optimisation problem is mapped to the continuous domain, optimised using linear programming, and the results converted back to discrete integer values.

In our solution approach, we represent the component tests as continuous-valued fractions of the total number of tests, maximise the N_{min} fraction using linear programming, then convert the optimal continuous test plan fractions back to a discrete integer test values for each component. The approach is described in more detail in the section below, and an example R [11] script implementation of the method is given in Appendix A.

4   Test Plan Optimisation Using Linear Programming

Let us introduce the following notation

m is the number of components;
$\mathbf{f} = (f_1, f_2, \ldots, f_m)' \in \mathbb{R}^m$ is the fraction of tests allocated to each component, i.e. $f_j = n_j/N, \ j = 1..m$;
s is the number of minimal cutsets;
$\mathbf{1}_s = (1, 1, \ldots, 1)'$ is a unit vector of size s;
Y is a $s \times m$ incidence matrix for minimal cutsets where $y_{ij} = 1$ if component c_j belongs to minimal cutset i, $y_{ij} = 0$ otherwise.

In order to maximise N_{min} for a given N, we are looking for the optimal test plan among all test plans that allocate the same fraction of tests g to all minimal cutsets in Y, by solving the following linear programming (LP) problem:

$$g \rightarrow \max \tag{6}$$

given

$$Y \cdot \mathbf{f} = g \cdot \mathbf{1}_s; \tag{7}$$

$$\sum_{j=1}^{m} f_j = 1; \tag{8}$$

$$f_j \geq 0, \ j = 1..m, \tag{9}$$

where $Y \cdot \mathbf{f}$ is the matrix product of matrix Y and vector $\mathbf{f}$ that computes the sum of the component test fractions for every cutset, hence constraint (7) requires that $\sum_{j=1}^{m}(y_{ij} \cdot f_j) = g, i = 1..s$.

We can now eliminate variable g by defining the following terms:

$$\mathbf{h} = \mathbf{f}/g \tag{10}$$

$$H = 1/g. \tag{11}$$

Rewriting the LP problem in these terms, g is maximised when H is minimised, i.e.:

$$\sum_{j=1}^{m} h_j = H \rightarrow \min \tag{12}$$

given

$$Y \cdot \mathbf{h} = \mathbf{1}_s; \tag{13}$$

$$h_j \geq 0, \ j = 1..m. \tag{14}$$

A simplex LP solver algorithm can be used to derive the solution to this problem. Conceptually, the feasible region for the solution is a multi-dimensional polyhedron where each face represents a different constraint. The simplex algorithm finds the optimal solution by locating a vertex of the polyhedron (the initial feasible point) and moving to the next vertex along an edge that is closer to the optimal value (in our case, the minimum value of H). In practice however, the solver can sometimes fail to find a solution when equality constraints are used – probably because it fails to generate an initial feasible point. To resolve the issue, we noted that H reaches its unconstrained minimum when $h_j = 0$, $j = 1..m$. Therefore, equality constraint (13) can be replaced with an inequality constraint $Y \cdot \mathbf{h} \geq \mathbf{1}$. This makes no difference to the final solution as the optimisation seeks to minimise H, so the final solution will still satisfy the constraint $Y \cdot \mathbf{h} = \mathbf{1}$. Thus, the LP problem can be reformulated as follows.

$$\sum_{j} h_j = H \rightarrow \min \tag{15}$$

given

$$Y \cdot \mathbf{h} \geq \mathbf{1}_s; \tag{16}$$

$$h_j \geq 0, \ j = 1..m. \tag{17}$$

This optimisation problem can solved by an R script that calls the LP solver *simplex()* as shown in Appendix A.

The resultant optimal test allocation fractions for the components are:

$$\mathbf{f}_{op} = \mathbf{h}_{op}/H_{op} \tag{18}$$

and the optimal minimal cutset fraction g_{op} is:

$$g_{op} = 1/H_{op}. \tag{19}$$

As in general these fractions are real values, the optimal apportionment of component tests i.e., $\mathbf{n} = \mathbf{f}_{op}N$ can be non-integer. An integer component test allocation can be derived by first finding the smallest number of tests, N_0, where all component test fractions scale to integer values, i.e.

$$\lfloor \mathbf{f}_{op}N_0 \rfloor = \mathbf{f}_{op}N_0. \tag{20}$$

N_0 can be found by incrementing an integer number k by 1 until all the products $k \cdot f_j$, $j = 1..m$ become integer.

It follows that the plan for a total number of tests

$$N^- = N - (N \mod N_0) \tag{21}$$

is always integer because it is a multiple of N_0.

If there is an option to add extra tests to the plan, one can consider a test plan for N^+ tests where

$$N^+ = N^- + N_0. \tag{22}$$

However, we know that the change in N_{min} between the plans for N^- and N^+ could be greater than one, i.e.

$$(N^+_{min} - N^-_{min}) \geq 1. \tag{23}$$

For example, if we start with the integer test plan for N^- and add one test to the k_p components on a single shortest success path, N_{min} increases by one. If $N_0 > k_p$ we know this solution is also an integer plan so the increase in N_{min} must be greater than 1.

For structures where $N_0 > k_p$, there will be intermediate integer test plans between N^- and N^+ where the non-zero component tests in each minimal cutset are not exactly equal, but the test plan still maximises the value of N_{min} for a given number of tests N.

In principle, there can be structures where $N_0 \gg k_p$, e.g. structures where the denominators of the component test fractions are differing prime numbers, so there could be an arbitrarily large number of intermediate test plans between a pair of perfectly balanced test plans with N^- and N^+ tests.

It would be possible derive optimal intermediate test plans where the non-zero component tests in the cutset are unequal, but this would require an entirely different, more complex algorithm (e.g. using integer programming). In practice, it is simpler to round up the fractional component tests to the next whole integer, i.e.

$$\mathbf{n}^\uparrow = \lceil \mathbf{f}_{op} N \rceil; \tag{24}$$

$$N^\uparrow_{min} = \min(Y \cdot \mathbf{n}^\uparrow); \tag{25}$$

$$N^\uparrow = \sum \mathbf{n}^\uparrow. \tag{26}$$

This plan for $N^\uparrow$ tests will include no more than m redundant tests to achieve the same N_{min} as a fully optimised integer test plan.

5   Example

Let us consider an example asymmetric structure with the reliability block diagram (RBD) given in Fig. 4.

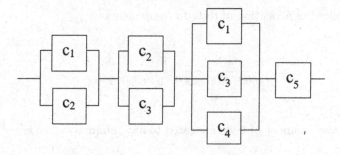

Fig. 4. Example asymmetric RBD

Its minimal cutsets are:

$$\{c_1, c_2\}$$
$$\{c_2, c_3\}$$
$$\{c_1, c_3, c_4\}$$
$$\{c_5\}$$

and its minimal cutset incidence matrix Y is shown in Table 2, where a "1" in a row indicates that the component is included in the minimal cutset.

Table 2. Minimal cutset incidence matrix

Cutset	Component j				
x	1	2	3	4	5
1	1	1	0	0	0
2	0	1	1	0	0
3	1	0	1	1	0
4	0	0	0	0	1

For this minimal cutset incidence matrix, the R script (see Appendix A) generates the following optimal test allocation fractions:

f_1	f_2	f_3	f_4	f_5	g_{op}
0.2	0.2	0.2	0.0	0.4	0.4

where zero tests are allocated to component c_4.

For this plan, sequential search gives $N_0 = 5$. Therefore, for a test campaign with a total number of tests $N = 20003$, the number of tests for an exact integer test plan is

$$N^- = 20003 - (20003 \ mod \ 5) = 20000 \tag{27}$$

with the following allocation of tests to components

n_1	n_2	n_3	n_4	n_5	N^-
4000	4000	4000	0	8000	20000

where the least number of tests allocated to any minimal cutset is

$$N_{min} = g_{op}N^- = 8000.$$

The R script also generates a rounded-up test plan where the test allocation is:

$n^{\uparrow}_1$	$n^{\uparrow}_2$	$n^{\uparrow}_3$	$n^{\uparrow}_4$	$n^{\uparrow}_5$	$N^{\uparrow}$
4001	4001	4001	0	8001	20004

and the least number of tests allocated to any minimal cutset is

$$N^{\uparrow}_{min} = \min(Y \cdot \mathbf{n}^{\uparrow})) = 8001.$$

This is not completely optimal because $N_{min} = 8001$ is possible with a test plan where $N = 20003$ by mapping the same test fraction values to different integer values, as shown the test plan below (the reduced tests are italicised).

n_1	n_2	n_3	n_4	n_5	N
4001	4001	*4000*	0	8001	*20003*

It can be seen that the simplified integerisation strategy of rounding up to the next integer only has a marginal impact on the number of tests required to achieve a given N_{min} value. It also allows test plans to be generated for every N_{min} value.

The choice of integerisation strategy only makes a marginal difference to the optimality of the plan. The main gain is achieved by identifying the optimal test fractions. For example, if we use the sub-optimal strategy proposed in [1] of allocating N/k_p tests equally to components on a single shortest success path, such as (c_1, c_2, c_5), then $k_p = 3$. This is clearly sub-optimal as the least tested cutsets only have $N_{min} = \lfloor N/k_p \rfloor = \lfloor 20003/3 \rfloor = 6667$ tests.

6   Discussion and Conclusions

In this paper, we have extended the test planning approach described in [1] so that optimal test plans can be produced for arbitrary structures by optimising test plans in the continuous domain. The fractions generated in the continuous domain are independent of the number of tests, so they only need to be generated once for any given structure. An integer test plan can be recalculated from these fractions for any given test budget – reducing the computing resources needed for a new plan.

We identified two options for converting the test fractions to integer component test values. The simplest method is to round up fractional values to the next whole integer. While not strictly optimal in all cases, there is only a minimal (and bounded) increase in the number of tests required to demonstrate a given confidence bound.

Other integer conversion methods are possible but the differences are marginal – the optimisation is primarily achieved by identifying the optimal test fractions.

In principle, it would be possible to create a library of optimal test plan solutions for different structures that can be converted to integer test plans for any specified total number of component tests. This approach might have broader application to other optimisation problems.

A   Test Plan Optimisation R Script

The test plan optimisation approach was implemented using the standard simplex solver available in the R statistical analysis library. The use of the test plan optimiser is illustrated using the non-symmetric structure shown in Fig. 4.

```
library("boot")

#----------------------------------------------
# lptplan_example <- function( N, alpha)
# N - total number of tests (default 20003)
# alpha = 1 - confidence level (default 0.05)
#----------------------------------------------

lptplan_example <- function(
N=20003,
alpha = 0.05
)
```

```
{
# minimal cutset matrix
    cutsets <- matrix(
    c(
    1,1,0,0,0,  # cutset: C1, C2
    0,1,1,0,0,  # cutset: C2, C3
    1,0,1,1,0,  # cutset: C1, C3, C4
    0,0,0,0,1   # cutset: C5
    ), 4, 5,
    byrow=TRUE
    )

# Generate optimised test plan
    print  ( lptestplan(cutsets, N, alpha) )
}


#-----------------------------------------
# lptestplan <- function(Y, N, alpha)
# Y   incidence matrix for the minimal cutsets
#      columns represent components
#      rows represent cutsets
# N    total number of tests
# alpha = 1 - confidence level
#-----------------------------------------

lptestplan <- function(Y, N, alpha)
{
# Number of components
    m <- ncol(Y)

# Number of minimal cutsets
    s <- nrow(Y)

# Unit vectors
    uvm <- rep(1,m)
    uvs <- rep(1,s)

# Solve LP
    lp0 <- simplex(
        a = uvm,
        A3 = Y,
        b3 = uvs
    )
    H <- as.numeric(lp0$value)
    h <- lp0$soln
```

```
# Optimal cutset test fraction
    g <- 1/H

# Optimal component test fractions
    f <- h * g

# Find exact integer test plan (<= N)
    k <- 1
    r <- 1
    while(r>0){
        r <- sum ((f*k)%%1)
        if(r>0) k <- k+1
    }
    NO <- k
    N_minus <- N - (N%%NO)

# Generate exact integer test plan
    N_min <- N_minus * g
    n <- N_minus * f

# Calculate upper confidence bound
    q_u <- log(1/alpha)/N_min

# Generate rounded-up integer test plan (>=N)
    n_up <- ceiling(N * f)
    N_min_up <- min(Y %*% n_up)
    N_up <- sum(n_up)

# Calculate rounded-up upper confidence bound
    q_u_up <- log(1/alpha)/N_min_up

# Return optimised results
  return
  (
    list(
    cutsets=Y,
    alpha = alpha,
    component_fractions = f,
    cutset_fraction = g,
    N = N,
    NO = NO,
    N_minus = N_minus,
    lptest_plan = n,
    N_min = N_min,
```

```
q_u = q_u,
N_up=N_up,
lptest_plan_up=n_up,
N_min_up=N_min_up,
q_u_up = q_u_up
)
)
}
```

References

1. Bishop, P., Povyakalo, A.: A conservative confidence bound for the probability of failure on demand of a software-based system based on failure-free tests of its components. Reliab. Eng. Syst. Saf. **203**, 107060 (2020)
2. Dantzig, G.B., Thapa, M.N.: Linear Programming 1: Introduction. Springer, Heidelberg (2006). https://doi.org/10.1007/b97672
3. Dommel, H.W., Tinney, W.F.: Optimal power flow solutions. IEEE Trans. Power Appar. Syst. **10**, 1866–1876 (1968)
4. Ehrenberger, W.: Statistical testing of real time software. In: Quirk, W.J. (ed.) Verification and Validation of Real-Time Software, pp. 147–178. Springer, Heidelberg (1985). https://doi.org/10.1007/978-3-642-70224-2_5
5. Hunns, D., Wainwright, N.: Software-based protection for Sizewell B: the regulator's perspective. In: 1992 International Conference on Electrical and Control Aspects of the Sizewell B PWR, pp. 198–203. IET (1992)
6. IEC: Functional safety of electrical/electronical/programmable electronic safety-related systems, Ed. 2, IEC 61508:2010 (2010)
7. King, T., Barrett, C., Tinelli, C.: Leveraging linear and mixed integer programming for SMT. In: 2014 Formal Methods in Computer-Aided Design (FMCAD), pp. 139–146. IEEE (2014)
8. May, J., Hughes, G., Lunn, A.: Reliability estimation from appropriate testing of plant protection software. Softw. Eng. J. **10**(6), 206–218 (1995)
9. NNB: Hinkley Point C pre-construction safety report 3 public version. Technical report, NNB Generation Company (HPC) Ltd. (2017)
10. Parnas, D.L., Asmis, G., Madey, J.: Assessment of safety-critical software in nuclear power plants. Nucl. Saf. **32**(2), 189–198 (1991)
11. Rizzo, M.L.: Statistical Computing with R. CRC Press, New York (2019)
12. Schrijver, A.: Theory of Linear and Integer Programming. Wiley, Hoboken (1998)

Author Index

Printed in the United States
by Baker & Taylor Publisher Services